The *Essentials* of the New Workplace

The *Essentials* of the New Workplace

A Guide to the Human Impact of Modern Working Practices

Edited by

David Holman, Toby D. Wall and Chris W. Clegg
University of Sheffield, UK

Paul Sparrow
University of Manchester, UK

and

Ann Howard
Development Dimensions International, New Jersey, USA

WILEY

Other Wiley Editorial Offices

John Wiley & Sons Inc., 111 River Street, Hoboken, NJ 07030, USA

Jossey-Bass, 989 Market Street, San Francisco, CA 94103-1741, USA

Wiley-VCH Verlag GmbH, Boschstr. 12, D-69469 Weinheim, Germany

John Wiley & Sons Australia Ltd, 33 Park Road, Milton, Queensland 4064, Australia

John Wiley & Sons (Asia) Pte Ltd, 2 Clementi Loop #02-01, Jin Xing Distripark, Singapore 129809

John Wiley & Sons Canada Ltd, 22 Worcester Road, Etobicoke, Ontario, Canada M9W 1L1

Wiley also publishes its books in a variety of electronic formats. Some content that appears in print
may not be available in electronic books.

Library of Congress Cataloging-in-Publication Data

The essentials of the new workplace : a guide to the human impact of modern working practices /
edited by David Holman . . . [et al.].
      p.   cm.
   Rev. ed. of : The new workplace. 2003.
   Includes bibliographical references and index.
   ISBN 0-470-02215-9 (pbk. : alk. paper)
      1. Quality of work life.   2. Job satisfaction.   3. Psychology, Industrial.   4. Work environment.
5. Work design.   6. Human-machine systems.   7. Industrial relations.   I. Holman, David (David J.)
II. New workplace.
   HD6955.N495   2005
   331.2–dc22

                                                                                    2004016048

British Library Cataloguing in Publication Data

A catalogue record for this book is available from the British Library

ISBN 0-470-02215-9

Typeset in 10/12pt Times by Techbooks Electronic Services Pvt Ltd, New Delhi, India
Printed and bound in Great Britain by TJ International Ltd, Padstow, Cornwall
This book is printed on acid-free paper responsibly manufactured from sustainable forestry
in which at least two trees are planted for each one used for paper production.

Contents

List of Illustrations

FIGURES

TABLES

About the Editors

David Holman is a Senior Research Fellow at the Centre for Organisation and Innovation, which is part of the Institute of Work Psychology, University of Sheffield. He obtained his degree in psychology, diploma in personnel management and doctorate from Manchester Metropolitan University. His main research interests are job design, well-being and emotions at work, learning at work, and management education and development. He is the author of *Management and Language: The Manager as a Practical Author* and has published articles in the *Journal of Applied Psychology, Journal of Occupational Health Psychology, Journal of Occupational and Organisational Psychology, Human Relations, Management Learning, Human Factors and Ergonomics in Manufacturing* and *Applied Ergonomics*.

Toby D. Wall is Professor of Psychology at the University of Sheffield, where he is Director of the Institute of Work Psychology and the ESRC Centre for Organisation and Innovation. He obtained his first degree and his doctorate from the University of Nottingham. His main research interests have been in industrial and organisational psychology and have recently focused on the effects of advanced manufacturing technology and shop floor work organisation on work performance and strain. His research has appeared in the *Journal of Applied Psychology*, the *Academy of Management Journal* and other leading publications. He is also the author of several books including *The Human Side of Advanced Manufacturing Technology* and *Job and Work Design*.

Chris W. Clegg is Professor of Organisational Psychology and Deputy Director of the Institute of Work Psychology at the University of Sheffield. He is a Co-Director of the ESRC Centre for Organisation and Innovation and Co-Director of the BAE – Rolls-Royce University Technology Partnership for Design. He currently chairs the Sociotechnical Sub-Group of the British Computer Society. He holds a BA (Hons) in Psychology from the University of Newcastle-upon-Tyne and an MSc in Business Administration from the University of Bradford. He is a Fellow of the British Psychological Society, a Fellow of the Royal Society of Arts, and a chartered psychologist. His research interests are in the areas of new technology, work organisation, information and control systems, sociotechnical theory and new management practices. He has published his work in a number of books and journals.

Paul Sparrow is the Ford Professor of International Human Resource Management at Manchester Business School. He graduated from the University of Manchester with a BSc (Hons) in Psychology and the University of Aston with an MSc in Applied Psychology and was then sponsored by Rank Xerox to study the impacts of ageing on the organisation for his Ph.D. at Aston University. He has written and edited a number of books including *European Human Resource Management in Transition, The Competent Organization: A*

Psychological Analysis of the Strategic Management Process, Human Resource Management: The New Agenda, International Human Resource Management and *Globalizing Human Resource Management*. He has also published articles in leading journals on the future of work, human resource strategy, the psychology of strategic management, international human resource management and cross-cultural management. He is the former Editor of the *Journal of Occupational and Organisational Psychology*.

Ann Howard is Manager of Assessment Technology Integrity for Development Dimensions International (DDI), a leading provider of human resource programs and services. She has served as president of the Leadership Research Institute, a non-profit organization that she co-founded in 1987. Ann is the author of more than 85 publications on topics such as assessment centers, management selection, managerial careers, and leadership. She is the senior author (with Dr Douglas W. Bray) of *Managerial Lives in Transition: Advancing Age and Changing Times*, which received the George R. Terry Award of Excellence from the Academy of Management in 1989. She has edited two books: *The Changing Nature of Work* (1995) and *Diagnosis for Organizational Change: Methods and Models* (1994). She is a past president of the Society for Industrial and Organizational Psychology and the Society of Psychologists in Management. Ann received her Ph.D. degree from the University of Maryland and her MS degree from San Francisco State University, both in industrial organizational psychology. She holds an honorary doctor of science degree from Goucher College, where she earned a BA degree in psychology.

List of Contributors

Professor Rosemary Batt, *School of Industrial and Labor Relations, Cornell University, 387 Ives Hall, Ithaca, NY 14853, USA*

Dr George S. Benson, *Department of Management, The University of Texas at Arlington, College of Business, BOX 19467, Arlington, TX 76019, USA*

Dr Bradley Chase, *Industrial and Systems Engineering, University of San Diego, 5998 Alcala Park, San Diego, CA 92110–2492, USA*

Dr Richard Cooney, *Department of Management, Monash University, Caulfield Campus, 27 Sir John Monash Drive, East Caulfield, Victoria 3145, Australia*

Professor John Cordery, *Department of Organizational and Labour Studies, University of Western Australia, Nedlands, Perth, WA 6907, Australia*

Professor Kevin Daniels, *Loughborough University Business School, University of Loughborough, Ashby Road, Loughborough LE11 3TU, UK*

Professor Rick Delbridge, *Cardiff Business School, Cardiff University, Colum Drive, Cardiff CF10 3EU, UK*

Virginia Doellgast, *School of Industrial and Labor Relations, Cornell University, 387 Ives Hall, Ithaca, NY 14853, USA*

Dr David Holman, *Institute of Work Psychology, University of Sheffield, Mushroom Lane, Sheffield S10 2TN, UK*

Dr Ann Howard, *Development Dimensions International, 21 Knoll Road, Tenafly, NJ 07670, USA*

Belén Icasati-Johanson, *Institute of Work Psychology, University of Sheffield, Mushroom Lane, Sheffield S10 2TN, UK*

Professor Waldemar Karwowski, *Center for Industrial Ergonomics, University of Louisville, Room 445, Lutz Hall, KY 40292, USA*

Dr Máire Kerrin, *Department of Psychology, Organisational Psychology Group, City University, Northampton Square, London EC1V 0HB, UK*

Professor David Lamond, *Sydney Graduate School of Management, University of Western Sydney, PO Box 6145, Paramatta Delivery Centre, NSW 2150, Australia*

Professor Edward E. Lawler III, *Center for Effective Organizations, Marshall School of Business, University of Southern California, Los Angeles, CA 90089–1421, USA*

Professor Harry Scarbrough, *Ikon Research Group, Warwick Business School, Warwick University, Coventry CV4 7AL, UK*

Professor Amrik Sohal, *Department of Management, Monash University, Caulfield Campus, 27 Sir John Monash Drive, East Caulfield, Victoria 3145, Australia*

Dr Peter Standen, *Department of Management, Edith Cowan University, Pearson St Churchlands, WA 6018, Australia*

Professor Toby D. Wall, *Institute of Work Psychology, University of Sheffield, Mushroom Lane, Sheffield S10 2TN, UK*

Professor Stephen Wood, *Institute of Work Psychology, University of Sheffield, Mushroom Lane, Sheffield S10 2TN, UK*

Preface

The make-up of today's workplace is characterised by the use of a wide array of modern working practices and technologies. Lean manufacturing, total quality management, advanced manufacturing technology, call centres, team working and knowledge management are just a few of the practices that organisations are using in their search for effectiveness. The introduction and use of these practices has provoked much debate and research on their nature and effects. A consistent theme within this has been that the social, psychological and organisational aspects of modern working practices and technologies must be considered in order to understand, design and manage them effectively. In order to bring this research together in one volume, we have invited leading authors from around the world to provide an up-to-date assessment of research on the main working practices that are shaping today's workplace. Most authors were invited to write on a particular practice, and to comment on its prevalence, to review its impact on employees' experience of work and to consider the human resource management implications of the practice. Where possible they also consider the impact of their chosen practice on performance. This theme is further developed in the final two chapters that examine, respectively, whether modern working practices and human resource practices more broadly have an effect on organisational performance in manufacturing and service sectors.

The breadth of working practices covered, the multi-disciplinary nature of the chapters and the focus on performance distinguish this book from others. We believe that this will help the reader gain a comprehensive understanding of the social, psychological and organisational aspects of modern working practices. Ultimately, though, this book is designed to make a contribution to the understanding, design and effective management of modern working practices. The book's breadth will appeal to those with an interest in industrial/ organisational psychology, human resource management, management and business studies, manufacturing, production engineering and change management, as well as those who are involved in the design, implementation and effective management of innovative working practices.

The editors would like to state that this book is an outcome of the programme of the ESRC Centre for Organisation and Innovation, at the Institute of Work Psychology, University of Sheffield, UK. The editors therefore acknowledge the support of the Economic and Social Research Council (ESRC) (UK). David Holman would particularly like to thank his family, Dave Wilson and family, Louise Wallace and family, and all his friends for their support throughout all the stages of preparing this book.

David Holman
Toby D. Wall
Chris W. Clegg
Paul Sparrow
Ann Howard

CHAPTER 1

Introduction to the *Essentials* of the New Workplace

David Holman, Stephen Wood and **Toby D. Wall**

Institute of Work Psychology, University of Sheffield, UK

and

Ann Howard

Development Dimensions International, New Jersey, USA

Modern working practices and technologies are typically designed to shape the nature of work and affect employees' behaviour. They include, for example, lean manufacturing, advanced manufacturing technology, total quality management, call centres, supply-chain partnering and knowledge management. Surveys show that these practices are increasingly prevalent in organisations in advanced industrial societies (Clegg, *et al.*, 2002; Lawler, Mohrman & Ledford, 1995; Osterman, 1994; Waterson *et al.*, 1999; Wood, Stride, Wall & Clegg, 2005). Yet when modern working practices are implemented they can alter work in unintended ways, have deleterious effects on employees and not produce the hoped for improvements in employee and organisational performance (Clegg *et al.*, 1997; Parker & Wall, 1998; Patterson, West, & Wall, 2004; Waterson *et al.*, 1999). Indeed, changing working practices often creates problems for employees at all levels in the organisation. It is therefore essential that we understand the nature of modern working practices, the extent of their use, and the effects that they have on employees and organisational performance so that they can be more effectively designed and managed.

Needless to say, considerable research has already been conducted on these issues in areas such as human resource management, occupational psychology, strategic management, operations management, economics and sociology; and one of the strongest messages to come out of this research is that the social, psychological and organisational aspects of working practices and technologies must be considered in order to understand, design and manage them effectively (Cherns, 1987; McLoughlin & Harris, 1997; Salvendy, 1997; Storey, 1994; Wall, Clegg & Kemp, 1987). As such, the main premise of this book is that the social and psychological side of modern working practices and technologies must be addressed. The aims of this book are therefore to examine:

1. The nature and extent of modern working practices and technologies.
2. The impact of modern working practices on how people work and their experience of work.

The Essentials *of the New Workplace: A Guide to the Human Impact of Modern Working Practices.*
Edited by David Holman, Toby D. Wall, Chris W. Clegg, Paul Sparrow and Ann Howard. © 2005 John Wiley & Sons, Ltd.

Table 1.1   Definition of the modern working practices

Modern working practice	Definition
Lean manufacturing	An integrated system of production with a single production flow that is pulled by the customer. Emphasis on small batch manufacture, just-in-time, team-based work and participation to eliminate non-value-adding activities and variabilities
Total quality management	A comprehensive, organisation-wide effort that is an integrated and interfunctional means of improving the quality of products and services and of sustaining competitive advantage
Advanced manufacturing technology	The application of computer-based technology to automate and integrate the different functions in the manufacturing system
Supply-chain partnering	Developing long-term, cooperative relationships with suppliers and customers
Team work	A collection of individuals who are interdependent in their tasks and outcomes, who see themselves and are seen by others as a distinct social entity within a larger social unit
Call centres	A work environment in which the main business is mediated by computer and telephone-based technologies that enable the efficient distribution of calls (or allocation of outgoing calls) to available staff, and permits customer–employee interaction to occur simultaneously with the use of display screen equipment and the instant access to, and inputting of, information
Knowledge management	The use of practices, particularly IT-based technologies and community- and network-based practices, to centralise, collectivise and create knowledge so that it can be exploited to increase organisational performance and to develop new opportunities
Employee involvement and empowerment	The use of practices to increase employee control, participation and involvement, and the supply of personal and organisational resources necessary to do the job
Teleworking/Virtual working	Working remotely from the home, remote offices or other sites for all or most of the working week, and connected to the main organisation by telephone and computer technologies

3. The human resource management implications of such practices.
4. The effect that these practices have on productivity and organizational performance.

These aims are covered throughout the book. Specifically, chapters 2–10 deal with the first three aims in relation to nine important modern working practices: lean manufacturing, total quality management, advanced manufacturing technology, supply-chain partnering, team work, call centres, knowledge management, employee involvement and virtual working. These practices are defined in Table 1.1 and were chosen because their use is thought to be on the increase and to be having a significant impact the nature of work. The last two chapters are concerned with the fourth aim of the book, the relationship between modern working practices, human resource management and organisational performance. Chapter 11 focuses on manufacturing organisations, Chapter 12 on service organisations. The rest of this chapter sets out some of the main issues that have concerned researchers when examining the area of modern working practices.

THE CONCEPTUALISATION AND NATURE OF MODERN WORKING PRACTICES

A working practice can be broadly defined as a set of technique- or technologically-based tasks that directly shape the labour process.[1] Technique-based tasks involve the practical application of a particular method, procedure or skill. Technologically-based tasks are those in which the practical application of a particular method or skill involves using technological hardware such as machinery or computers. According to this definition, working practices are likely to differ in the extent to which they use technique- or technology-based tasks. Advanced manufacturing technology primarily involves technology-based tasks; team work primarily involves technique-based tasks, whereas knowledge management appears to be a combination of technological and technique-based tasks. However, while this definition is useful in highlighting the basic nature of a working practice, and while general definitions of each working practice can be made (see Table 1.1), they hide a degree of conceptual variation within definitions of each practice. For example, Cooney and Sohal (Chapter 3) point out that TQM is "something of a fungible concept and one that is sometimes difficult to pin down. There is not one TQM, but a range of TQMs" (p. 34). They illustrate this by stating that TQM "may be seen as a technically-focused quality management programme, as a philosophy of business concerned with strategic business issues or as an organizational-behavioural intervention designed to promote the more effective use of human resources" (pp. 33–34). Similar degrees of conceptual variability are found in the concepts of advanced manufacturing technology, lean manufacturing, supply-chain partnering, call centres, team working and knowledge management.

In parallel with this conceptual variability, there is also a degree of variation in the actual form of a working practice. There are a number of reasons for this heterogeneity. First, working practices are used to achieve multiple aims, and different aspects of a practice may be emphasised in order to achieve those aims. Second, working practices rarely occur on their own as independent entities. Delbridge (Chapter 2) notes that lean manufacturing will contain TQM practices, team work and supply-chain partnering initiatives, while Benson and Lawler (Chapter 9) show how TQM can be an integral part of an employee involvement initiative. Even "remote" practices such as telework may be part of a supply-chain initiative or involve team working, albeit virtually.

Third, a modern working practice is always embedded within a broader social system and is best considered as a socio-technical system (Cherns, 1987). As a consequence, the nature of a working practice—and its effects—will be affected by the social system of which it is part. Significant aspects of the social system, and ones that are a core concern in this book, are job design and human resource practices. These two aspects will be discussed in more depth shortly, but job design varies along a continuum that runs from "Taylorist" to "Empowered" (Parker & Wall, 1998). In Taylorist jobs, employees have little discretion

---

[1] That working practices have direct effects on the labour process helps to distinguish it from human resource practices, which are likely to have indirect effects on the labour process.

over how they do their work and tasks tend to be unskilled and repetitive. In empowered jobs, employees are given responsibility for a broad range of varied tasks, a high degree of discretion in how they work, and opportunities to use and develop their skills and participate in decision-making processes. Human resource practices vary in the extent to which they are present in an organisation, and in their degree of sophistication. One organisation may make extensive use of high quality and continued training, regular performance appraisals, well-resourced recruitment procedures and performance-contingent payment systems (such as profit sharing); another organisation may use these for a specific group of employees, while another may use little or no induction, sophisticated selection or training practices regardless of the type of employees. It is often assumed in characterising the modern organisation that sophisticated human resource practices will be combined with empowered jobs to form what is called a high-commitment or involvement approach, while the minimal use of sophisticated human resource practices and Taylorist jobs are taken to form the low-commitment/involvement approach assumed to characterise the organisational model of the past (Lawler, 1986; Walton, 1985; see also Benson & Lawler, Chapter 9; Wood, Chapter 11; Batt & Doellgast, Chapter 12).

Throughout the book the reader will see how variations in job design and human resource practices affect the nature of a modern working practice. For example, Cooney and Sohal (Chapter 3) suggest that TQM can be used with either Taylorist or empowered jobs and that this leads to two very different sorts of TQM (cf., the distinction between total quality control and total quality learning forms of TQM; Sitkin, Sutcliffe & Schroeder (1994)). Moreover involvement initiatives, which are generally associated with empowered jobs, can be accompanied by Taylorist jobs (for an example of the latter see Adler and Borys'(1996) description of enabling or learning bureaucracies).

In sum, modern working practices are likely, so theory suggests, to be bundled together with other working practices and are embedded within a social system in which two significant aspects are job design and human resource practices. The mixture of technical and social practices means that a single practice can take on a variety of forms, and that the effects of a practice may ultimately depend on the form it takes.

CHANGE AND CONTINUITY IN THE WORKPLACE

Most of us are now fairly well versed in the changes occurring in the economic, political and social landscape. These include: the internationalisation of the economy; a reduction in trade barriers between countries; the deregulation of markets; privatisation and the ending of state monopolies; increasing demands for greater accountability and efficiency in the public sector; and changing consumer demand (e.g. a desire for more customised products or better quality) (Appelbaum & Batt, 1994; Doganis, 2000; Gabriel & Lang, 1998; Katz, 1997; Pollitt, 1993). The changes have intensified competition and achieving a competitive advantage will depend on the simultaneous pursuit of cost minimisation, quality, innovation and customisation (Appelbaum, Bailey, Berg & Kalleberg, 2000; Piore & Sabel, 1984). Similar demands for cost efficiencies, quality and customised services are evident in the public and not-for-profit sectors (e.g., in universities; see Peters, 1992). In addition, the creation, ownership and management of knowledge-based assets is increasingly recognised as a basis for competition (see Scarbrough, Chapter 8, on Knowledge Management, and Hodgkinson and Sparrow (2002), for the implications of knowledge management for organisational learning processes, the co-ordination of distributed cognition and top team behaviour).

Organisational change is undoubtedly taking place in response to these general economic and societal changes and in the expectation of such changes (Sparrow & Cooper, 2003). The chapters in this book provide evidence for this organisational change through the adoption of new working practices.[2] There appears to be fairly widespread use (in some 40–60% of organisations) of TQM, team work and supply-chain partnering, particularly in UK manufacturing companies (Clegg et al., 2002; Wood et al., 2005), while the service sector has witnessed a rise in the use of team work, TQM and information technology since the 1990s (Batt & Doellgast, Chapter 12). Advanced manufacturing technology is reported as being used, at least to a moderate extent, by some 40% of all manufacturing organisations and lean manufacturing appears to be fairly widespread in the automotive industry but less extensively used in other parts of the manufacturing sector (Clegg et al., 2002; Delbridge, Chapter 3). There is also evidence of initiatives that empower employees occurring in about one quarter of UK, Japanese, Australian and Swiss manufacturing organisations (Clegg et al., 2002; Wood et al., 2005), although Benson and Lawler (Chapter 9) do question the extent to which firms strongly embrace such initiatives and show that involvement initiatives declined in the US in the mid-1990s. Less extensive but growing in popularity are newer practices such as teleworking and knowledge management, while call centres now employ 1–2% of the working population in many industrialised nations and are of growing importance in developing economies such as India and Malaysia.

The common interpretation of the prevalence of modern working practices is that they represent part of a radical move away from the "old workplace", characterised by Fordist large-scale, hierarchical bureaucracies designed for mass production and mass service (see Wood, 1989, pp.10–11, for a definition of Fordism). This old workplace is being replaced by a "new workplace" characterised by the co-occurrence of four factors: flexible modern working practices; high-involvement human resource practices; a managerial orientation that views these two sets of practices as integrated and complementary; and an employee orientation that is flexible and pro-active (Amin, 1994; Kumar, 1992; Lawler et al., 1995; Schneider & Bowen, 1995; Storey, 1994; Unsworth & Parker, 2003; see also Wood, Chapter 11). This implies that "the new workplace" can be defined as comprising an "historical new", i.e., the presence of new working practices, types of HR practices or bundles of practice, and an "experiential new", i.e., the presence of qualitatively different managerial and employee orientations and experiences of self and work.

However, we must exercise some caution when applying these categories to the real world. First, a substantial proportion of organisations have not adopted many modern working practices, nor are modern working practices necessarily accompanied by high-involvement HRM. Second, "old workplace" ideas are still influencing how "modern" working practices are designed and managed, as is illustrated by the influence of Taylorism in some call centres and other service organisations (Ritzer, 1998; Taylor & Bain, 1999), and the extension and revitalisation of Fordist principles in just-in-time, an essential component of lean manufacturing (Tomaney, 1994; Wood, 1993). Third, modern working practices are

---

[2] Two caveats on this are that much of the available data comes from the US and the UK, and that not all changes are in the direction of new working practices, as some firms may be introducing practices for the first time or reformatting those associated with Taylorism.

not always accompanied by flexible, pro-active employee orientations and fundamentally different experiences of self and work. At this stage of knowledge it is safest to assume that throughout the economy there will be considerable variation across organisations. Combining our historical and experiential categories, there are logically four possible types of workplace:

1. *The "new/new" workplace* in which modern working practices are associated with a qualitatively different experience of work. For example, workplaces with a combination of TQM and employee involvement initiatives that are accompanied by qualitatively different employee orientations to work, customers and their lives.
2. *The "new/old" workplace* in which modern working practices are associated with a quantitative change in how jobs are designed but employees' experiences of work are not radically or qualitatively different as a consequence. For example, an organisation implements TQM and it results in employees experiencing less control and more stress. However, the introduction of TQM does not alter their sense of self or orientation to work, and thus the change has been one of degree, not type.
3. *The "old/new" workplace* in which traditional working practices are associated with qualitatively new experiences of work, for example when young employees have been socialised in a different economic climate and have radically different work expectations from those normally associated with the traditional practices prevalent in their place of work.
4. *The "old/old" workplace* in which traditional working practices are associated with a relatively unchanged experience of work.

We do not have the knowledge to identify the relative prevalence of these different types of workplace. For example, we do not know enough about the exact co-occurrence of modern working practices, HRM practices, managerial orientations and employee experiences. We know even less about the effects of such practices on how people experience or approach their work.[3] It is probable that all four types of workplaces will exist, but we might also speculate that it is likely that a sizeable proportion of contemporary workplaces will be a mixture of "old" and "new" (Blyton & Turnbull, 1994) and employees' experiences will mirror this. Just as there are questions about the extent and nature of workplace change, questions are also being asked about whether the effects of change are as beneficial as many imply (Knights & Willmott, 2000; Philimore, 1989). Modern working practices and high-involvement human resource practices are often portrayed as leading to a win–win situation for the employee and the organisation. But, while there is research that demonstrates that the introduction of modern working practices can lead to more interesting work, more skilled work and lower levels of employee stress, there are also studies that show that the introduction of modern working practices can intensify work, de-skill employees and reduce well-being (Adler & Borys, 1996; Braverman, 1974; Klein, 1989; Knights, Willmott & Collinson, 1985; Parker & Wall, 1998; Sturdy, Knights & Willmott, 1992).

---

[3] This lack of understanding of the employees' experience partly reflects the fact that the measures typically used to assess employee experience, such as job satisfaction and job control, are not designed to assess qualitative shifts in experience, and because factors tend to be examined independently, making it harder to ascertain global aggregate changes in individual experience. Qualitative shifts in the experience of work might be discerned more readily if other factors, such as identity or the psychological contract, were assessed, or if individual change was examined in a more aggregated manner (Jermier, Knights and Nord, 1994; Rousseau, 1995; Sennett, 1998).

While definitive answers cannot yet be made about the nature of change in the workplace, this book will equip the reader with a means of achieving a critical, nuanced understanding of the contemporary workplace and its social and psychological effects on employees. To help further achieve this, it is necessary to appreciate the three main traditions in which research on the human side of working practices has been conducted. They are:

* job design theory
* human resource management and its link to organisational performance, and
* socio-political perspectives on the design and management of working practices.

JOB AND WORK DESIGN THEORY

Historically, the main focus of job design research has been on the psychological conse-quences of work simplification brought about through the pervasive adoption of Taylorist and Fordist approaches to work organisation. Two approaches, job characteristics and socio-technical theories, have been particularly influential.[4] The job characteristics approach to job design has been strongly influenced by Hackman and Oldham's (1976) Job Character-istics Model (JCM). They proposed five core job dimensions (autonomy, feedback, skill variety, task identity, task significance) that determine one of three "critical psychological states". In particular, autonomy affects experienced responsibility, feedback affects knowl-edge of results, and skill variety, task identity and task significance affect the experienced meaningfulness of work. Collectively, these critical psychological states affect the level of work satisfaction, internal work motivation, performance, absence and labour turnover. Research has generally demonstrated that the core job characteristics all predict affective outcomes such as satisfaction and motivation, but evidence for their affects on employee behaviour, performance, turnover and absence, is less consistent (Parker & Wall, 1998, pp. 15–16). The motivating potential of job design has been a central issue within this research tradition (Campion & McClelland, 1993; Wall & Martin, 1987), as it also has been within debates on modern working practices and high-commitment human resource practices.

Karaseck and Theorell's (1990) control-demands model is another job characteristic approach that has been influential. It predicts that "high-strain jobs" are those characterised by high work demands and low control. Although the evidence for interactive effect of control and demand assumed in this prediction is inconclusive (Van Der Doef & Maes, 1999), numerous studies have confirmed that the absence of control and the presence of high job demands are consistent predictors of job-related strain (see O'Driscoll and Cooper (1996) and Parker and Wall (1998) for summaries).

The second main approach to job design has been socio-technical theory. Socio-technical theory is concerned with the design of work systems and posits that these are comprised of a technical system and a social system. These subsystems are seen as interdependent and should therefore be jointly designed in such a way that the overall system is optimal (de Sitter, den Hertog & Dankbaar, 1997). Socio-technical theory has made a number of contributions to our understanding of job design. It is best known for its articulation of a set of design principles and for its advocacy of autonomous work groups (Cherns, 1987; Clegg, 2000; Emery, 1964). These design principles include: methods of working should be minimally

---

[4] For a fuller discussion of the main job design traditions, their limitations and future prospects, see Bakker, Demerouti & Schaufeli, 2003; Holman, Clegg & Waterson, 2002; Parker, Wall, & Cordery, 2001.

specified; variances in work processes should be handled at source; boundaries between tasks should not be drawn to impede the sharing of information, learning and knowledge. Desirable job characteristics thus include a reasonable level of demand, opportunities for learning, and an area of decision-making owned by the operator. These principles of design for desirable jobs are seen to be best expressed in autonomous work groups (AWGs), and much socio-technical research and practice has been focused at a group level. Although it has been suggested that an "underlying lack of specificity about the nature and effects of such initiatives [i.e. AWGs] makes a coherent assessment of their outcomes difficult" (Parker *et al.*, 2001, p. 416), research demonstrates that AWGs can have positive effects on well-being and productivity (Parker & Wall, 1998).

Another notable feature of job design research is that it has reflected many of the debates and issues concerned with the changing nature of work. For example, the recent interest in cognition and knowledge at work has focused attention on cognitive job characteristics, such as problem-solving demands and attention demand (Jackson, Wall, Martin & Davids, 1993), and the opportunity to develop and utilise skills (O'Brien, 1986; Holman & Wall, 2002), as well as knowledge-based job outcomes, such as skill and self-efficacy (Holman & Wall, 2002; Parker & Wall, 1998). Consideration has also been given to the development of skills and knowledge as a mediator of the link between job characteristics and performance, as these make employees better able to deal with variances in the work process (Miller & Monge, 1986) and to decide the best strategy to deal with a particular situation (Frese & Zapf, 1994; Wall, Corbett, Martin, Clegg & Jackson, 1990; Wall, Jackson, & Davids, 1992).

HUMAN RESOURCE MANAGEMENT AND ORGANISATIONAL PERFORMANCE

Key concepts in human resource management (HRM) theory are fit and synergy (Wood, 1999). Three types of fit can be identified:

1. The internal fit between human resource management practices.
2. The organisational fit between HRM systems—coherent sets of HRM practices—and other systems within the organisation.
3. The strategic fit between HRM systems and organisational strategy.

The discussion of internal fit centres on the idea that some HRM practices combine better than others, and that coherent bundles of practice will have synergistic effects. A corollary of this is that any difference in organisational performance between organisations will be partly explained by the differential usage of bundles of practice. Two main bundles of HRM practice are normally identified, at least as ideal types, that correspond to the high-involvement (or high-commitment) approach and low-involvement approach (Lawler, 1986; Walton, 1985; see also Benson and Lawler, Chapter 9; Batt & Doellgast, Chapter 12).

The rationale of the high-involvement approach is that a particular bundle of HRM practices is needed to recruit, develop and maintain a workforce with the high-level technical, cognitive and interpersonal skills that are assumed to be necessary if organisations are to deal with rapidly changing demands, to provide a high quality service or product, and, crucially, to realise the full potential of complex modern working practices (Becker & Huselid, 1998;

Lawler *et al.*, 1995; Steedman & Wagner, 1987; see also Chapter 8 on knowledge management). The human resource practices used to achieve this include: employee involvement schemes; job flexibility; continued training; performance appraisal; well-resourced selection and recruitment procedures; and performance-contingent payment systems (Wood, 1999). In addition, jobs must be designed so as to provide employees with a high degree of discretion and responsibility so that employees can use their skills and abilities in the most effective manner, respond to variances in the work process as they occur and exhibit discretionary behaviours (Susman & Chase, 1986).

The rationale of the low-involvement approach is that it may not be desirable, possible or strategically necessary to use a costly but highly skilled workforce. For example, an organisation may offer a simple service or product to a mass market in which profit margins are low and in which they compete on low cost. Organisational effectiveness depends on keeping costs low. This is achieved by using simplified, Taylorist jobs with low variety and discretion so that less skilled, cheaper labour can be used. The use of unskilled labour also means that less sophisticated recruitment practices can be used and that little training is needed.

The current emphasis on the high-involvement HRM system as a replacement for an outmoded Taylorist, bureaucratic and low-involvement approach implies that it will have positive effects on organisational performance in all circumstances. From this "universalistic" perspective, modern working practices are most effective when underpinned by a highly skilled and committed workforce and secured through appropriate human resource management practices (Becker & Huselid, 1998; Lawler *et al.*, 1995; Walton, 1985). This implies that the high-involvement HRM system is a necessary but not sufficient basis for high performance. The added ingredient is modern working practices, such as TQM and lean manufacturing. It is matching or aligning high-involvement systems and modern working practices that will maximise performance (Wood, Chapter 11; Beaumont, 1995; Kochan & Osterman, 1995).

An alternative to this approach is the "contingency" approach, which places emphasis on strategic fit, and on the need for the HRM system to be chosen in the light of the organisation's strategy. A common formulation of this is that a high-involvement system will fit an innovation/quality strategy and a low-involvement system will fit a cost-minimisation strategy (Batt, 2000; Hoque, 1999; Schuler & Jackson, 1987). These different approaches are presented and discussed in more depth in Chapters 9, 11 and 12.

SOCIAL AND POLITICAL PROCESSES IN THE DESIGN AND MANAGEMENT OF MODERN WORKING PRACTICES

A basic assumption of this book is that job design and human resource management are fundamental to an understanding of modern working practices. However, much job design and HRM literature neglects the issue of why a particular practice takes its current form. Neither does it have much to say on the active role that employees play in shaping practices. In contrast, interpretivist research has illuminated how the political and social assumptions of those involved in the design and introduction of new technology become embedded within the technology, in the form of prescriptive design rationales that prescribe a particular view of how work is undertaken (Moran & Carroll, 1996). The configuration of a technology and the social practices that surround them can be seen, at any one point in time, as an outcome of social and political negotiation between various groups (Barley, 1990; Buchanan & Boddy, 1983; Mueller *et al.*, 1986; Orlikowski, 1992). Technologies can therefore be understood as "a frozen assemblage of practices, assumptions, beliefs [and] language" that has become "fixed" in a material form (Cooper & Woolgar, 1993, p. 2) and, because of this, design processes have lasting effects on job design, productivity and the quality of working life.

Critical research within the labour process tradition has drawn attention to how management attempt to instil within workers the belief that organisational objectives are their own and to ensure that these objectives are considered when making judgements at work. From this perspective, managements try to use working practices as mechanisms through which employees are encouraged into making positive productive responses (Grenier, 1988; Knights & Sturdy, 1990). But workers need not be seen as passive reactors to management initiatives. Rather, labour process theory treats workers as active agents who have to consciously comply with managerial efforts to control them and may equally resist these, and that these psychological processes in turn shape working practices (Burawoy, 1979; Collinson, 1994; Knights, 1990; Sturdy *et al.*, 1992).

These two approaches that emphasise the social and political processes involved in the design, introduction and management of modern working practices paint a dynamic picture of organisational life in which employees actively shape working practices and one in which there may be conflicting interests over their uses and aims (see Chapter 7 on call centres).

CONCLUSION

The main purpose of this chapter has been to set the scene for the rest of the book by discussing the working practices that organisations are using to respond to the changing social and economic landscape and introducing the main issues and theoretical approaches to the social and psychological side of modern working practices. This brief introduction suggests that a number of critical questions that the reader can bear in mind when reading this book. They are:

The New Workplace

- How prevalent are modern working practices?
- What is the evidence for the co-occurrence of working practices, job design and human resource practices?
- What is the evidence for the co-occurrence of working practices and particular types of managerial and employee orientations and experiences?
- To what extent does a new workplace exist?

Job and Work Design

- What are the impacts of new technologies and new working practices on job content?
- How do the job and work designs of modern working practices vary?
- What are the core job characteristics of modern working practices?
- What effects do the particular job designs of working practices have on employee well-being and performance?

- Through what mechanisms do job characteristics affect job outcomes in modern working practices?

Human Resource Management

- What human resource practices are used in conjunction with modern working practices?
- How do HRM practices affect the form of a practice?
- How do HRM and modern working practices affect employee and organisational performance?

Social and Political Factors in the Design and Management of Modern Working Practices?

- How do the designs of modern working practices arise?
- How are working practices shaped and configured by the various actors?
- What are the values and goals of the actors?
- Do these values conflict and, if they do, how is this expressed?

REFERENCES

Adler, P. & Borys, B. (1996). Two types of bureaucracy: enabling and coercive. *Administrative Science Quarterly*, **41**, 61–89.

Amin, A. (Ed.) (1994). *Post-Fordism: A Reader*. Oxford: Blackwell.

Appelbaum, E., Bailey, T., Berg., P. & Kalleberg, A. (2000). *Manufacturing Advantage: Why High Performance Work Systems Pay Off*. Ithaca, NY: ILR Press.

Appelbaum, E. & Batt, R. (1994). *The New American Workplace: Transforming Work Systems in the United States*. Ithaca, NY: Cornell ILR Press.

Bakker, A. B., Demerouti, E. & Schaufeli, W. B. (2003). Dual processes at work in a call centre: an application of the job demands-resources model. *European Journal of Work and Organisational Psychology*, **12**, 393–428.

Barley, S. R. (1990). The alignment of technology and structure through roles and networks. *Administrative Science Quarterly*, **35**, 61–103.

Batt, R. (2000). Strategic segmentation in front line services: matching customers, employees and human resource systems. *International Journal of Human Resource Management*, **11**, 540–561.

Beaumont, P. (1995). *The Future of Employment Relations*. London: Sage.

Becker, B. E. & Huselid, M. A. (1998). High performance work systems and firm performance: a synthesis of research and managerial implications. In G. R. Ferris (Ed.), *Research in Personnel and Human Resources*, Vol. 16. Stamford, CT: JAI Press.

Blyton, P. & Turnbull, P. (1994). *The Dynamics of Employee Relations*. London: Macmillan.

Braverman, H. (1974). *Labour and Monopoly Capital*. New York: Monthly Review Press.

Buchanan, D. & Boddy, D. (1983). *Organizations in the Computer Age*. Aldershot: Gower.

Burawoy, M. (1979). *Manufacturing Consent*. Chicago: Chicago University Press.

Campion, M. A. & McClelland, C. L. (1993). Follow-up and extension of the interdisciplinary cost and benefits of enlarged jobs. *Journal of Applied Psychology*, **78**, 339–351.

Cherns, A. (1987). Principles of socio-technical design revisited. *Human Relations*, **40**, 153–162.

Clegg, C.W. (2000). Socio-technical principles for system design. *Applied Ergonomics*, **31**, 463–477.

Clegg, C. W., Axtell, C. M., Damodaran, L., Farbey, B., Hull, R., Lloyd-Jones, R., Nicholls, J., Sell, R. & Tomlinson, C. (1997). Information technology: a study of performance and the role of human and organizational factors. *Ergonomics*, **40**, 851–871.

Clegg, C. W., Wall, T. D., Pepper, K., Stride C. B., Woods, D., Morrison, D., Cordery, J., Couchman, P., Badham, R., Kuenzler, C., Grote, G., Ide, W., Takahashi, M. & Kogi, K. (2002). An International Survey of the Use and Effectiveness of Modern Manufacturing Practices. *Human Factors and Ergonomics in Manufacturing*, **12**, 171–191.

Collinson, D. (1994). Strategies of resistance: power, knowledge and subjectivity in the workplace. In J. Jermier, D. Knights & W. Nord (Eds), *Resistance and Power in Organizations: Agency, Subjectivity and the Labour Process* (pp. 25–68). London: Routledge.

Cooper, G. & Woolgar, S. (1993). *Software Is Society Made Malleable: the Importance of Conceptions of Audience in Software Research and Practice*. PICT Policy Research Paper 25. London: Programme in Information and Communication Technologies.

Doganis, R. (2000). *The Airline Business in the Twenty-first Century*. London: Routledge.

Emery, F. (1964). *Report of the Hunfoss Project*. Tavistock Document Series. London: Tavistock.

Frese, M. & Zapf, D. (1994). Action as the core of work psychology: a German approach. In H. C. Triandis, M. D. Dunnette & L. M. Hough (Eds), *Handbook of Industrial and Organisational Psychology* (pp. 271–340). Palo Alto, CA: Consulting Psychologists Press.

Gabriel, Y. & Lang, T. (1998). *The Unmanageable Consumer: Contemporary Consumption and Its Fragmentations*. London: Sage.

Grenier, G. (1988). *Inhuman Relations: Quality Circles and Anti-unionism in American Industry*. Philadelphia, PA: Temple University Press.

Hackman, J. & Oldham, G. (1976). Motivation through the design of work: test of a theory. *Organizational Behaviour and Human Performance*, **15**, 250–279.

Hodgkinson, G. P. & Sparrow, P. R. (2002). *The Competent Organisation*. Maidenhead: McGraw-Hill.

Holman, D., Clegg, C. W. & Waterson, P. (2002). Navigating the territory of job design. *Applied Ergonomics*, **33**, 197–205.

Holman, D. & Wall, T. D. (2002). Work characteristics, learning outcomes and strain: a test of competing direct effects, mediated and moderated models. *Journal Of Occupational Health Psychology*, **7**, 283–301.

Hoque, K. (1999). Human resource management and performance in the UK hotel industry. *British Journal of Industrial Relations*, **37**, 419–443.

Jackson, P. R., Wall, T. D., Martin, R. & Davids, K. (1993). New measures of job control, cognitive demand and production responsibility. *Journal of Applied Psychology*, **78**, 753–762.

Jermier, J., Knights, D. & Nord, W. (Eds) (1994). *Resistance and Power in Organizations: Agency, Subjectivity and the Labour Process*. London: Routledge.

Karasek, R. & Theorell, T. (1990). *Healthy Work: Stress, Productivity, and the Reconstruction of Working Life*. New York: Basic Books.

Katz, H. C. (1997). *Telecommunications: Restructuring Work and Employment Relations Worldwide*. Ithaca, NY: ILR Press.

Klien, J. A. (1989). The human costs of manufacturing reform. *Harvard Business Review*, **67**, 60–66.

Knights, D. (1990). Subjectivity, power and the labour process. In D. Knights & H. Willmott (Eds), *Labour Process Theory* (pp. 297–336). London: Macmillan.

Knights, D. & Sturdy, A. (1990). New technology and the self-disciplined worker in the insurance industry. In I. Varcoe, M. McNeil & S. Yearly (Eds), *Deciphering Science and Technology* (pp. 126–154). London: Macmillan.

Knights, D. & Willmott, H. (2000). *The Reengineering Revolution: Critical Studies of Organisational Change*. London: Sage.

Knights, D., Willmott, H. & Collinson, D. (Eds) (1985). *Job Redesign: Critical Perspectives on the Labour Process*. Aldershot: Gower.

Kochan, T. & Osterman, P. (1995). *Mutual Gains*. Boston, MA: Harvard Business School.

Kumar, K. (1992). New theories of industrial society. In P. Brown & H. Lauder (Eds), *Education for Economic Survival: From Fordism to Post-Fordism*. London: Rouledge.

Lawler, E. E. (1986). *High-Involvement Management*. San Fransisco, CA: Jossey-Bass.

Lawler, E. E., Mohrman, S. & Ledford, G. (1995). *Creating High Performance Organisations: Practices and Results of Employee Involvement and Total Quality Management in Fortune 1000 Companies*. San Fransisco, CA: Jossey-Bass.

McLoughlin, I. & Harris, M. (1997). *Innovation, Organizational Change and Technology*. London: Thompson Business Press.

Mueller, W. *et al.* (1986). Pluralist beliefs about new technology within a manufacturing organization. *New Technology, Work and Employment*, **1**, 127–139.

Miller, K. I. & Monge, P. R. (1986). Participation, satisfaction and productivity: a meta-analytic review. *Academy of Management Journal*, **29**, 727–753.

Moran, T. P. & Carroll, C. M. (1996). *Design Rationale*. Hove: Erlbaum.

O'Brien, G. E. (1986). *Psychology of Work and Unemployment*. Chichester: Wiley.

O'Driscoll, M. P. & Cooper, C. L. (1996). Sources and management of excessive job stress and burnout. In P. B. Warr (Ed.), *Psychology at Work*, 4th edn. Harmondsworth: Penguin.

Orlikowski, W. (1992). The duality of technology: rethinking the concept of technology in organizations. *Organizational Science*, **3**, 398–427.

Osterman, P. (1994). How common is workplace transformation and who adopts it? *Industrial and Labour Relations Review*, **47**, 173–188.

Parker, S. K. & Wall, T. D. (1998). *Job and Work Design*. London: Sage.

Parker, S. K., Wall, T. D. & Cordery, J. L. (2001). Future work design and practice: towards an elaborated model of work design. *Journal of Occupational and Organisational Psychology*, **74**, 413–440.

Patterson, M. G., West, M. A. & Wall, T. D. (2004). Integrated manufacturing, empowerment and company performance. *Journal of Organizational Behaviour*, **25**, 1–25.

Peters, M. (1992). Performance and accountability in the "Post-Industrial Society": the crisis of British universities. *Studies in Higher Education*, **17**, 123–139.

Philimore, J. (1989). Flexible specialisation, work organisation and skills. *New Technology, Work and Employment*, **4**, 79–91.

Piore, M. & Sabel, C. (1984). *The Second Industrial Divide*. New York: Basic Books.

Pollitt, C. (1993). *Managerialism and the Public Services: Cuts or Change in the 1980s*. Oxford: Blackwell.

Ritzer, R. (1998). *The McDonaldization Thesis: Explorations and Extensions*. Thousand Oaks, CA: Sage.

Rousseau, D. M. (1995). *Psychological Contracts in Organizations: Understanding Written and Unwritten Agreements*. Thousand Oaks, CA: Sage.

Salvendy, G. (Ed.) (1997). *Handbook of Human Factors and Ergonomics*, 2nd edn. New York: Wiley.

Schneider, B. & Bowen, D. (1995). *Winning the Service Game*. Boston, MA: Harvard Business School Press.

Schuler, R. & Jackson, S. (1987). Linking competitive strategies with human resource management practices. *Academy of Management Executive*, **1**, 207–219.

Sennett, R. (1998). *The Corrosion of Character: The Personal Consequences of Work in the New Capitalism*. London: Norton.

Sitkin, S. B., Sutcliffe, K. M. & Schroeder, R. G. (1994). Distinguishing control from learning in Total Quality Management: a contingency perspective. *Academy of Management Review*, **19**, 574–564.

de Sitter, L., den Hertog, J. & Dankbaar, B. (1997). From complex organizations with simple jobs to simple organizations with complex jobs. *Human Relations*, **50**, 497–534.

Sparrow, P. R. & Cooper, C. L. (2003). *The Employment Relationship: Key Challenges for HR*. Oxford: Butterworth Heinemann.

Steedman, H. & Wagner, K. (1987). A second look at productivity, machinery and skills in Britain and Germany. *NI Economic Review*, November.

Storey, J. (1994). *New Wave Manufacturing Practices: Organizational and Human Resource Management Dimensions*. London: Chapman Hall.

Sturdy, A., Knights, D. & Willmott, H. (Eds) (1992). *Skill and Consent*. London: Routledge.

Susman, G. & Chase R. (1986). A sociotechnical systems analysis of the integrated factory. *Journal of Applied Behavioral Science*, **22**, 257–270.

Taylor, P. & Bain, P. (1999). An assembly line in the head: the call centre labour process. *Industrial Relations Journal*, **30**, 101–117.

Tomaney, J. (1994). A new paradigm of work organisation and technology? In A. Amin (Ed.), *Post-Fordism: A Reader*. Oxford: Blackwell.

Unsworth, K. L. & Parker, S. K. (2003). Pro-activity and innovation: promoting a new workforce for the new workplace. In D. Holman, T. D. Wall, C. W. Clegg, P. Sparrow & A. Howard (Eds),

The New Workplace: A Guide to the Human Impact of Modern Working Practices (pp.175–196). Chichester: Wiley.

Van Der Doef, M. & Maes, S. (1999). The job demand-control (-support) model and psychological well-being: a review of 20 years of empirical research. *Work and Stress*, **13**, 87–114.

Wall, T. D., Clegg, C. W. & Kemp, N. J. (Eds) (1987). *The Human Side of Advanced Manufacturing Technology*. Chichester: Wiley.

Wall, T. D., Corbett, J. M., Martin, R., Clegg, C.W. & Jackson, P. R. (1990). Advanced manufacturing technology, work design and performance: a change study. *Journal of Applied Psychology*, **75**, 691–697.

Wall, T. D., Jackson, P. R., & Davids, K. (1992). Operator work design and robotics system performance: a serendipitous field study. *Journal of Applied Psychology*, **77**, 353–362.

Wall, T. D. & Martin, R. (1987). Job and work design. In C. L. Cooper & I. T. Robertson (Eds), *International Review of Industrial and Organisational Psychology*. Chichester: Wiley.

Walton, R. (1985). From "control" to "commitment" in the workplace. *Harvard Business Review*, **63**, 77–84.

Waterson, P. E., Clegg, C. W., Bolden, R., Pepper, K., Warr, P. B. & Wall, T. D. (1999). The use and effectiveness of modern manufacturing practices: a survey of UK industry. *International Journal of Production Research*, **37**, 2271–2292.

Wood, S. (1989). *The Transformation of Work? Skill, Flexibility and the Labour Process*. London: Unwin Hyman.

Wood, S. (1993). The Japanization of Fordism? *Economic and Industrial Democracy*, **14**, 538–55. (Reprinted in B. Jessop) (Ed.) (2000). *Regulation Theory and the Crisis of Capitalism: Regulationist Perspectives on Fordism and Post-fordism* (pp. 318–337). Cheltenham: Edward Elgar.

Wood, S. (1999). Human resource management and performance. *International Journal of Management Review*, **1**, 367–413.

Wood, S. J., Stride, C. B., Wall, T. D. and Clegg, C. W. (2005). Revisiting the use and effectiveness of modern management practices. *Human factors and Ergonomics in Manufacturing*, **15**.

CHAPTER 2

Workers Under Lean Manufacturing

Rick Delbridge

Cardiff Business School, Cardiff University and Advanced Institute of Management Research, UK

Few management ideas have been as influential in their field as lean production techniques in manufacturing industry. Initially, the interest surrounded a relatively small number of companies that were perceived to be operating in a different way to that prescribed under traditional Western manufacturing methods. Particularly since the rise of the Japanese economy in the 1980s, there has been an increasing interest in the company philosophy and management techniques utilized by such companies as Toyota (Fujimoto, 1999), Nissan (Wickens, 1995) and Toshiba (Fruin, 1997). During the 1980s, numerous authors advocated the adoption of Japanese techniques (e.g. Pascale & Athos, 1982) or the moulding of such approaches to Western contexts (e.g. Ouchi, 1981). In addition to the research on Japanese organizations in Japan, there has been an enormous amount of research undertaken to assess the activities of Japanese organizations operating overseas, for example in the USA (e.g. Abo, 1994; Fucini & Fucini, 1990; Kenney & Florida, 1993; Milkman, 1991), in the UK (e.g. Morris, Munday & Wilkinson, 1993; Oliver & Wilkinson, 1992) and in the Asia–Pacific region (e.g. Dedoussis, 1995; Abdullah & Keenoy, 1995). There has also been prolonged debate over the "transferability" of "Japanese" techniques by Western capital (e.g. Ackroyd, Barrell, Hughes & Whitaker, 1988; Elger & Smith, 1994; Oliver & Wilkinson, 1992). As I will discuss, the origins of lean manufacturing lie firmly in Japanese industry. However, over the past decade the association of lean manufacturing with Japan has weakened and "lean" has become an international standard in many industry sectors.

Lean manufacturing is now understood as an integrated system of production that incorporates work organization, operations, logistics, human resource management and supply chain relations. While there is debate over whether lean manufacturing represents a "toolbox" of techniques or a "philosophy" of management (see Oliver & Wilkinson, 1992), a consensus has emerged over the key organizational and operating principles of the system. This level of consensus has not been sustained when assessment has turned to the implications for workers that such a system may involve.

In this chapter, we begin with an outline of the origins of lean manufacturing, commencing with an overview of the Toyota Production System and, in particular, the ideas of Taiichi Ohno, the main architect of just-in-time (JIT). Following this we review the emergence

The Essentials *of the New Workplace: A Guide to the Human Impact of Modern Working Practices.*
Edited by David Holman, Toby D. Wall, Chris W. Clegg, Paul Sparrow and Ann Howard. © 2005 John Wiley & Sons, Ltd.

of "lean" with specific reference to the main work which popularized the ideas of lean production—the International Motor Vehicle Program (IMVP) and the major publication from that study, *The Machine that Changed the World* (Womack, Jones & Roos, 1990). In the next section, we distil and articulate the key organizing principles of lean manufacturing. Following this, there are two sections which review, first, competing views on the potential implications for workers and then the research evidence on the shopfloor experience of working under lean manufacturing. A final section reviews current debates and flags future issues.

THE ORIGINS OF LEAN MANUFACTURING

While there has been some debate over how "Japanese" the different components of the "Japanese manufacturing system" are (see Graham, 1988), the origins of JIT can be clearly traced to the Toyota Motor Company of Japan, and in particular the work of one of its industrial engineers during the 1960s and 1970s, Taiichi Ohno. Ohno (1988) clearly outlines his ideas in his book, *Just-in-Time: For Today and Tomorrow*. The holistic and integrative nature of lean manufacturing is to be found in his initial comments that "the business world is a trinity of the market, the factory and the company as a whole," with company strategy designed to fine-tune the factory's processes in line with the immediate and real-time needs of the marketplace. Ohno's overarching concern is the elimination of the different forms of waste, which he associates with traditional Fordist methods of production. He lists various forms of waste, including overproduction, waiting time, transportation costs, unnecessary stock, unnecessary movement and the production of defective goods. He contrasts the Toyota production system with the Fordist production system and, in particular, with the fact that Fordism is a planned production system which "pushes" products onto the market, rather than a system building to market demand (see Table 2.1 for a full comparison of the Ford and Toyota production systems).

According to Ohno, the Toyota system has two pillars—JIT and "autonomation", or "automation with a human touch". The primary focus of this is to have machines sense

Table 2.1 Ohno's comparison of production systems at Toyota and Ford

Toyota production system	Ford production system
Builds what is needed when it is needed	Planned mass production
Market "pulls" necessary items from factory	Producing to a plan "pushes" products onto the marketplace
Production of small lots of many models	Production of similar items in large lots
Emphasis on decreasing machine set-up times and increasing frequency	Emphasis on decreasing number of set-ups
Create a production flow to produce JIT	Goods pushed through with high levels of work-in-progress stock
One person attends several processes, requiring multiskilling	One person attends one process; single skill and job demarcation
Stopping work to prevent defects is encouraged	Stopping the line is discouraged
The amount produced equals the amount sold	Amount produced based on calculations in production plan

Source: Adapted from Ohno (1988).

problems and automatically stop producing when defective work arises. A fully automated machine operating smoothly does not need a worker in attendance. Only when a problem occurs is an operator summoned to the machine, generally through a light and/or alarm system. The concept of pokeyoke, or foolproofing, attempts to guard against defective production by having automatic cut-outs in a similar way. While the latter idea of autonomation impacts directly on the role of labour, e.g. in the expectation that workers will mind several machines or processes, giving rise to Ohno's prospect of multiskilling for those workers, the former pillar also has significant direct and indirect implications. In Toyota, a simple physical pull system involving coloured cards, called kanban, is utilized to try to smooth flow and tie upstream and downstream production processes. The cards cycle between processes triggering build at upstream operations to replenish those downstream. Kanban work in a number of ways to reduce the prospects of waste; for example, by restricting the number of cards, inventories cannot build up; by acting as a work order, the cards prevent overproduction; and, since the card moves with goods in small lots, it allows a swift tracing of any goods found to be defective. The heightened visibility and close coupling of work activities have a number of implications for workers. Ohno himself describes kanban as the "autonomic nervous system" of the plant, not only making clear the role of controllers and supervisors, but also indicating to workers when operations should begin and when overtime is necessary (Ohno, 1988, p. 20).

A central feature of the Toyota production system is its close linking of supplier and customer plants, as well as work stations internal to the factory. In the advanced form of JIT adopted by Toyota and key suppliers, kanban cards flow between organizations, triggering build, managing inventory and providing identification of batches. The close linking and transparency between buyer and supplier are an important context to the activities of shopfloor employees. Ohno ascribes the successful adoption of JIT across the supplier base to the economic shock of the first oil crisis in 1973. It was at this time that both Toyota and its suppliers became convinced of the benefits of JIT. As Ohno makes clear, running a JIT system places heavy responsibility on both suppliers and customers. Customers must supply smooth and reliable schedule information upon which suppliers can depend, while the suppliers must deliver reliable quality and to tight time horizons. Organizational slack is removed both within and between members of the supply chain. It is for these reasons that right-first-time build quality is so important in lean manufacturing systems. For many years it has been common to talk of the Japanese system as a combination of JIT and total quality management (TQM).

Along with tight internal process control and the close operational integration of the supply chain, the third significant aspect of the Toyota production system, as outlined by Ohno, is "innovation". Again, Ohno is at pains to emphasize a holistic and integrated view. With regard to innovation within an organization, he comments that technological innovation is only possible when the marketplace, the factory and the research and development (R&D) department are united. He argues that:

> Workplace management does not aim simply for cost reduction through vigorous use of production management techniques. The ultimate goal must be the attainment of innovation through the aggressive development of new products and new techniques (Ohno, 1988, p. 81).

Notably, he recognizes both the importance of top-down management leadership and the bottom-up contribution of shopfloor employees in achieving improvement. Here again, the

Toyota production system represents a significant break from Western manufacturing traditions, in this instance regarding the division of labour. Under Fordist production, drawing on the ideas of Taylor's scientific management, there was a clear demarcation of responsibility between those who planned production and those who carried out the manual tasks prescribed. Under the Toyota system, it is expected that workers will make a contribution to improving how their own job is designed and organized. Moreover, Ohno argues that JIT and autonomation create a synergy between individual skill and team work. The importance of formalized team working and small-group problem solving represent a further departure from much that is commonly associated with traditional Western work organization practices.

From JIT to Lean

As we have seen, the work of Ohno provides an integrated and holistic manufacturing management template, at least with regards to the operations aspects. Concern with the human resource issues of Japanese manufacturing initially focused on the unique nature of Japan's sociocultural and historical context. Authors such as Pascale and Athos (1982) and Ouchi (1981) placed great emphasis on Japan's culture and traditions when seeking to explain the success of its manufacturing industry. However, this success soon led to debates over what could and should be learned from the Japanese and adopted by Western manufacturers. An important contribution to this transferability debate was made by the various researchers involved in the International Motor Vehicle Program (IMVP), coordinated at Massachusetts Institute of Technology (MIT).

   The IMVP was a five year, $5 million study of the world's major car assemblers. The main publication from the programme, which still runs, was *The Machine that Changed the World* (Womack *et al.*, 1990). This has been perhaps the single most influential book on manufacturing management of the last 20 years and its primary objective was to "de-Japanize" the Toyota production system and argue for its efficacy and efficiency irrespective of context. The book reported data from the various projects within the IMVP, including claims that the adoption of "lean production" led to major gains in both productivity and quality performance, although some of these findings have been contested (see Williams, Haslam, Johal & Williams, 1994). As can be seen from the summary in Table 2.2, much of the substantive content of the lean production model is readily recognizable as the Toyota production system

Table 2.2   What is lean production?

- Integrated single piece production flow, with low inventories, small batches made just in time
- Defect prevention rather than rectification
- Production is pulled by the customer and not pushed to suit machine loading, and level scheduling is employed
- Team-based work organization, with flexible multiskilled operators and few indirect staff
- Active involvement in root-cause problem solving to eliminate all non-value-adding steps, interruptions and variability
- Close integration of the whole value stream from raw material to finished customer, through partnerships with suppliers and dealers

Source: Derived from Womack *et al.* (1990).

described by Ohno (1988) and others (e.g. Monden, 1983; Shingo, 1988). Womack *et al.* (1990, p. 49) themselves cite Toyota as "the birthplace" of lean production. The book contains relatively little about the nature or practices of lean production that is distinct from what had been reported previously, but its major success was in propagating the ideas of Toyota and advocating the wholesale adoption of what were previously seen as "Japanese" management practices.

From the outset, Womack *et al.* (1990, p. 9) distance themselves from those who attributed Japanese corporate success to the country's culture or history, "We believe that the fundamental ideas of lean production are universal—applicable anywhere by anyone—and that many non-Japanese companies have already learned this". They are also unequivocal in advocating the adoption of lean production techniques:

> Our conclusion is simple: lean production is a superior way for humans to make things . . . It follows that the whole world should adopt lean production, and as quickly as possible (Womack *et al.*, 1990, p. 225).

For Womack *et al.*, the "one best way" of Fordism has been supplanted by the "one best way" of lean production. Such universalism has, of course, attracted considerable criticism (e.g. Elger & Smith, 1994; Thompson & McHugh, 1995).

The book itself concentrates primarily on the technical aspects of the system and there is little detail on the role of workers or the likely implications of adopting lean production techniques. There are stylized accounts contrasting "dispirited" General Motors' workers with the "sense of purposefulness" to be found amongst Toyota's shopfloor employees, but there is little depth to the discussion of workers' experiences under lean manufacturing. The role of labour is dealt with in a broad-brush manner:

> The truly lean plant . . . transfers the maximum number of tasks and responsibilities to those workers actually adding value to the car on the line . . . It is the dynamic work team that emerges as the heart of the lean factory (Womack *et al.*, 1990, p. 99).

The authors contrast the "mind-numbing stress" of mass production with the "creative tension" of lean production which is particularly engendered by the expectation for worker participation in problem solving and continuous improvement. Rather optimistically, they anticipate that shop floor work will begin to resemble that of professionals and that management will need to encourage "reciprocal obligation" in order that employees contribute to solving problems. Womack *et al.* (1990, p. 102) expect to see investment in automating repetitive tasks and thus anticipate that ". . . by the end of the [twentieth] century we expect that lean-assembly plants will be populated almost entirely by highly skilled problem solvers whose task will be to think continually of ways to make the system run more smoothly and productively". We will review the research evidence on the extent to which this appears an accurate prediction in a later section of the chapter. Before this, in the following sections we outline the key organizing principles of lean manufacturing and tease out the likely implications for workers.

ORGANIZING PRINCIPLES OF LEAN MANUFACTURING

Particularly in early research into Japanese manufacturing during the 1980s, the emphasis was very much upon the technical/systems aspects of practice (e.g. Schonberger, 1982; Voss & Robinson, 1987). However, increasingly the debates have turned to the organizational and work implications of lean manufacturing. Some consensus has emerged that the innovative interdependent and interorganizational nature of the system requires "new types of relationships among workers, between workers and management, and between firms and their buyers and suppliers" (Sayer, 1986, p. 43). It is the implications of these new types of relationship that have been hotly debated.

Oliver and Wilkinson (1992), in their book exploring the prospects for the "Japanization" of British industry, argue that the essence of understanding Japanese methods lies in the recognition that they:

> ... dramatically increase the interdependencies between the actors involved in the whole production process, and that these heightened dependencies demand a whole set of supporting conditions if they are to be managed successfully (Oliver & Wilkinson, 1992, p. 68).

Greater interdependence is founded upon the removal of "organizational slack" or loose coupling arrangements both between processes and between firms. Organizational slack has been the traditional approach to managing uncertainty; actions consistent with coping with uncertainty tend to lead to the creation of slack or "buffers", for example buffers may take the form of large levels of stock between firms or between processes or of lengthy order to delivery time periods. Such buffers may be characteristic of Western manufacturers but constitute the "waste" that Ohno set out to eradicate with the Toyota production system. Thus, if firms are not to accept reduced levels of performance, managers are left to seek ways of reducing uncertainty or of coping with it in ways that do not increase slack.

In removing the buffers or safeguards against disruption typically present under traditional Fordist mass production, lean manufacturing requires that uncertainty be minimized and, where possible, eradicated. Equally, in increasing the various actors' interdependence, organizations face a greater imperative to manage these relationships, both internally and externally, so as to reduce uncertainty. For example, if inventories are minimized, then production equipment must be reliable. Similarly, while introducing internal production, flexibility can partially compensate for unpredictability in market demand; supplier performance in terms of quality and delivery must be reliable and predictable if buffers are removed. Thus, the necessity for lean manufacturers to minimize uncertainty results in a need for a fundamentally reliable and largely stable and predictable set of external relations with other actors. This has led to considerable attention being focused on the nature of supply chain relations in lean manufacturing, particularly the Japanese automotive industry (Turnbull, Oliver & Wilkinson, 1989; Sako, 1992). A number of commentators have concluded that these relationships are best characterized as "high-trust partnerships" (e.g. Lamming, 1993; Womack *et al.*, 1990).

In a very similar fashion to the mutual dependence of the supply chain, lean manufacturers are also highly dependent upon their workforce working reliably and flexibly, since a central aspect of lean is to operate with the minimum possible level of employees. This has dual implications for individual workers. The first is that, since market demand is unlikely to prove entirely predictable and stable, employees must work on tasks as they become necessary. While some workers may concentrate their efforts in a narrowly defined area, at least some workers are likely to have to rotate through different tasks as and when required by demand. Second, the desire to run at minimal levels of staffing means that absenteeism poses a particular problem for management. Under a lean system there simply is not the spare labour to cover illness or other forms of absence. Workers must themselves meet the need for reliability and predictability central to lean manufacturing. Similarly, the emphasis is on stable industrial relations. As Turnbull (1988) notes, lean production is highly susceptible to disruption through even low-cost forms of industrial action. Rather as with the buyer–supplier relations of lean manufacturers, some commentators have concluded that these demands result in high trust partnerships between labour and management (Wickens, 1987; Womack *et al.*, 1990). We will discuss this in more detail below.

Alongside reliability of current processes, the further feature of lean manufacturing is its dynamic nature—the continual search for ways of improving performance. The drive for continuous improvement under lean manufacturing is derived from the Japanese concept of kaizen. As with the other aspects of lean manufacturing, this feature of management "best practice" has permeated widely through industry. Increasingly, contemporary manufacturing is characterized as involving (semi-) permanent innovation (Kenney & Florida, 1993; Cooke & Morgan, 1998) as managers seek to continually improve operating efficiencies and develop and introduce new products to the market. For its advocates, kaizen is the primary feature of the Japanese manufacturing model:

> KAIZEN strategy is the single most important concept in Japanese management—the key to Japanese competitive success. KAIZEN means improvement . . . KAIZEN means *ongoing* improvement involving *everyone*—top management, managers and workers (Imai, 1986: xxix, emphasis in original).

There are a number of organizational structures and processes that are associated with kaizen. Most notable of those involving lower-level workers are employee suggestion schemes and small group problem-solving activities, or quality circles, which involve shopfloor workers in meeting, discussing problems and generating ideas and solutions. Such activities offer the opportunity for employees to make suggestions for change. Clearly the effective operation of such activities places an emphasis on training and development of workers' skills and on engendering the appropriate employment relationship, such that workers feel willing and able to make such contributions. These further considerations compound the importance of workers and employment relations given the fragility of lean manufacturing discussed above.

The nature of HRM and industrial relations under lean manufacturing, and particularly in Japanese firms, has been a major area of study and debate. Indeed, Japanese companies have made an influential contribution to the emergence of HRM, providing role models for the West, with their so-called "Type J" organization characterized by high levels of worker commitment and company loyalty (Ouchi, 1981; Alston, 1986). The key objectives for Japanese personnel practices, and for HRM in support of lean manufacturing more broadly, are clearly derived from the nature of the production system outlined above. Thurley (1982) identifies these as being performance, motivation, flexibility and mobility, secured through an array of complementary policies, such as self-appraisal and feedback, consultation, status/grading progress, organizational or group bonuses, job rotation and retraining, transfer policies, self-education and organizational redesign. These are portrayed as characteristic of Japanese employers, although it should be remembered that at best they refer to the employment relationship of the "permanent" staff in large Japanese corporations and that Japan has a significant duality to its economy (Chalmers, 1989). Nevertheless, the approach to HRM of lean manufacturers outside Japan has drawn heavily upon the perceived advantages of the Japanese model.

According to Peter Wickens, the Personnel Director of Nissan Motor Manufacturing UK when it was founded in the mid-1980s, the secret of Japan's success was a so-called "Japanese tripod" of team work, quality consciousness and flexibility. Wickens himself promoted Nissan's approach to HRM through published articles (Wickens, 1985) and books (Wickens, 1987). He argued that workers at Nissan regarded themselves as part of the team (and company), that quality was emphasized through actual work, and that the employees' genuine involvement in the company through team work and quality led naturally to flexibility. The result, according to the company, was to create a "harmonious and productive working environment" (*The Guardian*, 8 September 1987). This view of the employment relationship at Nissan was specifically criticized by research conducted with workers from the plant (Garrahan & Stewart, 1992) and the perceived harmony and mutuality of Japanese IR and HRM has been questioned more generally (e.g. Delbridge & Turnbull, 1992; Gordon, 1985).

The link between workplace harmony and manufacturing productivity has been questioned on two different but inter-related points. First, while the distinctive production methods of lean manufacturing have been linked to high productivity in Japanese plants (Oliver, Delbridge & Lowe, 1996), there has been no such clear link evident for loyalty, commitment or "corporate culture" (Dunphy, 1986). Neither do Japanese HRM policies necessarily generate higher levels of worker satisfaction (Briggs, 1988; Dunphy, 1986). As Lincoln and Kalleberg (1990, p. 60) comment, "... a striking finding, which has appeared with remarkable consistency in comparative survey research on industrial attitudes, is that the levels of job satisfaction reported by the Japanese are lower than in the Western industrialized countries". Second, as discussed above, the key role of HRM as a strategically integrated subsystem within the organizing principles of lean manufacturing is to make workers feel *obliged* to contribute to the performance of the organization and to identify with its competitive success. For this reason, Wickens' "tripod of success" has been re-labelled a "tripod of subjugation", where team work represents "management through compliance", quality consciousness results in "management through blame" and flexibility leads to "management by stress" (Delbridge & Turnbull, 1992). These competing interpretations of the HRM approach needed to underpin to lean manufacturing may be characterized as a divergence of opinion over whether workers are prepared to meet the demands of the production system because of their levels of commitment or due to their subordination to management and their subsequent coercion to comply with production requirements. Both schools of thought concur, however, that the particular technical/systems characteristics of lean manufacturing—minimal buffers, tight coupling, high quality and the drive for continuous improvement—make specific demands upon workers and consequently require supportive HR practices. A schematic representation of the key organizing principles, both within and between plants operating under lean manufacturing, is given in Figure 2.1.

The clearest research-based articulation and advocacy of these principles and their relationship to organizational performance has been provided by the work of MacDuffie (1995a), who was a researcher on the original IMVP and has subsequently further developed this work. He presents data from a survey of 62 car assembly plants in support of two related arguments: first, that what he calls "innovative HR practices" affect performance as inter-related elements in an internally consistent HR "bundle"; second, that these bundles contribute most to assembly plant productivity and quality when they are integrated with manufacturing policies under the "organizational logic" of a "flexible production

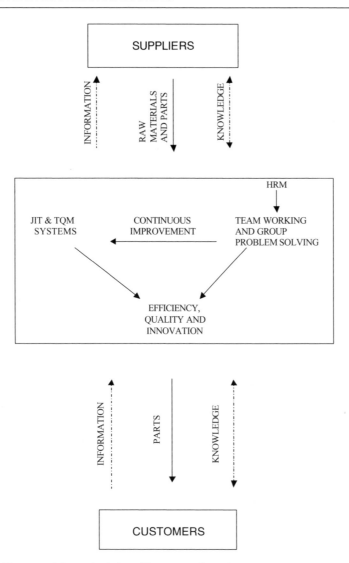

Figure 2.1   Key organizing principles of lean manufacturing

system", MacDuffie's term for lean manufacturing. His research shows that flexible production plants with team-based work systems, "high-commitment" HR practices and low
inventory consistently outperformed "mass production plants".

MacDuffie (1995a, p. 198) suggests that his work "explores the role of human resources
in the 'organizational logic' of a production system more deeply than previous descriptive
work", such as Womack *et al.* (1990). He continues:

> Although mass and flexible (or "lean") production systems implicitly require different
> approaches to managing human resources, Womack *et al.* did not explain how HR
> practices are integrated into these different production systems, nor did they test the
> relationship between HR practices and performance. Indeed, the term "lean production"

Table 2.3   MacDuffie's measures of work systems and HRM policies

"High-involvement" work systems have	High percentage of workforce involved in formal work teams
	High percentage of work force involved in employee involvement groups
	Large number of production-related suggestions received per employee
	High percentage of production-related suggestions implemented
	Frequent job rotation within and across teams and departments
	Production workers responsible for quality inspection and data gathering
"High-commitment" HRM policies	Hiring criteria that emphasize openness to learning and interpersonal skills
	Pay systems contingent upon performance
	Single status workplace (common uniform, common parking, common cafeteria, no ties)
	High levels of initial training for new recruits (workers, supervisors and engineers)
	High levels of ongoing training for experienced employees

Source: Derived from MacDuffie (1995a).

used by Womack *et al.* appropriately captures the minimization of buffers but neglects the *expansion* of work force skill and conceptual knowledge required for problem solving under this approach (MacDuffie, 1995a, p. 198).

Thus, MacDuffie's work represents an attempt to capture the nature of the integrated system of operations, organization and supporting management approach and to incorporate the implications of the systemic demands made upon labour for reliable, flexible and innovative working. The main measures that he uses to identify whether a plant has "high involvement" work practices and "high commitment" HR practices are outlined in Table 2.3.

IMPLICATIONS FOR WORKERS

A key theme running throughout discussions of "Japanese" and lean manufacturing has been the implications that such systems of production have for the workforce. It is on this issue that the debate has polarized, with critics deeply scathing of those who anticipate beneficial working conditions. Early assessments of lean manufacturing argued that it represented "management by stress" (Parker & Slaughter, 1988; Delbridge & Turnbull, 1992) and led to "work intensification" (Dohse, Jürgens & Malsch, 1985; Delbridge, Turnbull & Wilkinson, 1992). The counter-claim was that in fact workers worked "smarter, not harder", at least if the systems were implemented appropriately (e.g. Wickens, 1995).

The critics anticipated that the system demands of just-in-time, total quality control and team working would have a severe and detrimental impact on the prospects for worker autonomy and the opportunity to exercise counter-control. Delbridge *et al.* (1992) anticipated that the likely outcome was work intensification, as a result of: (a) increased monitoring and surveillance of workers' activities; (b) heightened responsibility and individual account-ability; (c) the harnessing of peer pressure within teams and via "customers"; and (d) the fostering of involvement in waste elimination and the continuous improvement of the pro-duction process. They concluded that lean factory regimes potentially consolidated and reproduced management control over the labour process in a more complete way than had been the case under traditional bureaucratic regimes. These conclusions contrast with the expectations of proponents of lean manufacturing, who have anticipated that workers will experience *increased* autonomy and involvement in decision making, primarily through their participation in problem-solving activities (e.g. Womack *et al.*, 1990). Before exam-ining this debate in more detail, we shall consider exactly what workers are expected to do under lean manufacturing.

MacDuffie (1995b) reviews the part of workers in lean production and identifies three primary roles. These are "doing" work, "thinking" work and "team" work. As he notes, and contrary to some of the wilder speculations of Womack *et al.* (1990), under lean manufacturing "first and foremost is the provision of manual effort" and, as he further recognizes:

> Most production work at an auto assembly plant continues to require difficult and demanding physical labor... The fact that lean production shares with mass production the use of a moving assembly line and a narrow division of labor means that the *physical* experience of "doing" work is not dramatically different in these two settings (MacDuffie, 1995b, p. 55).

It is with regard to the notions of "thinking" and "team" work that MacDuffie sees a break from Taylorist traditions. For him, the key distinction surrounds the demands which stem from the drive for continuous improvement. These mean that workers must have a broader contextual knowledge of their production system so that they can link their specific, and often tacit, knowledge of their tasks to the upstream and downstream processes to which they are coupled. Further, he cites the "deliberate organization of work to encourage worker ideas to be surfaced, specified, and legitimized as an input to making changes in the production process", i.e. the process of kaizen (MacDuffie, 1995b, p. 56). However, he is realistic about where the decision-making authority lies under the system, recognizing that workers are not the dominant influence within a lean factory and that engineers still establish the initial process specifications. Moreover, worker suggestions for change are closely scrutinized and must be approved by engineers or managers before adoption. Even an advocate like MacDuffie realizes that there are important limits to the extent to which workers are empowered to take decisions and make changes within lean manufacturing. On the other hand, it is important to acknowledge that under these systems the cognitive inputs of workers are legitimized and valued; this reverses the separation of conception and execution under Taylorism.

The third role raised by MacDuffie is that of team member. This, he argues, "legitimizes the informal social network in a company as an important source of coordination and commitment" (MacDuffie, 1995b, p. 57). However, on closer inspection, MacDuffie's view is rather unitarist:

> The most important social relationship under lean production is with the company: identification with company goals around performance, competitiveness and survival pulls workers towards identifying their interests as overlapping with managers at *their* company... (MacDuffie, 1995b, p. 57; emphasis in original).

The other aspect of organizing the informal social network in the production system is aligning employee interests as closely as possible with company goals. This is vital, as MacDuffie anticipates, because of the strain that lean manufacturing can put on inter-worker relationships, particularly when buffers are reduced to a minimum and quality control requires a tracing of all faults to the root cause (and culpable worker). He notes that the peer controls under such circumstances can "easily turn poisonous" unless there is group cohesion, a process of close and swift dispute resolution, personal influence based on expertise rather than seniority, and incentives that align team member interests with each other and the other teams within the organization. As we will see in the following section, case evidence suggests that organizations operating a lean manufacturing system appear to have had difficulty in meeting the requirements needed to avoid the negative perception of peer pressure amongst workers themselves.

The role of workers in teams has been a major area of study across all sectors of business and industry (see Procter & Mueller, 2000). Since team working is seen to lie at the heart of the lean shopfloor, it is worth looking at the role of workers in lean teams in more detail. Delbridge, Lowe and Oliver (2000) report managerial views of the responsibilities of teams, team members and functional specialists based on an international study of lean production practices in the automotive components industry. The paper reports management responses at 30 plants using lean team working to questions regarding the distribution of responsibility for different types of shopfloor task. The findings provide something of a contrast to those of MacDuffie and Pil (1997), who concluded that lean production results in fewer functional specialists and more multiskilled workers, greater decentralization of authority and a higher degree of integration between conceptual activity and production tasks from their research into car assembly plants.

According to the managers in the study of automotive components plants, the technical role of production workers in lean manufacturing is rather limited. Operators have primary responsibility for routine quality tasks, but have not been significantly upskilled in order to play major roles in more technically complex areas, such as maintenance. Indeed, these technical tasks remain the responsibility of blue-collar skilled specialists and typically lie outside of the individual team. These results are not consistent with the findings of MacDuffie and Pil (1997). Neither is the fact that respondents report very little responsibility at operator level for the management of production activities. The findings show limited evidence of worker autonomy under lean team working. However, there is evidence to support the changing role of labour with regard to innovation and improvement activities. Managers reported significant worker responsibility for problem solving and both quality and process improvements, and this does match the findings of MacDuffie and Pil (1997) at the car assembly plants. Thus, the Taylorist separation of planning and execution appears to be partially reversed, but the position that emerges for workers is one of increasing responsibility without any increase in autonomy.

The other important finding of the research into roles under lean team working was the relative significance of the team's leader. The team leaders had primary responsibility for process improvement, the allocation of work amongst the team and the setting of work pace, as well as training and the settling of grievances. These findings suggest a pivotal role for the leaders of lean teams as the first line of management, able to contribute through both technical competence and social skills. In combination with the continuing importance of skilled blue-collar specialists, the significance of the team leader appears to have "hollowed out" the roles of middle management in the areas of engineering and quality. The findings of Delbridge *et al.* (2000) suggest that lean manufacturing may have even greater implications for the roles and work experiences of first-line supervisors, specialists and middle managers than it does for shopfloor operators. These are questions that currently remain under-researched.

In our final substantive section, we turn attention to the case study evidence regarding the experience of shopfloor workers under lean manufacturing.

CASES OF LEAN WORKING

The evidence reported in Womack *et al.* (1990), MacDuffie (1995a), MacDuffie and Pil (1997) and Delbridge *et al.* (2000) was all gathered through a similar research approach, namely, plant-level questionnaires completed with managers during plant visits by the research teams. This approach provides valuable data, but does not give the best insights into the experience of workers under lean manufacturing. For this we need a research approach that is focused on the workers and the shopfloor specifically. Of necessity, these more in-depth studies are concentrated on particular organizations and there have been a number of such case studies conducted into lean manufacturing sites over the last decade or so. Naturally enough, given the rise of lean in the motor industry, the majority of these have been centred upon car assembly plants (e.g. Fucini & Fucini, 1990; Garrahan & Stewart, 1992; Graham, 1995). Each of these studies has reported criticism of the implications of lean production for workers and has reported worker dissatisfaction and negative experiences. There has been a fair degree of consistency in these findings across different case plants.

In this section we review the work of Rinehart, Huxley and Robertson (1997) in more detail, as a good and representative example of the findings of case-based studies at car assembly plants; their research findings are reported in a book entitled *Just Another Car Factory?*, which reports a longitudinal study of the CAMI Automotive car assembly plant located in Ontario, Canada. CAMI is a joint venture between General Motors and Suzuki, which was heralded as a model of lean production when it opened in 1989. The research was jointly conducted by academics and the Canadian Auto Workers (CAW) trade union and involved worker surveys, interviews and observations conducted by a team between early 1990 and mid-1996. The authors report that, when it opened, CAMI promised workers something different from traditional plants—a humane work environment, team-based empowerment and cooperative labour–management relations—as is to be expected under the lean manufacturing model. The book systematically documents the degree to which CAMI, in the eyes of its own workers, lives up to these expectations, particularly with regard to its own "core values" of empowerment, kaizen, open communications and team spirit. According to Rinehart *et al.* (1997), the initial enthusiasm felt by workers during their recruitment and orientation steadily dissipated, as indeed did their willingness to be involved in discretionary participation activities. Workers came to describe CAMI as "just another car factory".

The authors report extensive and detailed findings on issues such as multiskilling, team working and continuous improvement and, for example, their chapter on team working confirms other work that has questioned the relative autonomy of the team, the significance and divisiveness of peer pressure and the central role of the team leader. Rinehart *et al.* (1997, p. 201) conclude that while the implementation of techniques such as JIT and kanban distinguishes CAMI from traditional mass production plants, these developments in the production system are better conceived as "refinements of Fordism" than a paradigmatic shift in organizational logic, since "The lean environment is characterized by standardized, short-cycled, heavily loaded jobs" (Rinehart *et al.*, 1997, p. 202). Some of the findings from the researchers' worker survey are particularly striking: 88.3% viewed CAMI as no different from other companies; over 90% felt that single status trappings merely masked power differentials; and over 80% felt that the plant environment was competitive and stressful (Rinehart *et al.*, 1997, p. 160).

Overall, the authors conclude that workers at CAMI were no more committed than workers elsewhere and report both formal and informal resistance, including strike action, as evidence of worker discontent. Graham's (1995) participant observation study of another North American car plant, Subaru-Isuzu, also reports evidence of both individual and collective worker resistance. Both studies call into serious doubt the extent to which workers are able to participate in decision making. Consistent with the plant survey findings reported in Delbridge *et al.* (2000), Graham (1995, p. 137) reports that the production system at Subaru-Isuzu "neither engages workers in managerial aspects of their jobs nor provides an avenue for real involvement in decision making . . . When workers did manage to have input into decisions affecting the quality of their lives, it was because they went outside the [Japanese/lean] model's boundaries and approached the company as its adversary". Rinehart *et al.* (1997) conclude from their results that lean production does not rely on committed workers and that the system works so long as everyone does his/her job competently and does not create disruptions. This position correlates with the need for reliable and flexible workers, as outlined in the earlier section on lean's key organizing principles. This conclusion, however, overlooks the discretionary contribution required of workers under kaizen activities if the lean model's innovation and continuous improvement dynamics are to be achieved.

This problem was prominent in the ethnographic study of a Japanese-owned colour television plant in the UK which was reported in Delbridge (1998). This research identifies a low trust–high surveillance shopfloor which workers find stressful and intimidating. The tight quality control in the plant results in a culture of blame and workers are actively engaged in seeking to avoid being held responsible for defects to the extent that on occasion they accuse each other, even within their own team. This fragments the notion of a shopfloor collective and undermines any suggestion that the team may provide some form of social or emotional support. Workers had responded by withdrawing from discretionary activities and did not participate in suggestion schemes nor in small group problem solving. Rinehart *et al.* (1997) also report the withholding of tacit knowledge by workers. If innovation and operational learning are seen as fundamental to the lean model, then these plants are failing to deliver. This suggests an essential tension in the lean model between the desire to operate without waste and at maximum efficiency, leading to stress and alienation on the part of workers, while at the same time anticipating active worker involvement in problem solving. Authors have differed in the extent to which they perceive these findings to reflect the unique history and context of the individual plants and the degree to which the problems reported are due to the inadequate or inappropriate implementation of lean production or this more deep-seated contradiction between control and commitment.

In contrast to the more critical and pessimistic accounts above, Adler's (1993) research at NUMMI, the GM–Toyota joint venture in California, found evidence of high levels of productivity, continuous improvement and employee motivation. He reported a standardized and formal set of work routines that had been designed to promote learning rather than to enforce compliance, a variation on bureaucracy which he labelled "learning bureaucracy".

Adler (1993, p. 111) shares MacDuffie's (1995b) unitarism and anticipates "a workforce assumed to share a common goal of production efficiency and quality". There may be some initial justification for this view, since the GM-Fremont plant had been closed and workers laid off in 1982 before the instigation of the joint venture which saved the operation in 1984. In his discussion, Adler (1993, p. 183) ascribes much of the situation to the "unique conditions of NUMMI's start-up". Nevertheless, the case of NUMMI is interesting in the way it appears to run contrary to the findings of other studies. The explanation may be found in Adler's own conclusion, when he comments that trust, respect, employee participation in defining key standards and policies, and the balancing of power between employees and management are "the conditions of existence" for a learning bureaucracy.

CURRENT DEBATES AND FUTURE ISSUES

Current debates surrounding the experience of working under lean manufacturing centre on the competing explanations for why case-based research, which looks in depth at the circumstances and views of shopfloor workers, fails to supply support for the proposition that lean systems can provide, indeed rely on, employment relations and work conditions that foster commitment and the willingness of workers to participate in discretionary activities. There are a range of views that extend from the radical critics of lean manufacturing, who argue that at its very heart lean production represents a system of management control wherein there is a false rhetoric of worker involvement, autonomy and upskilling (e.g. Parker & Slaughter, 1988), through to the more contingent view of those who ascribe the negative findings of individual case studies to failings in implementation or the strategic choices made by managers (e.g. Klein, 1989).

In a recent review of research into lean production, and in particular evidence on the impact on worker health, Landsbergis, Cahill and Schall (1999, p. 122) conclude that recent survey work has tended to confirm case evidence that lean production in auto manufacturing creates an intensified work pace, modest or temporary increases in decision authority and skill, with the decision-making latitude of workers remaining low. Such work has inherent strains, and Landsbergis, Cahill and Schall (1999) argue that these may lead to various health problems, such as work-related musculoskeletal disorders (e.g. tendinitis and carpal tunnel syndrome) and the potential for increases in hypertension and cardiovascular disease. However, Landsbergis et al. (1999) acknowledge the limits of current evidence and note that there have been few well-designed research studies looking specifically at the impact of lean manufacturing and worker health. This is an area where further research is overdue.

One particular avenue for fruitful further research is more systematic assessment of the psychological impact of working under lean manufacturing systems. This is the conclusion put forward in a recent article by Conti and Gill (1998), who review current understanding of work under lean manufacturing and proceed to identify a series of hypotheses regarding the potential effects of JIT and lean production on job stress. Their primary concern is to seek to generalize from the detailed case evidence that has highlighted the potentially negative effects of lean production. Their position is consistent with the contingent view, and is that there will be varying job stress effects, dependent upon the range of management choices exercised in the design and operation of a lean production system.

Conti and Gill (1998) draw upon the Karasek–Theorell model of job stress, which suggests that high levels of stress are associated with high job demands, low job control and low levels of social support. Coming from the contingent view of lean implementation, Conti and Gill (1998, p. 163) suggest that the implications for job demands are not determined and argue that, "There is nothing inherent in the structure of JIT/LP that requires the use of greater than normal pace and intensity [work] levels", but note that "there are structural characteristics of JIT/LP that inherently restrict worker control and autonomy". Thus, one of their hypotheses is that, "The stress levels exhibited in firms will increase as the proportion of production organized as JIT/LP increases" (Conti and Gill, 1998, p. 164). From this, however, they argue that management has two avenues open to it through which job stress may be alleviated: "the proper use of continuous improvement programs and providing some degree of autonomy in job design" (Conti and Gill, 1998, p. 165).

The prospect for meaningful involvement in decision making is a central component of the rhetoric of lean manufacturing but the case evidence suggests that often managers do not make available the opportunities for workers to secure any form of autonomy and/or other aspects of the employment relationship, or workers' experiences, lead them to decline from any voluntary participation. It has been argued that off-line activities, such as quality circles, give workers a degree of job control and that these may thus help to offset the low level of on-line control (e.g. Conti and Gill, 1998). The case evidence does not support this view, however, and recent analysis of the Workplace Employment Relations Survey, which has responses from 28 323 employees (see Cully *et al.*, 1998), also indicates that workers do not perceive that narrow, "point of production" participation schemes, such as quality circles, provide meaningful opportunity for influence over their jobs (Delbridge & Whitfield, 2001). The other way, according to Conti and Gill (1998), that the stress inherent in the JIT system may be offset is through the resources and emotional support provided by working in teams. Again, this is an empirical question worthy of further investigation, but the case study evidence indicates that the particular pressures of lean manufacturing may fragment team loyalties and undermine the prospects of team-based support. At the very least, the research evidence indicates that managers seeking to ensure that innovation and improvement are a central part of their lean manufacturing system will need to reflect carefully on how they can mediate the stressful aspects inherent in such a system. In addition, they will need to integrate work, organization and supporting HR policies, such that workers perceive they have a vested interest in contributing their discretionary effort and tacit knowledge in order to make the lean shopfloor an ever more efficient and yet harmonious workplace. The current signs are that, even if managers are so inclined, this may prove beyond them.

REFERENCES

Abdullah, S. & Keenoy, T. (1995). Japanese managerial practices in the Malaysian electronics industry: two case studies. *Journal of Management Studies*, **32**(6), 747–766.

Abo, T. (1994). *The Hybrid Factory: the Japanese Production System in the United States*. Oxford: Oxford University Press.

Ackroyd, S., Burrell, G., Hughes, M. & Whitaker, A. (1988). The Japanisation of British industry. *Industrial Relations Journal*, **19**(1), 11–23.

Adler, P. (1993). The "learning bureaucracy": New United Motor Manufacturing, Inc. *Research in Organizational Behavior*, **15**, 111–194.

Alston, J. (1986). *The American Samurai: Blending American and Japanese Managerial Practices*. New York: de Gruyter.

Briggs, P. (1988). The Japanese at work: illusions of the ideal. *Industrial Relations Journal*, **19**(1), 24–30.

Chalmers, N. (1989). *Industrial Relations in Japan: the Peripheral Workforce*. London: Routledge.

Conti, R. & Gill, C. (1998). Hypothesis creation and modelling in job stress studies: the effect of just-in-time and lean production. *International Journal of Employment Studies*, **6**(1), 149–173.

Cooke, P. & Morgan, K. (1998). *The Associational Economy: Firms, Regions and Innovation*. Oxford: Oxford University Press.

Cully, M., O'Reilly, A., Millward, N., Forth, J., Woodland, S., Dix, G. & Bryson, A. (1998). *The 1998 Workplace Employee Relations Survey: First Findings*. London: HMSO.

Dedoussis, V. (1995). Simply a question of cultural barriers? The search for new perspectives in the transfer of Japanese management techniques. *Journal of Management Studies*, **32**(6), 731–745.

Delbridge, R. (1998). *Life on the Line in Contemporary Manufacturing*. Oxford: Oxford University Press.

Delbridge, R., Lowe, J. & Oliver, N. (2000). Shopfloor responsibilities under lean teamworking. *Human Relations*, **53**(11), 1459–1479.

Delbridge, R. & Turnbull, P. (1992). Human resource maximisation: the management of labour under a JIT system. In Blyton, P. & Turnbull, P. (Eds), *Reassessing Human Resource Management* (pp. 56–73). London: Sage.

Delbridge, R., Turnbull, P. & Wilkinson, B. (1992). Pushing back the frontiers: management control and work intensification under JIT/TQM factory regimes. *New Technology, Work and Employment*, **7**(2), 97–106.

Delbridge, R. & Whitfield, K. (2001). Employee perceptions of job influence and organizational participation. *Industrial Relations*, **40**(3), 472–489.

Dohse, K., Jürgens, U. & Malsch, T. (1985). From "Fordism" to "Toyotism"? The social organization of the labour process in the Japanese automobile industry. *Politics and Society*, **14**(2), 115–146.

Dunphy, D. (1986). An historical review of the literature on the Japanese enterprise and its management. In Clegg, S., Dunphy, D. & Redding, G. (Eds), *The Enterprise and Management in East Asia* (pp. 343–368). Hong Kong: Centre for Asian Studies, University of Hong Kong.

Elger, T. & Smith, C. (Eds) (1994). *Global Japanization? The Transnational Transformation of the Labour Process*. London: Routledge.

Fruin, M. (1997). *Knowledge Works: Managing Intellectual Capital at Toshiba*. Oxford: Oxford University Press.

Fucini, J. & Fucini, S. (1990). *Working for the Japanese: Inside Mazda's American Auto Plant*. New York: Free Press.

Fujimoto, T. (1999). *The Evolution of a Manufacturing System at Toyota*. Oxford: Oxford University Press.

Garrahan, P. & Stewart, P. (1992). *The Nissan Enigma: Flexibility at Work in a Local Economy*. London: Mansell.

Gordon, A. (1985). *The Evolution of Labor Relations in Japan: Heavy Industry, 1853–1945*. Boston, MA: Harvard University Press.

Graham, I. (1988). Japanisation as mythology. *Industrial Relations Journal*, **19**(1), 69–75.

Graham, L. (1995). *On the Line at Subaru-Isuzu: the Japanese Model and the American Worker*. Ithaca, NY: ILR Press.

Imai, M. (1986). *Kaizen: the Key to Japan's Competitive Success*. New York: McGraw Hill.

Kenney, M. & Florida, R. (1993). *Beyond Mass Production: the Japanese System and its Transfer to the United States*. Oxford: Oxford University Press.

Klein, J. (1989). The human cost of manufacturing reform. *Harvard Business Review*, **March–April**, 60–66.

Lamming, R. (1993). *Beyond Partnership: Strategies for Innovation and Lean Supply*, New York: Prentice Hall.

Landsbergis, P., Cahill, J. & Schall, P. (1999). The impact of lean production and related new systems of work organization on worker health. *Journal of Occupational Health Psychology*, **4**(2), 108–130.

Lincoln, J. & Kalleberg, A. (1990). *Culture, Control and Commitment*. Cambridge: Cambridge University Press.

MacDuffie, J. (1995a). Human resource bundles and manufacturing performance: organizational logic and flexible production systems in the world auto industry. *Industrial and Labor Relations Review*, **48**(2), 197–221.

MacDuffie, J. (1995b). Workers' roles in lean production: the implications for worker representation. In S. Babson (Ed.), *Lean Work: Empowerment and Exploitation in the Global Auto Industry* (pp. 54–69). Detroit: Wayne State University Press.

MacDuffie, J. & Pil, F. (1997). Changes in auto industry employment practices: an international overview. In T. Kochan, R. Lansbury, & J. MacDuffie (Eds), *After Lean Production: Evolving Employment Practice in the World Auto Industry* (pp. 9–42). Ithaca, NY: ILR Press.

Milkman, R. (1991). *Japan's California Factories: Labor Relations and Economic Globalization.* Los Angeles, CA: University of California Press.

Monden, Y. (1983). *Toyota Production System: Practical Approach to Production Management.* Norcross: Industrial Engineering and Management Press.

Morris, J., Munday, M. & Wilkinson, B. (1993). *Working for the Japanese: The Economic and Social Consequences of Japanese Investment in Wales.* London: Athlone.

Ohno, T. (1988). *Just-in-Time: For Today and Tomorrow.* Cambridge: Productivity Press.

Oliver, N., Delbridge, R. & Lowe, J. (1996). The European auto components industry: manufacturing performance and practice. *International Journal of Operations and Production Management,* **16**(11), 85–97.

Oliver, N. & Wilkinson, B. (1992). *The Japanization of British Industry: New Developments in the 1990s.* Oxford: Blackwell.

Ouchi, W. (1981) *Theory Z: How American Business Can Meet the Japanese Challenge.* Reading: Addison Wesley.

Parker, M. & Slaughter, J. (1988). *Choosing Sides: Unions and the Team Concept.* Boston, MA: Labor Notes.

Pascale, R. & Athos, A. (1982). *The Art of Japanese Management.* New York: Simon and Schuster.

Procter, S. & Mueller, F. (Eds) (2000). *Teamworking.* Basingstoke: Macmillan.

Rinehart, J., Huxley, C. & Robertson, D. (1997). *Just Another Car Factory? Lean Production and its Discontents.* Ithaca, NY: ILR Press.

Sako, M. (1992). *Prices, Quality and Trust: Inter-firm Relations in Britain and Japan.* Cambridge: Cambridge University Press.

Sayer, A. (1986). New developments in manufacturing: the just-in-time system. *Capital and Class,* **30**, 43–72.

Schonberger, R. (1982). *Japanese Manufacturing Techniques: Nine Hidden Lessons in Simplicity.* New York: Free Press.

Shingo, S. (1988). *Non-stock Production: the Shingo System for Continuous Improvement.* Cambridge: Productivity Press.

Thompson, P. & McHugh, D. (1995). *Work Organizations.* Basingstoke: Macmillan.

Thurley, K. (1982). The Japanese model: practical reservations and surprising opportunities. *Personnel Management,* February, 36–39.

Turnbull, P. (1988). The limits to "Japanisation"—just-in-time, labour relations and the UK automotive industry. *New Technology, Work and Employment,* **3**(1), 7–20.

Turnbull, P., Oliver, N. & Wilkinson, B. (1989). Recent developments in the UK automotive industry: JIT/TQC and information systems. *Technology Analysis and Strategic Management,* **4**(1), 409–422.

Voss, C. & Robinson, S. (1987). The application of just-in-time techniques. *International Journal of Operations and Production Management,* **7**(4), 46–52.

Wickens, P. (1985). Nissan: the thinking behind the union agreement. *Personnel Management,* August, 18–21.

Wickens, P. (1987). *The Road to Nissan.* Basingstoke: Macmillan.

Wickens, P. (1995). *The Ascendant Organization.* Basingstoke: Macmillan.

Williams, K., Haslam, C., Johal, S. & Williams, J. (1994). *Cars.* Providence: Berghahn Books.

Womack, J., Jones, D. & Roos, D. (1990). *The Machine that Changed the World.* New York: Rawson Macmillan.

CHAPTER 3

The Human Side of Total Quality Management

Richard Cooney and **Amrik Sohal**

Department of Management, Monash University, Victoria, Australia

Total quality management (TQM) has been a singular organizational practice. Management scholars and consultant-practitioners speak of a quality "era" and a quality "revolution" when discussing the manifold changes that have been effected under the banner of TQM. TQM programs have been implemented in a wide variety of manufacturing and service industries and they have been significant in the reshaping of public institutions and the delivery of public services. Few management practices in the modern era have been as widely disseminated as has TQM.

Within organizations, TQM has had profound effects upon the way in which senior management exercises its strategic leadership function, the way in which middle management carries out its function of supervision and control, but above all TQM has radically changed the experience of work for employees. The delegation of responsibility for quality and quality improvement has led to a dramatic expansion of the work role of employees. Employees are now directly responsible for managing manufacturing and service delivery processes to ensure that customers receive a quality product or service.

Along with this expansion of the work role to deliver quality products and services has come a reorientation on the part of employees towards their work role. Employees have been encouraged to identify more closely with the mission and values of the organization and to take a more proactive stance in achieving that mission. The implementation of TQM has, in some cases, meant that employees have assumed greater responsibility for overall organizational performance and not just quality performance. Employees have been encouraged to see themselves as, in effect, small business managers, responsible for the output of their own "business unit". It is not simply the expansion of the work role through the delegation of enhanced responsibilities for quality that has been a feature of TQM programs; equally important has been the reorientation of employees towards their work and their organization.

TQM has transformed the experience of work for employees and this chapter outlines some of the dimensions of this change. The chapter begins by investigating the multiple meanings of TQM as a management practice. TQM may be seen as a technically focused quality management program, as a philosophy of business concerned with strategic business

The Essentials *of the New Workplace: A Guide to the Human Impact of Modern Working Practices.*
Edited by David Holman, Toby D. Wall, Chris W. Clegg, Paul Sparrow and Ann Howard. © 2005 John Wiley & Sons, Ltd.

issues, or as an organizational–behavioural intervention designed to promote the more effective use of human resources.

After outlining the elements that may appear in a TQM program, the chapter moves on to examine the impact of TQM on managers, supervisors and employees. Different kinds of TQM programs have differing effects upon the work employees and the design of jobs in contemporary work systems. The differing effects of the technical and the organizational–behavioural or, as they are often called, the "hard" and the "soft" elements of TQM, are emphasized. The chapter first analyses the effects of quality control techniques and continuous improvement activities upon employees' work design, before moving on to examine the impact of human resource practices and organizational change techniques upon employees' orientation towards their work and organization.

The chapter concludes by examining the research evidence for the efficacy of the various types of TQM program but, it transpires, the evidence is mixed. Improved enterprise competitiveness is a key goal of any TQM program but the routes to that improved performance are seemingly disparate. The available research evidence provides support for the efficacy of many varieties of TQM. Hard TQM can be effective, soft TQM can be effective and the implementation of more broadly based TQM programs can also be effective. TQM in its many guises can be an effective practice from a management perspective, but the chapter ends by questioning why seemingly little attention has been paid to the outcomes of TQM for employees.

THE VARIETIES OF TQM

TQM is a contemporary management practice that contains a number of elements and entails an number of related organizational interventions. TQM encompasses a number of themes about management itself and is an umbrella concept for a set of related organizational interventions (Hackman & Wageman, 1995). For this reason, TQM is something of a fungible concept and one that is sometimes difficult to pin down. There is not one TQM but a range of TQMs, each dependent upon the themes and the practices that are employed in the name of TQM (Dean & Bowen, 1994, Hill & Wilkinson, 1995, Wilkinson, 1995).

It is not possible to give a clear definition of TQM, but it is rather more useful to identify the major themes and practices that are said to constitute TQM. At its most basic, TQM is a program of management action to improve quality performance. Evans and Dean (2000, p. 5) define TQM as:

> A comprehensive, organization-wide effort to improve the quality of products and services

and this definition underlines both the systematic nature of TQM interventions, as well as their clear focus upon quality goals. The application of quality management and quality control tools, techniques and practices, in order to improve quality performance, is one clear focus of TQM programs (Crosby, 1980; Feigenbaum, 1983; Ishikawa, 1985).

Other writers, however, go further than this and identify TQM as a philosophy of management, as well as a management program of quality improvement. Wilkinson, Redman, Snape and Marchington (1998, p. 11) define TQM as:

A general business management philosophy, which is about the attainment of continuously improving customer satisfaction by quality-led company-wide management.

Definitions such as this highlight the fact that TQM may be about more than simple quality
improvement. TQM is often about the reorientation of management thinking from a focus
upon internal operational control, towards a strategic focus upon customers and markets.
Increasing globalization has led to a renewed focus upon market position, and this has
led to a rethinking of management approaches developed during the long post-war boom.
TQM provides a philosophy of business that can guide management efforts in an uncertain
business environment and it can help to reorientate management thinking about strategic
business issues (Deming, 1982, 1986).

As well as being a philosophy of management, TQM may provide a focus for strategic management change efforts. Flynn, Schroeder and Sakakibara (1995, p. 660) develop
this theme and state that "Quality management is an integrated, interfunctional means of
achieving and sustaining competitive advantage". Such definitions emphasize the way in
which quality programs can facilitate the integration of work systems, quality systems and
business process systems, to develop a seamless and strategically focused organization
(Dawson, 1994b). Whilst the broad quality strategy of the organization is critical, this may
also serve as a catalyst for other change interventions.

Many activities are carried out in the name of TQM and not all are directly related to
quality. Quality programs may entail the development of changed approaches to employee
relations to encourage greater employee participation and involvement in the business; they
may entail the redesign of work to establish teams and *ad hoc* work groups; they may entail
greater expenditure on training and the development of human capital; they may entail
significant organizational change and restructuring; and they may involve the review of
business processes and product or service delivery systems. Many varied organizational
interventions are conducted in the name of TQM, as part of the development of a quality
strategy (Spencer, 1994).

Other scholars focusing on the strategic change initiatives entailed in a TQM program
go even further and emphasize the behavioural and attitudinal elements of TQM, over and
above the quality system elements and the philosophy of business elements. Cole (1998,
p. 43) says that "Quality means maximizing organizational behaviour to enhance the satisfaction of present and potential customers". Here, it is the employee's orientation to work
and to the company that is critical. Employees are seen as important contributors to the
success of the business, capable of self-regulating their work, of monitoring performance
against the goals set by management, of being accountable for that performance and of
continuously improving business outcomes. Such definitions underline a new conceptualisation of the role of the employee within the enterprise, one that focuses upon their
normative alignment to the organizational mission and their capacity for self-management,
as work tasks are increasingly delegated to those directly producing value at the front
line.

The great variety of themes and practices that fall under the banner of TQM create a
perception that TQM can be all things to all people and, consequently, that it is of little
conceptual value. In fact, this seeming limitation of TQM contains a practical advantage.
TQM programs can be customized to suit the needs of individual enterprises and TQM practices can be selected that appeal to a range of organizational participants. Senior managers,
middle managers and employees can all make sense of TQM in ways that resonate with

their own experience, and they can relate to quality principles and practices that directly affect the way that they do their work.

MANAGERS, SUPERVISORS, EMPLOYEES AND TQM

For senior managers, TQM can be seen as a philosophy of management. TQM provides a coherent framework of principles and practices that can be used to steer the firm and develop its competitive position (Garvin, 1991; Schonberger, 1992). In this view, TQM is seen as providing a total approach to the problems encountered in the management of contemporary organizations. Critical themes of leadership, customer and market focus, organizational structure, management process and organizational change are all embraced by TQM. These themes give senior managers a clear interpretation of contemporary business trends and provide a structured program of management action.

Senior executive managers may also embrace TQM, as it offers them a way of managing organizational performance to improve quality, productivity and competitiveness. The tools and practices identified by TQM can assist with the identification of the organizational mission and goal setting by senior management; they can help with the planning of quality and general business improvement efforts; and they can help with the development of appropriate business metrics. As well as offering a coherent view of the purpose of management, TQM also offers a set of tools and techniques with which to guide the development of management systems in the enterprise and carry out the executive management role (Crosby, 1980; Imai, 1997; Juran & Godfrey, 1999).

TQM has both a technical and a rhetorical appeal to senior managers and this can create a dilemma for those implementing TQM. An over-emphasis on the technical elements of TQM may lead to it being seen, by employees, as a specialised technical program of marginal relevance to their work. On the other hand, an under-emphasis on the techniques of TQM, may lead to it being seen as little more than vacuous management rhetoric (Hackman & Wageman, 1995). The approach of senior managers towards TQM, the themes and practices that they choose to implement under the umbrella of TQM, is a critical factor in the success of TQM programs (Choi & Behling, 1997; Zbaracki, 1998).

For middle managers, TQM may have mixed effects, depending upon the version of TQM that is implemented. TQM, in its quality system guise, may enhance the expert power of middle managers and their ability to supervise and control subordinates. The clarification of work roles in the work system and the establishment of clear reporting systems may enhance the position of a supervisor, whilst the implementation of quality control techniques may enhance their expert power. Middle managers may thus embrace TQM because its scientific and technical practices augment their control over subordinates.

In other respects, however, TQM may pose a significant challenge to middle managers. Other versions of TQM, those that focus upon the attitudinal and behavioural elements, may challenge supervisors to relinquish their positional power and to act in new ways. Middle managers may be expected to act as facilitators, coaches, coordinators and mentors, building the lines of communication with senior management and developing trust. They may become responsible for employee skill development, for facilitating improvement activities and for championing change initiatives. These new role demands can create significant role conflict for those middle managers unwilling or unable to relinquish direct control of subordinates (Coyle-Shapiro, 1999; Dawson, 1994a; Yong & Wilkinson, 1999).

The organizational restructuring associated with the transfer of greater authority to employees has also had some dramatic effects upon middle managers and supervisors. Downsizing and delayering has drastically reduced the numbers of middle managers and it has reduced the power and influence of those remaining, as what were formerly management responsibilities are transferred to those directly producing products and services (Clinton, Williamson, & Bethke, 1994; Grant, Shani & Krishnan, 1994).

The implementation of quality programs may thus have drastic effects upon the work roles of middle managers. Middle managers may, in fact, pose the strongest point of resistance to the implementation of TQM programs, as their job security, power and authority are undermined by the changes entailed in adopting TQM. Even where TQM is embraced by middle managers, it may have a pronounced effect upon their work, making their jobs more complex and demanding as they respond to those below them in new ways (Wilkinson, Redman & Snape, 1994).

When we turn to look at employees' experience of TQM, the picture is similar to that of middle managers. The impact of TQM programs varies, depending upon whether they are implemented with a "hard" quality system/quality process orientation or with a "soft" attitudinal–behavioural orientation (Wilkinson, Godfrey & Marchington, 1997).

TQM, WORK DESIGN AND EMPLOYEES

TQM can be broadly divided into its hard and soft elements. Each of these have differing impacts upon the work of employees and it is the hard elements of TQM that have the most direct impact upon work design. Thus, TQM programs may facilitate low-skill job expansion as more tasks of the same or lesser skill levels are added to the work role. In manufacturing processes, such simple task enlargement of the work role may consist of the addition of basic tasks, such as housekeeping, simple quality inspection and quality record keeping. In such circumstances, inspection may consist of little more than visual inspection and basic gauge checking. Visual inspections may simply involve inspecting a work sample or comparing a work sample with a master sample, to check for obvious flaws. Basic gauge checking may involve the use of fixed gauges, such as "go" and "no-go" gauges, to check product attributes, and it may involve some elementary record keeping, such as the use of simple tally sheets, defect logs or defect concentration diagrams (Evans & Lindsay, 1999; Montgomery, 1991). Such simple techniques of quality control require little skill in measurement or the use of measuring instruments and demand only minimal levels of numeracy to keep and interpret quality records.

In cases where simple tools are used, operator control of quality may be supplemented by the work of quality technicians and supervisors, leading to the development of systems where limited operator control is complemented by inspection and expert control measures. Quality technicians, supervisors and middle managers may use the more sophisticated statistical quality control techniques to monitor operational processes and may take most of the decisions regarding changes to the quality control system. These quality control measures may also be supplemented by statistically-based inspection measures, such as acceptance sampling.

A similar phenomenon of limited work role expansion can be observed in the services sector, where the work of frontline service personnel may be expanded by the addition of a wider range of customer service tasks. Customer service officers may deal with a wider range of customer enquires and transactions but the interactions may be tightly scripted and organized in a lock-step sequence. In these circumstances, employees are merely called upon to deliver the scripted response, with non-routine enquiries and transactions being escalated to supervisors and senior workers. Such scripted interactions may require little product or service knowledge on the part of the frontline service personnel and may require minimal development of communicative and interpersonal skills.

The limited expansion of the work role, then, may lead to an expansion of work tasks and increased responsibility for quality, but it does not necessarily lead to any increase in skill or expansion of decisional authority. In such circumstances, operators and customer service personnel may have little or no say in the design of the quality system, little involvement in the improvement of the quality system and a limited role in the conduct of quality assurance itself.

Even this low-skill job expansion is seen, however, to be motivational, improving key work design criteria. Where frontline employees have responsibility for quality, a greater range of tasks are undertaken and so skill variety is enhanced; employees have more holistic control of the production process and so task identity is enhanced; and the work of front-line employees is more integral to the success of the enterprise, thereby enhancing task significance (Davis & Wacker, 1987, Hackman, 1977, 1991; Hackman & Oldham, 1980).

The more extensive implementation of TQM involves high-skill job enrichment, where more complex tasks requiring greater levels of skill are undertaken. Employees may be given greater responsibility for the management of quality and may be given some authority to make decisions about the operation of the quality system. Craft-like skills may be developed as employees are taught to use statistically-based tools, such as histograms, Pareto analysis, run charts and control charts. They may be authorised to take preventative and corrective actions and to deal directly with customers and customer complaints. This latter aspect is especially important in service industries, where employees may be authorised to deal with non-routine enquiries and to rectify customer complaints by providing refunds or replacement services.

Employees experiencing high-skill work redesigns may also be engaged in system design tasks. They may be involved in the design of work methods, testing and inspection methods. Employees may also be involved in the continuous redesign and improvement of both their own jobs and quality procedures. Such empowerment of employees is seen to overcome the limitations of the narrow, fragmented tasks found in routine production and service work (Adler, 1993; Adler & Borys, 1996). The high-skill redesign of work is also associated with long-term changes to employee perceptions about tasks and the work role, and thus may become the basis upon which perceptions about co-workers, managers and the firm are changed (Griffin, 1991).

The more complex work redesigns entail employees developing a broader range of skills in order to respond flexibly to changing product, service, customer and market requirements, and these increased skill demands are often reflected in greater training (Schonberger, 1994). Employees require some training in order to manage the expansion of their work role following the delegation of responsibilities for quality, but they also require some training in non-technical skills to be able to participate in quality improvement activities and the redesign of organizational systems. The provision of such training is, however, contingent, with low-skill redesigns entailing minimal training, while high-skill designs require significantly more (Gee & Nystrom, 1999).

Enhanced work motivation and the development of broad-based skills may flow from the delegation of responsibility for quality to frontline employees, but there are other effects of the implementation of hard TQM. The implementation of quality control measures improves the manufacturability or ease of manufacture of products, thus establishing a more even and steady work flow for employees. Quality problems are identified by employees and recurring quality issues are eliminated. The stress of trying to rectify defective parts and assemblies in-process may be reduced, disruptions to work flow are reduced and this may also contribute to enhanced employee satisfaction (Conti & Warner, 1997; Shingo, 1986, 1989).

Job enrichment, employee empowerment and upskilling are the positive effects of TQM programs, but such programs also have some deleterious effects upon the work of employees. The major limitation of hard TQM is that it introduces a high level of task standardization and hence limits employee discretion. Employee control of work methods is reduced as these methods are standardized, and bureaucratic procedures may have to be followed to log and record preventative, corrective and containment actions. Standardization is introduced in TQM programs to improve the consistency and reliability of processes, but the application of process disciplines, such as standardized work, limits the autonomy of employees. System standardization means that whilst employees may have a greater say in the design and improvement of the quality system, non-routine tasks are progressively eliminated and hence employee autonomy is progressively reduced. As Klein (1991) observes, whilst quality management systems encourage "task design" autonomy on the part of employees as they solve problems and improve the system, the use of TQM practices limits employees autonomy in "task execution" compared to that found in non-TQM work environments.

The standardization of work methods limits employee autonomy and it also increases the interdependencies in the processing system. Upstream and downstream processes are increasingly linked together and the increased reliance upon those in other work areas to maintain production flow and meet production targets limits employee self-regulation of work. The scope for employees in a particular work area to self-manage that area is reduced as standardized, plant-wide quality procedures and work methods are implemented (Dawson & Webb, 1989; Delbridge, Turnbull & Wilkinson, 1992).

The implementation of hard TQM may thus have mixed effects upon the work of employees. TQM may be typified by low-skill job expansion or by high-skill job enrichment. It may contribute to employee empowerment by enhancing their decisional autonomy or it may lead to reduced autonomy in the execution of tasks, as procedures are standardized. TQM leads to an expansion of the work role of employees, but this expansion may have seemingly contradictory effects, enabling employees in some respects but constraining them in others.

CONTINUOUS IMPROVEMENT AND TQM

One element of TQM programs that is often seen as contributing to employee empowerment is employee involvement in continuous quality improvement activities. Employees in TQM programs are often called upon to identify problems and then work together in groups to analyze those problems. Employees may also be involved in generating solutions and implementing and evaluating those solutions. Involvement in these continuous improvement activities is seen to enhance employee decisional autonomy, but once again, the scope of that enhancement is contingent upon the nature of the improvement activities being undertaken (Wilkinson *et al.*, 1997).

When introduced in conjunction with low-skill work expansion, employee involvement in decision making may be limited to consultation rather than participation. Employees may be simply consulted by management and asked to identify quality problems or to contribute suggestions and ideas for quality improvement. The actual implementation of these ideas is then left to management and there is little further employee involvement. Employee suggestion schemes frequently operate on this basis. Employees contribute ideas for improvement, but the selection of ideas for implementation, and the work of implementation itself, remains the provenance of management alone.

Where employees participate directly in improvement activities, their authority to make decisions may also be constrained by the nature of the participative structures employed. A variety of *ad hoc* and temporary teams and work groups are often used to implement continuous improvement activities—quality circles, taskforces, problem-solving groups, improvement project groups, customer-response groups and so on—and these groups are not always well integrated into the management hierarchy of the enterprise. Such groups may in fact form parallel organizational structures established outside, but in parallel to, the decisional hierarchy. Such parallel structures are dependent upon the support of management. Projects and improvement activities are not undertaken without management support and are not implemented without management approval. If employees do not secure the approval of management for their improvement projects and, more importantly, secure from management the resources necessary to implement their projects, then the projects usually do not proceed (Cordery, 1996; Cotton, 1993; Cotton, Vollrath, Froggatt, Lengnick-Hall & Jennings, 1988; Hill, 1991).

The limitations of these parallel structures—involvement without decisional autonomy— go a long way towards explaining why they so often fail to secure ongoing employee interest in quality improvement activities. The use of groups such as quality circles has been found to lead to few (Marks, Mirvis, Hackett & Grady, 1986) or temporary (Griffin, 1988) improvements in quality performance and employee satisfaction, and consequently the use of such groups within TQM programs has often been dismissed as a fad (Lawler & Mohrman, 1985).

When introduced in conjunction with high-skill work enrichment, improvement activities may be integrated with the normal organizational structures through the delegation of responsibility for improvement to autonomous work teams. These ongoing, permanent work groups may undertake improvement activities as part of their normal work, but even here employees face the limitations of the quality improvement techniques themselves. These problem solving and data analysis techniques are frequently heavily standardized and so offer limited scope for employee initiative (Cole, 1994; Sitkin, Sutcliffe & Schroeder, 1994).

Involvement in improvement activities should emphasize information sharing between employees and management, intra- and intergroup cooperation in problem solving and the development of cross-functional work. This should lead to an emphasis upon learning and employee development, with consequent positive effects upon the organizational climate and employee satisfaction (Waldman, 1994). Employees should see improvements in quality outcomes but also in employee-related outcomes, such as improvements to the work environment and occupational health and safety. Too often, however, the scope of such benefits is limited by the constraints upon employee decision making entailed in the application of TQM improvement techniques (Wilkinson, Marchington, Goodman & Ackers, 1992).

TQM AND HUMAN RESOURCE MANAGEMENT

In order to make the most of TQM programs, some researchers argue that hard TQM must be combined with the extensive use of soft TQM. Innovations in quality control and employee involvement, it is argued, must be supported by innovative human resource management (HRM) practices, such as team working, performance-based compensation and single-status facilities (Kochan, Gittell & Lautsch, 1995; Schonberger, 1994).

The difficulty faced by researchers, however, is that whilst there is some overlap between TQM and HRM, the two are not identical and there is no identifiable set of HRM practices that are consistently used in TQM programs. Employee training and employee involvement are two practices that are widely accepted as part of a TQM program (Ahire, Golhar & Waller, 1996; Black & Porter, 1996; Dean & Bowen, 1994; Saraph, Benson & Schroeder, 1989) but the use of practices such as team work (Black & Porter, 1996) and performance-based rewards and recognition (Dean & Bowen, 1994) are more contentious. Some would see these practices as central to TQM programs, others not so. There is little evidence of a convergence between contemporary strategic HRM and TQM, despite some similarities.

Whilst the significance of HRM practices for TQM may be in dispute, there is wide agreement that good HRM practice is needed to support TQM initiatives and that line managers should be more highly skilled in people management, in order to facilitate employee involvement in quality management and organizational change activities.

ORGANIZATIONAL CHANGE AND TQM

The soft side of TQM may have a tenuous connection to HRM practices but it has a much stronger connection to organizational change and development practices. TQM, as a strategic management tool, often requires significant organizational structural change and it requires some broad cultural change. In the first case, change may entail reducing layers of management to improve communication and facilitate the delegation of enhanced responsibilities for quality to employees, and, in the latter case, it may entail the reorientation of employee attitudes and behaviours to enhance their focus upon customer needs and their involvement in improvement activities.

TQM entails an element of normative reorientation on the part of employees towards their work role. Employees are encouraged to embrace change as an empowering process, and to more closely identify with the firms' mission and quality values. This reorientation towards the work role is effected through the development of a quality discourse by senior management. The rhetorical presentation of quality initiatives seeks to explain change to employees, but also to shape the meaning of "quality" and the vocational identity of employees. The discourse of quality often emphasizes the unity of the work of the organization, outlining the benefits for employees, management and owners of the quality transformation. Quality is often presented as win–win change, and something that transcends sectional interests and petty organizational politics. The introduction of TQM is presented as an opportunity for employee empowerment, as a program of change that will lead to enhanced work designs, high skill development and greater decisional authority for employees (Hackman & Wageman, 1995; Tuckman, 1994; Reger, Gustafson, Demarie & Mullane, 1994; Zbaracki, 1998).

The discourse of TQM provides for the normative orientation of employees towards change and this normative alignment is enhanced by the developmental perspective found within TQM. The development of problem solving and continuous improvement activities entails systemic learning and the development, both for employees and the organization (Adler & Cole, 1993; Cole, 1994; Sitkin *et al.*, 1994). This learning leads to the development of new capacities amongst employees and this may influence employee attitudes (Zeitz, Mittal & McAulay, 1999).

TQM has its limitations as a model for organizational change, however, and these are four-fold. In the first instance, the TQM model is often top-down in its approach to change, and hence it is not necessarily the most effective. TQM places a strong emphasis upon senior management leadership to develop strategies and plan change initiatives. This approach leaves little room for bottom-up initiatives and little scope for broad-based participation in the change effort. The use of quality practices that promote standardization and the use of standard procedures may also be inimical to the change effort, promoting bureaucratic inflexibility rather than an openness to change (Dawson, 1998; Dawson & Palmer, 1995; Hunter & Beaumont, 1993). TQM programs may thus be caught on the horns of a dilemma, torn between the need to standardize to improve reliability and the need to innovate and respond to changing customer requirements (Sitkin *et al.*, 1994).

A further limitation of TQM is that the disparate nature of TQM practices can often lead to fragmented change efforts, as one failed quality initiative after another is tried and abandoned. The management literature is replete with failed quality fads, such as quality circles, quality function deployment, customer first programs and so on. These practices are often introduced in a piecemeal fashion and hence do not become embedded within the organization. Change pursued through the introduction of quality fads may be only short-term, with high initial interest but a quick return to the *status quo ante* thereafter (Reger *et al.*, 1994; Yong & Wilkinson, 1999; Zeitz *et al.*, 1999).

The total quality approach to change also often ignores the context of that change. TQM requires the development of open communications and a high level of trust between units and departments, employees and managers, and yet it is often implemented in conjunction with major changes to operations that undermine the very preconditions for success. Total quality programs are often implemented at same time as plant closures and downsizing is occurring, for example, or as outsourcing and increased use of contingent labour to increase labour flexibility, and thus change efforts may be cynically received and perceived as little more than work intensification (Hunter & Beaumont, 1993; McCabe & Wilkinson, 1997; Parker & Slaughter, 1993).

A final limitation of the TQM model is that the quality discourse within the firm promotes the creation of a unitary organizational culture. Identification with the mission and goals of the organization by all employees leaves little room for the assertion of difference, and does not provide any recognition of the multiple identifications that employees may have with the immediate work unit, vocational peers or unions and employee representatives (Dawson, 1998; Edwards, Collinson & Rees, 1998). The quality discourse developed by senior management may also reflect management priorities and interests, and so may be perceived as self-serving by employees. The actual implementation of quality practices may in fact be perceived as an attempt to implement even greater control by management, with the consequent surfacing of withdrawal behaviours and a lack of cooperation and trust on the part of employees (Hunter & Beaumont, 1993; McCabe & Wilkinson, 1997; Zbaracki, 1998).

TQM, in its guise as a philosophy of management, offers a vision of organizational transformation, but it lacks the tools with which to implement that transformation. The TQM approach to change often fails to grasp the magnitude of change and has no clear techniques to implement change, other than the introduction of quality control techniques and employee involvement practices (Redman & Grieves, 1999). The failure of TQM as a program for organizational change may lead to the perception that it is merely rhetorical, with little workplace change and employee empowerment actually taking place (Hackman & Wageman, 1995; Reger et al., 1994; Tuckman, 1994).

TQM AND ORGANIZATIONAL PERFORMANCE

TQM is widely used and has a variety of impacts upon employees. The implementation of quality control and improvement practices leads to an expansion of the work role, whilst the development of a quality discourse leads to a reorientation on the part of employees towards that work role. How effective these changes are and what contribution they make towards improving the performance and competitive position of an enterprise, however, remains unclear. There have been a variety of attempts to assess the effectiveness of TQM, by scholars and by those promoting TQM programs, but to date a clear and comprehensive assessment remains elusive.

Some initial studies of the effect of TQM programs compared high-performing and low-performing firms to see whether there was a difference in the kind of TQM programs adopted by these firms. High-performing firms seemed to make greater use of all elements of a TQM program, and hence the inference was drawn that the adoption of comprehensive TQM programs was more efficacious than the adoption of single practices (Australian Manufacturing Council, 1994; Ferdows & De Meyer, 1990). Other studies along similar lines examined the performance of quality award winners and compared their practice with that of lower-ranked competition entrants. Once again, the main conclusion of such studies was that firms with comprehensive TQM programs seemed to perform better than firms with partially implemented TQM programs, on a range of financial and operational measures (General Accounting Office, 1991; Easton, 1995; Helton, 1995). Studies examining the longer-term impact of TQM have also found significant differences in performance between firms with comprehensive TQM programs and those with partially implemented TQM programs, adding further weight to the claims that TQM is a singularly effective management practice (Easton & Jarrell, 1998).

These general studies of TQM effectiveness, however, aggregate TQM practices together and thus do not provide much of a picture of the relationships between practices. It was the development of more sophisticated TQM frameworks that enabled researchers to examine the role of particular TQM practices in relation to organizational performance. The development of analytical frameworks that attempted to: (a) clearly specify the elements of a TQM program (Ahire et al., 1996; Black & Porter, 1996; Saraph et al., 1989); (b) conceptualize the relationships between the elements of a TQM program (Flynn et al., 1995); and (c) elaborate the dimensions of quality performance (Garvin, 1984), enabled scholars to develop a more detailed account of the relationship between quality practice and organizational performance. Quality was found to be a multi-dimensional construct and the strength of the relationships between the elements of a TQM program and organizational performance was found to vary. The assumption that there was a necessary interrelationship between all TQM practices began to be questioned (Dow, Samson & Ford, 1999; Powell, 1995; Samson & Terziovski, 1999).

Some studies found that it was the "hard" quality management practices that were significant in lifting performance, rather than the broader set of hard and soft TQM practices (Flynn *et al.*, 1995). These studies lend support to the view that TQM is, first and foremost, a program of management action designed to lift quality performance by using established quality control tools and techniques. The hard, technical elements of TQM, in other words, can be effective in lifting performance.

Many other studies indicated that it was senior management support for TQM programs that was critical, developing a strategic vision for the organization and providing support for the numerous change initiatives that accompany the implementation of a TQM program (Samson & Terziovski, 1999). Such findings lend support to the view that TQM can be seen as a successful philosophy of management which, if embraced whole-heartedly by senior management, can lead to significant improvements in performance.

Other studies, however, supported the view that the attitudinal and behavioural elements of a TQM program were the most critical to organizational success. These studies lend support to the view that TQM is principally an organizational–behavioural intervention and that it is the soft elements of a TQM program that have the greatest effect upon direct product quality and overall organizational performance (Ahire *et al.*, 1996; Curkovic, Vickery & Droge, 2000; Dow *et al.*, 1999; Powell, 1995; Samson & Terziovski, 1999).

There is, then, some evidence that TQM is an effective management program of action. Support can be found for the effectiveness of most varieties of TQM and there is no conclusive evidence that would support the efficacy of one version of TQM over another. Notwithstanding the recent attempts to specify the complex interdependencies between TQM practices, much work remains to be done to establish the mechanisms by which TQM programs affect organizational performance (Das, Handfield, Calantone & Ghosh, 2000; Douglas & Judge, 2001; Ho, Duffy & Shih, 2001; Kaynak, 2003).

CONCLUSION

This chapter has investigated the many facets of TQM. TQM may refer to simple programs of quality improvement, to a business philosophy embraced by senior management, or to a program of organizational change that focuses upon the behavioural and attitudinal aspects of organizational life. This chapter has emphasized the importance of the first and third of these aspects of TQM, for their impact upon employees. What are often referred to as the "hard" and "soft" aspects of TQM have been the focus of attention here. The hard, technical elements of TQM have been shown to have the greatest effect on work design, whilst the soft, organizational–behavioural aspects of TQM have the greatest effect upon employee orientation towards the work role.

Hard TQM has been found to lead to an expansion of the work role that enhances employee motivation and improves work design. This conception of the impact of TQM can be readily accommodated within existing work design theories and, in this respect, TQM may be seen as simply another in the long line of job redesign initiatives implemented by management (Hackman & Wageman, 1995). TQM has also been found to have effects upon the decisional autonomy given to employees, enabling or constraining their participation in workplace decision making. Once again, this change can be accommodated within existing theories of employee participation and the outcomes explained within the framework of existing work design theories (Cotton, 1993; Cotton *et al.*, 1988; Davis & Wacker, 1987; Hackman, 1977, 1991; Hackman & Oldham, 1980).

The technical elements of TQM are, however, often implemented in ways that do not challenge underlying organizational structures, social–affective systems or work cultures. Here it is the soft elements of TQM that have the greatest impact. The implementation of the soft aspects of TQM—the restructuring of hierarchical role relationships within organizations and the reorientation of employees towards their work role—introduces new dimensions to the discussion of work design, and yet this change has been little studied. The efforts within TQM programs to provide for the normative integration of employees into unitary organizational cultures have not been touched upon by previous work design theories, and there is a need to elaborate more fully a theory of work roles in contemporary work systems (Parker, Wall & Jackson, 1997).

More pragmatically, little research has focused upon the outcomes of TQM programs for employees. Few studies have examined the impact of TQM programs on employee satisfaction, employee commitment, job satisfaction or job security (Coyle-Shapiro, 1999; Cowling & Newman, 1995; Lam, 1995). TQM programs should enhance work design, and the improvements wrought by TQM should enhance the competitive position of the organization and hence job security. These effects of TQM programs are widely hypothesised, but there has been little direct study of the veracity of such claims (Edwards *et al.*, 1998).

The link between TQM and improved outcomes for employees is supported indirectly by studies of strategic HRM systems (Arthur, 1994; Becker & Gerhart, 1996; Huselid, 1995) and high-performance work systems (Brown, Reich & Stern, 1993; MacDuffie, 1995). Many of the practices examined in these studies may be said to overlap with TQM practices, but TQM is not identical to either HRM or high-performance work systems, and so direct inferences cannot be drawn. Studies of human resource management practices and employee outcomes have also been complemented by studies of advanced manufacturing practices and employee outcomes. Once again, there is some overlap with TQM; however, these studies do not look solely at TQM, but rather examine the impact of TQM practices in conjunction with advanced manufacturing technology, just-in-time flow and other new manufacturing techniques (Jayaram, Droge & Vickery, 1999; Youndt, Snell, Dean & Lepak, 1996).

There is thus a need to reconceptualise the study of employee outcomes of TQM programs. There has been some study of employee satisfaction and commitment, but little study of the impact of TQM upon employees' vocational identities or upon significant outcomes such as job security (Edwards *et al.*, 1998; Redman & Grieves, 1999). The experience of TQM, reflected here, points to the limitations of viewing such programs simply as a management initiative. The implementation of TQM has profound effects upon the work of employees and these effects need to be more extensively researched and more clearly theorised.

REFERENCES

Adler, P. S. (1993). Time-and-motion regained. *Harvard Business Review*, **January–February**, 97–108.

Adler, P. S. & Borys, B. (1996). Two types of bureaucracy: enabling and coercive. *Administrative Science Quarterly*, **41**, 61–89.

Adler, P. S. & Cole, R. E. (1993). Designed for learning: a tale of two auto plants. *Sloan Management Review*, **Spring**, 85–94.

Ahire, S. L., Golhar, D. Y. & Waller, M. A. (1996). Development and validation of TQM implementation constructs. *Decision Sciences*, **27**(1), 23–56.

Arthur, J. B. (1994). Effects of human resource systems on manufacturing performance and turnover. *Academy of Management Journal*, **37**(3), 670–687.

Australian Manufacturing Council (1994). *Leading the Way. A Study of Best Manufacturing Practices in Australia and New Zealand*. Melbourne: AMC.

Becker, B. & Gerhart, B. (1996). The impact of human resource management on organizational performance: progress and prospects. *Academy of Management Journal*, **39**(4), 779–801.

Black, S. A. & Porter, L. J. (1996). Identification of the critical factors of TQM. *Decision Sciences*, **27**(1), 1–21.

Brown, C., Reich, M. & Stern, D. (1993). Becoming a high-performance work organization: the role of security, employee involvement and training. *International Journal of Human Resource Management*, **2**(4), 247–275.

Choi, T. Y. & Behling, O. C. (1997). Top managers and TQM success: one more look after all these years. *Academy of Management Executive*, **11**(1), 37–47.

Clinton, R. J., Williamson, S. & Bethke, A. L. (1994). Implementing total quality management: the role of human resource management. *SAM Advanced Management Journal*, **Spring**, 10–16.

Cole, R. E. (1994). Different quality paradigms and their implications for organizational learning. In M. Akoi & R. Dore (Eds), *The Japanese Firm. The Sources of Competitive Strength* (pp. 66–83). Oxford: Oxford University Press.

Cole, R. E. (1998). Learning from the quality movement: what did and didn't happen and why. *California Management Review*, **41**(1), 43–73.

Conti, R. F. & Warner, M. (1997). Technology, culture and craft: job tasks and quality realities. *New Technology, Work and Employment*, **12**(2), 123–135.

Cordery, J. L. (1996). Autonomous work groups and quality circles. In M. A. West (Ed.), *Handbook of Work Group Psychology* (pp. 225–246). Chichester: Wiley.

Cotton, J. L. (1993). *Employee Involvement. Methods for Improving Performance and Work Attitudes*. Newbury Park, CA: Sage.

Cotton, J. L., Vollrath, D. A., Froggatt, K. L., Lengnick-Hall, M. L. & Jennings, K. R. (1988). Employee participation: diverse forms and different outcomes. *Academy of Management Review*, **13**(1), 8–22.

Cowling, A. & Newman, K. (1995). Banking on people: TQM, service quality and human resources. *Personnel Review*, **24**(7), 25–41.

Coyle-Shapiro, J. A-M. (1999). Employee participation and assessment of an organizational change intervention. A three-wave study of total quality management. *Journal of Applied Behavioural Science*, **35**(4), 439–456.

Crosby, P. B. (1980). *Quality Is Free: the Art of Making Quality Certain*. New York: Mentor Books.

Curkovic, S., Vickery, S. & Droge, C. (2000). Quality-related action programs: their impact on quality performance and firm performance. *Decision Sciences*, **31**(4), 885–905.

Das, A., Handfield, R. B., Calantone, R. J. & Ghosh, S. (2000). A contingent view of quality management—the impact of international competition on quality. *Decision Sciences*, **31**(3), 649–690.

Davis, L. E. & Wacker, G. J. (1987). Job design. In G. Salvendy (Ed.), *Handbook of Human Factors* (pp. 431–452). New York: Wiley.

Dawson, P. (1994a). *Organizational Change. A Processual Approach*. London: Paul Chapman.

Dawson, P. (1994b). Total quality management. In J. Storey (Ed.), *New Wave Manufacturing Strategies* (pp. 103–121). London: Paul Chapman.

Dawson, P. (1998). The rhetoric and bureaucracy of quality management. A totally questionable method. *Personnel Review*, **27**(1), 5–19.

Dawson, P. & Palmer, G. (1995). *Quality Management. The Theory and Practice of Implementing Change*. Melbourne: Longman.

Dawson, P. & Webb, J. (1989). New production arrangements: the totally flexible cage. *Work, Employment and Society*, **3**(2), 221–238.

Dean, J. W. Jr & Bowen, D. E. (1994). Management theory and total quality: improving research and practice through theory development. *Academy of Management Review*, **18**(3), 392–418.

Delbridge, R., Turnbull, P. & Wilkinson, B. (1992). Pushing back the frontiers: management control and work intensification under JIT/TQM factory regimes. *New Technology, Work and Employment*, **7**(2), 97–106.

Deming, W. E. (1982). *Quality, Productivity and Competitive Position*. Cambridge, MA: MIT Centre for Advanced Engineering Study.

Deming, W. E. (1986). *Out of the Crisis*. Cambridge, MA: Cambridge University Press.

Douglas, T. J. & Judge, W. Q. (2001). Total Quality Management implementation and competitive advantage: the role of structural control and exploration. *Academy of Management Journal*, **44**(1), 158–169.

Dow, D., Samson, D. & Ford, S. (1999). Exploding the myth: do all quality management practices contribute to superior performance? *Production and Operations Management*, **8**(1), 1–27.

Easton, G. S. (1995). A Baldrige Examiner's assessment of US total quality management. In R. E. Cole (Ed.), *The Death and Life of the American Quality Movement* (pp. 11–58). New York: Oxford University Press.

Easton, G. S. & Jarrell, S. L. (1998). The effects of total quality management on corporate performance: an empirical investigation. *Journal of Business*, **71**(2), 253–307.

Edwards, P., Collinson, M. & Rees, C. (1998). The determinants of employee response to total quality management: six case studies. *Organization Studies*, **19**(3), 449–475.

Evans, J. R. & Dean, J. W. Jr (2000). *Total Quality. Management, Organization and Strategy*. Cincinnati, OH: South-Western College Publishing.

Evans, J. R. & Lindsay, W. M. (1999). *The Management and Control of Quality*, 4th Edn. Cincinnati, OH: South-Western College Publishing.

Feigenbaum, A. V. (1983). *Total Quality Control*. New York: McGraw-Hill.

Ferdows, K. & De Meyer, A. (1990). Lasting improvements in manufacturing performance: in search of a new theory. *Journal of Operations Management*, **9**(2), 168–184.

Flynn, B. B., Schroeder, R. G. & Sakakibara, S. (1995). The impact of quality management practices on performance and competitive advantage. *Decision Sciences*, **26**(5), 659–691.

Garvin, D. (1984). What does product quality really mean? *Sloan Management Review*, **36**(1), 25–43.

Garvin, D. (1991). *Managing Quality: the Strategic and Competitive Edge*. New York: Free Press.

General Accounting Office (1991). *Report to the House of Representatives on Management Practices: US Companies Improve Performance Through Quality Efforts*. Washington DC: US General Accounting Office.

Gee, M. V. & Nystrom, P. C. (1999). Strategic fit between skills training and levels of quality management: an empirical study of American manufacturing plants. *Human Resource Planning*, **22**(2), 12–23.

Griffin, R. (1988). Consequences of quality circles in an industrial setting: a longitudinal assessment. *Academy of Management Journal*, **31**(2), 338–358.

Griffin, R. (1991). Effects of work redesign on employee perceptions, attitudes, and behaviours: a long-term investigation. *Academy of Management Journal*, **34**(2), 425–435.

Grant, R. M., Shani, R. & Krishnan, R. (1994). TQM's challenge to management theory and practice. *Sloan Management Review*, **Winter**, 25–35.

Hackman, J. R. & Oldham, G. R. (1980). *Work Redesign*. The Philippines: Addison-Wesley.

Hackman, J. R. & Wageman, R. (1995). Total quality management: empirical, conceptual and practical issues. *Administrative Science Quarterly*, **40**, 309–342.

Hackman, R. J. (1977). Work design. In R. J. Hackman & J. L. Suttle (Eds), *Improving Life at Work. Behavioral Science Approaches to Organizational Change* (pp. 96–159). Santa Monica, CA: Goodyear.

Hackman, R. J. (1991). Work design. In R. M. Steers & L. W. Porter (Eds), *Motivation and Work Behaviour*. New York: McGraw-Hill.

Helton, B. R. (1995). The Baldie play. *Quality Progress*, **28**(2), 43–45.

Hill, S. (1991). Why quality circles failed but total quality management might succeed. *British Journal of Industrial Relations*, **29**(4), 541–569.

Hill, S. & Wilkinson, A. (1995). In search of TQM. *Employee Relations*, **17**(3), 8–25.

Ho, D. C. K., Duffy, V. G. & Shih, H. M. (2001). Total Quality Management: an empirical test for mediation effect. *International Journal of Production Research*, **39**(3), 529–548.

Hunter, L. & Beaumont, P. B. (1993). Implementing TQM: top down or bottom up? *Industrial Relations Journal*, **24**(4), 318–327.

Huselid, M. A. (1995). The impact of human resource management practices on turnover, productivity and corporate financial performance. *Academy of Management Journal*, **38**(3), 635–672.

Imai, M. (1997). *Gemba Kaizen: A Commonsense, Low-cost Approach to Management.* New York: McGraw-Hill.

Ishikawa, K. (1985). *What Is Total Quality Control? The Japanese Way.* Englewood Cliffs, NJ: Prentice-Hall.

Jayaram, J., Droge, C. & Vickery, S. K. (1999). The impact of human resource management practices on manufacturing performance. *Journal of Operations Management*, **18**, 1–20.

Juran, J. M. & Godfrey, A. B. (Eds) (1999). *Juran's Quality Control Handbook*, 5th Edn. New York: McGraw-Hill.

Kaynak, H. (2003). The relationship between Total Quality Management practices and their effects on firm performance. *Journal of Operations Management*, **21**(4), 405–435.

Klein, J. A. (1991). A reexamination of autonomy in light of new manufacturing practices. *Human Relations*, **44**(1), 21–38.

Kochan, T. A., Gittell, J. H. & Lautsch, B. A. (1995). Total quality management and human resource systems: an international comparison. *International Journal of Human Resource Management*, **6**(2), 201–223.

Lam, S. S. K. (1995). Quality management and job satisfaction. *International Journal of Quality & Reliability Management*, **12**(4), 72–79.

Lawler, E. E. & Mohrman, S. A. (1985). Quality circles after the fad. *Harvard Business Review*, **January–February**, 64–71.

MacDuffie, J. P. (1995). Human resource bundles and manufacturing performance: organizational logic and flexible production systems in the world auto industry. *Industrial and Labor Relations Review*, **48**(2), 197–221.

McCabe, D. & Wilkinson, A. (1997). The rise and fall of TQM: the vision, meaning and operation of change. *Industrial Relations Journal*, **29**(1), 18–29.

Marks, M. L., Mirvis, P. H., Hackett, E. J. & Grady, J. F. Jr (1986). Employee participation in a quality circle program: impact on quality of work life, productivity and absenteeism. *Journal of Applied Psychology*, **71**(1), 61–69.

Montgomery, D. C. (1991). *Introduction to Statistical Quality Control*, 2dn Edn. Toronto: Wiley.

Morrow, P. C. (1997). The measurement of TQM principles and work-related outcomes. *Journal of Organizational Behaviour*, **18**(2), 363–376.

Parker, M. & Slaughter, J. (1993). Should the labour movement buy TQM? *Journal of Organizational Change Management*, **6**(4), 43–56.

Parker, S. A., Wall, T. D. & Jackson, P. R. (1997). "That's not my job": developing flexible employee work orientations. *Academy of Management Journal*, **40**(4), 899–929.

Powell, T. C. (1995). Total quality management as competitive advantage: a review and empirical study. *Strategic Management Journal*, **16**(1), 15–28.

Redman, T. & Grieves, J. (1999). Managing strategic change through TQM: learning from failure. *New Technology, Work and Employment*, **14**(1), 45–61.

Reger, R. K., Gustafson, L. T., Demarie, S. M. & Mullane, J. V. (1994). Reframing the organization: why implementing total quality is easier said than done. *Academy of Management Review*, **19**(3), 565–584.

Samson, D. & Terziovski, M. (1999). The relationship between total quality management practices and operational performance. *Journal of Operations Management*, **17**, 393–409.

Saraph, J. V., Benson, P. G. & Schroeder, R. G. (1989). An instrument for measuring the critical factors of quality management. *Decision Sciences*, **20**(4), 810–829.

Schonberger, R. J. (1992). Is strategy strategic? Impact of total quality management on strategy. *Academy of Management Executive*, **6**(3), 80–87.

Schonberger, R. J. (1994). Human resource management: lessons from a decade of total quality management and reengineering. *California Management Review*, **Summer**, 103–123.

Shingo, S. (1986). *Zero Quality Control: Source Inspection and the Poka-Yoke System* (Trans. A. P. Dillon). Cambridge, MA: Productivity Press.

Shingo, S. (1989). *A Study of the Toyota Production System from an Industrial Engineering Viewpoint* (Trans. A. P. Dillon). Cambridge, MA: Productivity Press.

Sitkin, S. B., Sutcliffe, K. M. & Schroeder, R. G. (1994). Distinguishing control from learning in total quality management: a contingency perspective. *Academy of Management Review*, **19**(3), 537–564.

Spencer, B. A. (1994). Models of organization and total quality management: a comparison and critical evaluation. *Academy of Management Review*, **19**(3), 446–471.

Tuckman, A. (1994). The yellow brick road: total quality management and the restructuring of organizational culture. *Organization Studies*, **15**(5), 727–751.

Waldman, D. A. (1994). The contributions of total quality management to a theory of work performance. *Academy of Management Review*, **19**(3), 510–536.

Wilkinson, A. (1995). Re-examining quality management. *Review of Employment Topics*, **3**(1), 187–211.

Wilkinson, A., Godfrey, G. & Marchington, M. (1997). Bouquets, brickbats and blinkers: total quality management and employee involvement in practice. *Organization Studies*, **18**(5), 799–819.

Wilkinson, A., Marchington, M., Goodman, J. & Ackers, P. (1992). Total quality management and employee involvement. *Human Resource Management Journal*, **2**(4), 1–20.

Wilkinson, A., Redman, T. & Snape, E. (1994). Quality management and the manager. *Employee Relations*, **16**(1), 62–70.

Wilkinson, A., Redman, T., Snape, E. & Marchington, M. (1998). *Managing with Total Quality Management*. Basingstoke: Macmillan Business.

Yong, J. & Wilkinson, A. (1999). The state of total quality management: a review. *International Journal of Human Resource Management*, **10**(1), 137–161.

Youndt, M. A., Snell, S. A., Dean, J. W. Jr & Lepak, D. P. (1996). Human resource management, manufacturing strategy and firm performance. *Academy of Management Journal*, **39**(4), 836–866.

Zbaracki, M. J. (1998). The rhetoric and reality of total quality management. *Administrative Science Quarterly*, **43**, 602–636.

Zeitz, G., Mittal, V. & McAulay, B. (1999). Distinguishing adoption and entrenchment of management practices: a framework for analysis. *Organization Studies*, **20**(5), 741–776.

CHAPTER 4

System Integration in Advanced Manufacturing Technology

Waldemar Karwowski

Center for Industrial Ergonomics, University of Louisville, KY, USA

and

Bradley Chase

Industrial and Systems Engineering, University of San Diego, CA, USA

Contemporary manufacturing enterprises are exposed to changing market demands, rapid technological development, legal provisions and social changes. Furthermore, today's customers often demand customised, high quality and competitively priced products with a timely delivery. These demands have put pressure on companies to produce products with shorter life cycles, to produce a greater variety of models, to adapt their manufacturing program to customers' wishes within short time scales, and to produce smaller batch sizes in order to keep the finished stock as low as possible (Stalk & Hout, 1990). Manufacturing enterprises have responded with a wave of massive restructuring and have increased their use of advanced manufacturing technologies (AMT), such as computer-integrated manufacturing, computer-aided design and manufacture, computer-numerical-controlled machines and automated inventory systems (Storey, 1994; Waterson *et al.*, 1999).

However, the effective implementation and use of AMT has proved to be no straightforward matter (Karwowski, Kantola, Rodrick & Salvendy, 2002; Majchrzak & Paris, 1995). In part this is due to the complexity of the technology itself, but research shows that the successful use of AMT depends on how the technology (e.g. computer-based technologies, information systems) is integrated with human factors (e.g. skill, expertise and cognition of users) and organisational factors (e.g. job design, human resource practices) (Goldman, Nagel & Preiss, 1995; Karwowski *et al.*, 1994; Karwowski & Salvendy, 1994; Kidd, 1994; Majchrzak & Wang, 1994). Conversely, a lack of integration can lead to poor outcomes; for example, Martin (1993) reported that many manufacturing automation projects have failed because of insufficient automability (automation flexibility), inadequate user–system interfaces (i.e. human–computer integration) and an incompatibility between human needs and system requirements.

Marchrzak & Paris (1995) concluded that high failure rates in the implementation of AMT are attributable to managers and designers lacking an understanding of the organizational and human changes that are often needed with new technology. Given the importance

The Essentials *of the New Workplace: A Guide to the Human Impact of Modern Working Practices.*
Edited by David Holman, Toby D. Wall, Chris W. Clegg, Paul Sparrow and Ann Howard. © 2005 John Wiley & Sons, Ltd.

of understanding these issues, the main aim of this chapter is to discuss the human and organizational factors that affect the operation of AMT and how these elements can be best integrated. It is important to note that space precludes a detailed discussion of all AMTs and the differences between them. This chapter therefore refers to AMT in its broadest sense and it is assumed to include computer-integrated manufacturing, computer-numerically-controlled machine tools and cellular manufacturing. Lean manufacturing can also be understood as a way of integrating AMT, people and organisation. As this practice is addressed in Chapter 2, it will not be covered in this chapter.

AMTs: COMPLEXITY AND INTEGRATION

Advanced manufacturing technology (AMT) can be defined as the application of computer-based systems to automate and integrate different functions in the manufacturing system, such as design, planning and manufacturing. Introducing AMT can significantly increase the complexity of operational systems (Karwowski *et al.*, 2002; Majchrzak & Paris, 1995), as the technologies used often serve multiple and flexibly interchangeable functions. The different parts of the system can also be highly interdependent. This means that the removal of a disturbance is more difficult, as a solution to a problem at one machine will need to be considered in relation to other parts of the system (Jarvinen, Vannas, Mattila & Karwowski, 1996). Designers and users of AMT therefore need to consider how best to integrate technologies by assuring effective interfacing and interactions between machines, and to consider how best to integrate different functional tasks, such as design, scheduling, maintenance and inventory control.

In addition to the integration of technological systems, the designers and users of AMT need to consider how to integrate AMT in the context of human factors. Human factors that have been identified as being important include the skills of the operator, hardware ergonomics (e.g. safety and prevention of accidental operation), software ergonomics (e.g. provision of informative feedback to enable the correct interpretation, evaluation and diagnosis of events), operator training requirements, boredom and stress at work, and safety (Clegg & Corbett, 1987; Cummings & Blumberg, 1987; Office of Technological Assessment, 1984). However, designers of AMT systems rarely give due consideration to the paramount need for effective human integration within AMT systems and primarily focus on technological integration (Kidd, 1994). In addition, human skill is perceived as a problem and the human operator as the source of error (Bainbridge, 1983; Sanderson, 1989; Wilson, Koubek, Salvendy, Sharit & Karwowski, 1994). Yet the successful operation of AMT depends upon human skill and knowledge to compensate for limitations of computer-based technology and relies on the human resource to provide a basis for the development and continuous improvement of AMT (Martin, 1990). Indeed, one of the ironies of AMT is that the role of the human becomes more important in less labour-intensive, automated AMT systems, not less (Wilson, 1991). Furthermore, it is the very fact that people are flexible, intelligent and able to solve complex novel problems that permits AMT to be used at all (Clegg & Corbett, 1987). These issues were exemplified in a study by Wobbe & Charles (1994), who concluded that:

1. The more complex products become, the more quality is dependent upon upgrading of all stages of manufacturing and demands the full dedication of employees at all levels.

2. The more sophisticated manufacturing technology becomes, the more it is vulnerable and dependent upon human skills for control and maintenance.
3. The more customized productions are, the more human intervention is necessary with regard to change-over, setting up machines, adaptation, adjustment and control.
4. If products demand a high service input and after-sales service and maintenance, skilled people are required to deal with this.
5. The shorter the life cycle of products becomes, the more innovativeness comes into play; take-off phases occur more frequently and their mastery is dependent upon experienced personnel with formal knowledge to overcome new challenges connected with the start of a new product.

In addition to being integrated with human factors, various studies have observed that AMT must be integrated with job and organizational factors. For example, the Manufacturing Studies Board (1986) in the USA concluded that realizing the full benefits of AMTs requires inter-related changes in human resource practices, planning, plant culture, plant organization, job and work design, and labour–management relations. These findings were also echoed by European studies on the fusion of flexible manufacturing systems and new information technologies (Brödner, 1987, 1991). These studies concluded that organizational factors are a key element in economic success of modern production systems, and should be valued and appreciated at the level equal to new technology.

A recurring theme in the literature on AMT is that its successful integration with human and organizational factors is fundamental to its effective use (Marchrzak, 1995). Human and organizational factors are important in AMT and must be addressed. The rest of this chapter is devoted to exploring the issues that need to be considered when attempting to integrate AMT, people and organization.

THE ROLES AND SKILLS OF THE OPERATOR IN AMT

AMT systems require operators to engage in a variety of mostly cognitive tasks. These include: monitoring the automated system to ensure that it is functioning properly and fine-tuning it, making adjustments as necessary; detecting, diagnosing and compensating for scheduling failures, infeasible routings and other system faults; planning what should be done and specifying how it should be done; communicating with colleagues and those in other departments; making some necessary trade-offs and negotiating among alternative solutions; and learning through feedback from the plant about the impact of the above four activities (Bi & Salvendy, 1994; Sinclair, 1986). Operators need to be skilled in all these areas and from this it is apparent that, in modern manufacturing systems, the emphasis has moved away from perceptual–motor skills and towards higher-order cognitive skills (e.g. problem solving and decision making) and interpersonal skills (Goodstein, Anderson & Olsen, 1988).

Rasmussen (1983) has offered an alternative way in which to conceptualize the skills needed by human operators in AMT systems. He has classified the skills needed into three major categories. They are skill-based behaviour, rule-based behaviour and knowledge-based behaviour. Skill-based behaviour refers to sensory–motor performance during acts or activities, which take place without conscious control as smooth, automated and highly integrated patterns of behaviour. In this view, human activities are considered as a sequence of skilled acts composed for the actual situation. Rule-based behaviour is based on explicit knowledge and knowing how to employ the relevant rules in the correct situation (Goodstein *et al.*, 1988; Johannsen, 1988). Knowledge-based behaviour refers to goal-controlled performance, where the goal is explicitly formulated, based on the knowledge of environment and aims of the person (Johannsen, 1988). The internal structure of the system is represented by a mental model. This kind of behaviour allows the operator to develop and test different plans under unfamiliar and uncertain conditions. It is particularly required when the skills and know-how of the individual are insufficient, so that conscious problem solving and planning are called for (Goodstein *et al.*, 1988). This implies that the effective use of AMT thus requires the use of higher-order cognitive knowledge-based skills.

The preceding paragraphs have shown that a range of tasks is performed in an AMT environment and that higher-order cognitive and interpersonal skills are needed to complete these tasks. Furthermore, because of the complexity and tight interdependencies of the AMT environment, it has been argued that operators need to be able to perform *all* these tasks (and have the appropriate skills) in order effectively to control variances in the work process. Only broad job roles and multiskilled operators will be able to deliver the full benefits of AMT (Marchrzak & Paris, 1995). As such, AMT has the potential to up-skill or re-skill when operators are given responsibility over a wide range of tasks, such as monitoring machines, machine maintenance, programming and problem solving (Cross, 1983; Wall, Corbett, Martin, Clegg & Jackson, 1990b). Yet it is not always the case that operators are given responsibility for a wide range of tasks within an AMT environment. Depending on how tasks are allocated, AMT can de-skill operators. This can occur, for example, when engineers and computer specialists rather than operators are given responsibility for maintaining machines, repairing machines and writing and fine-tuning the machines' programs. In these circumstances, not only will the operator be engaged in a restricted range of activities, but he/she may have little opportunity to use and develop high-order cognitive skills (Blumberg & Gerwin, 1983; Wall, Corbett, Clegg, Jackson & Martin, 1990a).

The aforementioned examples are concerned with the allocation of tasks between humans; also addressed has been task allocation between humans and machines. Attention has focused on the type of planning and scheduling tasks and the type of fault diagnosis procedures that are best carried out by either humans or machines (Nakamura & Salvendy, 1994; Karwowski, Warnecke, Hueser & Salvendy, 1997) and researchers have sought to understand the ways in which the capabilities of machines and humans can complement each other (Clegg & Corbett, 1987), e.g. a computer can generate plans or schedules far quicker than a human and, under normal conditions, can check the difference between the planned and actual schedule. However, in unusual conditions, or when a plan needs to be modified and rescheduled according to competing priorities, a human operator is normally far more effective at generating work plans and schedules. Task allocation should therefore rely on a clear understanding of the capabilities and limitations of humans and machines (see also Bi & Salvendy, 1994). It should be noted that one of the ironies of allocating human functions to machines, i.e. of automation, is that it can mystify the production process (Artandi, 1982), as operators may not be able to learn adequately about the production process as a whole. One consequence of this is that operators become unable to deal with or anticipate difficulties in the production process (Sanderson, 1989). This problem is exacerbated when the tasks of the operator are restricted and when the skills of the operator are reduced. Widening the operators' roles is one way of overcoming this problem.

JOB AND WORK DESIGN

To ensure the effective application of AMT, the following job design factors need to be addressed: job content, particularly the variety, breadth and integration of tasks (e.g. uniting planning, execution, monitoring and problem solving); job control; job demands; performance monitoring and feedback; supervisory style; social interaction; and participation in the design of technology and other work systems (Corbett, 1988; Cummings & Blumberg, 1987; Smith & Carayon, 1995).

Most emphasis has been placed on job content (e.g. task and skill variety, as discussed above) and job control. With regard to job control, much of the debate has focused on whether AMT technologies reduce or increase control. Studies indicate that the effects of AMT on operator control depend on the choices made by the designers of the technology (Clegg, 1988; Wall *et al.*, 1990a), for example decentralization principles can be followed to increase the control of operators (Badham & Shallock, 1991). First, operators' tasks can be widened as far as possible. Second, computer-aided planning facilities can be located at the shop floor level rather than the planning department level. Third, planning and scheduling functions can be supported at the production level, rather than the foreman/area control level. Cooley (1989) demonstrated control could be increased in a manufacturing cell by giving operators, rather than a specialist technician, control over the creation of machine programmes using high-level software tools, the improvement of software tools, machine scheduling and the programming the work handler to load and unload. Yet, while AMT may increase operator control over some aspects of work, it can reduce it with regard to other aspects. An operator may have little individual control over how he/she does his/her work, due to high levels of standardisation, but have a high degree of group or collective autonomy over the specification of these standards (Klein, 1991). Similarly, an operator may have little control over the timing of his/her work, but have a high degree of control over work methods (Wall *et al.*, 1990a).

In addition to job control, job demands, particularly cognitive demands, are likely to be affected by AMT (Jackson, Wall, Martin & Davids, 1993; Wall *et al.*, 1990a). One of the main roles of the operator is to monitor the manufacturing process, to ensure that it is running smoothly and to be alert to problems. Attention demands are therefore likely to be high, even though little intervention in the system may be required. Furthermore, the problems that are presented to the operator may be complex and difficult to solve—although whether operators have the authority to deal with them may depend on how tasks are allocated. Another demand placed on operators has been called "production responsibility" (Jackson *et al.*, 1993). In AMT systems, machine operators may have considerable responsibility for valuable machinery and, in some cases, costly products. The failure to anticipate or identify a problem may damage the machine and lead to a costly loss of production. Furthermore, since the CNC machines used in AMT can produce a proportionally greater amount, machine downtime incurs greater costs for the firm. In total, AMT systems can increase the cognitive load on the operator.

The use of AMT also affects cognition in two other ways: hierarchically and horizontally (Sanderson, 1989). The hierarchical effect of AMT manifests itself through the process of automation, and leads to human operators acting as supervisors of the artificially intelligent manufacturing processes. The horizontal effect of AMT can be described in information-processing terms, and illustrates the situation in which the human operators have access to information about all aspects of the manufacturing system. It is clearly important that attention in the design process be given to the cognitive tasks involved when working within

AMT systems, and to ensure that these are concomitant with operators' skill levels and cognitive mental models. Failure to consider an operator's skill level and mental model can increase the levels of operator error, which in an AMT environment can be costly (Reason, 1990). One approach that has sought to address this need is cognitive engineering (Harris, 1997; Hollnagel & Woods, 1983), in which human knowledge and skill are considered as an inherent part of system design requirements.

Social contact is another important work characteristic as, at a basic level, it fulfils a human need for significant social relationships (Wall & Martin, 1987). AMT can affect the extent of social contact although, as in other cases, the effect of AMT on this job characteristic is not uniform or deterministic. On the one hand, a number of studies have shown that AMT can isolate employees from each other physically and limit social interaction, due to high monitoring requirements (Argote, Goodman & Schkade, 1983; Kostecki, Mrela & Pankow, 1984). On the other hand, the interdependencies between different aspects of the AMT system can increase the need for operators to collaborate with each other and with other departments and functional roles (Blumberg & Alber, 1982; Boddy & Buchanan, 1986). In highly interdependent AMT systems, performance may therefore be enhanced by group-level re-design, such as the introduction of team work, semi-autonomous work groups and manufacturing cells, that facilitate collaboration.

Research on the effects of job characteristics on job strain and job dissatisfaction in AMT indicates that the following characteristics have the most consistent effects (Keita & Sauter, 1992; Smith, Carayon, Sanders, Lim & LeGrande, 1992; Wall *et al.*, 1990a): a lack of control over the timing of work and the methods used (Wall & Martin, 1987); a lack of social contact and social support (Kiggundu, 1981; Warr, 1987); high problem-solving and attention/monitoring demand (Jackson *et al.*, 1993; Wall, Kemp, Jackson & Clegg, 1986) and high production responsibility.[1]

Given that contemporary enterprises have a choice about how to organise work, a human-centred approach to AMT can be adopted to reduce employee strain. This was shown by Seppälä, Touminen and Koskinen (1992), who investigated the effects of introducing AMT and a flexible production philosophy on job contents, work demands and employee well-being in nine Finnish companies. The components of the AMT systems studied included flexible manufacturing systems, computer-numerical-controlled machine centres, and robotized machining cells. The results showed that, if management design the production system on a human-centred approach that assumes a flexible and multiskilled workforce, then AMT does not inevitably result in the impoverishment of job contents, de-skilling or employee strain.

Studies on job characteristics and well-being generally point to universal effects, whereas the effects of job design on performance appear to be contingent on factors such as operational uncertainty; for example, Wall *et al.* (1990b) examined whether the effect of job control on performance is greater when task uncertainty is high. The study compared two work design styles used to manage and operate CNC stand-alone systems. The work designs of interest were "specialist control" and "operator-centred control". In the specialist control mode, engineers and computer specialists maintain, repair, write and fine-tune the programs, while the operator has minimal involvement. In the operator-centred control mode,

---

[1] With regard to demand characteristics and production responsibility, it is clear that extremes on any of the ranges may cause low well-being, but within the ranges found in organizations, the effects can be assumed to be linear.

the operator is responsible for monitoring and maintenance and programming of problems as they occur. A socio-technological criterion for predicting performance through the concept of production variance was used. It was hypothesized that increasing operator control will improve performance to a greater extent in high-variance manufacturing systems than in low-variance ones. The study results revealed that introduction of enhanced operator control over CNC assembly machines led to a reduction in downtime for high-variance machines. Also of interest was the fact that work redesign improved intrinsic job satisfaction and reduced feelings of job pressure among operators. It was argued that performance improved because operators were able to immediately deal with problems and variances in the work processes in the most effective manner. It is also worth noting that several authors have proposed that AMT increases the degree of technological and operational uncertainty (Cummings & Blumberg, 1987; Majchrzak, 1988), a general implication being that job control should be high in AMT systems.

Work on the mechanisms through which job design might have its effects on AMT performance has looked at knowledge- or learning-based mechanisms and quick-response mechanisms. Evidence for these mechanisms comes from two field experiments that observed strong effects of job control on CNC machine down-time and output (Jackson & Wall, 1991; Wall *et al.*, 1990b). The authors of these studies noticed that different measures of down-time could be used to test for different mechanisms. One measure was of the reduction in time per incident, used to examine a quick-response mechanism; and the other measure was a decrease in the number of incidents which could be used to show that operators were learning to prevent faults, i.e. a knowledge-based mechanism. The results supported the latter explanation. However, interpreting the results with regard to the quick-response mechanism is not straightforward. It could have been the case that the faults that were prevented were of shorter duration, masking a real effect on down-time per incident. Wall, Jackson and Davids (1992) addressed this problem by tracking particular types of faults on a robotics line, both before and after there had been an increase in operator control. The results were very clear. There was an instant and lasting reduction in down-time per fault, and a progressive reduction in faults. This demonstrates that both a quick-response and a knowledge-based mechanism can explain the effect of job control on performance. A more general implication is that increased job control affects performance in two ways, first by allowing the operator to use existing knowledge more effectively (e.g. to immediately rectify faults when they occur), and second, through the development of predictive knowledge and other strategies that prevents faults occurring. This clearly shows that, since AMT relies on operator knowledge and operators' use of higher-order cognitive skills, job designs that allow the opportunity to use and develop knowledge and skills are imperative for their effective use.

ADVANCED MANUFACTURING TECHNOLOGY: THE NEED FOR INTEGRATED, OPEN, HUMAN-CENTRED APPROACHES

At present, many AMT systems remain poorly integrated with the inherent capabilities of the human operators, expressed by their skills and knowledge necessary for the effective control and monitoring of these systems, and other systems within the organization (Karwowski &

Rahimi, 1990; Kidd, 1994). Such incompatibility arises at all levels of the human, machine and human–machine functioning. Problems with integrating people and technology occur early at the AMT design stage. These problems can be conceptualized (Karwowski *et al.*, 1994) using the following model of the complexity of interactions (I) between contemporary manufacturing designers (D) and users (U) of AMT technology, and the AMT technology (T) itself:

$$I(U, T) = F[I(U, D), I(D, T)]$$

where: I stands for relevant interactions and F indicates functional relationships between designers (D), users (U), and technology (T).

The above model points out that the interactions between users and AMT technology are determined by the outcome of the integration of the two earlier interactions, i.e. those between the designers and potential users, and those between the designers and manufacturing technology (at the level of machines and system integration). Although strong interactions typically exist between designers and technology, only a few examples of strong connections between designers and human operators can be found.

To assure full benefits from AMT, designers need a broad vision that includes people, organization and technology (Karwowski *et al.*, 2002; Kidd, 1991), and one in which organizational structures, work practices and technologies allow people to adapt their work strategies to the AMT systems (Kidd, 1990). As such, work practices and technologies need to be designed and developed as open systems. The term "open system" is used to describe a system that receives inputs from, and sends outputs to, the systems environment (Kidd, 1992). The term was associated in manufacturing with system architectures based on the International Standards Organization Open Systems Interconnection model (ESPRIT Consortium AMICE, 1989). The idea can be applied not only to system architectures and organizational structures, but also to work practices, human–computer interfaces and the relationship between people and technologies, such as scheduling, control systems and decision support systems (Kidd, 1990).

An open manufacturing system allows people a large degree of freedom to define the systems operation and adapt the system to the context of use. In the open, adaptable manufacturing system, the relationship between the user and the computer is determined by the user and not by the designer. The role of the designer of an open manufacturing system is to create a system that will satisfy the users' personal preferences, and allow the users to work in a way that they find most appropriate. Kidd (1990) has demonstrated the concept of an open manufacturing system for the human–computer interface in workshop-orientated computer-numerically-controlled (CNC) systems. An open human–computer interface allows the human operator to customize the interface to his/her own personal preferences by changing the dialogue, the screen layout, etc. Another example of an open system can be seen in the operator-centred work design described by Wall *et al.* (1990b), where the operator was responsible for monitoring and maintenance and programming of problems as they occurred. In a closed manufacturing system, the system designer, through hardware, software or performance constraints on the actions of the user, restricts their autonomy and, in some cases, can force the user to use the manufacturing system in a particular way. A simple example of this is where the human–computer interface of a CNC machine tool is pre-set by the manufacturing designers. Another example is where a particular task is automated but, when the manufacturing system fails, the system leaves the user without the necessary computer-based decision support.

A core feature of an open system is that it is human-centred. Corbett (1988) suggests that a human-centered AMT system should:

1. Accept the present skill of the user and provide opportunities for the user to develop new skills. Conventional technological design tends to incorporate this skill into the machine itself, with the resultant de-skilling of the human.
2. Offer a high degree of freedom to users, so that they can shape their own working behaviour and objectives.
3. Unite the planning, execution and monitoring component of work. Hence, the division of labour, which predominates present-day practice in manufacturing, is minimized.
4. Encourage social communication (both formal and informal) between users, preserving the face-to-face interaction in favour of electronically transmitted data exchange.
5. Provide a healthy, safe and efficient work environment.

The types of job and work designs and human resource practices that would support a move towards a more human-centred approach and help employees to deal with the complexity of AMT systems include the following (Liker, Fleischer & Arndorf, 1993; Majchrzak, 1988):

1. Broadening manufacturing operators' job responsibilities to include machine repair, process improvements and inspection.
2. Enlarging maintenance workers' job responsibilities to include teaching, ordering parts, scheduling and machine operations.
3. Extending supervisory job responsibilities to include working with other departments to solve problems.
4. Employing more maintenance people to compensate for increasing equipment responsibility.
5. Increased use of work teams to provide a coordinated response to broad problems.
6. Operator selection based more on human relations skills than seniority, to ensure necessary communication and coordination capabilities.
7. Increased training in problem solving and how the various manufacturing processes function to handle the increased scope of problems.

Another human-centered approach to AMT systems is based on idea of the anthropocentric production system (APS). APS are called anthropocentric because they are focused on skilled human labour instead of technology as the main resource for highly flexible, customer-orientated and quality-based production. As discussed by Wobbe and Charles (1994), the anthropocentric production system assumes that people play a central role in manufacturing, and relates the production system to work organization, the management structure and organizational culture. The defining characteristics of APS are: work in semi-autonomous groups; holistic task assignment to the groups, including both horizontal task integration (e.g. integration of technical maintenance and quality assurance into groups) and vertical task integration (e.g. integration of numerical control programming, planning and scheduling); a decentralized factory organisation, with comprehensive delegation of planning and controlling functions to semi-autonomous units; internal rotation of tasks, leading to job enlargement and job rotation for group members; and high and polyvalent skills and continuous up-skilling at work.

TOOLS AND METHODS FOR AMT JOB AND WORK RE-DESIGN

A number of different tools have been proposed as useful for the introduction and design of AMT systems. In general, these tools conform to the socio-technological principle that both the social and technological aspects of a system must be designed in congruence with each other, i.e. that they are jointly optimized. One such tool is the HITOP system, which stands for high integration of technology, organization and people (Majchrzak, Fleischer, Roitman & Mokray, 1991). HITOP involves the design team completing a series of checklists and forms to describe their organization, current technology and plans. It then helps the design team to consider the implications of those plans for factors such as role requirements and organizational design. A more detailed description of the HITOP framework can be seen in Table 4.1.

Another framework that has been developed for integrating technological, human and organisational factors is GOPRIST. Karwowski *et al.* (1994) proposed this conceptual framework to address the long-term issues related to competitiveness, complexity and uncertainty issues relevant to the human side of contemporary manufacturing enterprises. The GOPRIST framework (see Figure 4.1) starts with the overall company goals, the set of design principles as a basis to fulfil these goals; a set of management and organizational structures, which correspond to the given principles; and the specific techniques to implement these principles.

The "goals" refer to the desired future state of the manufacturing enterprise. Karwowski *et al.* (1994) argues that existing functional organizations of the manufacturing enterprises

Table 4.1   The HITOP framework

1. *Organisational readiness*—how ready is the organisation to make the changes recommended by a HITOP analysis?
2. *Critical technical features*—those features of the technology that are most likely to impact on the integration with people and organisation
3. *Essential role requirements*—for the four primary functions in a manufacturing workforce (operators, support, supervisors and management). HITOP identifies eight role requirements, including degree and type of interdependence, information exchange, decision authority and involvement and complexity of strategic goal setting
4. *Job designs*—the HITOP analysis requires the design team to develop a set of job design values, such as "workers should have control over resources for those areas for which they are responsible"
5. *Skill requirements (including selection and training)*—the minimal skill requirements (characterized by perceptual, conceptual, manual dexterity, problem solving, technical and human relations) for each role requirement are determined in this set and a determination of which skills will be trained vs. selected
6. *Rewards systems*—forms are provided to help the design team to make three decisions about rewards: basis for pay (e.g. merit, hours, performance), basis for non-financially recognising and rewarding performance, and future career paths
7. *Organisation design*—forms are provided to help the design team work through five organisational design changes typically seen with the implementation of AMT: changes in reporting lines; procedural formality; unit grouping; cross-unit coordination mechanisms; and organisational culture

Source: After Majchrzak *et al.* (1991).

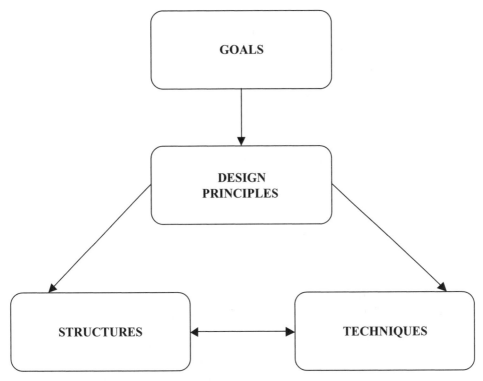

Figure 4.1   A framework for competitive advanced manufacturing enterprise (after Karwowski *et al.*, 1994)

are too rigid to cope with external complexity and dynamics of the markets, and with rapid changes in products and processes suitable to meet the market demands. Rather, contemporary manufacturing companies should aim to create self-configurable and highly adaptive organizational structures that have a rapid response capacity and rapid product innovation. These goals are thought to be realizable if guided by a set of human factors design "principles" that include the following topics: (a) work organization; (b) job design, new forms of organizing manufacturing processes; (c) skill-orientated control and responsibility; (d) ideas for managing the change process by assessing the critical change factors and developing systems, procedures and tactics to address them; (e) evaluating change by aiming to make problems visible; (f) determining the cost/benefit of alternatives; and (g) specific tools, techniques and methods in the above-listed and other areas.

The organizational "structures" of the GOPRIST framework corresponds to the given design principles. Such structures translate these principles into specific actions by utilizing a set of available organizational design techniques. In general, the organization subsystem focuses on work processes (tasks, procedures), work group design, communication and decision-making processes, and it includes the learning organization and a set of integrated organization design principles. The learning organization principle allows for the high level of cooperation, open communication and continuous improvement, and leads to an integrated organization design principle. The technology subsystem focuses on the "technology as a tool" design principle.

Finally, knowledge of the implementation process should be translated into a comprehensive set of methods and "techniques". Elements to be included into such tools are: (a) risk assessment; (b) cost-benefit analysis; (c) predictive models; (d) methods to constantly assess and modify and adjust the end state; and (e) specific application of change management theory at each stage of the change process. Examples of organizational design techniques that can be used to implement specific organizational structures include: (a) joint technological and organizational design; (b) job design principles; (c) user participation (participatory design); (d) organizationally appropriate technologies, and (e) comprehensive training and professionalization of personnel.

The use of design tools and frameworks such as HITOP and GOPRIST also needs to be seen within the wider context of the management of technology implementation. Sun and Riis (1994) have proposed the following stages for the implementation of AMT:

1. *Initiation and justification.* At this stage, a champion starts to specify the problems and to recommend the potential AMT for top management approval.
2. *Preparation and design.* The design and planning of both the physical and work organization issues related to the AMT are conducted. It is recommended that the users of the AMT are involved at this early stage and that there are early discussions with the vendor.
3. *Installation and training.* The AMT is installed and the necessary changes in work organization and human resource management practices introduced. Staff are trained in the new equipment.
4. *Routinization and learning.* All employees need to gain experience with working in the new set-up. Adjustments to the AMT and work organizations are made.

From the above, it is possible to view design and implementation as a process that continues after the machinery has been installed. This has a number of implications (Majchrzak, 1993). First, AMT is not best conceived as a generic model or type of equipment, but rather as a configuration of technical options, workplace decisions, human factors and socio-political factors. Second, the technological innovation process occurs continually, going to and fro between design and implementation and from one generation of technology to the next. Third, the design of technology should not be conceived as a single point in time but as an extended process that is extended in time to include post-adoption incremental design changes.

CONCLUSION

AMT technologies increase the complexity and interdependencies of the manufacturing process. One of the ironies of AMT is that human and organizational factors become more, not less, important. To successfully manage AMT, these factors must be addressed and successfully integrated with the AMT technology. Of course, AMT may be implemented and used in such a way that it reduces the skill of the operators and reduces role breadth and job control. It would appear that not only will this increase the level of employee stress, but it will not permit the efficient use of AMT. Rather, the full benefits of AMT may only be realised when accompanied by appropriate job designs that include wide job roles and high levels of operator control. This type of "empowered" job design is particularly important in uncertain conditions. Attention also needs to be given to how organizations can be designed so that they are self-adaptive to the requirements and changes in technology.

A further implication of AMT is that it increases cognitive task demands and the need for higher-order cognitive skills. As such, the cognitive demands of the workplace and cognitive characteristics of the workers need to be considered in the design and management of contemporary manufacturing systems, in order to assure their compatibility with the worker's internal models that describe the operations and functions of these systems. Using approaches such as cognitive engineering, new methods for cognitive task analysis need to be developed in order to identify the operator's model of a system. The challenge to the human factors profession is to assist in design of contemporary manufacturing systems, which incorporate the characteristics of human cognition and explicitly build into the design process both physical and cognitive images of the workers.

Acknowledgements

The authors would like to thank David Holman for his extensive work on earlier versions of this chapter.

REFERENCES

Argote, L., Goodman, P. S., & Schkade, D. (1983). The human side of robotics: how workers react to a robot. *Sloan Management Review*, **24**, 31–41.

Artandi, S. (1982). Computers and the post-industrial society: symbiosis or information tyranny? *Journal of the American Society for Information Science*, **33**, 302–307.

Badham, R. & Schallock, B. (1991). Human factors in CIM: a human-centered perspective from Europe. *International Journal of Human Factors in Manufacturing*, **1**(2): 121–141.

Bainbridge, L. (1983). Ironies of automation. *Automatica*, **19**, 775–779.

Bi, S. & Salvendy, G. (1994). Analytical modeling and experimental study of human workload in scheduling of advanced manufacturing systems. *International Journal of Human Factors in Manufacturing*, **4**, 205–234.

Blumberg, M. & Alber, A. (1982). The human element: its impact on the productivity of advanced manufacturing systems. *Journal of Manufacturing Systems*, **1**, 43–52.

Blumberg, M. & Gerwin, D. (1983). Coping with advanced manufacturing technology. *Journal of Occupational Behavior*, **5**, 113–130.

Boddy, D. & Buchanan, D. A. (1986). *Managing New Technology*. Oxford: Blackwell.

Brödner, P. (Ed.) (1987). *Strategic Options for New Production Systems—CHIM: Computer and Human Integrated Manufacturing*. FAST Occasional Papers. Brussels, Belgium: Directorate General for Science, Research and Development, Commission of the European Communities.

Brödner, P. (1991). Design of work and technology in manufacturing. *International Journal of Human Factors in Manufacturing*, **1**(1), 1–16.

Clegg, C. W. (1988). Appropriate technology for management: some management issues. *Applied Ergonomics*, **19**, 25–34.

Clegg, C. W. & Corbett, J. M. (1987). Research and development in "humanizing" advanced manufacturing technology. In T. D. Wall, C. W. Clegg & N. J. Kemp (Eds), *The Human Side of Advanced Manufacturing Technology*. Chichester: Wiley.

Cooley, M. (1989). Human-centred systems. In H. H. Rosenbrock (Ed.), *Designing Human-centred Technology* (pp.133–143). New York: Springer-Verlag.

Corbett, J. M. (1988). Ergonomics in the development of human-centered HAS. *Applied Ergonomics*, **19**, 35–39.

Corbett, J. M. (1990). Human-centered advanced manufacturing systems: from theoretics to reality. *International Journal of Industrial Ergonomics*, **5**, 83–90.

Cross, M. (1983). *Changing Requirements for Craftsmen in Process Industries. Stage 1, Interim Report.* London: Technical Change Centre.

Cummings, T. G. & Blumberg, M. (1987). Advanced manufacturing technology and work design. In T. D. Wall, C. W. Clegg & N. J. Kemp (Eds), *The Human Side of Advanced Manufacturing Technology.* Chichester: Wiley.

ESPRIT Consortium AMICE (1989). *Open System Architecture for CIM.* Berlin: Springer-Verlag.

Goldman, S. L., Nagel, R. N. & Preiss, K. (1995). *Agile Competitors and Virtual Organizations.* New York: Van Nostrand Reinhold.

Goodstein, L. P., Anderson, H. B. & Olsen, S. E. (Eds) (1988). *Tasks, Errors and Mental Models.* London: Taylor & Francis.

Harris, D. (Ed.) (1997). *Engineering Psychology and Cognitive Ergonomics, Vol. 2: Job Design and Product Design.* Aldershot: Ashgate.

Hollnagel, E. & Woods, D. (1983). Cognitive systems engineering: new wine in new bottles. *International Journal of Man–Machine Studies,* **18**, 583–600.

Jackson, P. R. & Wall, T. D. (1991). How does operator control enhance performance of advanced manufacturing technology? *Ergonomics,* **34**, 1301–1311.

Jackson, P. R., Wall, T. D., Martin, R. & Davids, K. (1993). New measures of job control, cognitive demand and production responsibility. *Journal of Applied Psychology,* **78**, 753–762.

Jarvinen, J., Vannas, V., Mattila, M. & Karwowski, W. (1996). Causes and safety effects of production disturbances in FMS installations: a comparison of field studies in the USA and Finland. *International Journal of Human Factors in Manufacturing,* **6**(1), 57–72.

Johannsen, G. (1988). Categories of human operator behavior in fault behavior situations. In L. P. Goodstain, H. B. Andersson & S. E. Olsen (Eds), *Tasks, Errors, and Mental Models* (pp. 251–277). London: Taylor and Francis.

Karwowski, W., Kantola, J., Rodrick, D. & Salvendy, G. (2002). Macroergonomics aspects of manufacturing in H. W. Hendrick & B. M. Kleiner (Eds)., *Macroergonomics: An Introduction to Work System Design* (pp. 223–248). Mahwah, NJ: Lawrence Erlbaum Associates.

Karwowski, W. & Rahimi, M. (Eds) (1990). *Ergonomics of Hybrid Automated Systems II.* Amsterdam: Elsevier.

Karwowski, W. & Salvendy, G. (Eds) (1994). *Organization and Management of Advanced Manufacturing.* New York: Wiley.

Karwowski, W., Salvendy, G., Badham, R., Brodner, P., Clegg, C., Hwang, L., Iwasawa, J., Kidd, P. T., Kobayashi, N., Koubek, R., Lamarsh, J., Nagamachi, M., Naniwada, M., Salzman, H., Seppälä, P., Schallock, B., Sheridan, T. & Warschat, J. (1994). Integrating people, organization and technology in advanced manufacturing. *Human Factors and Ergonomics in Manufacturing,* **4**, 1–19.

Karwowski, W., Warnecke, H. J., Hueser, M. & Salvendy, G. (1997). Human factors in manufacturing. In G. Salvendy (Ed.), *Handbook of Human Factors and Ergonomics,* 2nd Edn. New York: Wiley.

Keita, G. P. & Sauter, S. L. (1992). *Work and Well-being.* Washington, DC: American Psychological Association.

Kidd, P. T. (1990). An open systems human computer interface for a workshop orientated CNC lathes. In W. Karwowski & M. Rahimi (Eds), *Human Aspects of Hybrid Automated Systems II* (pp. 537–544). Amsterdam: Elsevier.

Kidd, P. T. (1991). Human and computer integrated manufacturing: a manufacturing strategy based on organization, people and technology. *International Journal of Human Factors in Manufacturing,* **1**(1), 17–32.

Kidd, P. T. (1992). Interdisciplinary design of skill-based computer-aided technologies: interfacing in depth. *International Journal of Human Factors in Manufacturing,* **2**(3), 209–228.

Kidd, P. T. (1994). *Agile Manufacturing: Forging New Frontiers.* Reading, MA: Addison-Wesley.

Kiggundu, M. N. (1981). Task interdependence and the theory of job design. *Academy of Management Review,* **6**, 499–508.

Klein, J. A. (1991). A re-examination of autonomy in light of new manufacturing practices. *Human Relations,* **44**, 21–38.

Kostecki, M. J., Mrela, K. & Pankow, W. (1984). Job design and automation in the polish machine industry: the case of non-programmed automation in a planned economy. In, F. Butera & J. Thurman (Eds), *Automation and Work Design.* Amsterdam: North-Holland.

Liker, J. K., Fleischer, M. & Arndorf, D. (1993). Fulfilling the promises. *Sloan Management Review*, **33**, 74–86.

Majchrzak, A. (1988). *The Human Side of Factory Automation*. San Francisco, CA: Jossey-Bass.

Majchrzak, A. (1993). Commentary. *International Journal of Human Factors in Manufacturing*, **3**, 89–90.

Majchrzak, A. (1995). *Tools for Analyzing Organizational Impacts of New Technology: Handbook of Technology Management*. New York: McGraw-Hill.

Majchrzak, A., Fleischer, M., Roitman, D. & Mokray, J. (1991). *Reference Manual for Performing the HITOP Analysis*. Ann Arbor, MI: Industrial Technology Institute.

Majchrzak, A. & Paris, M. L. (1995). High performing organizations match technology and management strategies: results of a survey. *International Journal of Industrial Ergonomics*, **16**, 309–326.

Majchrzak, A. & Wang, Q. (1994). The human dimension of manufacturing: results of a survey of electronics manufacturers. *Journal of Applied Manufacturing Systems*, **7**(1), 5–15.

Manufacturing Studies Board (1986). *Toward a New Era in U.S. Manufacturing: the Need for National Vision*. Washington, DC: National Academy Press.

Martin, T. (1990). The need for human skills in production: the case of CIM. *Computers in Industry*, **4**, 203–211.

Martin, T. (1993). Considering social effects in control-system design—a summary. In *Pre-prints of IFAC 12th World Congress*, Vol. 7 (pp. 325–330), Sydney, Australia, July 18–23.

Nakamura, N. & Salvendy, G. (1994). Human planner and scheduler. In G. Salavendy & W. Karwowski (Eds), *Design of Work and Development of Personnel in Advanced Manufacturing Systems* (pp. 331–354). New York: Wiley.

Office of Technology Assessment (OTA) (1984). *Computerized Manufacturing Automation: Employment, Education and the Workplace (OTA-CIT-235)*. Washington, DC: Office of Technology Assessment, US Government Printing Office.

Rasmussen, J. (1983). Skills, rules, and knowledge: signals, signs, and symbols; and other distinctions in human performance models. *IEEE Transactions on Systems, Man and Cybernetics, SMC* **13**(3), 257–266.

Reason, J. (1990). *Human Error*. Cambridge: Press Syndicate of the University of Cambridge.

Sanderson, P. M. (1989). The Human Planning and Scheduling Role in Advanced Manufacturing Systems (unpublished report). Urbana-Champaign, IL: Department of Mechanical and Industrial Engineering, University of Illinois.

Seppälä, P., Touminen, E. & Koskinen, P. (1992). Impact of flexible production philosophy and advanced manufacturing technology on organization and jobs. *International Journal of Human Factors in Manufacturing*, **2**, 172–192.

Sinclair, M. A. (1986). Ergonomics aspects of the automated factory. *Ergonomics*, **29**(12), 1507–1523.

Smith, M. J. & Carayon, P. (1995). New technology, automation, and work organization: stress problems and improved implementation strategies. *International Journal of Human Factors in Manufacturing*, **5**, 99–116.

Smith, M. J., Carayon, P., Sanders, K. J., Lim, S. Y. & LeGrande, D. (1992). Employee stress and health complaints in jobs with and without monitoring. *Applied Ergonomics*, **23**, 17–27.

Stalk, G. & Hout, T. M. (1990). *Competing Against Time*. New York: Free Press.

Storey, J. (1994). *New Wave Manufacturing Practices: Organizational and Human Resource Management Dimensions*. London: Paul Chapman.

Sun, H., & Riis, H. O. (1994). Organisational, technical, strategic, and managerial issues along the implementation process of advanced manufacturing technology—a general framework of implementation guide. *International Journal of Human Factors in Manufacturing*, **4**, 23–36.

Wall, T. D., Corbett, M., Clegg, C. W., Jackson, P. R. & Martin, R. (1990a). Advanced manufacturing technology and work design: towards a theoretical framework. *Journal of Organizational Behavior*, **11**, 201–219.

Wall, T. D., Corbett, J. M., Martin, R., Clegg, C. W. & Jackson, P. R. (1990b). Advanced manufacturing technology, work design and performance: a change study. *Journal of Applied Psychology*, **75**, 691–697.

Wall, T. D., Jackson, P. R. & Davids, K. (1992). Operator work design and robotics system performance: a serendipitous field study. *Journal of Applied Psychology*, **77**, 353–362.

Wall, T. D., Kemp, N. J., Jackson, P. R. & Clegg, C. W. (1986). Outcomes of autonomous work groups. *Academy of Management Journal*, **29**, 280–304.

Wall, T. D. & Martin, R. (1987). Job and work design. In C. L. Cooper & I. T. Robertson (Eds), *International Review of Industrial and Organizational Psychology*. Chichester: Wiley.

Warr, P. B. (1987). *Work, Unemployment and Mental Health*. Cambridge: Cambridge University Press.

Waterson, P. E., Clegg, C. W., Bolden, R., Pepper, K., Warr. P. B. & Wall, T. D. (1999). The use and effectiveness of modern manufacturing practices: a survey of UK industry. *International Journal of Production Research*, **37**, 2271–2292.

Wilson, J. R. (1991). Personal perspective: critical human factors contributions in modern manufacturing. *International Journal of Human Factors in Manufacturing*, **1**, 281–297.

Wilson, J. R., Koubek, R., Salvendy, G., Sharit, J. & Karwowski, W. (1994). Human factors in advanced manufacturing: a review and reappraisal. In W. Karwowski & G. Salvendy (Eds), *Organization and Management of Advanced Manufacturing* (pp. 379–415). New York: Wiley.

Wobbe, W. & Charles, T. (1994). Human roles in advanced manufacturing technology. In W. Karwowski & G. Salvendy (Eds), *Organization and Management of Advanced Manufacturing*. New York: Wiley.

CHAPTER 5

Supply-chain Partnering

Máire Kerrin

Organisational Psychology Group, City University, London

and

Belén Icasati-Johanson

Institute of Work Psychology, University of Sheffield, UK

Over recent years, organisations have begun to recognise that there are strong competitive advantages and performance improvements to be gained from developing cooperative relationships with suppliers (Dyer & Ouchi, 1993; Lamming, 1993). Supply-chain partnering has therefore developed as an important trend in the context of new work practices and philosophies. It also has many links to other new working practices discussed in this section of the book, for example total quality management (TQM) (Chapter 3), lean manufacturing and just-in-time (JIT) (Chapter 2), and knowledge management (KM) (Chapter 8), which provide a wider context to the changes in the supply chain literature.

This chapter focuses the discussion of supply-chain partnering around the three central aims of the book. First, a review is presented of the nature and extent of supply-chain partnering. The aim is to provide a recent history of customer supplier relationships, so that the features of supply-chain partnering can be understood within a context of previous paradigms. The second aim is to explore the impact that supply-chain partnering has on the way people work and how they experience work. In particular, this section will focus on the impact and role of two psychological concepts and theories, that of trust and perspective taking. There are many concepts that could have been examined in relation to how people experience work within supply-chain partnering. However, these two were chosen as they illustrate one concept that has consistently been the focus of academic and practitioner analysis (trust), and a second that is suggested to play an important part in the future of supply-chain partnering (perspective taking).

The final part of the chapter will contemplate the implications for practice and the role of human resource management (HRM) in influencing supply-chain partnering. For example, which HRM practices might contribute to improving the experience of work within a partnership? This will be addressed generally and also in relation to the two concepts of trust and perspective taking. The chapter will also consider the design choices that are open to organisations when implementing and managing supply-chain partnering.

The Essentials *of the New Workplace: A Guide to the Human Impact of Modern Working Practices.*
Edited by David Holman, Toby D. Wall, Chris W. Clegg, Paul Sparrow and Ann Howard. © 2005 John Wiley & Sons, Ltd.

THEORETICAL APPROACHES TO CUSTOMER–SUPPLIER RELATIONSHIPS

The traditional view of customer–supplier transactions is one that is often based on the customer being passive while activity in the transaction comes from the supplier. The notion of a "relationship" between the customer and the supplier is one that has only come about in the last decade or so (Bessant, 1991; Farmer & Ploos von Amstel, 1991; Sako, 1992; Slack, 1991). The shift in focus has been away from the formal contract made between two organisations, towards a system that involves conducting multiple exchanges. This is now recognised or known as the "relationship" between two companies, and primarily recognises that buyers and sellers are both active in the transactions and hence take an *interactive* approach.

Theoretical approaches to customer–supplier relationships draw on many different academic subdisciplines, such as marketing, purchasing, economics and inter-organisational theory, to name a few. While the focus of this chapter is to explore how changes in customer–supplier relations may affect people's experience of work (through a psychological and human relations perspective), it is important to detail some of the key academic contributions to the relationship concept. For example, Williamson's (1975) transaction cost analysis (TCA) theory combines economic theory and management theory to determine the best type of relationship a firm should develop in the marketplace. The approach is based on minimising the sum of production and transaction costs by simplifying the interfaces between the stages, either by removing them completely (vertical integration) or by effectively cancelling them by creating perfectly competitive supply markets. Put another way, TCA considers how closely the purchasing organisation should become involved with its supplier. This was later developed into a model of "obligational contracting", where certain areas became the crucial factor in deciding upon how developed a relationship should be. Dore's (1987) contribution of "relational contracting" was based upon the concept of perceived and actual high levels of trust and moral trading in Japan.

Both Williamson's and Dore's concepts are brought together by Sako (1992), who constructed two ideal types of customer–supplier relationships, which are situated at either end of a continuum, and captured the complex variations in customer–supplier relationships. Any organisation can be placed on the continuum, based on the patterns of relationship with their supplier and regardless of nationality. The features of the continuum can be seen in Table 5.1 (Sako, 1992). At one extreme, organisations rely on arm's-length contract relations (ACR) if they want to retain control over their destiny. Independence is the motivating principle here, with the desire to be unaffected by the decisions of other companies. This type of company would disclose the minimum information about costings and future plans to existing and potential buyers and suppliers. The "arm's-length" nature of contracts enables the company to engage in hard commercial bargaining to obtain competitive prices. In this competitive relationship (ACR), both buyer and supplier attempt to get the best deals solely for themselves, potentially at the expense of the other party. The advantages are that the resultant insecurity ensures that suppliers are continually trying to improve their level of competitiveness, but the disadvantage is that the customer must monitor the supplier, as low trust exists. This can be carried out, for example, through heavy goods inwards inspection to ensure quality goods.

Table 5.1 Features of arm's-length contract relations (ACR) and obligational contract relations (OCR) (Sako, 1992)

	ACR<———— CONTINUUM ————>OCR	
Transactional dependence	**Customer** seeks to maintain low dependence by trading with a large number of competing suppliers within the limits permitted by need to keep down transaction costs. **Supplier** seeks to maintain low dependence by trading with a large number of customers within limits set by scale economies and transaction costs	For a **customer**, avoidance of dependence is not a high priority; it prefers to give security to few suppliers, although may still be dual or triple source for flexibility. For a **supplier**, avoidance of dependence is not a high priority, but it may well have several OCR customers
Ordering procedure	Bidding takes place; buyer does not know which supplier will win the contract before bidding. Prices negotiated and agreed before an order is commissioned	Bidding may or may not take place. With bidding, buyer has a good idea of which supplier gets the contract before bidding. Without bidding, there is a straight commission to the supplier. Prices are settled after decision about who gets contract
Projected length of trading	For the duration of the current contract. Short-term commitment by both buyer and supplier	Continued beyond the duration of the current contract. Mutual long-term commitment
Documents for exchange	Terms and conditions of contract are written, detailed and substantive	Contracts contain procedural rules, but substantive issues are decided case by case. Contracts may be oral rather than written
"Contractualism"	Contingencies are written out and followed strictly	Case-by-case resolution, with much appeal to the diffuse obligation of long-term relationships
"Contractual trust"	Supplier never starts production until written orders are received	Supplier often starts production on the basis of oral communication, before written orders are received
"Goodwill trust"	Multiple sourcing by supplier, combined with supplier's low transactional dependence	Sole sourcing by buyer, combined with supplier's transactional dependence
"Competence trust"	Thorough inspection on delivery; the principle of *caveat emptor* predominates	Little or no inspection on delivery for most parts (customer may be involved in establishing supplier's quality-control systems)
Technology transfer and training	Only the transfer, training and consultancy that can be costed and claimed for in the short run	Not always fully costed, as benefits are seen as partly intangible and/or reaped in the distant future
Communication channels and intensity	A narrow channel between the buyer's purchasing department and the supplier's sales department, with frequency kept to minimum necessary to conduct business	Extensive multiple channels, between engineers, quality assurance personnel, top managers, as well as between purchasing and sales managers. Frequent contact, often extending beyond the immediate business into socialising
Risk sharing	Little sharing of risk; how risk, resulting from price and demand fluctuations, is to be borne by each party is spelt out in explicit prior agreement	Much sharing of risk, in the sense that the relative share of unforeseen loss or gain is decided case by case, by applying some principle of fairness

Obligational contract relations (OCR) is at the other extreme of the continuum to ACR, in that it depends on high-trust cooperativeness, with a commitment to long-term trade. This commitment may include unusual requests and obligations not traditionally accepted, such as late unexpected orders. The benefits lie in good quality and service, growing or stable orders and other non-price aspects of trading (Sako, 1992). Cooperative relationships, often referred to as obligational or relational contracting, most evident in Japan, gives both parties a sense of obligation to assist one another and to protect the other's interests. It is characterised by a tightly integrated system of supply and assembly, with a minimum of waste in terms of inventories and inspection activities. In this relationship, the larger purchasing company places "trust" in its supplier's competencies only after a thorough investigation of these competencies and a lengthy probation period, and often only when financial leverage is gained through a direct stakeholding in the firm (Carr & Truesdale, 1992). Hoyt and Huq (2000) provide a useful review of how customer–supplier relationships have evolved over the past two decades from transaction processes to collaborative processes.

MODELS AND DEFINITIONS OF SUPPLY-CHAIN PARTNERING

Lamming's (1986, 1993) research detailing the development of the customer–supplier relationship is a useful starting point in providing an understanding of how supply-chain partnering can take different forms. His research involved in-depth interviews in the UK, where he distinguished between three types of customer–supplier relationships. Lamming characterised these as the traditional model, the stress model and the resolved model. A fourth type was added, the partnership model, to incorporate existing best practice. The model is detailed in Table 5.2, with the key factors selected for analysing customer–supplier relationships, for example the nature of competition, basis of sourcing decisions, role of research and development (R&D). This original model was validated in a further 129 companies in 12 countries across four continents. As Lamming (1993) suggests, the resulting model could be said to "serve the functions of recording part of the transition from mass production to its successor (i.e. the decline of the old paradigm) and of indicating some characteristics of that successor (a new 'best practice' for customer–supplier relationships in the automotive components industry)" (p. 150).

The effective management of supply chains is said to be characterised by developing close, long-term working relationships with a limited number of supply chain partners. As is apparent in Table 5.2, mutually beneficial inter-organisational partnerships have to be developed in which information is freely shared, and where partners work together to attain common goals (Spekman, Kamauff & Myhr, 1998b). Supply-chain partnering occurs when organisations in the supply chain agree to work in a cooperative rather than an adversarial manner. Boddy, Macbeth, Charles and Fraser-Kraus (1998) define partnering as ". . . a situation in which there is an attempt to build close long-term links between organisations in a supply chain that remain distinct, but which choose to work closely together" (p. 1004). Finally, Macbeth (1998) argues that partnering is an approach to business in which companies expect a long-term relationship, develop complementary capabilities, share more information and engage in more joint planning than is customary.

Table 5.2 illustrates the different types of customer–supplier relationships that had been developed up until the practice of supply-chain partnership in the 1990s. The purpose of

Table 5.2 Models of customer-supplier relations (Lamming, 1993)

Model	Nature of competition	Basis of sourcing decision	Role of data/information exchange	Management of capacity	Delivery practice	Dealing with price changes	Attitude to quality	Role of R&D	Level of pressure
Traditional	Closed but friendly; plenty of business	Wide: enquiries; lowest bid; price-based	Very restricted— minimum necessary	Few problems: some poor scheduling	Large quantities; buyer's choice: steady	General negotiation (annual): a game (win/lose)	Inspection: arguments/ laissez-faire	One-sided: either assembler or supplier	Low/ medium: steady: predictable
Stress	Closed and deadly: chaotic	"Dutch Auctions": price-based	A weapon: one-way; supplier must open books	Spasmodic: no system to deal with chaos	Unstable; no control; variable; no notice of changes	Conflict in negotiation; a battle (lose/lose)	Aggressive campaigns	Shared, but only for cost reduction	High/ unbearable; volatile
Resolved	Closed: some collaboration; strategic	Price, quality and delivery	Two-way: short-term, e.g. forward build	Gradually improving; linkages appearing	Smaller quantities; buyer's demands stabilizing	Annual economics plus; negotiation; (win/lose)	Joint effort towards improvements	Shared for developments	Medium: some sense of relief
Partnership	Collaboration; tiering; still dynamic	Performance history; long-term source; costs	Two-way: long-term, e.g. knowledge of costs	Coordinated and jointly planned	Small quantity; agreed basis; dynamic (JIT)	Annual economics, planned reductions (win/win?)	Joint planning for developments	Shared: some black or grey box	Very high: predictable

this chapter is to focus on supply-chain partnering and the implications of this new way of working for employees within both the customer and supplier organisation.

ADVANTAGES AND DISADVANTAGES OF SUPPLY-CHAIN PARTNERING

In today's business environment, the advantages of supply-chain partnering are becoming more evident, as conventional exchange relationships based on arm's-length transactions between independent suppliers and customers often do not allow for effective coordination of marketing activities (Anderson & Weitz, 1992). Moreover, companies that try to operate independently may be at a competitive disadvantage. This is due to the advantage in having networks of companies in supply-chain partnerships, in which more creative solutions are developed, adaptation to market changes is more speedy and services or products are brought to market in shorter periods of time (Currall & Judge, 1995). In light of this, relationships among firms are increasingly gaining importance for understanding competitive advantage at both the individual firm and network level (Dyer & Singh, 1998).

The benefits claimed for partnering are numerous, particularly when companies are operating in competitive and volatile environments and may focus multi-lateral efforts on improving areas of mutual concern, such as improved delivery, quality performance, customer service and technology sharing, as well as reduced administration costs, inventories and prices (Pagel, 1999). Furthermore, partnerships provide firms with access to new technologies, knowledge beyond the boundaries of the firm, and access to complementary skills (Mohr & Spekman, 1994). In addition, effective buyer–supplier partnerships help promote cross-functional activity within individual firms, which in turn stimulates cross-functional improvements between firms (Landeros, Reck & Plank, 1995). Indeed, because closer ties between exchange partners are usually long-term-orientated, they also help safeguard relationship-specific investments and facilitate adaptation to uncertainty (Heide & John, 1990). Sharing information during design may also support more rapid product innovation.

In terms of disadvantages to UK suppliers, Turnbull, Delbridge, Oliver and Wilkinson (1993) suggest that many UK firms will struggle to meet the exacting standards required of preferred suppliers within supply-chain partnering, and that it will lead to the survival of fewer, more talented and larger suppliers. Despite all of the benefits, the problem of implementation is one which is seen as a major problem, and many partnerships fail because partners do not have processes in place to maintain the relationship. Barratt (2004) notes that supply-chain collaboration has proved difficult to implement. He proposes the need for a greater understanding of the elements that make up supply-chain collaboration, and in particular how the relevant cultural, strategic and implementation elements interrelate with each other.

The concerns regarding implementation make it even more crucial to examine those factors that promote success in a collaborative relationship (Boddy, Macbeth & Wagner 2000; Landeros et al., 1995). Case study evidence provides particular insights into how supply-chain partnering at Toyota (Langfield-Smith & Greenwood, 1998; Winfield & Kerrin, 1996) and Kodak (Ellram, Edis & Owen, 1996) was implemented successfully. These examples discuss the factors that enable an organisation to move from relationships characterised by strong buyer power and bargaining position to partnerships based on trust and cooperation. Langfield-Smith and Greenwood (1998) conclude that the factors that influence the development of a cooperative customer–supplier relationship include a consideration of similarities between the industries and technologies of the customer and supplier, prior experiences of change among suppliers, effective customer–supplier communication, and the importance of experiential learning in the acceptance of change. Wagner, Macbeth and Boddy's (2002) case study research on implementation also provides an insight into some of the key issues.

In terms of uptake, early surveys into the practice in the UK of supply-chain partnering include those reported by Oliver and Wilkinson (1992). They found an increase in use from their 1987 data of JIT supplies and quality-assured supplies. They also reported that, "practices indicating close buyer–supplier relations—supplier involvement in design, supplier development activities and single sourcing—all show significant usage, with approximately two-thirds of companies using or planning to use each practice" (p. 191). More recently, Leverick and Cooper (1998) detailed the responses from 88 suppliers of their relationships with their customers. They found substantial levels of supplier–manufacturer partnering, based on measures of the duration and nature of the relationship, the involvement of the suppliers in design and product development, the price-setting process, the nature of supplier–manufacturer communication and the level of external awareness among suppliers. However, one survey of 100 companies that had attempted to introduce supply-chain partnering found that less than half of the respondents considered that their organisation had been successful in implementing the change (Boddy *et al.*, 1998). More recently, a survey of supply-chain management practices in small- to medium-sized enterprises indicates a lack of effective adaptation from traditional adversarial relationships to more collaborative relationships (Quayle, 2003). In a wider analysis of alliances, Spekman, Forbes, Isabella and MacAvoy (1998a) estimate that 60% of all alliances fail.

In summary, the model of customer–supplier relations (Table 5.2) illustrates that supply-chain partnering is different from previous forms of customer–supplier relationships, with different expectations of employees in both the customer and supplier organisation. Given this understanding of the shift in practices from the traditional model to supply-chain partnering, the next section will examine the impact of this new working practice on employees' work and experience of work.

IMPLICATIONS OF SUPPLY-CHAIN PARTNERING FOR EMPLOYEES' EXPERIENCE OF WORK

There are many areas where changes in the customer–supplier relationship could have an impact on the experience of work. Drawing on one of the theoretical models outlined earlier (Sako, 1992), moving away from ACR to OCR would have a major impact on the way work is carried out, particularly in areas of quality management and continuous improvement (Kerrin, 2002); for example, Table 5.1 illustrates differences in "communication channels" and "competence trust" between ACR and OCR. Both involve changes in working practices for the customer and the supplier organisation. The recent changes in customer–supplier relationships also provide indications of changes in work practices (see Table 5.2), for example "management of capacity" under a partnership model is coordinated and jointly planned, while "attitude to quality" illustrates the move away from inspection towards joint planning for developments. Finally, the role of R&D involves the sharing of information, requiring personnel from multiple levels within both organisations to change the way that they interact with each other.

The impact of supply-chain partnering may therefore include changes in work roles, trust, workload, innovation, perspective taking and knowledge sharing activities. For example, supply-chain partnering may increase or decrease workload, or mean that different tasks are required of employees within a supply-chain partnership. Increased workload and additional tasks may not necessarily be manual, but may relate to increasing need for communication and information to and from suppliers, and also in increasing levels of information and communication within the organisation, for example in response to senior managers' requests for information on quality and costings.

Changes in workload due to demands from partnership relationships and changing job roles affect knowledge sharing. Previous models of customer–supplier relationships encouraged individuals to retain knowledge regarding processes and products (in order to maintain a competitive edge), but with supply-chain partnering, knowledge sharing between organisations and individuals is vital. However, while information and data may be more easily transferred across organisations within the partnership (e.g. through websites, intranets and extranets), exchange of knowledge—in particular *tacit* knowledge—relating to products and processes is less straightforward (Blackler, 1995; Brown & Duguid, 1991; Cook & Brown, 1999; Lam, 1997; Lave & Wenger, 1991). The scope of this chapter precludes a detailed discussion of the issues involved in knowledge sharing, but to make the most of partnerships, organisations need to be able to harness this tacit knowledge so that it can be absorbed by both organisations. Questions such as how this is carried out, what resistance might there be, and what is the overall value of it, have an impact on planning HR policies and practice. The development of systems that suit both organisations in the partnership need to be developed if knowledge is to be shared at the individual, team and organisational level.

As can be seen from the examples of workload and knowledge sharing, it would be impossible to discuss the impact of supply-chain partnering on all of the issues raised above, so two areas have been selected for special analysis. The first is the impact and role of trust in supply-chain partnering. This concept has been chosen as it is often the most frequently cited issue within successful or unsuccessful partnering and yet is often poorly defined and understood in practice. The second concept is that of the role of perspective taking in supply-chain partnering. This is a concept that is less frequently discussed but it is proposed that it has potential to have a major impact on employees' experience of supply-chain partnering. Both concepts are of particular interest because of their inclusion in future developments in job and work design research and practice. For example, in a recent analysis of the future of work design research and practice, Parker, Wall and Cordery (2001), suggest that the parameters of work design, traditionally set within models such as Hackman and Oldham (1976), will be limited in explaining individuals' interactions with their workplace. In particular, they suggest an expanded model of work design which includes interpersonal trust and perspective taking as factors likely to be of importance, but yet to be considered within existing models. It is for these reasons that we now choose to concentrate on these emerging areas.

SUPPLY-CHAIN PARTNERING AND TRUST

So far, little attention has been paid to the processes needed to build and nurture effective partnerships. Given both the risks and costs associated with mismanaging a

supply-chain partnership, it is crucial to explore the determinants of partnership success (Mohr & Spekman, 1994). Granovetter (1985) and Powell (1990) urge researchers
to recognise the role that socially embedded personal relationships (such as those of suppliers and customers in a supply chain) play in economic exchange. In light of this, it
follows that the customer–supplier relationship should be considered a key determinant
of the success of the supply-chain partnership. The management and marketing litera-
tures (e.g. Anderson & Narus, 1990; Dion, Easterling & Miller, 1995; Ganesan, 1994)
have described trust as one of the key contributing factors to customer–supplier relationship success. Yet, despite the strength of the evidence linking trust to successful
customer–supplier relationships and to organisational competitiveness, there is little universal agreement as to the actual definition of the trust construct. Thus, the section below
will attempt to highlight the issues relating to trust as it is presently conceived in the
literature.

What Is Trust?

Numerous authors (e.g. Gambetta, 1988; Powell, 1996; Williamson, 1993) have highlighted
the elusive meaning of trust. A careful examination of the trust literature reveals a lack of
clarity concerning the concept of trust, with probably as many definitions of the construct
as there are studies examining it (e.g. Anderson & Weitz, 1989; Barney & Hansen, 1994;
Crosby, Evans & Cowles, 1990; Currall & Judge, 1995; Hagen & Choe, 1998; Rotter,
1967, 1980; Schurr & Ozanne, 1985). Several authors have argued that to advance our
understanding of trust and to usefully inform research and theory, the concept of trust
requires clear contextual boundaries rather than a universal definition (Rousseau, Sitkin,
Burt & Camerer, 1998). They have thus called for an approach to the definition of trust that
takes into account the context in which the construct is being studied (Bigley & Pearce,
1998; Rousseau et al., 1998). This is particularly important because, as noted by Bigley and
Pearce (1998), when attempting to arrive at a universal conceptualisation of trust we run
the "risk of producing constructions that are either too elaborate for theoretical purposes or
relatively meaningless in the realm of empirical observation" (p. 408). Thus, the definition
used here does not claim to be a universal definition of trust. Rather, it aims to define trust
in a supply-chain partnering context, i.e. in the context of interpersonal relations across
organisational firm boundaries in customer–supplier dyads. Before trust in supply-chain
partnering can be defined, however, there are a number of assumptions that must be made
explicit (Hagen & Choe, 1998) because they relate to the many criticisms made in the past
about previous attempts to define the construct.

Interpersonal Trust and Interorganisational Trust
in Supply-chain Partnering

One of the key criticisms concerning the notion of trust in the inter-firm relations literature
concerns the issue that ideas about inter-personal trust are transferred to inter-organisational
matters (e.g. Blois, 1999). The key issue here is whether trust, which originates as an individual level construct, has meaning at the organisational level (e.g. Blois, 1999; Jensen &
Meckling, 1976); for example, some authors have suggested that "interorganisational and

interpersonal trust are different, because the focal object differs" (Zaheer, McEvily & Perrone, in press, as cited in Rousseau *et al.*, 1998).

Similarly, Sako and Helper (1998) have argued that psychology's focus on interpersonal trust in the context of business organisations is "deficient". They argue that "while psychologists tend to study inter-personal trust, business firms are concerned just as much with inter-organisational trust. It is this latter construct that might survive a breakdown of inter-personal relationships due to labour turnover or personality clash, and which provides the stability necessary for firms to pursue innovative and competitive activities" (p. 389). Thus, they suggest that because of this, the determinants of interpersonal and inter-organisational trust may be different.

However, while interpersonal trust may be different from inter-organisational trust in that the focal object is different, it can be argued that interpersonal trust is one of the factors that comprises inter-firm trust. If a person in a boundary role does not trust their counterpart in the partner firm, this could ultimately influence the overall level of inter-organisational trust. For instance, if a buyer perceives his/her immediate contact at the supplier firm as untrustworthy, this may have detrimental influence upon how trustworthy that supplier's firm is. Moreover, Aulakh, Kotabe and Sahay (1996) highlight that trust can be extended to exchanges between organisations because "inter-organisational relationships are managed by individuals in each organisation" (p. 1008). So, in line with Rousseau *et al.* (1998), trust is seen here as a multilevel construct (individual, group and organisational), "integrating micro-level psychological processes and group dynamics with macro-level institutional arrangements" (p. 393). In other words, trust is "a psychological state composed of the psychological experiences of individuals, dyads and firms" (Rousseau *et al.*, 1998, p. 398). As such, interpersonal trust contributes to inter-organisational trust, which is key to the success of the supply-chain partnership (as argued below).

Multidimensional Nature of Trust

Past research has often approached the notion of trust as a unidimensional construct. Such an approach, however, fails to identify the various aspects that comprise the concept. As Blois (1999) has noted, "a person may completely trust another with regard to certain aspects of their behaviour" but "they may positively distrust them in other matters" (p. 200). In line with Blois' criticism, the stance taken here is that trust is a construct comprised of various aspects that can only be tapped into if both the definition of the concept, and the measures utilised, acknowledge this diversity. Thus, trust is here assumed to be a multidimensional construct, where trust or distrust in some aspect of the relationship does not preclude trust or distrust in other aspects of that relationship.

Definition of Trust in Supply Chain Partnering

In light of the issues raised above, Icasati-Johanson, Clegg and Axtell (2000) conducted a study of trust in supply chains, and grounded their definitions and measures of trust on the views of relevant stakeholders. Icasati-Johanson *et al.* (2000, p. 15) developed a definition of trust, anchored in the context of supplier–buyer relationships, as:

> In an exchange relationship, under conditions of risk and interdependence, trust is the belief that a voluntarily accepted duty will prevail, ensuring that no party exploits the other's vulnerabilities.

Further, the authors noted that trust entails having optimistic expectations of positive future behaviour. Participants described a set of elements that made them trust their supply chain partners:

- An expectation that the partner will behave with *integrity*, i.e. be honest in their dealings with the partner and not take advantage or act in self-interest at the expense of the other party.
- Confidence in the *competence*, dependability and reliability of the partner, i.e. a belief that a partner is capable of doing a good quality job, delivering on time and fulfilling requirements.
- An expectation that the partner will be *fair* and act in a spirit of cooperation. This usually entails discussing and working through changes without imposing them.
- A belief that a partner will be *loyal* and display benevolent motives. This involves behaving in a non-bullying manner, displaying a long-term orientation towards the relationship, and allowing partners time to react when faced with a threat to the relationship.
- An expectation of *frankness* and *openness*. This entails being straight with one another regarding issues relevant to the relationship, such as being open and direct about the fact that other market possibilities, e.g. competitors, might be approached.

Why Is Trust Important?

Numerous authors (e.g. Agarwal & Shankar, 2003; Allison, 1999; Anderson & Weitz, 1989; Anderson & Narus, 1990; Dion *et al.*, 1995; Dwyer, Schurr & Oh, 1987; Mohr & Spekman, 1994) have highlighted the critical role of trust as a facilitator of interfirm relationships and as a key source of competitive advantage; for example, the role of trust has been described as pivotal to the development of long-term customer–supplier relations (Dwyer *et al.*, 1987), the continuity of those relations (Anderson & Weitz, 1989; Aulakh *et al.*, 1996; Landeros *et al.*, 1995) and as one of the primary characteristics of successful trade relationships (Anderson & Narus, 1990; Corrigan, 1995; Dion *et al.*, 1995; Mohr & Spekman, 1994).

Relationships where there is greater trust can withstand greater stress and offer greater adaptability (Anderson & Weitz, 1989; Sullivan & Peterson, 1982). More specifically, trust in customer–supplier interaction influences satisfaction with profit (Mohr & Spekman, 1994), sales outcomes and performance (Dion & Banting, 1988; Dion *et al.*, 1995; Moore, 1998). In contrast, a lack of trust has been associated with partnering failure (Ellram, 1995). Riddalls, Icasati-Johanson, Axtell, Bennett and Clegg (2002) found that, in certain circumstances, low levels of trust can increase total supply-chain costs considerably. From this evidence it is clear that trust can facilitate interfirm relationships and act as a key source of competitive advantage to the supply chain.

How Trust Works

Trust contributes to the creation of a lasting bond and promotes cooperation in inter-organisational exchanges through a number of inter-related mechanisms (Aulakh *et al.*, 1996; Ganesan, 1994). First, trust in inter-firm exchanges reduces the perception of risk. Therefore, trust offers assurance that individual benefits will not be placed before the partnership goals, and that members of one firm will not knowingly distort information or otherwise subvert the other firm's members' interests (Crosby *et al.*, 1990). Second, trust acts as an important deterrent of opportunistic behaviour (Hagen & Choe, 1998; Hill, 1990). Third, trust assures partners that short-term inequities, which are inevitable in any relationship, will be corrected in time, to yield a long-term benefit (Anderson & Weitz, 1989). And fourth, trust can facilitate inter-organisational relationships by lowering transaction costs in uncertain environments (Allison, 1999; Doney, Cannon & Mullen, 1998; Ganesan, 1994; Ring & Van de Ven, 1992).

This latter mechanism has been corroborated through a great deal of empirical evidence. For instance, Aulakh *et al.* (1996), found that trust was a substitute for hierarchical governance (i.e. where "formal authority structures based on ownership are used to enforce contractual obligations" p. 1009). Similarly, Gulati (1995) and Smith, Carroll and Ashford (1995) observed that trust served to replace legal relationships, like equity sharing, as a governance system (i.e. whereby partners are given formal control over each other). Moreover, Nooteboom, Berger and Noorderhaven (1997) observed that, by reducing the specification and monitoring of contracts, trust made transactions "cheaper, more agreeable and more flexible" (p. 311). Finally, McAllister (1995) found that trust was inversely and directly related to the need for monitoring, formal rules and administrative costs. This evidence lends support to the argument that trust promotes a spirit of cooperation (Smith *et al.*, 1995) that can "lower the costs of a transaction by reducing the extent of opportunism by one or more of the transacting parties, as well as the need to guard against opportunism by the other party" (Hagen & Choe, 1998, p. 589). Therefore, trust is complementary to economic factors in the governance of customer–supplier relationships in supply chains (Zaheer & Venkatraman, 1995).

How Does Trust Change People's Work Roles? Implications for Supply-chain Partnering

From the above discussion, it follows that the presence of trust in supply-chain relationships will almost inevitably lead to changes in people's work roles across the partnering organisations. The roles of boundary spanners (e.g. sales and commercial managers, buyers, account controllers, etc.) may change as awareness of the impact of inter-personal trust upon inter-organisational trust is increased (e.g. Rousseau *et al.*, 1998). Thus, people in boundary positions may be required to actively promote and place their trust on those with whom they have perhaps had an adversarial relationship in the past, shifting the focus towards cooperation rather than opportunism. For this, however, organisations may need to use a broader range of measures to assess supply-chain partners' performance. This may in turn impact upon how one's own performance is measured; for example, the traditionally adversarial role of the buyer, whose performance is often measured mostly in terms of lowest price obtained for purchases, may need to be reviewed to incorporate other important factors, such as reliability.

An approach to supply-chain partnering based on trust may assume a greater deal of flexibility in people's work roles and their attitude to formal contracts. Employees may need to be prepared to go beyond what is stipulated in the contract (e.g. Sako, 1992) and become less reliant on detailed written contracts. Moreover, an approach to supply-chain partnering based on trust requires that people collaborate more with their partners and take a more macro approach, whereby they take into account not only the needs of their own organisation but also the needs of the other organisations that make up the chain through to the consumer end, hence the need to see the world not only from one's own company's perspective, but also from the perspective of the other companies that make up the chain. That is, as a result of supply-chain partnering practices, a need arises for perspective taking. Just as trust in supplier–buyer relationships is crucial for inter-organisational relationship success (Anderson & Narus, 1990), so too is understanding others' points of view.

SUPPLY-CHAIN PARTNERING AND PERSPECTIVE TAKING

Mohrman and Cohen (1995) have argued that perspective taking will become more important given the changes in organisational structure towards a more lateral structure, where individuals no longer work within a "box". They suggest that the cognition of individuals within lateral organisational structures will be of central importance. In order to work with people across organisational interfaces and disciplines, "individuals will have to develop an understanding of ideas and frameworks different from their own" (Mohrman & Cohen, 1995, p. 381).

As such, perspective taking is emerging as a concept that will have a major role to play in both employees' experience of work and it is important to understand how perspective taking is operationalised at an individual level, what role might it play in the relationships within supply-chain partnering and what the implications for practice might be.

HOW IS PERSPECTIVE TAKING OPERATIONALISED AT AN INDIVIDUAL LEVEL?

Perspective taking at the individual level is not a new concept, as it has been shown to be a fundamental aspect of child development (Piaget & Inhelder, 1968). The concept of perspective taking has also been important in clinical situations, where it is often assumed that therapy can only be successful if the clinician empathises with the client (Duan & Hill, 1996). However, most of the discussion in the management literature on perspective taking and knowledge sharing has focused on the organisational or team level, although the role of perspective taking is argued to be central to customer–supplier relations in order for organisational learning and knowledge-creation to occur in Japanese companies such as Hitachi (Lincoln, Ahmadjian & Mason, 1998). "Learning by taking the customer's role" enables one company to gain an intimate familiarity with one or more others. Imai, Nonaka and Takeuchi (1985) have documented learning in Fuji Xerox, where the learning process is one in which the firm "takes the role of the other", a core concept in symbolic interactionist social psychology (Stone, 1962). Within organisations, such role taking can be promoted by boundary-spanning activities, such as short-term visits, long-term transfers or stable interorganisational teams. In this way, it is interorganisational "learning by doing". The people of each firm immerse themselves in the routines of the other, thereby gaining access to the partner's stock of tacit knowledge. Learning takes place without the need to first convert tacit knowledge to explicit knowledge (Nonaka & Takeuchi, 1995).

Whilst this organisational level analysis is important to the perspective-taking process, there is a need to examine perspective taking at the level of the individual. As identified by Mohrman and Cohen (1995), there have been few studies of perspective taking in organisations, let alone in examining its impact on supply-chain partnerships.

Parker and Axtell (2001) suggest that perspective taking at the individual level is generally agreed to be a cognitive or intellectual process that results in the *affective response of empathy*. How people experience empathy depends on the level at which they cognise others. When people engage in active perspective taking they are more likely to empathise with the target, such as feeling concern at their misfortune (Betancourt, 1990; Davis, 1983), understanding or identifying with their experiences and experiencing pleasure at their achievements. Parker and Axtell (2001) argue that perspective taking is also a state that has other cognitive manifestations, such as changed attribution processes. This involves making positive attributions about another person's behaviour and outcomes, including recognising the effects of external circumstances and acknowledging the role of internal factors such as hard work and ability when things go wrong. Often people explain the behaviour of others in more negative terms, for example different explanations are often given according to whether there is a positive or negative outcome. Individuals attribute their own success to internal factors (e.g. ability, hard work) and failure to external factors (e.g. task difficulty), whereas they tend to give situational explanations for others' success and dispositional explanations for others' failure. Evidence suggests that these biases are reduced when individuals take the perspective of the other (Galper, 1976; Regan & Totten, 1975).

WHAT IS THE ROLE OF PERSPECTIVE TAKING IN SUPPLY-CHAIN RELATIONSHIPS?

Although we have noted some positive organisational outcomes (e.g. increased interorganisational learning) from encouraging perspective taking between supply-chain partners (Lincoln *et al.*, 1998), this research was only based on a small number of case study organisations within Japan. One study, which has taken a more psychological approach, has tested a model of the antecedents and outcomes of supplier perspective taking at the individual level. The study, carried out by Parker and Axtell (2001), used a sample of front-line production employees within a UK-based manufacturing company. Whilst the study asked the participants to think about their "main internal supplier" (the team upstream in the process who provided materials or products for employees to work on), rather than an external supply partner, it offers some interesting findings to extrapolate to the wider supply chain.

In summary, Parker and Axtell (2001) tested a model of antecedents and outcomes of supplier perspective taking, using correlations and structural equation modelling. In terms of outcomes, they proposed that perspective taking would enhance interpersonal facilitation. In particular, they argued that supplier perspective taking (measured by positive supplier attributions and supplier empathy) would be associated with cooperative and helping behaviours towards suppliers. They also examined individual (experience of supplier job; production ownership; integrated understanding of the workplace) and job-related (interaction with supplier; job autonomy) antecedents that are directly or indirectly associated with perspective taking. In short, they found that supplier perspective taking was associated with team-leader ratings of employees' contextual performance, i.e., helping and cooperative behaviours. Production ownership and integrated understanding predicted supplier perspective taking, and these antecedents were in turn predicted by job autonomy. Although it is only one study, it offers some support to the need to examine perspective taking as a key psychological process involved within the supply-chain relationship.

We have argued that trust and perspective taking are two important concepts within supply-chain partnering that influence the way in which employees experience work. While we have reviewed the research evidence for the impact of these concepts on employees work within this context, we now turn to examine what the implications will be for practice. What influence can human resource management practices have in supporting supply-chain partnering in general, and particularly in relation to the role of trust and perspective taking?

IMPLICATIONS FOR PRACTICE AND THE ROLE OF HUMAN RESOURCE MANAGEMENT (HRM)

Whilst we have outlined the possible impact of supply-chain partnering on employees' experience of work, it is important to consider the available mechanisms that could contribute to either improving the experience of work and/or ensuring the success of supply-chain partnering. Human resource management (HRM) policies and practices constitute one mechanism that has the potential to contribute to this area. However, although research into the mechanisms of supply-chain partnerships and alliances is beginning to be documented, there is as yet little reference made to possible HRM implications (Partnership Sourcing, 1991; Williamson, 1985). This section will begin with a general discussion of the contribution of HRM within supply-chain partnerships, before assessing how it may impact on the issues that we have raised in relation to trust and perspective taking.

Research that has addressed the role of HRM has rightly identified that in moving towards supply-chain partnering, the management and workforce capabilities of the two organisations become paramount (Hunter, Beaumont & Sinclair, 1996). In particular, this includes each partners' ability to engage in joint development activity, to communicate effectively with each other, to participate in joint cross-functional teams and to share a common approach to problem identification and solution. These abilities highlight the contribution to the partnership of the HRM function, which for many is rarely considered. In other words, the underpinning of many of the systems that are central to supply-chain partnering depends on the capabilities, training and organisation of the human resources involved in the partnership. This has been identified by Briscoe, Dainty and Millett (2001), who examined the knowledge skills and attitudes required for effective supply-chain partnership in the UK construction industry. They ask whether deficiencies in these areas act as barriers to effective supply-chain partnering.

Hunter, Beaumont and Sinclair (1996) present evidence that suggests that in earlier stages of partnership development, the HRM function at the customer end is often only marginally involved. They recognise that the information gathered from the supplier is often technical in nature (e.g. quality, efficiency and productivity data) and is not concerned with matters such as employee commitment, work organisation or communication methods. Hunter *et al.* (1996) put forward two principal means by which HRM in the partner organisation can be influenced. First are the indirect effects, in which there are a number of ways that the HR department within the supplier can become involved. These might include developing training programmes in support of the business development objectives, or helping to clear away perceived industrial relations obstacles (e.g. negotiating collective agreements, permitting greater flexibility).

The second avenue that Hunter *et al.* (1996) identify is where HRM is considered as one of the major criteria for the development of a successful supply chain partnership. In this way, HRM policies and practices are central to the partnership and actually drive interventions, rather than being reactive to incompatibilities between the two organisations. Having outlined different avenues for general involvement for the HR function, we now return to the specific issues of trust and perspective taking within the supply-chain relationship and suggest areas where the HR function may contribute.

A final important point made by Van Hoek, Chatham and Wilding (2002) is that attracting and training the right supply-chain managers will be a critical challenge to the realisation of future supply-chain partnering. They argue for a shift in focus towards selecting and training managers in more "human aspects" and "people" dimensions to ensure a broader range of capability.

TRUST AND HRM POLICIES AND PRACTICES

It has been established that to manage supply-chain relationships better and to ensure success it is necessary to have dedicated resources to effectively manage the interface between customers and suppliers. HR practices can contribute to better aligning partners' expectations, goals and objectives. In the area of trust, there need to be measures that promote the development of trust. Although not intended as the only solution to the issues raised earlier, what follows is a set of practical recommendations that supply-chain partners may wish to consider as ways of addressing relationship problems and building trust.

Training and Development

Given the critical role that trust plays in the customer–supplier relationship, it is crucial that supply-chain partners take measures to ensure the development and/or maintenance of trust. Supply-chain partners could promote the development (or further enhance) the key characteristics of trust in their own relationships. For instance, induction programmes for newly appointed boundary role people (i.e. sales and purchasing directors and managers) could emphasise the importance of trust and its individual dimensions (e.g. integrity, competence, fairness, loyalty, and openness and frankness).

Reward Systems and Performance Measures

A way of encouraging the development of a trust approach would be, for example, the alignment of reward systems with a view to promoting close, trusting relationships. Thus, reward systems in the case of buyers should not only consider hard issues such as profit margins, but also soft aspects such as quality of the customer–supplier and inter-firm relationship. The absence of standardised or universal performance measures across the supply chain, however, is often a cause of problems arising. If supply-chain partners do not know what the goalposts are, or if these are confusing or ambiguous, the chances of effective performance across the supply chain are decreased. Thus, supply-chain partners should endeavour to identify and agree universally acceptable supply-chain performance measures. In light of the importance of trust, trust levels in the relationship should also be included as an important performance indicator. A simple tool designed to identify and measure levels of trust in interorganisational relationships may be the first step towards identifying and resolving issues that prevent trust from arising.

Communication and Information Sharing

Mohr and Spekman (1994) have suggested that to develop and maintain trust with other supply chain partners, communication both within and across organisations is crucial. Communication across different organisational functions and across organisational boundaries therefore needs to be tightly integrated, and new work roles may need to specifically and explicitly account for this. Regular review meetings, where partners voice their concerns about the relationship and update one another on order progress and business development, would ensure effective and frequent communication across businesses. Further, knowing what is going on in one's firm could impact upon the perception of competence of a particular firm (with competence being a key dimension in trust). In light of this, it is crucial that supply-chain partners evaluate their internal communication systems in an effort to identify existing areas of weakness. Moreover, such systems should ensure that clear and common objectives are agreed across departments prior to involving another member of the supply chain.

Collaboration and Commitment

The adoption of a long-term approach towards a relationship would help enhance its quality and trust levels. Indeed, relationships that were seen as difficult to substitute were described as the most trusting. In a relationship that is perceived as easily substitutable, a lower level of trust might develop. In contrast, an environment more conducive to the emergence of trust would be created by supply-chain partners approaching the relationship as one that is difficult to substitute.

Approaches to Conflict Resolution

In interorganisational relationships, such as those of a supplier and customer firm, disagreements often arise due to a conflict of interests. In such cases, buyers have traditionally resorted to threats of ending the commercial relationship if their wishes are not granted. This, however, is often described by suppliers as very harmful and counterproductive to the relationship (e.g. Icasati-Johanson et al., 2000). The use of more constructive approaches to conflict resolution should therefore be promoted. This could entail joint regular meetings where the relevant parties would raise, examine and discuss any issues and their proposed solutions.

PERSPECTIVE TAKING AND HRM POLICIES AND PRACTICES

Further studies are required in order to replicate the evidence from the above studies within the external supply chain. However, the potential implications for practice are considerable. For example, the evidence to date supports the idea that the extent to which employees see multiple viewpoints can be enhanced via organisational intervention, although Parker and Axtell (2001) do state that causality has not been firmly established. These authors suggest two ways to enhance supplier perspective taking and hence contextual performance (cooperative behaviours towards suppliers), first to increase employee interaction with suppliers and second to enrich job content. Both of these can be facilitated by HR interventions once the partnership is set up, or by taking the more direct avenue as detailed by Hunter *et al.* (1996) and designing them into the partnership agreement at the outset.

In terms of interaction, Parker and Axtell's findings suggest that the more contact employees have with their suppliers, the more likely they will be to make positive attributions about supplier behaviour and empathise with them. Regardless of the actual mechanisms involved in providing this outcome, there is major scope for HRM interventions in increasing interactions. Many of the interventions recommended to encourage perspective taking are complementary to those proposed for developing trust between supply-chain partners (e.g. training and development, collaboration and commitment, and communication). For example, training programmes or events (e.g. one-day workshops) could be devised to promote mutual understanding of the needs of customers and suppliers. Scenarios planning, a tool that helps people understand and evaluate existing ways of working and helps identify and evaluate alternative ways of working, could be used in this context. Supply-chain partners could set up a working group to explore how they currently work together and how they may work together in the future. Such an intervention would, for instance, help in promoting more interaction across companies in the chain. The perception that one member of the supply chain has different objectives to those of the remaining chain members is a source of tension that needs careful consideration. Steps therefore need to be taken to understand, and if possible align, the objectives of each member of the supply chain.

Understanding of the business of supply-chain partners can also be enhanced through the use of employee visits or exchange programmes and other events (such as meetings to discuss problems, etc.). Such collaborative programmes should be frequent enough for mutual understanding and empathy to develop. The use of cross-functional teams to work on problem-solving activities could also aid interaction and hence perspective taking. Finally, it is possible that recruitment and selection practices may also play a part in selecting individuals that have the ability to take the perspective of others. This is particularly relevant if you take a dispositional approach to empathy, which considers it as a relatively stable trait (Sawyer, 1975).

The emphasis on interaction as a facilitator to perspective taking is also relevant to the recent work in the area of knowledge sharing. Here, it is recognised that the appreciation of another's perspective (to contribute to the knowledge-sharing process) typically requires an extensive amount of social interaction and face-to-face communication (Kerrin & Currie, 2001; Lam, 1997; Leonard-Barton, 1995). It is suggested that it is this face-to-face interaction and interventions (rather than formal training courses outlining the supplier's role) that will be more successful in developing perspective taking.

Autonomy was an important predictor of employees' level of production ownership and associated with integrated understanding. Job redesign is therefore a potential approach that can be used to develop perspective taking, in addition to traditional outcomes measures of job satisfaction and stress (Parker & Axtell, 2001), although the design of work tasks provides challenges for the HR function in the development of job descriptions, which allow autonomy in employees' work.

The proposals put forward here in relation to the role of the HR function provides support for many of the practices already existing in some organisations, in an attempt to encourage better customer–supplier integration through short-term visits or long-term transfers (Lincoln *et al.*, 1998). However, what we have tried to argue here is that there is a specific role for HRM in developing trust and perspective taking within a supply-chain partnership. There are also choices for organisations to make in terms of the stages at which they involve the HR function. Given some of the interventions (e.g. training and development, job redesign), we would argue that the HR function needs to be involved directly, rather than indirectly and after the partnership has begun. This would allow the organisation to design in to the partnership key elements to provide support for perspective taking and the development of trust.

CONCLUSION

Supply-chain partnering and the mechanisms involved in its development are becoming increasingly better understood (Lamming, 1993; Sako, 1992). As a relatively new working practice, it is likely to have a significant impact on employees' experience of work in the future. This chapter has identified two areas, trust and perspective taking, where there are opportunities and choices for managers and work psychologists. It has assessed their contribution to this area by first identifying the impact of such concepts on the experience of work and second by examining their practical implications for HRM. It is evident from the discussion of HR interventions that there are different design issues and different paths to follow in the structure of supply-chain partnerships that will have an impact on trust and perspective taking.

However, this chapter is not advocating a "best practice" route, which was prominent following the emergence of other new forms of working practices, such as lean production. The criticisms put forward by Lowe, Delbridge and Oliver (1997) of the "best practice" approach are recognised as relevant here. Their findings on adaptation of lean practices in the automotive components industry did not support the notion that one style of work organisation and human resource policy represents one best way. In the same way, the choices for organisations in supply-chain partnering in utilising the HR function needs to be context-specific (e.g. recognising the importance of specific organisational characteristics and choices for understanding performance). This is particularly true when dealing with issues such as trust and perspective taking. What this chapter has tried to do is to provide an indication of what is important to address within these concepts and which may then be assessed in terms of its relevance to certain contexts. Finally, given the emergence of the global organisation, contextual issues may be particularly important in considering international factors when choosing HR practices to support the development of trust and perspective taking within supply-chain partnering.

REFERENCES

Agarwal, A. & Shankar, R. (2003). On-line trust building in e-enabled supply chain. *Supply Chain Management: An International Journal*, **8**(4), 324–334.

Allison, D. (January 9, 1999). Making and Acting Upon Trustworthiness Assessments in Buyer–Supplier Relations. Unpublished manuscript, Center for Research on Social Organisation, University of Michigan.

Anderson, J. & Narus, J. (1990). A model of distribution firm and manufacturing firm working partnerships. *Journal of Marketing*, **54**(1), 42–59.

Anderson, E. & Weitz, B. (1989). Determinants of continuity in conventional industrial channel dyads. *Marketing Science*, **3**(4), 310–323.

Anderson, E. & Weitz, B. (1992). The use of pledges to build and sustain commitment in distribution channels. *Journal of Marketing Research*, **XXIX**(February), 18–34.

Aulakh, P. S., Kotabe, M. & Sahay, A. (1996). Trust and performance in cross-border marketing partnerships: a behavioural approach. *Journal of International Business Studies*, **27**(5), 1005–1032.

Barney, J. B. & Hansen, M. H. (1994). Trustworthiness as a source of competitive advantage. *Strategic Management Journal*, **15**: 175–190.

Barratt, M. (2004). Understanding the meaning of collaboration in the supply chain. *Supply Chain Management: An International Journal*, **9**(1), 30–42.

Bessant, J. R. (1991). *Managing Advanced Manufacturing Technology: the Challenge of the Fifth Wave*. Oxford: NCC Blackwell.

Betancourt, H. (1990). An attribution–empathy model of helping behavior: behavioral intentions and judgements of help giving. *Personality and Social Psychology Bulletin*, **16**: 573–591.

Bigley, G. A. & Pearce, J. L. (1998). Straining for shared meaning in organisation science: problems of trust and distrust. *Academy of Management Review*, **23**(3), 405–421.

Blackler, F. (1995). Knowledge, knowledge work and organisations: an overview and interpretation, *Organisation Studies*, **16**(6), 1021–1046.

Blois, K. J. (1999). Trust in business to business relationships: an evaluation of its status. *Journal of Management Studies*, **36**(2) (March), 197–215.

Boddy, D., Macbeth, D. K., Charles, M. & Fraser-Kraus, H. (1998). Success and failure in implementing partnering. *European Journal of Purchasing and Supply Management*, **4**, 143–151.

Boddy, D., Macbeth, D. K. & Wagner, B. (2000). Implementing collaboration between organizations: an empirical study of supply chain partnering. *Journal of Management Studies*, **37**(7), 1003–1017.

Briscoe, G., Dainty, A. R. J. & Millett, S. (2001). Construction supply chain partnerships: skills, knowledge and attitudinal requirements. *European Journal of Purchasing and Supply Management*, **7**(4), 243–255.

Brown, J. S. & Duguid, P. (1991). Organisational learning and communities of practice: toward a unified view of working, learning and innovation. *Organisation Science*, **2**(1) 40–57.

Carr, C. H. & Truesdale, T. A. (1992). Lessons from Nissan's British Suppliers. *International Journal of Operations and Production Management*, **12**(2), 49–57.

Cook, S. & Brown, J. (1999). Bridging epistemologies: the generative dance between organizational knowledge and organizational knowing. *Organization Science*, **10**(4), 381–400.

Corrigan, S. (1995). Determinants of Success in the Buyer/Supplier Relationship. Unpublished MSc Thesis, Institute of Work Psychology, University of Sheffield.

Crosby, L. A., Evans, K. R. & Cowles, D. (1990). Relationship quality in services selling: an interpersonal influence perspective. *Journal of Marketing*, **54**(July), 68–81.

Currall, S. C. & Judge, T. A. (1995). Measuring trust between organisational boundary role persons. *Organisational Behaviour and Human Decision Processes*, **64**(2, November), 151–170.

Davis, M. H. (1983). The effects of dispositional empathy on emotional reactions and helping: a multidimensional approach. *Journal of Personality*, **51**, 167–184.

Dion, P. A. & Banting, P. M. (1988). The purchasing agent, friend or foe to the salesperson. *Journal of Academy of Marketing Science*, **16**.

Dion, P., Easterling, D. & Miller, S. J. (1995). What is really necessary in successful buyer/seller relationships? *Industrial Marketing Management*, **24**, 1–9.

Doney, P. M., Cannon, J. P. & Mullen, M. R. (1998). Understanding the influence of national culture on the development of trust. *Academy of Management Review*, **23**(3), 601–620.

Dore, R. P. (1987). *Taking Japan Seriously*. Stanford, CT: Stanford University Press.

Duan, C. & Hill, C. E. (1996). The current state of empathy research. *Journal of Counselling Psychology*, **43**, 261–274.

Dwyer, R. F., Schurr, P. H. & Oh, S. (1987). Developing buyer–seller relationships. *Journal of Marketing*, **51**(April), 11–27.

Dyer, J. H. & Ouchi, W. G. (1993). Japanese style business partnerships: giving companies a competitive edge. *Sloan Management Review*, **35**(1), 51–63.

Dyer, J. H. & Singh, H. (1998). The relational view: cooperative strategy and sources of interorganizational competitive advantage. *Academy of Management Review*, **23**(4), 660–679.

Ellram, L. M. (1995). Partnering pitfalls and success factors. *International Journal of Purchasing and Materials Management*, **Spring**, 36–44.

Ellram, L., Edis, M. & Owen, R. V. (1996). A case study of successful partnering implementation. *International Journal of Purchasing and Materials Management*, **32**(4), 20–28.

Farmer, D. H. & Ploos von Amstel, R. (1991). *Effective Pipeline Management: How to Manage Integrated Logistics*. Aldershot: Gower.

Galper, R. E. (1976). Turning observers into actors: differential causal attributions as a function of "empathy". *Journal of Research in Personality*, **10**, 328–335.

Gambetta, D. G. (Ed.) (1988). *Trust: Making and Breaking Co-operative Relations*. New York: Basil Blackwell.

Ganesan, S. (1994). Determinants of long-term orientation in buyer–seller relationships. *Journal of Marketing*, **58**(April), 1–19.

Granovetter, M. (1985). Economic action and social structures: the problem of embeddedness. *American Journal of Sociology*, **91**(3), 481–510.

Gulati, R. (1995). Does familiarity breed trust? The implications of repeated ties for contractual choice in alliances. *Academy of Management Journal*, **38**(1), 85–112.

Hackman, J. R. & Oldham, G. (1976). Motivation through the design of work: test of a theory. *Organizational Behaviour and Human Performance*, **16**, 250–279.

Hagen, J. M. & Choe, S. (1998). Trust in Japanese interfirm relations: institutional sanctions matter. *Academy of Management Review*, **23**(3), 589–600.

Heide, J. B. & John, G. (1990). Alliances in industrial purchasing: the determinants of joint action in buyer–supplier relationships. *Journal of Marketing Research*, **XXVII**(February), 24–36.

Hill, C. W. L. (1990). Co-operation, opportunism, and the invisible hand: implications for transaction cost theory. *Academy of Management Review*, **15**(3), 500–513.

Hoyt, J. & Huq, F. (2000). From arms-length to collaborative relationships in the supply chain. *International Journal of Physical Distribution and Logistics Management*, **30**(9), 750–764.

Hunter, L., Beaumont, P. & Sinclair, D. (1996). A "partnership" route to human resource management. *Journal of Management Studies*, **33**(2), 235–257.

Icasati-Johanson, B., Clegg, C. W. & Axtell, C. M. (2000). *The Role of Trust in Supplier–Buyer Relationships in Packaging Supply Chains. Feedback Report to Participating Companies.* Sheffield: ESRC Centre for Organization and Innovation. Institute of Work Psychology, University of Sheffield, April 2000.

Imai, K., Nonaka, I. & Takeuchi, H. (1985). Managing the new product development process: how Japanese companies learn and unlearn. In K. B. Clark, R. H. Hayes & C. Lorenz (Eds), *The Uneasy Alliance: Managing the Productivity–Technology Dilemma*. Boston, MA: Harvard Business School Press.

Jensen, M. C. & Meckling, W. M. (1976). Theory of the firm: managerial behaviour, agency costs, and ownership structure. *Journal of Financial Economics*, **3**, 305–360.

Kerrin, M. (2002). Continuous improvement along the supply chain: the impact of customer–supplier relations. *Integrated Manufacturing Systems*, **13**(3), 141–149.

Kerrin, M. & Currie, G. (2001). Utilising HRM practices to mediate the impact of organizational structures and processes upon shared learning: case study evidence from a global pharmaceutical company. *Proceedings of the Managing Knowledge: Conversations and Critiques Conference*, University of Leicester Management Centre.

Lam, A. (1997). Embedded firms, embedded knowledge: problems in collaboration and knowledge transfer in global co-operative ventures. *Organization Studies*, **18**(6), 973–996.

Lamming, R. (1993). *Beyond Partnership: Strategies for Innovation and Lean Supply*. London: Prentice Hall.

Lamming, R. (1986). For better or for worse—impacts of technical change upon the UK automotive components sector. In C. Voss (Ed.), *Managing Advanced Manufacturing Technology*. Proceedings of the 1st UK Operations Management Association Conference. Bedford: IFS.

Landeros, R., Reck, R. & Plank, R. E. (1995). Maintaining buyer–supplier partnerships. *International Journal of Purchasing and Materials Management*, **Summer**, 3–11.

Langfield-Smith, K. & Greenwood, M. (1998). Developing co-operative buyer–supplier relationships: a case study of Toyota. *Journal of Management Studies*, **35**(3), 331–354.

Lave, J. & Wenger, E. (1991). *Situated Learning: Legitimate Peripheral Participation*. Cambridge: Cambridge University Press.

Leonard-Barton, D. (1995). *Wellsprings of Knowledge: Building and Sustaining the Sources of Innovation*. Boston, MA: Harvard Business School Press.

Leverick, F. & Cooper, R. (1998). Partnerships in the motor industry: opportunities and risks for suppliers. *Long Range Planning*, **31**(1), 72–81.

Lincoln, J. R, Ahmadjian, C. L. & Mason, E. (1998). Organizational learning and purchase–supply relations in Japan: Hitachi, Matsushita, and Toyota compared. *California Management Review*, **40**(3), 241–264.

Lowe, J. Delbridge, R. & Oliver, N. (1997). High-performance manufacturing: evidence from the automotive components industry. *Organization Studies*, **18**(5), 783–798.

Macbeth, D. K. (1998). Partnering—why not? *Proceedings of the 2nd Worldwide Symposium on Purchasing and Supply Chain Management* (pp. 351–362). Stamford, UK: Chartered Institute of Purchasing and Supply.

McAllister, D. J. (1995). Affect- and cognition-based trust as foundations for interpersonal co-operation in organisations. *Academy of Management Journal*, **38**(1), 24–59.

Mohr, J. & Spekman, R. (1994). Characteristics of partnership success: partnership attributes, communication behavior and conflict resolution techniques. *Strategic Management Journal*, **15**, 135–152.

Mohrman, S. A. & Cohen, S. G. (1995). When people get out of the box: new relationships, new systems. In Mohrman, S. A. & Cohen, S. G. (Eds), *The Changing Nature of Work*. San Francisco, CA: Jossey-Bass.

Moore, K. R. (1998). Trust and relationship commitment in logistics alliances: a buyer perspective. *International Journal of Purchasing and Materials management*, **January**.

Nonaka, I. & Takeuchi (1995). *The Knowledge-creating Company: How Japanese Companies Create the Dynamics of Innovation*. New York: Oxford University Press.

Nooteboom, B., Berger, H. & Noorderhaven, N. G. (1997). Effects of trust and governance on relational risk. *Academy of Management Journal*, **40**, 308–338.

Oliver, N. & Wilkinson, B. (1992). *The Japanization of British Industry*. Oxford: Blackwell.

Pagel, D. (1999). Managing for optimal performance through effective coordination of the supply chain. *Production and Inventory Management Journal*, **40**(1), 66–70.

Parker, S., Wall, T. & Cordery, J. (2001). Future work design research and practice: towards an elaborated model of work design. *Journal of Occupational and Organizational Psychology*, **74**(4), 413–440.

Parker, S. & Axtell, C. (2001). Seeing another view point: antecedents and outcomes of employee perspective taking activity. *Academy of Management Journal*, **44**(6), 1085–1100.

Partnership Sourcing Ltd (1991). *Partnership Sourcing*. Reading: DTI/CBI.

Piaget, J. & Inhelder, B. (1968). *The Psychology of the Child*. New York: Basic Books.

Powell, W. W. (1990). Neither market nor hierarchy: network forms of organizations. *Research in Organizational Behavior*, **12**, 295–336.

Powell, W. W. (1996). Trust-based forms of governance. In R. M. Kramer & T. R. Tyler (Eds), *Trust in Organisations: Frontiers of Theory and Research* (pp. 51–67). Thousand Oaks, CA: Sage.

Quayle, M. (2003). A study of supply chain management practice in UK industrial SMEs. *Supply Chain Management: An International Journal*, **8**(1), 79–86.

Regan, D. & Totten, J. (1975). Empathy and attribution: turning actors into observers. *Journal of Personality and Social Psychology*, **32**, 850–856.

Riddalls, C. E., Icasati-Johanson, B., Axtell, C. M., Bennett, S. & Clegg, C. (2002). Quantifying the effects of trust in supply chains during promotional periods. *International Journal of Logistics*, **5**(3), 257–274.

Ring, P. S. & Van de Ven, A. H. (1992). Structuring co-operative relationships between organisations. *Strategic Management Journal*, **13**, 483–498.

Rotter, J. B. (1967). A new scale for the measurement of interpersonal trust. *Journal of Personality*, **35**, 651–665.

Rotter, J. B. (1980). Interpersonal trust, trustworthiness, and gullibility. *American Psychologist* **35**(1), 1–7.

Rousseau, D. M., Sitkin, S. B., Burt, R. S. & Camerer, C. (1998). Not so different after all: a cross-discipline view of trust. Introduction to a special topic forum. *Academy of Management Review*, **23**(3), 393–404.

Sako, M. (1992). *Prices, Quality and Trust: Inter-firm Relations in Britain and Japan*. Cambridge: Cambridge University Press.

Sako, M. & Helper, S. (1998). Determinants of trust in supplier relations: evidence from the automotive industry in Japan and the United States. *Journal of Economic Behaviour & Organisation*, **34**, 387–417.

Sawyer, F. H. (1975). A conceptual analysis of empathy. *Annual of Psychoanalysis*, **3**, 37–47.

Schurr, P. H. & Ozanne, J. L. (1985). Influences on exchange processes: buyers' preconceptions of a seller's trustworthiness and bargaining toughness. *Journal of Consumer Research*, **11**, 939–953.

Slack, N. (1991). *The Manufacturing Advantage*. London: Mercury Business Books.

Smith, K. G., Carroll, S. J. & Ashford, S. J. (1995). Intra- and interorganizational co-operation: toward a research agenda. *Academy of Management Journal*, **38**(1), 7–23.

Spekman, R., Forbes, T., Isabella, L. & MacAvoy, T. (1998a). Alliance management: a view from the past and a look to the future. *Journal of Management Studies*, **35**(6), 747–772.

Spekman, R. E., Kamauff, J. W. Jr & Myhr, N. (1998b). An empirical investigation into supply chain management: a perspective on partnerships. *International Journal of Physical Distribution and Logistics Management*, **28**(8), 630–650.

Stone, G. P. (1962). Appearance and the self. In A. M. Rose (Ed.), *Human Behavior and Social Processes: an Interactionist Approach*. Boston, MA: Houghton Mifflin.

Sullivan, J. & Peterson, R. B. (1982). Factors associated with trust in Japanese–American joint ventures. *Management International Review*, **22**: 30–40.

Turnbull, P., Delbridge, R., Oliver, N. & Wilkinson, B. (1993). Winners and losers—the 'tiering' of component suppliers in the UK automotive industry. *Journal of General Management*, **19**(1), 48–63.

Van Hoek, R. I., Chatham, R. & Wilding, R. (2002). Managers in supply chain management, the critical dimension, *Supply Chain Management: An International Journal*, **7**(3), 119–125.

Wagner, B. A., Macbeth, D. K. & Boddy, D. (2002). Improving supply chain relations: an empirical case study. *Supply Chain Management: An International Journal*, **7**(4), 253–264.

Williamson, O. E. (1975). *Markets and Hierarchies*. New York: Free Press.

Williamson, O. E (1985). *The Economic Institutions of Capitalism*. New York: Free Press.

Williamson, O. E. (1993). Calculativenesss, trust, and economic organisation. *Journal of Law and Economics*, **36**, 453–486.

Winfield, I. J. & Kerrin M. (1996). Toyota motor manufacturing in Europe: lessons for management development. *Journal of Management Development*, **15**(4), 49–56.

Zaheer, A. & Venkatraman, N. (1995). Relational governance as an interorganizational strategy: an empirical test of the role of trust in economic exchange. *Strategic Management Journal*, **16**, 373–392.

CHAPTER 6

Team Work

John Cordery

Department of Organizational and Labour Studies,
University of Western Australia, Perth, Australia

The growth of interest in how groups or teams function in work settings has been nothing short of dramatic over recent decades (Ilgen, 1999; Katzell, 1994; Stewart, 2000). This reflects the fact that surveys of management practices around the globe have repeatedly shown that implementing teams is amongst the most popular initiatives aimed at improving organizational effectiveness (e.g. Clegg *et al.*, 2002; Godard, 2001; Gittleman, Horrigan & Joyce, 1998; Lawler, Mohrman & Ledford, 1995; Osterman, 2000). Why is the concept of team so popular in contemporary organizations? In this chapter, I seek to answer this question, and to describe how team working can be most effectively deployed to support the operation of modern work systems.

To understand the phenomenon, one first needs to understand what is meant by team working in a modern organizational context. The chapter thus begins by identifying the key parameters of team working, and looks at what it promises to deliver in terms of productivity and organizational effectiveness. This is followed by a review of evidence as to the actual effectiveness of team working in modern work settings, and by a discussion of contexts within which teams are more likely to be an effective work design option. This leads on to a discussion of elements of team structure and process that influence their effectiveness. Next, features of the broader management and organizational context that are needed to justify and support the use of teams are discussed. Finally, areas where our knowledge of how teams operate in real organizations is weak, along with promising avenues for further research, are identified.

THE ESSENCE OF TEAMS

If one were to identify the single most important prerequisite for describing an organisational unit as a team, it would have to be the degree to which members are truly reliant on each other's actions. This requisite reliance can take two forms (Wageman, 1995). First, there is task interdependence—the extent to which successful task performance of one team member is dependent on tasks performed by others in the team. In its simplest form, task interdependence arises where work flows sequentially from one team member to another;

for example, the driver of an ore truck on a minesite cannot begin the trip to the crusher until another member of his operating team has finished loading it. More complex work systems involve reciprocal forms of task interdependence, where work flows backwards and forwards between team members (as with treatment of patients by members of a primary healthcare team). A second form of reliance, outcome interdependence, refers to the extent to which team members are dependent on each other for significant outcomes or rewards. That is, members are collectively responsible for team outcomes. For example, even though task interdependence may be relatively weak, rewards to individuals within a customer service team may depend on levels of performance achieved by the team as a whole.

More than just a group of interdependent employees—after all, all organizational members are this to some degree—teams also involve an agreed collective purpose and boundaries protected by membership criteria. They are thus readily identifiable social entities that serve some legitimate organizational purpose, as well as providing a source of social identification for their members (Hogg & Terry, 2000). As a coherent social unit, they manage their interactions with others (e.g. customers, suppliers, other organizational teams) in ways that reflect their collective perspectives, interests and goals.

In summary, an organizational team may be defined as a:

> ... collection of individuals who are interdependent in their tasks, who share responsibility for outcomes, who see themselves and who are seen by others as an intact social entity embedded in one or more larger social systems (e.g. business unit or the corporation), and who manage their relationships across organizational boundaries (Cohen & Bailey, 1997, p. 242).

Of course, teams meeting the above definition can be found in many different parts of the organization, performing many different functions. For example, Cohen and Bailey (1997) offer a taxonomy of four main team types, differentiated by organizational level and function: work teams are relatively permanent groups found at the base of the operating core of the organization, and perform tasks associated with the organization's primary production or service functions (e.g. customer service team, process operator team). Parallel teams operate outside the formal authority structure, performing specific functions such as problem-solving, quality improvement and employee involvement (e.g. quality circles, process improvement teams). Project teams are temporary, and are formed for a specific time-delimited purpose, such as solving a particular problem or performing a one-off task (e.g. fighting a bushfire, designing a new building). With the increasingly rapid permeation of information technology into work organizations, there has been a rapid rise in the use of virtual project teams (Duarte & Tennant-Snyder, 2000; Majchrzak, Rice, Kink, Malhotra & Ba, 2000), so-called because members are not co-located and may never meet face-to-face. Finally, management teams operate towards the strategic apex, coordinating and controlling key business processes across the organization.

THE POPULARITY OF TEAM-BASED WORK ORGANIZATION

As indicated earlier, the popularity of organizing work around teams is reflected in statistics regarding their useage. Lawler *et al.* (1995) reported that the percentage of leading US firms organizing work in their operating core around self-managing teams had risen from 28% in 1987 to 68% in 1993. At around the same time, Osterman (1994) also estimated that around

50% of US organizations were using teams, with around 40% of organizations having teams covering 50% or more of their employees. In Osterman's study, teams emerged as the single most popular work practice innovation, ahead of total quality management, job rotation and quality circles. In a follow-up study, it was also found that the use of teams had remained relatively constant over the 5-year period 1992–1997 (Osterman, 2000). More recently, in an international survey carried out 1996–1998, Clegg *et al.* (2002) have reported the use of team-based work in manufacturing organizations in the UK (35%), Japan (22%), Australia (45%) and Switzerland (50%) as significant, although at levels generally lower than in the USA.

What lies behind this level of uptake? Richard Guzzo has noted that perspectives on the importance and role of teamwork in organisations have changed over the years:

> In the 1960s teams were instruments of training and experience, thought to impart skills essential to effective management. In the 1970s teams became an antidote to worker alienation. In the 1980s teams were a solution to problems of quality and productivity that permitted foreign (especially Japanese) firms to surpass our own. And in the 1990s teams make for lean and flexible organizations (Guzzo, cited in Church, 1996).

Staw and Epstein (2000) have suggested that there is an element of fashion driving the popularity of teams. In a longitudinal study of 100 large US industrial corporations, they found no evidence to support the direct economic or efficiency benefits of management innovations such as teams. However, they did find reputational effects, namely that "companies were more admired, seen as being more innovative, and rated as having higher-quality management when they followed management trends such as quality, teams and empowerment". This, in turn, translated into higher levels of CEO remuneration.

However, Osterman (2000) argues that the rise in popularity of so-called high-performance work practices such as teams over the past two decades has occurred because they seemed to make possible benefits for both employees and employers. This idea of mutuality of benefits for organizations and employees alike stems from arguments that employees working as a team are likely to be more productive and satisfied than those working alone (Campion, Medsker & Higgs, 1993; Cohen & Ledford, 1994; Leavitt, 1975; Mohrman, Cohen & Mohrman, 1995). Three principal productivity-related advantages have been associated with team-based work structures (Pfeffer, 1998). First, the introduction of teams makes possible a shift in the nature of control processes from traditional hierarchical forms of control (e.g. through managerial supervision and direction) to more decentralized peer-based forms of control. This, in turn, leads to more direct and efficient control over performance, not simply because of the power of peer pressure to regulate individual employee behaviour (Barker, 1993) but also because key sources of performance variance may be controlled more rapidly (Cummings, 1978). When a problem arises, for example in relation to a production process or a customer service, the problem is more likely to be resolved quickly if a decision does not need to be referred to someone higher up in the organization. It has also been suggested that this peer-based control is associated with increased feelings of employee accountability for organizational outcomes, and that this "increased sense of responsibility stimulates more initiative and effort on the part of everyone involved" (Pfeffer, 1998, p. 75). This potential for decentralized team structures to enhance the motivational properties of work for their members has been a long-standing theme in the job design literature (e.g. Hackman, 1987; Hackman & Oldham, 1980) and also in the recent literature on psychological empowerment (e.g. Kirkman & Rosen, 2000).

The second main argument in favour of the productivity of teams relates to their potential to enhance the quality of work outcomes. For example, the range and depth of physical and cognitive resources (e.g. knowledge and skill, information-processing capacity) that can be brought to bear on a problem by the team as a whole may be considerably greater than any individual employee (including a manager or supervisor) possesses. Team working thus increases the probability of a solution to any given problem being found. Teams have also been credited with an increased likelihood of creative and innovative solutions, in the sense that synergistic outcomes may arise from the required interactions between individuals of diverse abilities, knowledge and backgrounds (Paulus, 2000).

Third, the introduction of teams has been linked to lowered operational costs associated with reductions in the levels of administrative and managerial support required. This arises as a result of improved coordination of interdependent tasks at the team level, but also because the devolution of authority and responsibility for outcomes that generally accompanies team formation means that many decisions once made by managers and supervisors are now made by team members themselves.

What about the benefits for employees themselves? Job design theory suggests that teams may offer increased scope for employees to satisfy higher-order needs and to obtain important intrinsic rewards through their work (Hackman, 1987). Psychologically significant job design characteristics, such as task autonomy and variety, can be enhanced at the team level as well as at the level of the individual job, e.g. being able to rotate between jobs within a team may increase the level of skill variety experienced by individuals. Similarly, levels of autonomy experienced by an individual can be enhanced when the team is given the responsibility to collectively manage its internal operations. Finally, teams also offer important opportunities for social interaction and also support for their members.

HOW EFFECTIVE ARE TEAMS IN PRACTICE?

Do teams actually live up to their billing as "high-performance" work systems? Is the promise of mutual benefits for employees and organizations actually realized? For some management commentators the answer is unequivocally in the affirmative; for example, O'Reilly and Pfeffer (2000) propose that team-based people management systems are a feature of many organizations that are regarded as highly successful. They observe that:

> Even in those organizations where the work might lend itself to significant specialization . . . there is an emphasis on collective responsibility. This emphasis on teams as an organizing principle derives not from a current fad but from a belief in the fundamental importance of teams as a way of both getting the work done and of promoting autonomy and responsibility—of tapping the ideas and energy of everyone (p. 242).

Good empirical studies demonstrating the positive impact of teamwork on organizational and employee outcomes are relatively rare, although they do exist; for example, Banker, Field, Schroeder and Sinha (1996) reported on the impact of work teams on manufacturing performance, using a longitudinal study of employees in an electro-mechanical assembly plant. Over a period of just under 2 years, and controlling for inter-team differences resulting from differences in managerial policies (e.g. overtime, product diversity, capacity utilization), they found that the introduction of "high-performance work teams" had a significant impact on both quality and labour productivity. For example, they found that there had been a 38% reduction in defect rates from the beginning to the end of the post-implementation measurement period. They also found a 20% improvement in labour productivity, assessed as a ratio of the number of units produced to the number of hours worked, over the same period.

Batt (1999) studied self-managing teams in the customer service area of a large telecommunications firm. As in Banker *et al.*'s (1996) study, significant performance effects were associated with the teamwork intervention. With customer sales as the performance criterion, improvements of 10–17% were observed. Ironically, these performance gains were not regarded as sufficient by management, who abandoned the trial of teams soon after the study was completed.

Other studies, however, provide less convincing evidence of the benefits of teams to organizations and their employees. As previously indicated, Staw and Epstein (2000) could find no evidence of economic benefits associated with the implementation of teams at the organizational level, although their uptake did seem to be linked to enhancement of the firm's external reputation. Osterman (2000) has questioned the "mutual benefits" associated with introducing teams. For example, he found that the presence of teams in 1992 was positively associated with lay-offs in the same organization in subsequent years. He also found that the adoption of teams was associated with decreases in average real wages for core staff in subsequent years, and to the employment of fewer managers and fewer temporary or contract staff. Hackman's (1990) collection of 33 case studies of teams in organizations appears to contain as many instances of problematic as of successful teams, and considerable variability in research findings regarding the consequences of work teams for productivity, work attitudes and employee behaviour has been consistently noted by reviewers (e.g. Goodman, Devadas & Griffiths-Hughson, 1988; Guzzo & Dickson, 1996).

Why might teams fail to deliver in line with earlier predictions? Several possible explanations arise. First, aspects of the social and technical context may be unsuited to the introduction of teams. Second, the design of the team structures may be deficient in some way. Third, ineffective internal processes may develop within the teams themselves. Finally, teams may be poorly supported by other aspects of the organisational context (Vallas, 2003). Each of these aspects are now discussed in greater detail.

CONTEXTS SUITABLE FOR TEAMS

In reviewing the evidence as to the effectiveness of teams, it should be remembered that teams form elements in larger organizational systems, interacting with other elements to influence effectiveness (Guzzo & Dickson, 1996). In addition, teams are frequently introduced along with other new work practices (Godard, 2001) and/or changes to other important influences on performance (e.g. selection and reward systems, new technology, quality management, etc.). However, it may be that there are some settings in which a team-based work design will be no more (or even less, because of potential process losses) effective than individual jobs, e.g. it seems logical to suggest that team-based work designs will only be more effective than individual job designs where (a) moderate levels of interdependence (task or goal) exist, and (b) employees have strong social needs. In some cases, it may be possible to create at least the perception of interdependence (e.g. by cross-training team members, or by providing performance feedback at the team level). However, in other cases, it may simply not be feasible (e.g. there is no natural interdependence at the level of the task or outcome, jobs are so specialized that cross-training is not possible, and team-level performance data is meaningless to team members). Similarly, giving self-management responsibilities to a team may have little effect on performance and member satisfaction where the predictability of the operating system (e.g. reliability of technology) is high, since the inherent requirement for exercising team decision-making discretion will also then be low. Each of these aspects is now discussed in more detail.

Technological Interdependence

The interdependence of tasks within a team may be seen as a fairly stable structural property of the technological system contained within the team boundaries (Thompson, 1967). This is not to say that this is the only source of task interdependence or that it is independent of managerial control (see later section on team design variables), but it is one that exerts considerable control over the way in which employees are required to interact and behave. For example, the process of refining alumina is a continuous unbuffered process, where employees performing tasks at various points in the process are directly and immediately affected by the actions of employees at other points in the sequence. To effectively perform their task of controlling the refinery operations, process operators must continually liaise over their actions. Wageman (1995) also points out that some tasks defined by the technical system may require very little interaction with others, whilst others are very interdependent, meaning that required interdependence may vary across time and tasks for the one team. In general, however, the higher the degree of task interdependence arising out of the technical system, the more likely it is that collaborative teams will offer performance advantages over employees performing alone.

Operational Uncertainty

Operational uncertainty may be defined as "a lack of knowledge about production require-ments, of when problems will be met and how best to deal with them (Wall, Cordery & Clegg, 2002, p. 159). Whatever its source (it may, for example, arise as a result of interde-pendencies between team members), it manifests itself as variability and unpredictability in work tasks and requirements. It may be argued that the coordination and control benefits of team-based work identified earlier are likely to be most readily observed in such con-texts, where the need for responsive control and coordination is intrinsically greater and the requirement for innovative decisions higher. A study by Cordery, Wright and Wall (1997) il-lustrates this. They investigated the effects of the introduction of self-managing work teams into a production environment concerned with the treatment of waste water prior to release into ocean and river systems. They found that where teams faced greater unpredictability associated with the process (e.g. as a consequence of using unstable biological processes to treat effluent, rather than stable mechanical processes), the reductions in the levels of pollutants in treated waste water were significantly greater. Teams in the high-uncertainty environments were able to make use of their autonomy and collective problem-solving power to effect greater improvements than those in low-uncertainty environments.

Cultural Values

It has been suggested that team-based work is likely to be less appropriate within certain cul-tures, specifically those where individualistic cultural values (Hofstede, 1980) predominate (Kirkman & Shapiro, 1997; Lemons, 1997; Tata, 2000). Clegg *et al.* (2002) found that significant cross-national differences existed in the perceived effectiveness of team-based work. It has also been found that people from countries where individualistic values predominate will tend to resist team working (Kirkman, Jones & Shapiro, 2000; Kirkman & Shapiro, 1997), and will be less influenced by group-focused training (Earley, 1994) than those from societies characterized by more collectivistic values. In a laboratory study of US and Hong Kong students, Gibson (1999) found that the impact of group efficacy (a team's belief in its capabilities) was related to features of the task (uncertainty and interdependence) and to cultural characteristics (collectivism). Where members of a team possessed low levels of collectivistic values and worked independently on uncertain tasks, no relationship was found between group efficacy and performance. Rather, the efficacy–performance relationship was maximized where collectivism and interdependence were high and task uncertainty was low.

DESIGNING A HIGH-PERFORMANCE TEAM

In general, and given a favourable context for their introduction, it is possible to identify three main variables associated with the creation of high-performing teams: team task characteristics, team composition and interdependence. These are usefully termed "team design variables", reflecting the fact that they can be engineered into the structural fabric of the team.

Team Task Characteristics

The motivational potential of the group task is the first major determinant of the level of effectiveness demonstrated by any given work team. Campion *et al.* (1993) examined the relationship between job design characteristics known to be influential in motivating task performance at the individual job level (Hackman & Oldham, 1976), particularly self-management (autonomy) and participation in decision making, and team effectiveness. Their study, which involved 80 financial services teams from the same organization, found that autonomy and self-management were amongst the most powerful predictors of team effectiveness, assessed in terms of productivity (in this case, unfinished work), employee job satisfaction, and managerial ratings of team effectiveness. Their findings are broadly consistent with other team-level research into factors that differentiate between effective and ineffective teams (Campion, Papper & Medsker, 1996; Hyatt & Ruddy, 1997). The concept of team empowerment (Kirkman & Rosen, 1999, 2000) views such task characteristics (along with group potency—see later discussion) as a powerful source of performance motivation for the team as a whole. Although there are inconsistencies in the observed strength of the autonomy–team performance relationship across studies (Cohen & Bailey, 1997; Godard, 2001; Guzzo & Dickson, 1996), as has already been observed, these most probably derive from differences in the level of operating uncertainty across different task environments. Where system variability and unpredictability is moderate to high, then it can reasonably be assumed that empowering task characteristics will be translated into increased motivation and performance by team members.

Team Composition

As would be expected, studies have demonstrated a positive relationship between team performance and constituent member abilities (Bottger & Yetton, 1987; Cohen, Ledford &

Spreitzer, 1996; Hill, 1982; Tannenbaum, Salas & Cannon-Bowers, 1996). Researchers have also recently begun to identify a range of specific knowledge skills and abilities (KSAs) associated with effective team working (Druskat & Kayes, 1999; Stevens & Campion, 1994). Stevens and Campion (1994) proposed that effective teamwork requires five broad clusters of KSAs, namely conflict resolution, collaborative problem-solving, communication, goal setting and performance management, and planning and task coordination KSAs. Is it possible, then, to select people for effective teamworking? In a recent validation study, the same authors (Stevens & Campion, 1999) developed a pencil and paper test for identifying these KSAs. Combined results from two studies generated criterion-related validities for the test of between 0.32 and 0.40 for various aspects of team performance. Interestingly, the test correlated very highly with a battery of traditional employment aptitude tests, suggesting that the ability to work in teams is strongly related to general mental ability (g). Given the fact that teams are frequently implemented as responses to complex and uncertain task environments (Cummings & Blumberg, 1987), the finding that ability to operate effectively in teams is strongly linked to g (with its known relationship with the ability to deal with novel situations) comes as no real surprise (Barrick, Stewart, Neubert & Mount, 1998).

The personality of team members has also been linked to team effectiveness, within the framework of the "big five" model of personality (Barrick & Mount, 1991). The composition of a team in terms of average levels of agreeableness, conscientiousness, extraversion and emotional stability has been linked to predict team effectiveness in a number of recent studies (Barrick *et al.*, 1998; Neuman & Wright, 1999). A more differentiated perspective on team personality composition has been provided by Neuman, Wagner and Christiansen (1999), who distinguish between the average level of a given personality trait within a group and the diversity of personality traits within a team. They studied teams of retail assistants, and found that the average levels of agreeableness, conscientiousness and openness to experience within a team was strongly predictive of team performance. However, heterogeneity of team personality traits was favoured when it came to predicting a positive relationship between extroversion and emotional stability and performance. In other words, too many extroverts or neurotics in a team will diminish effectiveness. What is striking about this study's findings is that, taken together, the indices of personality strength and personality diversity at the team level predicted nearly half the variance in team performance across the 82 work teams. As a well-known captain of a national sports team once put it, "seen from a distance, a successful team may look well organised and cohesive; get closer up and you see . . . the vigour and rivalries of a group of strong personalities" (Brearly, 2000, p. 1141). Reinforcing the importance of team personality composition, Neuman and Wright (1999) found that aggregate team-level agreeableness and conscientiousness predicted a range of team performance measures for human resource work teams, whilst agreeableness also predicted team interpersonal skills.

The size of a team is also a factor that has to be considered. Empirical research has failed to provide a clear-cut answer to the question of ideal team size, as a range of empirical findings attest (Cohen & Bailey, 1997). On the one hand, increasing the numbers of members in a team increases the range of resources available to the team. On the other, one might expect that group "process losses", such as arise from imperfect communication and conflict, would be magnified in large vs. small groups, leading to an inverted curvilinear relationship between size and performance (Steiner, 1972). Generally speaking, conventional wisdom suggests that the ideal team size depends on the nature of the task and the effectiveness of group processes (Wageman, 1997). Stewart's (2000) meta-analytic study reported that team size had a small negative influence on team member satisfaction and a small positive influence on team performance.

Another perspective on team composition considers the "fit" between the components of team membership. As Newman *et al.*'s (1999) study of personalities within teams suggests, the degree of balance amongst elements of team composition may facilitate or constrain effectiveness. One of the most researched aspects of team composition relates to team heterogeneity/homogeneity. Guzzo and Dickson (1996) concluded that the relationship between team heterogeneity (in terms of the diversity of personalities, ability, gender, age, etc.) and effectiveness is "a complicated matter", with the relationship dependent on the particular focus of diversity, and with the potential interactions with other group composition variables, such as team size. Williams and O'Reilly (1998) have attempted to summarize the extensive research relating demographic diversity to group performance. Somewhat surprisingly, they concluded "that at the micro level, increased diversity typically has negative effects on the ability of the group to meet its members' needs and to function effectively over time" (p. 116). Interestingly, only functional diversity was found to be positively related to both performance and satisfaction across a range of studies (see also Randel & Jaussi, 2003).

Interdependence

As discussed earlier, task interdependence may be regarded as an inherent property of the task environment, requisite levels of which determine the need for teams in the first place. Some work processes may be regarded as inherently more interdependent than others, such that their effective control necessitates collective action. However, task interdependence can also be seen as a manipulable design feature of teams, something that arises from managerial decisions about how employees are grouped, from instructions given to employees about how to carry out their tasks, and which is reflected in the characteristic way people behave in performing their work (Wageman, 1995). For example, instead of grouping employees performing a single function together (e.g. packing, on an assembly line), teams may be formed around the complete set of functions required to manufacture a given product. Employees in a financial services team may be required to rotate through a number of positions within the team, and to check each other's work.

Other forms of interdependence can be "designed" into the team environment. Campion *et al.* (1993) refers to two such forms of interdependence as goal interdependence and interdependent feedback and rewards. Goal interdependence is the degree to which a team shares a clear engaging direction, a common sense of purpose (Wageman, 1997). As noted by Campion *et al.* (1993), the evidence relating group goals to effectiveness is less firm than it is at the individual level—nevertheless, studies do show that such a relationship exists (Hollensbe & Guthrie, 2000; O'Leary-Kelly, Martocchio & Frink, 1994; Sawyer, Latham, Pritchard & Bennett, 1999). Interdependence of feedback and rewards refers to the extent to which team members are dependent on each other for either (a) information on their own task performance or (b) receipt of rewards. Campion *et al.* (1993) found that interdependent feedback and rewards (also termed outcome interdependence) was significantly related to levels of employee job satisfaction within teams. Wageman's (1995) study of service technicians found that task and outcome interdependence each influenced different aspects of team effectiveness, with the former influencing cooperation amongst team members, whilst the latter influenced task motivation. Wageman's study helps confirm the primary role played by both task and outcome interdependence in determining teams effectiveness. She concluded that "The pivot, then, is how the work is structured . . . whenever cooperative behavior is critical to excellent task performance, it is most essential to create real task interdependence and then support the task design with interdependent rewards" (1995, p. 173).

EFFECTIVE WITHIN-TEAM PROCESSES

Interactions between team members have received a good deal of attention in the teams literature and studies have shown that intra-team processes (e.g. conflict, collaboration, communication, patterns of influence, decision-making, cohesiveness and potency) strongly influence both team performance and member satisfaction (Campion *et al.*, 1993, 1996; Guzzo & Dickson, 1996; Stewart, 2000). However, it is important to recognise that it is not the presence or absence of processes such as conflict or communication in teams that determines team effectiveness. Cohesiveness (the level of interpersonal attraction and liking) in a group may facilitate performance (Mullen & Cooper, 1994), or it may lead to the development of dysfunctional outcomes, such as groupthink (Esser, 1998; Janis, 1982; McCauley, 1989), social loafing (Shepperd & Taylor, 1999), risky shift (Friedkin, 1999; Isenberg, 1986; Whyte, 1998) or encourage the development of inappropriate norms (Barker, 1993).

As a consequence, researchers have been urged to develop more fine-grained models of the sorts of process configurations associated with high levels of team performance and member satisfaction (Goodman, Ravlin & Schminke, 1987). A number of such prescriptions exist (e.g. Hackman, 1987; Katzenbach & Smith, 1993; Wageman, 1997). In this vein, Wright, Barker and Cordery (2003) contend that the ideal set of internal conditions to promote team effectiveness is approached when:

1. *Team members share responsibility and leadership, and are adaptable and flexible in task execution.* Campion *et al.*'s (1993) study found that participation in decision-making at the team level was consistently related to team effectiveness. Such participation is encouraged when leadership is decentralized and where it is allowed to emerge naturally, in the absence of formally assigned leadership roles. Recently, Taggar, Hackett and Saha (1999) found that teams performed best when leadership behaviours were exhibited by *all* team members, and that leadership emergence within a team was related to the general cognitive ability and personality characteristics of individual team members. Research by Cannon-Bowers, Salas, Blickensderfer and Bowers (1998) and Kirkman and Rosen (1999) confirms the value of flexible cross-skilling within teams. The ability of team members to communicate effectively, to empathize with others, and to respond to shifting task demands is likely to be enhanced where members of the team have a flexible orientation to who does what and when.

2. *The team as whole has clear goals and objectives and systems of control to maintain discipline in achieving those goals and objectives.* It flows from the earlier discussion of goal interdependence that teams who develop processes for setting clear and difficult collective goals for their performance are likely to expend more effort, persist longer in pursuit of that goal, and achieve higher levels of performance than groups without goals. However, it is also that case that teams need to develop internal processes to

regulate behaviours in pursuit if those goals. Barker (1993, 1999) has observed that teams frequently develop powerful values-driven normative rules for behaviour within the team, designed to ensure that all members work towards the common goal. Linked to goal-setting processes within teams is the development of collective efficacy beliefs. Collective or group efficacy refers to the aggregate belief of team members that their team can be effective in performing their overall job (Gibson, 1999; Lindsley, Brass & Thomas, 1995; Little & Madigan, 1997; Prussia & Kinicki, 1996). Sometimes this construct is referred to as group potency (Guzzo, Yost, Campbell & Shea, 1993), and it is considered a core element in the psychological empowerment of teams (Kirkman & Rosen, 2000). Little and Madigan (1997) studied the performance of self-managing work teams in a manufacturing setting and found that the strength of collective efficacy beliefs accounted for significant differences in performance between teams. Campion *et al.* (1993) found that potency was the strongest correlate of team effectiveness.

3. *The team has a sharing and supportive environment, promoting openness and trust.* One of the reasons why teams may be more effective is that their members develop an internal climate characterized by greater willingness to trust and support one another, along with a stronger sense of collective pride and commitment to the task (Wright *et al.*, 2003). Interpersonal trust may be defined as a "willingness to be vulnerable to the actions of another party, based on the expectation that the other will perform a particular action important to the trustor, irrespective of the ability to monitor or control the other party" (Mayer, Davis & Schoorman, 1995, p. 712). Effectively, trust between team members amounts to an acceptance of the risk that comes with interdependence, the risk of others impacting negatively on one's work. Team members with a low level of trust in others (either as a result of earlier bad experiences, or because they have this predisposition) are likely to try to limit their dependence on other team members, resisting changes which might increase their reliance on other team members (Bigley & Pearce, 1998; Zand, 1972). Trust within teams is also related to team composition. For example, Mayer *et al.*'s (1995) model specifies a number of antecedents of trustworthiness, which include the benevolence, integrity and competence of the trustee, and the trustor's propensity to trust. The distinction between ability and both benevolence and integrity suggests that it is possible to like other team members, but not to be willing to put one's faith in their technical competence. Recent research on interpersonal trust in work teams has established that trust acts to moderate the influence of motivation on team performance, channelling motivational energy into productive group processes (Dirks, 1999). Trust has also been linked to spontaneous sociability (Fukuyama, 1995); "the myriad forms of cooperative, altruistic, and extra-role behavior in which members of a social community engage, that enhance collective well-being and further the attainment of collective goals" (Kramer, 1999, p. 583).

Related to the existence of trust in teams is the existence of positive environment characterized by openness among group members. Edmondson (1999) defined "team psychological safety" as the existence of "a shared belief that the team is safe for interpersonal risk taking" (p. 354). Similarly, West (1990) used the term "participative safety" to refer to an environment that is supportive of individuals and their contributions, such that group members feel able to participate fully in the team's affairs without fear of sanction or ridicule. West (1990) saw this particular aspect of group functioning as central to unlocking the potential of teams to generate creative and innovative solutions to problems. Edmondson's (1999) study of manufacturing teams suggests that cohesive teams that develop such shared beliefs are more likely to exhibit learning behaviours designed to improve team performance.

4. *There are systems in place to manage group knowledge, whether formal or informal.* A recent development in the study of intra-team processes has involved the study of how knowledge is accumulated, stored and accessed by teams as they perform their work. These systems for knowledge management, commonly called "team mental models", may relate to shared knowledge concerning the operation of technology and equipment, about the best way to approach a task, about team roles and responsibilities and characteristic ways of interacting, and about the personal attributes of team members (Mathieu, Heffner, Goodwin, Salas & Cannon-Bowers, 2000). Mathieu *et al.* (2000) used flight-combat simulations to demonstrate that as mental models regarding the task and other team members converged, team process improved, and so did performance. They concluded that the "knowledge organization—and the relationship among the ways various team members organize their own task knowledge—is a crucial concept" (p. 280). Recently, Stout, Cannon-Bowers, Salas and Milanovich (1999) were able to demonstrate that pre-performance planning activities carried out by a team assisted the formation of shared mental models, which in turn led to more efficient communication and improved coordination during task performance. A related approach to describing knowledge structures in teams involves the study of transactive memory systems (Wegner, 1987). A transactive memory system (TMS) is defined as "a set of individual memory systems in combination with the communication that takes place between individuals" (Wegner, Guiliano & Hertal, 1985: 186). By means of a TMS, individuals supplement their own cognitive capacity by using other team members as units for storing knowledge. Studies have indicated that the existence of TMS within work groups is associated with improved group performance (Austin, 2003; Moreland & Myakovsky, 2000).

5. *The team and its members have a proactive and innovative orientation.* The way a group frames its task is important in ensuring that team processes develop along constructive lines, for example, Alper, Tjosvold and Law (1998) and Tjosvold and Tjosvold (1994) discuss the significance of constructive controversy, "the open-minded discussion of opposing positions" (Alper *et al.*, 1998, p. 36), to the development of group potency or efficacy, and thereby to team effectiveness. Thus, although too much intra-group conflict can hinder team effectiveness, conflict that is regulated through constructive norms relating to problem solving can give rise to beneficial outcomes. West (1996) has further proposed that the success of teams will be dependent on the extent to which they are "reflexive", i.e. they analyse and reflect on their objectives, processes, performance and environment and adapt their internal operations accordingly (Schippers, Den Hartog, Koopman & Wienk, 2003). According to West, Borrill and Unsworth (1998, p. 8), reflexive teams are likely to "have a more comprehensive and penetrating intellectual representation of their work; a longer time-frame; a larger inventory of environmental cues to which they respond; a better knowledge and anticipation of errors; and a more active orientation towards their work".

Finally, Kirkman and Rosen (1999) found that empowerment in teams was associated with members having a more proactive orientation to their work which, in turn, was strongly related to measures of performance effectiveness. Similarly, Wall *et al.* (2002) have suggested that empowerment practices (such as high-performance work teams) provide opportunities for both the improved application of knowledge and the development of new knowledge, alongside a more proactive employee orientation (Parker, Wall & Jackson, 1997) and improved work performance (Lawler, 1992).

A final point to note in relation to effective intra-team processes: it should be noted that some team process variables have strong relationships with some input variables, including team autonomy and individual characteristics (Stewart, 2000), indicating that it may be possible to some extent to enhance intra-team process by manipulating team design variables. For example, enhanced autonomy may encourage proactivity, potency and innovation. Similarly, the composition of the group (diversity) would also influence internal group functioning.

SUPPORTING HIGH-PERFORMANCE WORK TEAMS

Once operational, a number of key organizational supports appear necessary to maintain the operation of teams at a high level of effectiveness. Broadly speaking, these relate to the availability of requisite material resources, rewards, information, and training (Hackman, 1987; Hyatt & Ruddy, 1997). Major determinants of such supports are human resource management policies and practices within the firm; for example, Kirkman and Rosen (1999) found that levels of team empowerment were positively related to the extent that the team was permitted to select new members, were rewarded as a team (rather than as individuals), were cross-trained to do different jobs, and evaluated the performance of their own team members. Campion *et al.* (1993) also found that access to training was significantly related to managerial judgements of a team's effectiveness. The importance of cross-training within teams, where members are trained to be able to take on the tasks, roles and responsibilities of their colleagues, has received particular attention from Cannon-Bowers, Tannenbaum, Salas and Volpe (1995) and Cannon-Bowers *et al.* (1998). Cross-training may improve team functioning by facilitating the development of interpositional knowledge, which helps in coordination and communication within teams, particularly under conditions of high workload (Cannon-Bowers *et al.*, 1998). Stevens and Campion's (1999) study suggests that the use of selection criteria that emphasise knowledge, skills and abilities relevant to working in teams will also help support team effectiveness.

Most studies investigating the influence of these elements of organizational context on team performance have focused on the role of leaders as sources of support for effective team functioning. External team leaders (i.e. first-line supervisors, managers) can influence team effectiveness in a number of ways. First, they act as agents through which the human resource policies and practices discussed above are operationalized at the team level; for example, one supervisor might allow team members more opportunities to attend cross-training sessions than another. Second, they have the potential to act as gatekeepers, controlling the flow of informational and material resources to the work team. Leader–member exchange theory (Graen & Uhl-Bien, 1995) suggests that leaders classify subordinates as ingroup or outgroup members, and favour ingroup members when it comes to the administration of rewards (e.g. praise and recognition). Third, external team leaders ration discretion, or team autonomy. Thus, different teams may be permitted different levels of discretion by the one supervisor, or the level of direct control over team-level decisions exerted by a supervisor may vary across time (e.g. depending on production pressure). It has been pointed out that the propensity of a supervisor to allow discretion at the team level may well reflect that manager's characteristic leadership style (Cordery & Wall, 1985). The propensity for external leader intervention to reduce the key design element autonomy at the team level has led some to suggest that teams perform best without formal leadership (e.g. Beekun, 1989).

Fourth, the style of leader may be related to key intra-group processes, such as the development of a sense of potency. In this light, Manz and Sims (1987) identified six features of effective leadership of self-managing work teams, namely to encourage the following amongst team members: self-observation/self-evaluation; self-goal setting; self-reinforcement; self-criticism; self-expectation; and self-rehearsal Cohen, Chang and Ledford (1997) used the Self-Management Leadership Questionnaire (SMLQ) developed by Manz and Sims (1987) and were able to empirically confirm their model. Interestingly, they found only modest relationships between self-managing leader behaviours and both employee quality of work life indicators and self-rated team effectiveness. More worrying is the finding of Spreitzer, Cohen and Ledford (1999) that those teams whose leaders were perceived by team members as doing most to encourage self-management (assessed in terms of Manz and Sims' dimensions) were rated as performing worst by senior managers.

A reason for the apparently contradictory findings is provided by Wageman (1997). She has argued that the primary responsibility of a team leader is to see that the team is designed right, with a clear sense of why it exists and what it is trying to achieve, and with access to organisational supports (e.g. information, resources, etc.). Once that has occurred (and only then, she argues), the conditions are right for the leader to focus on coaching the team. Positive coaching behaviours include helping the team deal with interpersonal problems, providing feedback and reinforcement related to how effectively the team is managing its own activities, and facilitating problem-solving. Possibly because of the proposed contingency relationship with team design factors, research into the effectiveness of team coaching behaviours has produced mixed results. Thus, Druskat and Kayes (1999) found that external leadership behaviours that provided "clear and engaging direction" for the team were associated with the development of team self-management competencies; however, those that focused on more direct "coaching" of team performance were negatively associated with performance (see also Druskat & Wheeler, 2003).

In another indication of the important role played by external team leadership in developing and maintaining effective teams, Stewart and Manz (1997) have suggested that teams frequently fail because supervisors resist their implementation and empowerment. They use the theory of reasoned action (Fishbein & Ajzen, 1975) to demonstrate that supervisory attitudes (e.g. empowering teams will reduce my job security; employees will take advantage of increased discretion to slack off; employees are not capable of effective self-management) and subjective norms (e.g. other supervisors do not support team empowerment) may act to impede effective team development by supervisors (see also Batt, 2004).

THE FUTURE FOR TEAMS

In this chapter, I have outlined the factors both within and outside teams that contribute to their internal effectiveness, and which make them a popular intervention with managers seeking to maximize the performance of work systems. The evidence suggests that, even though they sometimes fail (Hackman, 1990), they can be made to work well under the right conditions and with appropriate organizational support.

There seems to be no reason to suggest that the existing popularity of teams in organizations will decline in future. However, it appears that the focus and purpose of teams is shifting once more. The combined influence of e-commerce and globalization is shifting the focus of teamwork away from physically co-located, fairly permanent work teams towards an emphasis on far more transient team structures, where interdependence is mediated via information technology, and where functioning work teams cross organizational and even national boundaries (Cascio, 2000; Kirkman, Rosen, Gibson, Tesluk & McPherson, 2002). We are also seeing transformations in the nature of work in many countries, whereby service and knowledge work is on the increase relative to manufacturing (Parker, Wall & Cordery, 2001). Developing and maintaining effective intra-team processes in teams whose membership is distributed and whose work processes are largely cognitive, centring on the development and transformation of knowledge, poses a particular challenge for managers.

There are also challenges for future research. Perhaps the most pressing is the need to develop more precise and dynamic models of how teams function. Our current input–process–output models of team effectiveness (e.g. Cohen & Bailey, 1997; Hackman, 1987; Sundstrom, DeMeuse & Futrell, 1990) say little about the mechanisms used by teams to transform inputs into outcomes. For example, much of the previous research into team effectiveness has been framed around motivational explanations of team performance (e.g. job characteristics and empowerment theories). Yet, we also know that cognitive processes may explain some of the same transformations. Increasing team autonomy may improve collective motivation, but it may also enable learning and knowledge-based action in furtherance of improved task performance (Parker *et al.*, 2001). Interdependence may make more likely the development of transactive memory systems, leading to efficiencies in the storage and retrieval of performance-relevant knowledge. Furthermore, whilst we have a fair idea which processes are influential in team effectiveness, we still know surprisingly little about their significance, both at varying stages in task performance and for different dimensions of effectiveness (Weldon, 2000). In this respect, Marks, Mathieu and Zaccaro's (2001) conceptual model of how intra-team processes may vary over time would seem to provide a fruitful starting point for advancing our knowledge.

A second area of pressing need for research has to do with how teams perform in different contexts, particularly across different types of work. For example, some research has suggested that teams are less common (or are designed differently) in service organizations compared to manufacturing (Osterman, 1994). It is not very clear why this might be. One reason that has been suggested lies in the nature of the service task, particularly where the product is "co-produced" by employee and customer and workloads and flows are customer-driven (Hunter, 1998). Given the growth in service sector jobs over recent decades, this issue needs further investigation. Furthermore, Cohen and Bailey (1997) clearly demonstrated the value of distinguishing between teams with different strategic purposes when it comes to understanding effective team design, yet the value of having generic vs. context-specific models of team effectiveness is little understood. Finally, the issue of how effective design and processes differ between traditional physically co-acting teams and distributed computer-mediated teams must be addressed as these forms of teamwork become more common.

REFERENCES

Alper, S., Tjosvold, D. & Law, K. (1998). Interdependence and controversy in group decision making: antecedents to effective self-managing teams. *Organizational Behavior and Human Decision Processes*, **74**, 33–52.

Austin, J. R. (2003). Transactive memory in organizational groups: the effects of content, consensus, specialization, and accuracy on group performance. *Journal of Applied Psychology*, **88**, 866–878.

Banker, R. D., Field, J. M., Schroeder, R. G. & Sinha, K. K. (1996). Impact of work teams on manufacturing performance: a longitudinal field study. *Academy of Management Journal*, **39**, 867–890.

Barker, J. R. (1993). Tightening the iron cage: concertive control in self-managing teams. *Administrative Science Quarterly*, **38**, 408–437.

Barker, J. R. (1999). *The Discipline of Teamwork: Participation and Concertive Control*. Newbury Park, CA: Sage.

Barrick, M. R. & Mount, M. K. (1991). The Big Five personality dimensions and job performance: a meta-analysis. *Personnel Psychology*, **44**, 1–26.

Barrick, M. R., Stewart, G. L., Neubert, M. J. & Mount, M. K. (1998). Relating member ability and personality to work-team processes and team effectiveness. *Journal of Applied Psychology*, **83**, 377–391.

Batt, R. (1999). Work organization, technology and performance in customer service and sales. *Industrial and Labor Relations Review*, **52**, 539–564.

Batt, R. (2004). Who benefits from teams? Comparing workers, supervisors, and managers. *Industrial Relations*, **43**, 183–212.

Beekun, R. I. (1989). Assessing the effectiveness of sociotechnical interventions: antidote or fad? *Human Relations*, **47**, 877–897.

Bigley, G. A. & Pearce, J. L. (1998). Straining for shared meaning in organization science: problems of trust and distrust. *Academy of Management Review*, **23**, 405–421.

Bottger, P. C. & Yetton, P. W. (1987). Improving group performance by training in individual problem solving. *Journal of Applied Psychology*, **72**, 651–657.

Brearly, M. (2000). Teams: lessons from the world of sport. *British Medical Journal*, **321**, 1141–1143.

Campion, M. A., Medsker, G. J. & Higgs, A. C. (1993). Relations between work group characteristics and effectiveness: implications for designing effective work groups. *Personnel Psychology*, **46**, 823–850.

Campion, M. A., Papper, E. M. & Medsker, G. J. (1996). Relations between work team characteristics and effectiveness: a replication and extension. *Personnel Psychology*, **49**, 429–452.

Cannon-Bowers, J. A., Tannenbaum, S. I., Salas, E. & Volpe, C. E. (1995). Defining team competencies and establishing team training requirements. In R. A. Guzzo & E. Salas (Eds), *Team Effectiveness and Decision Making in Organizations* (pp. 333–380). San Francisco, CA: Jossey-Bass.

Cannon-Bowers, J. A., Salas, E., Blickensderfer, E. & Bowers, C. A. (1998). The impact of cross-training and workload on team functioning: a replication and extension of initial findings. *Human Factors*, **40**, 92.

Cascio, W. F. (2000). Managing a virtual workplace. *Academy of Management Executive*, **13**, 81–90.

Church, A. H. (1996). From both sides now: the power of teamwork—fact or fiction? Society for Industrial and Organizational Psychology, Inc. Accessed online at http://siop.org/tip/backissues/tipoct96/church.htm

Clegg, C. W., Wall, T. D., Pepper, K., Stride, C., Woods, D., Morrison, D., Cordery, J., Couchman, P., Badham, R., Kuenzler, C., Grote, G., Ide, W., Takahashi, M. & Kogi, K. (2002). An international survey of the use and effectiveness of modern manufacturing practices. *Human Factors and Ergonomics in Manufacturing*, **12**(2), 171–191.

Cohen, S. G. & Bailey, D. E. (1997). What makes teams work: group effectiveness research from the shop floor to the executive suite. *Journal of Management*, **23**, 239–290.

Cohen, S. G. & Ledford, G. E. (1994). The effectiveness of self-managing teams: a quasi-experiment. *Human Relations*, **47**, 13–43.

Cohen, S. G., Ledford, G. E. & Spreitzer, G. M. (1996). A predictive model of self-managing work team effectiveness. *Human Relations*, **49**, 643–676.

Cohen, S. G., Chang, L. & Ledford, G. E. Jr (1997). A hierarchical construct of self-management leadership and its relationship to quality of work life and perceived group effectiveness. *Personnel Psychology*, **50**, 275–308.

Cordery, J. L. & Wall, T. D. (1985). Work design and supervisory practice: a model. *Human Relations*, **38**, 425–441.

Cordery, J. L., Wright, B. & Wall, T. D. (1997). Towards a more comprehensive and integrated approach to work design: production uncertainty and self-managing work-team performance. Paper presented at 12th Annual Conference of the Society for Industrial and Organisational Psychology, St. Louis, MO, April.

Cummings, T. G. (1978). Self-regulating work groups: a socio-technical synthesis. *Academy of Management Review*, **3**, 624–634.

Cummings, T. G. & Blumberg, M. (1987). Advanced manufacturing technology and work design. In T. D. Wall, C. W. Clegg & N. J. Kemp (Eds), *The Human Side of Advanced Manufacturing Technology* (pp. 37–60). New York: Wiley.

Dirks, K. T. (1999). The effects of interpersonal trust on work group performance. *Journal of Applied Psychology*, **84**, 445–455.

Druskat, V. U. & Kayes, D. C. (1999). The antecedents of team competence: toward a fine-grained model of self-managing team effectiveness. In M. A. Neale & E. A. Mannix (Series Eds) & R. Wageman (Vol. Ed.). Research on managing groups and teams: Context (Volume 2, pp. 201–231). Stanford, CT: JAI Press.

Druskat, V. U. & Wheeler, J. V. (2003). Managing from the boundary: the effective leadership of self-managing work teams. *Academy of Management Journal*, **46**, 435–457.

Earley, P. C. (1994). Self or group? Cultural effects of training on self efficacy and performance. *Administrative Science Quarterly*, **39**, 89–117.

Edmondson, A. (1999). Psychological safety and learning behavior in work teams. *Administrative Science Quarterly*, **44**, 350–383.

Esser, J. K. (1998). Alive and well after 25 years: a review of groupthink research. *Organizational Behavior and Human Decision Processes*, **73**, 116–141.

Fishbein, M. & Ajzen, I. (1975). *Belief, Attitude, Intention and Behavior: an Introduction to Theory and Research*. Reading, MA: Addison-Wesley.

Friedkin, N. E. (1999). Choice shift and group polarization. *American Sociological Review*, **64**, 856–875.

Fukuyama, F. (1995). *Trust: the Social Virtues and the Creation of Prosperity*. New York: Free Press.

Gibson, C. B. (1999). Do they do what they believe they can? Group efficacy and group effectiveness across tasks and cultures. *Academy of Management Journal*, **42**, 138–152.

Gittleman, M., Horrigan, M. & Joyce, M. (1998). 'Flexible' work practices: evidence from a nationally representative survey. *Industrial and Labor Relations Review*, **52**, 99–115.

Godard, J. (2001). High performance and the transformation of work? The implications of alternative work practices for the experience and outcomes of work. *Industrial and Labor Relations Review*, **54**, 776–805.

Goodman, P. S., Devadas, R. & Griffiths-Hughson, T. L. (1988). Groups and productivity: analyzing the effectiveness of self-managing teams. In J. P. Campbell & R. J. C. & Associates (Eds), *Productivity in Organisations* (pp. 295–327). San Francisco, CA: Jossey-Bass.

Goodman, P. S., Ravlin, E. & Schminke, M. (1987). Understanding groups in organizations. In B. M. Staw & L. L. Cummings (Eds), *Research in Organizational Behavior*, Vol. 9 (pp. 121–173). Greenwich, CT: JAI Press.

Graen G. B. & Uhl-Bien M. (1995). Development of leader–member exchange (LMX) theory of leadership over 25 years: applying a multi-level multi-domain perspective. *Leadership Quarterly*, **6**, 219–247.

Guzzo, R. A., Yost, P. R., Campbell, R. J. & Shea, G. P. (1993). Potency in groups: articulating a construct. *British Journal of Social Psychology*, **32**, 87–106.

Guzzo, R. A. & Dickson, M. W. (1996). Teams in organizations: recent research on performance and effectiveness. *Annual Review of Psychology*, **47**, 307–338.

Hackman, J. R. (1987). The design of effective work teams. In J. W. Lorsch (Ed.), *Handbook of Organizational Behavior* (pp. 316–341). Englewood Cliffs, NJ: Prentice-Hall.

Hackman, J. R. (Ed.) (1990). *Groups that Work (and Those that Don't)*. San Francisco, CA: Jossey-Bass.

Hackman, J. R. & Oldham, G. R. (1976). Motivation through the design of work: test of a theory. *Organisational Behavior and Human Performance*, **15**, 250–279.

Hackman, J. R. & Oldham, G. R. (1980). *Work Redesign*. Reading, MA: Addison-Wesley.

Hill, G. W. (1982). Group vs. individual performance: are $n + 1$ heads better than one? *Psychological Bulletin*, **91**, 517–539.

Hofstede, G. (1980). *Culture's Consequences: International Differences in Work-related Values*. Newbury Park, CA: Sage.

Hogg, M. A. & Terry, D. J. (2000). Social identity and self-categorization processes in organizational contexts. *Academy of Management Review*, **25**, 121–140.

Hollensbe, E. C. & Guthrie, J. P. (2000). Group pay-for-performance plans: the role of spontaneous goal setting. *Academy of Management Review*, **25**, 864–872.

Hunter, L. W. (1998). Services, high-involvement management, and strategic fit. Paper presented at 1988 meeting of the Academy of Management, San Diego, CA.

Hyatt, D. & Ruddy, T. M. (1997). An examination of the relationship between work group characteristics and performance: once more unto the breach. *Personnel Psychology*, 50: 553–585.

Ilgen, D. (1999). Teams embedded in organizations: some implications. *American Psychologist*, **54**, 129–139.

Isenberg, D. J. (1986). Group polarization: a critical review and meta-analysis. *Journal of Personality and Social Psychology*, **50**, 1141–1151.

Janis, I. L. (1982). Groupthink: a study of foreign policy decisions and fiascos (2nd Edn). Boston, MA: Houghton Mifflin.

Katzell, R. A. (1994). Contemporary meta-trends in industrial and organizational psychology. In H. C. Triandis, M. D. Dunnette & L. M. Hough (Eds), *Handbook of Industrial and Organizational Psychology*, Vol. 4 (pp. 1–93). Palo Alto, CA: Consulting Psychologists Press.

Katzenbach, J. R. & Smith, D. K. (1993). *The Wisdom of Teams: Creating the High Performance Organization*. Boston, MA: Harvard Business School Press.

Kirkman, B. L., Jones, R. G. & Shapiro, D. L. (2000). Why do employees resist teams? Examining the "resistance barrier" to work team effectiveness. *International Journal of Conflict Management*, **11**, 74–92.

Kirkman, B. L. & Shapiro, D. L. (1997). The impact of cultural values on employee resistance to teams: toward a model of self-managing work team effectiveness. *Academy of Management Review*, **22**, 730–737.

Kirkman, B. L. & Rosen, B. 1999. Beyond self-management: antecedents and consequences of team empowerment. *Academy of Management Journal*, **42**, 58–75.

Kirkman, B. L. & Rosen, B. (2000). Powering up teams. *Organizational Dynamics*, **28**, 48–66.

Kirkman, B. L., Rosen, B., Gibson, C. B., Tesluk, P. E. & McPherson, S. O. (2002). Five challenges to virtual team effectiveness. *Academy of Management Executive*, **16**, 67–79.

Kramer, R. M. (1999). Trust and distrust in organizations: emerging perspectives, enduring questions. *Annual Review of Psychology*, **50**, 569–588.

Lawler, E. E. III (1992). *The Ultimate Advantage: Creating the High Involvement Organisation*. San Francisco, CA: Jossey-Bass.

Lawler, E. E. III, Mohrman, S. A. & Ledford, G. E. (1995). *Employee Involvement and Total Quality Management: Practices and Results in Fortune 1000 Companies*. San Francisco, CA: Jossey-Bass.

Leavitt, H. J. (1975). Suppose we took groups seriously . . . In E. L. Cass & F. G. Zimmer (Eds), *Man, Work and Society*. New York: Van Nostrand Reinhold.

Lemons, M. A. (1997). Work groups or work teams? Cultural and psychological dimensions for their formation. In M. M. Beyerlein, D. A. Johnson & S. T. Beyerlein (Eds), *Advances in Interdisciplinary Studies of Work Teams*, Vol. 4 (pp. 97–113), Greenwich, CT: JAI Press.

Lindsley, D. H., Brass, D. J. & Thomas, J. B. (1995). Efficacy-performance spirals: a multilevel perspective. *Academy of Management Review*, **20**, 645–678.

Little, B. L. & Madigan, R. M. (1997). The relationship between collective efficacy and performance in manufacturing work teams. *Small Group Research*, **28**, 517–534.

McCauley, C. (1989). The nature of social influence in groupthink: compliance and internalization. *Journal of Personality and Social Psychology*, **57**, 250–260.

Majchrzak, A., Rice, R. E., Kink, N., Malhotra, A. & Ba, S. (2000). Computer-mediated interorganizational knowledge-sharing: insights from a virtual team innovating using a collaborative tool. *Information Resources Management Journal*, **13**, 44.

Manz, C. C. & Sims, H. P. Jr (1987). Leading workers to lead themselves: the external leadership of self-managing work teams. *Administrative Science Quarterly*, **32**, 106–128.

Marks, M. A., Mathieu, J. E. & Zaccaro, S. J. (2001). A temporally based framework and taxonomy of team processes. *Academy of Management Review*, **26**, 356–376.

Mathieu, J. E., Heffner, T. S., Goodwin, G. F., Salas, E. & Cannon-Bowers, J. A. (2000). The influence of shared mental models on team process and performance. *Journal of Applied Psychology*, **85**, 284–293.

Mayer, R. C., Davis, J. H. & Schoorman, F. D. (1995). An integrative model of organizational trust. *Academy of Management Review*, **20**(3), 709–734.

Mohrman, S. A., Cohen, S. G. & Mohrman, A. M. (1995). *Designing Team-based Organizations*. San Francisco, CA: Jossey-Bass.

Moreland, R. L. & Myaskovsky, L. (2000). Exploring the performance benefits of group training: transactive memory or improved communication? *Organizational Behavior and Human Decision Processes*, **82**, 117–133.

Mullen, B. & Cooper, C. (1994). The relation between group cohesiveness and performance: an integration. *Psychological Bulletin*, **115**, 210–227.

Neuman, G. A., Wagner, S. H. & Christiansen, N. D. (1999). The relationship between work-team personality composition and the job performance of teams. *Group and Organization Management*, **24**, 28–45.

Neuman, G. A. & Wright, J. (1999). Team effectiveness: beyond skills and cognitive ability. *Journal of Applied Psychology*, **84**, 376–389.

O'Leary-Kelly, A. M., Martocchio, J. J. & Frink, D. D. (1994). A review of the influence of group goals on group performance. *Academy of Management Review*, **37**, 1285–1302.

O'Reilly, C. A. & Pfeffer, J. (2000). *Hidden Value: How Great Companies Achieve Extraordinary Results with Ordinary People*. Boston, MA: Harvard Business School Press.

Osterman, P. (1994). How common is workplace transformation and who adopts it? *Industrial and Labor Relations Review*, **47**, 173–188.

Osterman, P. (2000). Work reorganization in an era of restructuring: trends in diffusion and effects on employee welfare. *Industrial and Labor Relations Review*, **53**, 179–196.

Parker, S. K., Wall, T. D. & Jackson, P. R. (1997). "That's not my job": developing flexible employee work orientations. *Academy of Management Journal*, **40**, 899–929.

Parker, S. K., Wall, T. D. & Cordery, J. L. (2001). Future work design research and practice: an elaborated work characteristics model. *Journal of Occupational and Organizational Psychology*, **73**, 414–440.

Paulus, P. (2000). Groups, teams, and creativity: the creative potential of idea-generating groups. *Applied Psychology: an International Review*, **49**, 237–262.

Pfeffer, J. (1998). *The Human Equation*. Boston, MA: Harvard Business School Press.

Prussia, G. E. & Kinicki, A. J. (1996). A motivational investigation of group effectiveness using social cognitive theory. *Journal of Applied Psychology*, **78**, 61–72.

Randel, A. E. & Jaussi, K. S. (2003). Functional background identity, diversity, and individual performance in cross-functional teams. *Academy of Management Journal*, **46**, 763–774.

Sawyer, J. E., Latham, W. R., Pritchard, R. D. & Bennett, W. R. (1999). Analysis of work group productivity in an applied setting: application of a time series panel design. *Personnel Psychology*, **52**, 927–967.

Schippers, M. C., Den Hartog, D. N., Koopman, P. L. & Wienk, J. A. (2003). Diversity and team outcomes: the moderating effects of outcome interdependence and group of longevity and the mediating effect of reflexivity. *Journal of Organizational Behavior*, **24**, 779–803.

Shepperd, J. A. & Taylor, K. M. (1999). Social loafing and expectancy-value theory. *Personality and Social Psychology Bulletin*, **25**, 1147–1158.

Spreitzer, G. M., Cohen, S. G. & Ledford, G. E. (1999). Developing effective self-managing work teams in service organizations. *Group and Organizational Management*, **24**, 340–366.

Staw, B. M. & Epstein, L. D. (2000). What bandwagons bring: effects of popular management techniques on corporate performance, reputation and CEO pay. *Administrative Science Quarterly*, **45**, 523–556.

Steiner, I. D. (1972). *Group Process and Productivity*. New York: Academic Press.

Stevens, M. J. & Campion, M. A. (1994). The knowledge, skill, and ability requirements for teamwork: implications for human resource management. *Journal of Management*, **20**, 503–530.

Stevens, M. J. & Campion, M. A. (1999). Staffing work teams: development and validation of a selection test for teamwork settings. *Journal of Management*, **25**, 207–228.

Stewart, G. L. (2000). Meta-analysis of work teams research published between 1977 and 1998. Paper presented at 2000 Academy of Management Conference, Organizational Behavior Division. Toronto.

Stewart, G. L. & Manz, C. C. (1997). Understanding and overcoming supervisor resistance during the transition to employee empowerment. In W. A. Pasmore & R. W. Woodman (Eds), *Research in Organizational Change and Development*, Vol. 10 (pp. 169–196). Greenwich, CT: JAI Press.

Stout, R. J., Cannon-Bowers, J. A., Salas, E. & Milanovich, D. M. (1999). Planning, shared mental models, and coordinated performance: an empirical link is established. *Human Factors*, **41**, 61.

Sundstrom, E., DeMeuse, K. P. & Futrell, D. (1990). Workteams: applications and effectiveness. *American Psychologist*, **45**, 120–133.

Taggar, S., Hackett, R. & Saha, S. (1999). Leadership emergence in autonomous work teams: antecedents and outcomes. *Personnel Psychology*, **52**, 899–926.

Tannenbaum, S. I., Salas, E. & Cannon-Bowers, J. A. (1996). Promoting team effectiveness. In M. A. West (Ed.), *Handbook of Work Group Psychology* (pp. 503–529). Chichester: Wiley.

Tata, J. (2000). The influence of national culture on work team autonomy. *International Journal of Management*, **17**, 266–271.

Thompson, J. D. (1967). *Organizations in Action*. New York: McGraw-Hill.

Tjosvold, D. & Tjosvld, M. M. (1994). Cooperation, competition, and constructive controversy: knowledge to empower self-managing teams. In M. M. Beyerlein & D. A. Johnson (Eds), *Advances in Interdisciplinary Studies of Work Teams*, Vol. 1 (pp. 119–144). Greenwich, CT: JAI Press.

Vallas, S. P. (2003). Why teamwork fails: obstacles to workplace change in four manufacturing plants. *American Sociological Review*, **68**, 223–250.

Wall, T. D., Cordery, J. L. & Clegg, C. W. (2002). Empowerment, performance and operational uncertainty: a theoretical integration. *Applied Psychology: An International Review*, **51**, 146–169.

Wageman, R. (1995). Interdependence and group effectiveness. *Administrative Science Quarterly*, **40**, 145–180.

Wageman, R. (1997). Critical success factors for creating superb self-managing teams. *Organizational Dynamics*, **26**, 37–49.

Wegner, D. M. (1987). Transactive memory: a contemporary analysis of the grown mind. In B. Mullin & G. R. Goethals (Eds), *Theories of Group Behavior* (pp. 185–208). New York: Springer-Verlag.

Wegner, D. M., Giuliano, T. & Hertel, P. (1985). Cognitive interdependence in close relationships. In W. J. Ickes (Ed.), *Compatible and Incompatible Relationships* (pp. 253–276). New York: Springer-Verlag.

Weldon, E. (2000). The development of product and process improvements in work groups. *Group and Organizational Management*, **25**, 244–268.

West, M. A. (1990). The social psychology of innovation in groups. In M. A. West & J. L. Farr (Eds), *Innovation and Creativity at Work* (pp. 309–333). Chichester: Wiley.

West, M. A. (1996). Reflexivity and work group effectiveness: a conceptual integration. In M. A. West (Ed.), *Handbook of Work Group Psychology* (pp. 555–579). Chichester: Wiley.

West, M. A., Borrill, C. S. & Unsworth, K. L. (1998). Team effectiveness in organizations. In C. L. Cooper & I. T. Robertson (Eds), *International Review of Industrial and Organizational Psychology*, Vol. 13 (pp. 1–48). Chichester: Wiley.

Whyte, G. (1998). Recasting Janis's groupthink model: the key role of collective efficacy in decision fiascoes. *Organizational Behavior and Human Decision Processes*, **2**, 185–209.

Williams, K. Y. & O'Reilly, C. A. (1998). Demography and diversity in organizations. *Research in Organizational Behavior*, **20**, 77–140.

Wright, B. M., Barker, J. & Cordery, J. L. (2003). The ideal participative state: a prelude to work group effectiveness. *Journal of Business and Management*, **9**, 171–188.

Zand, D. E. (1972). Trust and managerial problem solving. *Administrative Science Quarterly*, **17**, 229–239.

CHAPTER 7

Call Centres

David Holman

Institute of Work Psychology, University of Sheffield, UK

Call centres have rapidly become an established and significant part of the global economy. They are now present in all sectors, occur in almost all national economies, and employ 1–3% of the working population in the European Union, the USA and Australia. Call centres are also of growing importance in emerging economies such as India and Malaysia (ACA Research, 2001; Sprigg, Smith & Jackson, 2003; Taylor & Bain, 2003; TOSCA, 2002). The prevalence of call centres is largely attributable to the benefits that organisations accrue from using them, such as the ability to reduce the cost of existing functions (e.g. centralising back office functions in banks), to extend and improve customer service facilities (e.g. telephone banking) and to develop new avenues of revenue generation (e.g. exploiting customer databases for direct selling). But although call centres offer organisations a number of clear benefits, the benefits for those employed in them, particularly front-line staff, are less clear. Indeed, while some front-line staff enjoy call centre work, for many it is boring, demanding and stressful. It is these workplace experiences that are thought to contribute to the high levels of staff turnover in the call centre industry (Holman & Wood, 2002; IRS/CCA, 2002; Michel, 2001; TOSCA, 2002) and that have led some to label call centres as "electronic sweatshops" (Garson, 1988; Incomes Data Services, 1997; Metcalf & Fernie, 1998).

One of the central issues in the study of call centres has been how work organization and human resource management practices (HRM) affect employee stress and turnover. Other concerns relate to the nature of HRM practices in call centres and how these affect call centre performance. The aim of this chapter is to review research on these topics. To meet this aim, the chapter is split into the following sections. The first offers a brief and basic definition of a call centre. The second section outlines most important features of call centres, while the third section focuses on how these features affect the experiences of front-line staff, particularly their well-being. Research on employee and call centre performance is then examined, followed by some concluding comments.

DEFINING CALL CENTRES

A call centre is a work environment in which the main business is mediated by computer and telephone-based technologies that enable the efficient distribution of incoming calls (or

The Essentials *of the New Workplace. A Guide to the Human Impact of Modern Working Practices.*
Edited by David Holman, Toby D. Wall, Chris W. Clegg, Paul Sparrow and Ann Howard. © 2005 John Wiley & Sons, Ltd.

allocation of outgoing calls) to available staff, and permit customer-employee interaction to occur simultaneously with the use of display screen equipment and the instant access to, and inputting of, information. It includes parts of companies dedicated to this activity, as well whole companies that specialise in such services (Smith & Sprigg, 2001; Waters, 1998).

This definition helps to distinguish a call centre from other working environments and highlights two distinctive features, the nature of call centre technology and the fact that customer–employee interaction is mediated by technology, particularly the telephone. However, the focus on technology tends to ignore other important though not unique call centre features, such as performance monitoring, work and job design, and HRM practices. The following section is devoted to a full exploration of these in order to delineate the distinctive and significant features of call centres.

FEATURES OF CALL CENTRES

Call Centre Technologies

Information and computer technologies are central to call centres and much of the debate among practitioners is on the technological possibilities afforded by, for example, automatic call distribution systems, interactive voice recognition or web enablement/joint browsing. Discussion often focuses on the extent to which these technologies can aid efficiency, cut costs, improve customer service and increase revenue. However, while technical systems play an important role in call centres, of equal importance are the social systems of a call centre, for example the work organisation and HRM practices. As such, the interest here is not on the details of call centre technology *per se*, but on the relationship between the technological and social practices in call centres. In other words, our interest is in call centres as socio-technical systems (Cherns, 1987).

A good starting point when examining this socio-technical relationship is to consider how one aspect of a social system, the stakeholders who are involved in the design and implementation of call centre technology, can affect the final form of that technology (Clark, McLoughlin, Rose & King, 1998; Orlinowski, 1992). Boddy (2000) described how, during the development of a call centre, management used the possibilities of the IT system by opting to introduce an individualised electronic monitoring and reporting system. They chose to do this in order to further their aim of achieving greater control over the work process. The interests of management, together with the capability of the technology, shaped the IT system's final form. Other case studies reveal how a cost minimisation strategy can shape call centre technology. One way of cutting costs is to employ cheaper, less skilled staff, a particularly attractive option in service industries where labour can account for up to 60% of total costs (Batt, 2000). However, to employ less skilled staff, work must be broken down into small, simple tasks (Callaghan & Thompson, 2001; Knights & McCabe, 1998; Taylor & Bain, 1999; for an example of task standardisation in professional work see Collin-Jacques, 2004). These simple tasks then become embedded within technology in the form of scripts or formal procedures. In this way, technology has enduring effects on other aspects of the social system, such as job design and customer–employee interaction. Furthermore, as these factors affect employee well-being (see later), attention to them in the design process would seem imperative. Yet, beyond an increased recognition that the design of display screen equipment ergonomics can affect physical and psychological well-being (Vandevelde, 2001), there is little evidence that this occurs. Rather, the technologically-driven concerns of management, as well as a singular focus on cost minimisation, can shape technology in ways that produce deleterious effects on users' well-being and often, interestingly, on service quality (Brooke, 2002). Any opportunity for customer service representatives (CSRs) to shape a technology according to their needs that management may provide often arises only during the latter stages of implementation, when, of course, the scope for change is much restricted (Boddy, 2000).

Customer–Employee Interaction

Although a distinctive feature of customer–employee interaction in call centres is that it is mainly telephone-based (but can also be supplemented by face-to-face, letter or e-mail contact), the nature of the service interaction may not be radically different to that occurring in other types of organisation. This becomes apparent when Gutek's distinction between service interactions as "relationships" and "encounters" is employed (Gutek, 1995, 1997; and see Table 7.1). In a relationship the participants have a shared history and attempt to know each other as individuals and as role occupants. This shared history and mutual understanding can be drawn on to make the service efficient, effective and customised. In time, this can lead to the development of trust, loyalty and satisfaction for both parties (Chaudhuri & Holbrook, 2001; Singh & Sirdeshmukh, 2000). Examples where such relationships may be especially important are in call centres dealing with counselling or stock brokering. Encounters are almost the reverse of relationships and typically involve a single, short interaction between strangers. The standardised nature of encounters makes them efficient and it is easy to change the provider without affecting the service. There is less room for authentic emotional expression, particularly for the service provider, and less opportunity to understand the reasons for another's behaviour; this can lead to errors of attribution, such as when a customer might attribute good service to organisational rules and

Table 7.1 Characteristics of relationships and encounters (based on Gutek, 1997)

Relationships	Encounters
Provider and customer are known to each other	Provider and customer are strangers: can be anonymous
All providers not equivalent	Providers interchangeable, functionally equivalent
Based on trust	Based on rules
Elitist: Customers treated differently	Egalitarian: all customers treated alike
Customised service	Standardised service
Difficult to start	Easy to enter
Difficult to end, loyalty is a factor	No obligation to repeat interaction
Does not need infrastructure	Is embedded in infrastructure
Fosters emotional involvement	Often requires emotional expressions not felt
Become more effective over time, e.g. therapist, doctor, financial advisor	Designed to be operationally efficient, e.g. fast-food worker, bank teller
Call centre examples: counsellor, stockbroker	Call centre examples: telephone banking, ticket sales, operator services

bad service to individual traits. An encounter is exemplified by a call to a directory service provider.

Initial research on call centre service interactions has found that they tend to be relatively short, with average call times of five to six minutes being common (Batt, 2000; Holman & Wood, 2002; Zapf, Isic, Bechtoldt & Blau, 2003). In addition, employees only interact with the same customer on a relatively infrequent basis. Holman and Wood (2002) discovered that, in a survey of 142 UK call centres, repeated interaction with the same customer occurred sometimes in 27% of the sample and never occurred in 37%. Such findings might lead one to conclude that encounters are more prevalent in call centres. Yet, Holman and Wood also discovered that a typical service interaction involved exchanging information, giving advice and building a relationship. This implied that efforts are made in many call centres to emulate the positive features of relationships in short one-off service interactions. In other words, call centres attempt to develop pseudo-relationships—encounters that are made to look like relationships (Gutek, 1995). A core aspect of a pseudo-relationship is the development of an "instant rapport". One method of doing this is to get CSRs to discover why a customer is using a service (e.g. getting a loan to finance a holiday) and using this information to express interest in the customers' affairs (e.g. where is the customer going on holiday, wishing them a happy holiday). Another method is to use customer-relationship management systems that track customers' interactions with the organisation and enable employees to anticipate their needs.

Current research in call centres indicates that encounters and pseudo-relationships service interactions may be more common than relationship-type service interactions. The relative scarcity of relationships is probably due to the fact that a relationship may not be needed, possible or desired for certain services (e.g. when getting a ticket) and also that work in call centres tends to be organised so that interactions are simple, short, one-off episodes. The lack of relationships in call centres is not due to interactions being telephone-based, as telephone interaction is unlikely to significantly inhibit the development of relationships, although it can make interaction more formal, make complex problems more difficult to solve and delay the development of trust (Grundy, 1998; Nohria & Eccles, 1992; Rutter, 1987; Short, Williams & Christie, 1976).

Another important feature of service interactions in call centres is the emotions that customers and employees express towards each other. For employees, the display of particular emotions is normally a job requirement, for example to appear enthusiastic towards customers, and the idea that employees regulate the expression of emotion in exchange for a wage is called emotional labour (Grandey, 2000; Hochschild, 1983). Central to theories of emotional labour is notion of emotional dissonance, which occurs when the required emotional expression does not match the emotions felt. When dissonance occurs the employee can either display his "true" emotions, thereby violating job requirements, or try to display the required emotions. If the employee chooses the latter option, two modes of emotional regulation may be used, namely surface acting or deep acting. Surface acting involves faking the display of the required emotion, with little attempt to feel that emotion. Deep acting involves trying to feel and display the required emotions, for example by reappraising the situation so that any inappropriate emotional impact is lessened.

One of the few studies on the emotional aspects of service interactions in call centres found that CSRs expressed positive emotions (e.g. happiness, enthusiasm) on a fairly regular basis but seldom expressed negative emotions (e.g. anger, anxiety) (Zapf *et al.*, 2003). The level of positive emotional expression was similar to that found in human service work (e.g. nursing, teaching) and significantly higher than that in service (e.g. banks, insurance) and non-service work (e.g. manufacturing). But, the level of negative emotional expression was significantly lower than for all other forms of work. Emotional dissonance was experienced fairly regularly by CSRs and this was at a similar level to that found in human service work but significantly higher than that in service and non-service work. Totterdell and Holman (2001, 2003) reported a similar pattern of emotional labour in a daily diary study. CSRs reported displaying more positive emotions than negative emotions over the course of each working day. With regard to emotional dissonance, they expressed more positive emotions than they felt on about 50% of occasions and expressed more negative feelings than they felt on about 20% of occasions. In other words, the CSRs hid negative feelings half the time but suppressed positive feelings about a fifth of the time. It seems likely that the CSRs suppressed positive feelings in order to appear professional. The CSRs also reported that they surface acted on 13% of occasions and deep acted on 43% of occasions. Overall, initial research on the emotional aspects of service interactions in call centres indicates that it is characterised by the frequent display of positive emotions, the infrequent expression of negative emotions, and that the emotions displayed tend to be more positive than the emotions felt. (The impact of this no employee well-being is considered later.)

Performance Monitoring

Performance monitoring is not unique to call centres. What is distinctive within many call centres is its overt and pervasive nature, and it is this that is perceived to have such a negative impact on employee well-being (Holman & Wood, 2002; TOSCA, 2002). This impact will be discussed later, but first performance monitoring will be described.

Performance monitoring involves the observation, examination, recording and feedback of employee work behaviours and exists in both "traditional" and "electronic" forms[1] (Carayon, 1993; Stanton, 2000). Traditional performance monitoring encompasses methods such as observation, work sampling and customer surveys. In a call centre, it is typified by a supervisor listening to a call, either at the side of a CSR or remotely (with or without the CSR's knowledge), and then evaluating its quality. As listening to a call is resource-rich, the actual number of calls listened to ranges from one per day in some call centres to once a month in others (Frenkel, Tam, Korczynski & Shire, 1998; Holman, Chissick & Totterdell, 2002). Holman and Wood (2002) found that one third of call centres listened to one or more of an agent's calls each week and another third listened to an agent's call once every few weeks or once a month. From this it would appear that traditional monitoring is not pervasive until it is remembered that increasing numbers of call centres have the capability to record all calls. A call's quality is normally evaluated against a mixture of knowledge-based, behavioural and attitudinal criteria that can include: adherence to a script; call opening and closing; accuracy of information; product knowledge; helpfulness; empathy; enthusiasm; and professional tone (Bain, Watson, Mulvey, Taylor & Gall, 2002; Holman et al., 2002). These evaluations are normally fed back in one-to-one discussions and summated results fed back in team meetings. In addition to call quality, CSRs are usually assessed against a range of non-call-related criteria, such as teamwork, helpfulness and attendance.

---

[1] While not ideal labels, we keep them as they are used by others in this field (cf. Stanton, 2000).

Electronic performance monitoring involves the continuous, automatic and remote collection of quantitative data (e.g. call times, call volumes, number of sales). Holman and Wood (2002) found that the results of electronic monitoring were fed back to agents daily in 30% of call centres and weekly in a further 32%. Similar rates have been reported in other studies (Bain & Taylor, 2000; Frenkel *et al.*, 1998; Holman, Chissick & Totterdell, 2002). It is also interesting to note that Holman and Wood (2002) found that 60% of call centres use overhead screens to provide continuous feedback on information, such as number of calls waiting.

The purpose of performance monitoring relates to the uses to which performance data is put. For example, performance monitoring can be deployed punitively to inform disciplinary proceedings. It can also be used to: improve employee performance, particularly through the identification of training needs and new goals; reduce costs; enhance customer satisfaction; and enable the correct allocation of resources by matching employee numbers to call levels (Aiello & Kolb, 1995; Betts, Meadows & Walley, 2000; Chalykoff & Kochan, 1989).

Job and Work Design

To some, CSR jobs are an expression of an advanced form of Taylorism (Bain *et al.*, 2002; Knights & McCabe, 1998; Taylor & Bain, 1999) However, not all CSR jobs are designed in this manner, and most can be placed on a job design continuum that runs from "Taylorist" to "Empowered" (Batt, 2000; Frenkel *et al.*, 1998; Frenkel, Korczynski, Shire & Tam, 1999; Holman, 2002). At the Taylorist end of the continuum, jobs are unskilled, repetitive and monotonous. Calls are of a short duration, are required to be completed within a specified time and there is no choice as to whether a call can be answered or not. Calls are often conducted in accordance to a script that specifies the opening and closing of the call and, in some cases, the entire call. These factors mean that CSRs have little control over the timing of their work, the methods they use and what they can say. CSRs also spend most of their time answering calls, a consequence being that little time is spent doing other tasks, such as administration. Variety comes from answering different call types, although actual differences may be small. The level of problem-solving demand is not high and when problems do arise there is a general expectation that these should be handed on to a supervisor. Taylorist jobs also tend to have low degrees of task interdependence. As a result, work is individualised and fewer interactions with other CSRs are needed to ensure service delivery, although co-workers may interact to offer social support and help each other to learn the job (Batt & Moynihan, 2004; Frenkel *et al.*, 1999).

In the "empowered" job, a semi-professional CSR has a high degree of control over how he or she works and is required to combine an extensive product or service knowledge (e.g. mortgages or computer repair) with advanced IT and customer service skills to provide a customised service (Frenkel *et al.*, 1998; Shah & Bandi, 2003). CSRs are engaged in a variety of calls and tasks in which problems are handled at source. Calls are longer and generally unscripted apart from the call's opening and closing. Empowered jobs often have higher degrees of task interdependence, as CSRs need to draw upon others' knowledge.

Current research indicates that that CSR jobs in call centres fall towards the lower/middle end of the Taylorist–Empowered job design continuum and are characterised by low control. Low levels of job control have been reported by CSRs in Switzerland, Denmark, the UK and

Germany (Grebner *et al.*, 2003; Jensen, Finsen, Søgaard & Christensen, 2002; Sprigg *et al.*, 2003; Zapf *et al.*, 2003). These studies also reveal that CSRs generally report low levels of demand, such as workload and, surprisingly, time pressure. There is, however, more reported variation in team and interpersonal factors such as group climate, supervisory relationships and co-operation.

Comparative studies show that the level of job control in call centre work is generally lower than that found in administrative, manufacturing, service and human service jobs. Call centre work contains more repetitive tasks and physical movements than other jobs where computer use is high (Jensen *et al.*, 2002). The findings from employee-level surveys were mirrored in the organisational-level survey of Holman and Wood (2002) who found that one third of call centres surveyed had CSR jobs with low variety and low control over most aspects of work. In another 19%, CSRs had jobs with moderate variety, low control over tasks and the pace of work but moderate control over customer interaction. In only 9% of call centres did CSRs have jobs with high variety and high levels of control.

Human Resource Management

Two models of service management have been proposed—the "mass service" model and the "high commitment service" (HCS) model. Each model specifies a range of factors relating to market segment, strategic aims, customer–employee interaction, HRM practices and work organisation. Three types of alignment between these factors are considered necessary in order to maximise organisational performance (Bowen & Schneider, 1988; Frenkel *et al.*, 1999; Levitt, 1972; Schlesinger & Heskett, 1991; Schuler & Jackson, 1995; Wright & McMahon, 1992).[2] The first is an *internal alignment* between HRM practices and work organisation, i.e. whether there is a coherent bundle of HRM and work organisation practices. The second is an *organisational alignment* between bundles of practice and operational requirements, which in the call centre is the service interaction. Batt (2000, p. 542) argues that "the customer–worker interface is a significant factor in defining the organisation of work and HRM practices in services". The third is a *strategic alignment* between the organisation's strategy and bundles of practices.

These two models of service management have been drawn on in the call centre literature to conceptualise two ideal types of call centre, the mass service call centre and the high commitment service call centre (see Table 7.2). The mass service call centre serves the mass market, in which profit margins are small and competition is based on low cost. In order to maximise profit, important strategic aims are to minimise costs, particularly labour costs, and to maximise volume. These aims are achieved by delivering standardised products and services through short, standardised interactions. Organising service delivery in this way means that cheap, unskilled labour and Taylorist job design can be used, which in turn permits low-cost HRM practices to be used to recruit, train and retain the workforce, for example, low rates of pay, minimal training and unsophisticated recruitment practices. Monitoring needs to be high, however, to ensure adherence to the standardised job requirements. The mass service call centre therefore contains: an internal alignment between

---

[2] These are the functional equivalent of the mass production and high commitment/involvement models present in the manufacturing literature (Ichniowski, Kochan, Levine, Olson & Strauss, 1996; Wood, 1995).

Table 7.2 Call centre models: "mass service" and "high commitment service"

Mass service	High commitment service

Customer segment
  Mass Market
	Customer Segment
	  High-value customers, e.g., Specialist,
	    high-earning private customers,
	    businesses

Market
  High-volume, low added value
	Market
	  Low-volume, high added value

Strategy
  Cost-minimisation
	Strategy
	  Customisation of service, cross-selling,
	    bundling of services

Product/service
  Simple, one or few product or services on
    offers
  Standardised service
	Product/service
	  Complex and/or multiple products and
	    services on offer
	  Customised service

Customer–employee interaction
  Encounter or pseudo-relationship
	Customer–employer interaction
	  Relationship or pseudo-relationship

Job design
  Taylorist, e.g. low control and variety, low
  skill, high use of scripts, short call times
	Job design
	  Empowered, e.g. high control and variety,
	  little scripting, long calls

Work design
  Low interdependence
  Work groups
  Off-line work groups
	Work design
	  High interdependence
	  High use of semi-autonomous work groups
	  Off-line work groups

Performance monitoring
  High levels of monitoring
  Emphasis on quality and quantity
  Higher tendency to use monitoring to
    discipline and control
	Performance monitoring
	  Low levels of monitoring
	  Emphasis on quality
	  Use of monitoring for developmental
	    purposes

Human resource practices
  Low cost
  Recruitment—minimal criteria
  Pay—relatively low rates of pay, low
    percentage of total pay that is
    commission-based
  Training—mainly induction training
  Career—little career structure, poor
    promotion prospects
  Job security—low, high use of temporary
    contracts in core workers
	Human resource practices
	  Sophisticated
	  Use of selection tests and competency
	    models
	  Relatively high rates of pay, higher
	    percentage of total pay that is
	    commission-based, good additional
	    benefits
	  Extensive induction and continued training
	  Good promotion prospects
	  High job security, lower use of temporary
	    contracts in core workers

Management/supervisor relations with CSRs
  Hierarchical
  Low trust
	Management/supervisor relations with CSRs
	  Supportive, facilitative
	  High trust

Taylorist job design and low cost HRM practices; an organisational alignment between Taylorist job design, low cost HRM practices and standardised service encounters; and a strategic alignment between these three factors and a mass market customer segment and a cost minimisation strategy.

The high-commitment service call centre serves a "high-value" customer segment from which high profit margins and sales revenue can be extracted by building a relationship with the customer and providing a customised, tailored service. To achieve this, the organisation needs to use sophisticated HRM practices to: build a skilled workforce, for example by effective recruitment and continuous training; reward discretionary behaviour, for example by performance-related pay; and, to cultivate employee commitment to the organisation, for example through job security and good terms and conditions. Empowered work designs are also needed in order to give the employee the opportunity to provide a customised service, display discretionary behaviour and build relationships with customers. Greater employee commitment means that less monitoring is needed to gain adherence to job requirements. The high commitment service call centre therefore contains; an internal alignment between empowered job design and sophisticated HRM practices; an organisational alignment between empowered job design, sophisticated HRM practices and relationship-type service encounters; and a strategic alignment between these three factors and a high-value customer segment.

These ideal types have been used to explain variation in HRM practices among call centres and to explain the performance effects of HRM practices in call centres (Batt, 2000; Holman, 2002; Kinnie, Purcell & Hutchinson, 2000; cf. Frenkel *et al.*, 1998, 1999). Research indicates that work organisation and HRM practices in call centres do vary in a manner similar to that predicted by these models. The strongest evidence comes from Batt's study of US telecommunications call centres that served four customer segments that were, in order of increasing value, operator services (low margin/mass market), residential consumers, small businesses and middle market (high value/specialised market) (Batt, 2000, 2002; Batt & Moynihan, 2004). Batt (2002) found that empowered jobs (high control, low scripting, high skill requirements) were associated with HRM practices such as low performance monitoring and high levels of discretionary pay. Batt amalgamated these practices into a "high-involvement" index. This high-involvement bundle was positively associated with relationship-type interactions; and the extent of the high involvement index and relationship-type interactions increased in line with the value of the market segment, i.e. they were lowest in operator services and highest in the middle market customer segment.

The respondents in Batt's study were managers. Evidence from employee-level data comes from Holman and Fernie (2000), who compared CSRs working in a banking call centre serving mass market customers with those in a call centre giving mortgage advice to residential customers. CSRs in the banking call centre reported more encounter-type interactions, lower job control and variety, lower skill use, higher monitoring and poorer relations with managers. Thus, there were different bundles of practice and the organisational alignments were as suggested by the models. A similar pattern was reported by Frenkel *et al.* (1999) who, using case study and CSR-level survey data, found that work roles, job designs and HRM practices consistent with the ideal mass service call centre were aligned with customer–employee encounters and a mass market customer segment. A case study by Hutchinson, Purcell and Kinnie (2000) also demonstrated that "the driving force for the adoption of HCM [high-commitment management] was the need to realign business strategy and organisational structure" (p. 74). In the call centre in question, HRM practices were changed in response to a new strategic aim of adding value, particularly for customers, and the provision of a more complex service that combined previously distinct sales and service tasks. The HRM changes included greater use of induction and continuing training, more sophisticated recruitment and selection techniques, a wider use of performance-related pay and greater involvement in quality improvement teams.

Work on HRM in call centres, while limited in extent, does indicate that practices do exhibit an internal, organisational and strategic alignment akin to that posited in both the mass service and the HCS call centre models. However, an important caveat to this conclusion is that there are many "anomalies" in the data. Batt (2000) found little difference among call centres serving different customer segments with regard to the use of self-managed teams, off-line teams (e.g. quality circles), training, promotion and job security. It would appear that some mass service call centres adopt high commitment work practices (e.g. self-managed work teams in mass service call centres; Batt, 2000, 2002; Houlihan, 2004) while some HCS call centres adopt mass service work practices (e.g. high levels of performance monitoring in HCS call centres; Kinnie *et al.*, 2000). Indeed, some call centres might be best characterised as a hybrid of mass service and HCS call centres, which Frenkel *et al.* (1998) have labelled "mass customized bureaucracies".

The fact that call centres adopt "anomalous" practices probably occurs because conflicting demands make it difficult to achieve an ideal alignment of practice, strategy and customer segment. For example, mass market customers may demand better service quality, to which managers respond by reducing call scripting and increasing training—even though this might negatively affect costs, service quantity (e.g. call volumes) and the need for standardised procedures (Bain *et al.*, 2002; Knights & McCabe, 1998; Korczynski, Shire, Frenkel & Tam, 2000; Sturdy, 2000). Managers may also have to contend with competitive local labour markets, which means that it may not be possible to use practices such as low pay or Tayloristic job designs that exacerbate recruitment and turnover problems (Houlihan, 2004). Other factors that influence the adoption of work practices include legal requirements, problems of implementation and, particularly in call centres that provide outsourced services, the demands of the client (Kinnie & Parsons, 2004). It must also be stated that the choices managers make on the adoption of HRM and work practices may not be the result of a top-down strategy informed by an underlying and well-conceived rationale. Rather, the practices that are adopted may result from the pragmatic choices made by managers when trying to make sense of the dynamic call centre environment, and this provides another reason why alignments appear to be messy and full of anomalies (Hutchinson *et al.*, 2000; Kinnie *et al.*, 2000).

THE EXPERIENCE OF CALL CENTRE WORK

Call centre work, particularly that of CSRs, has attracted much attention due to its perceived impact on job-related stress. In response, there is a growing literature on the causes of stress in call centres. Another body of work has focused on how CSRs actively resist managerial control and deleterious working practices. The latter work is heavily influenced by labour process theory but not entirely disconnected from the literature on stress and well-being.

The Experience and Causes of Stress, Stress-related Outcomes and Affect

Job design, performance monitoring, customer–employee interaction and HRM practices all have a significant impact on employee stress and stress-related outcomes in call centres.[3]

---

[3] Nearly all research on stress in call centres has been in relation to CSRs. The following relates to this group unless otherwise stated.

Research into the effects of job design reports similar findings to research on this topic conducted in other types of organisation (Karasek & Theorell, 1990; Terry & Jimmieson, 1999; Tittiranonda, Burastero, & Rempel, 1999). In short, research in call centres has demonstrated that high job demands (e.g. workload, call volume, concentration demands, problem solving demand, role ambiguity) and low job resources (e.g. method control, timing control, interaction control, social support, participation, supervisor relationships, skill utilisation) are associated with various indicators of poor psychological well-being such as anxiety, depression, emotional exhaustion, psychosomatic complaints, absenteeism and turnover (Bakker, Demerouti, & Schaufeli, 2003; Batt & Appelbaum, 1995; Batt & Moynihan, 2004; Deery, Iverson & Walsh, 2002; Grebner *et al.*, 2003; Holman, 2002; Sprigg *et al.*, 2003; Workman & Bommer, 2004; Zapf, Vogt, Seifert, Mertini & Isic, 1999). In addition, poor work-station design, prolonged computer use, repetitive physical movements due to computer-based work, and job demands have been linked to musculoskeletal disorders (MSDs) of the wrist, neck, shoulder and back (Bakker Demerouti & Schaufeli, 2003; Ferreira & Saldiva, 2002; Halford & Cohen, 2003; Jensen *et al.*, 2002).

Performance monitoring has been found to have positive and negative effects on stress. On the one hand, Chalykoff and Kochan (1989) discovered that the performance-related content of the monitoring system in a call centre (i.e. immediacy of feedback, the use of constructive feedback and the clarity of the rating criteria) was positively related to satisfaction with the monitoring system, which in turn was related to job satisfaction. Likewise, Bakker *et al.* (2003) showed that performance feedback reduced feelings of emotional exhaustion in CSRs. It is thought that this occurs because, as a job resource, feedback helps employees improve their performance and develop new skills (Grant & Higgins, 1989), which in turn helps the CSR to cope better with demands (Aiello & Shao, 1993; Stanton, 2000). On the other hand, field and laboratory studies have found that monitored employees (or participants) experience higher levels of stress and dissatisfaction than non-monitored employees (Aiello & Kolb; 1995; Irving, Higgins & Safeyeni, 1986; Smith, Carayon, Sanders, Lim & LeGrande, 1992). This implies that performance monitoring can be experienced as a demand, as effort has to be expended thinking about one's performance, or a threat, as the information gained from monitoring may affect remuneration or relationships with coworkers (Alder, 1998; Smith *et al.*, 1992).

The positive and negative associations between performance monitoring and employee stress suggests that various performance monitoring characteristics may have differential effects. In other words, certain characteristics of performance monitoring reduce stress, whilst other aspects of it increase stress. This proposition found support in a study by Holman *et al.* (2002) that examined the relationship between well-being and three performance monitoring characteristics in a call centre, viz. its performance-related content (i.e. immediacy of feedback, clarity of performance criteria), its beneficial purpose (i.e. does it have developmental rather than punitive aims?), and its perceived intensity (i.e. was it felt to be pervasive?). The results revealed that the performance-related content of performance monitoring was negatively associated with depression, that the beneficial purpose of monitoring was negatively associated with depression, anxiety and emotional exhaustion, whilst perceived intensity had a positive relationship with anxiety, depression and emotional exhaustion. Furthermore, the perceived intensity of monitoring had a much stronger relationship to these stress outcomes than the other two performance monitoring characteristics. This implies that while performance monitoring can reduce stress if it is conducted in a developmental manner and is based on regular feedback and clear criteria, these positive effects can be wiped out if monitoring is perceived by CSRs to be too intense. Indeed, excessive monitoring may, over the long term, make employees more depressed, less enthusiastic and have the opposite effect of that intended.

Like performance monitoring, customer–employee interaction can have both positive and negative associations with employee stress. Unpleasant interactions with customers— something that has been recorded as occurring in about 10% of all calls—have been shown to be highly associated with emotional exhaustion (Grandey, Dickter, & Sin, 2004; Totterdell & Holman, 2003). Interestingly, Grandey *et al.* (2004) found that CSRs were more likely to experience unpleasant customer interactions as stressful when they had low job control. Unpleasant interactions are also related to emotional dissonance, which in turn is associated with emotional exhaustion, and employee efforts to regulate their emotions. In particular, surface acting has been shown to increases stress, as the suppression of feelings is probably more demanding on personal resources than other forms of regulation such as deep acting (Grebner *et al.*, 2003; Holman *et al.*, 2002; Zapf *et al.*, 1999). In contrast, customer– employee interaction displays a negative relationship with employee stress when customers are pleasant, when positive emotions are expressed (as this is pleasant in itself), and when the provision of good customer service leads to a sense of personal accomplishment (Frenkel *et al.*, 1999; Holman *et al.*, 2002; Totterdell & Holman, 2003; Zapf *et al.*, 1999).

Research on other causes of stress in call centres is less comprehensive. However, with regard to HRM practices, the perceived fairness of the payment system, the usefulness of performance appraisal and the adequacy of training, all have been linked to low anxiety, low depression and job satisfaction (Batt & Appelbaum, 1995; Frenkel *et al.*, 1998; Holman, 2002).

The types of practices that are associated with employee stress are more commonly found in mass service than HCS call centres. As a result, it would be expected that employee well-being should differ accordingly. Batt (2002) confirmed this by showing that quit rates were lower in HCS type call centres. Holman and Fernie (2000) compared levels of employee stress among a mass service-type call centre, an HCS-type call centre and a hybrid type. Depression and job dissatisfaction were generally lower at the HCS and hybrid call centres. Against expectations, however, anxiety was lower at the mass service call centre. It was argued that CSRs were managing their anxiety by leaving the mass service call centre. CSRs at the other call centres, which had better pay, were more likely to stay and endure the conditions.

Call centre work has been highlighted as particularly stressful and, by implication, as being more stressful than other forms of work. Some studies support such an assertion. In one of the more comprehensive surveys that covered CSRs from across a wide range of business sectors in the UK, Sprigg *et al.* (2003) revealed that CSRs were more anxious than shop floor manufacturing staff, clerical staff, technical support staff and supervisory staff—and had comparable levels of anxiety to managers. CSRs also had higher depression than all occupational groups except workers in non-manufacturing organisations, and had lower job satisfaction than all occupational groups except workers in manufacturing and non-manufacturing organisations. Likewise, Frenkel *et al.* (1999) found call centre workers to be less satisfied than sales workers and knowledge workers (e.g. IT systems designers). However, other studies do not show such clear differences between call centre work and other types of work. Grebner *et al.* (2003) compared call centre workers to a sample of younger workers in a range of occupations (e.g. cooks, sales assistants, nurses, bank clerks). Call centre workers reported higher psychosomatic complaints, were no different with regard to job satisfaction but reported lower irritation and intention to quit. In another study, call centre work compared favourably with shop floor manufacturing work and clerical work with regard to anxiety, depression and job satisfaction (Holman, 2002). However, as this latter study was conducted in the financial services sector, where employee well-being in call centres tends to be higher, the findings may be sector specific (Sprigg *et al.*, 2003, p. 27). It can therefore be concluded that, while there are not totally consistent differences in well-being between call centre workers and their counterparts in more traditional organisations, the general trend indicates that well-being is lower in call centre workers. Furthermore, variations in levels of employee stress between different call centres and between call centre work and other forms of work appear largely attributable to differences in job design and HRM practices.

Control and Resistance in Call Centre Work: the Active Agent

Research on stress in call centres tends to paint the CSR as a rather passive figure—as someone simply responding to work conditions. In contrast, studies inspired by labour process theory have illustrated CSRs active consent, compliance and resistance to managers' efforts to control their work (Sturdy, Knights & Willmott, 1992). Management control practices in call centres are fairly wide-ranging and, to remind the reader, include technical and normative methods such as:

- The measurement of output through IT systems.
- The measurement of behaviour through call monitoring.
- The inculcation of norms and skills through training, customer awareness programmes, socialisation, coaching, performance appraisal and feedback (Thompson, Callaghan & van den Broek, 2004).
- The structuring of work tasks through scripts and IT systems.

However, despite managers' best efforts, CSRs may not consent to managerial control practices. CSRs may have different ideas about how the call centre should be run and will probably disagree with practices viewed as damaging. CSRs may therefore resist such practices and labour process theory has illuminated the individual and collective ways in which this occurs (see Table 7.3; Taylor & Bain, 2003; van den Broek, 2004). For example,

Table 7.3   Individual and collective forms of CSR resistance to management control

Individual resistance	Collective resistance
Cutting customers off	Traders union activity
Not following the script	Humour
Not selling	Sharing knowledge of how to beat the system
Deliberately cheating the IT system	
Pretending to be speaking to a customer	
Challenging targets set	
Not filling in information properly	

at an individual level, a CSR may resist managerial exhortations to deal with calls more rapidly as a means of improving customer service. This may occur because a CSR's sense of customer service is different. The CSR may have an embodied sense of customer service, i.e. to the customer she is serving, and this makes her attend to the needs of the individual without regard to those other customers waiting in the queue (Korczynski *et al.*, 2000; Sturdy, 2000). At a collective level, resistance may take the form of trade union activity that aims to alter job design or performance monitoring (Keefe & Batt, 2001; Taylor & Bain, 2001; Trades Union Congress, 2001). Finally, the labour process literature has highlighted how CSRs are confronted by similar demands to management (e.g. quality vs. quantity, service vs. selling, etc.), but while managers have to contend with these issues at a system level, the CSR has to manage these conflicting demands in every call.

CALL CENTRE PERFORMANCE

A small number of studies have examined employee-level and organisational-level performance in call centres. At the employee-level, self-reported service quality has been found to be higher with team self-regulation (akin to the processes involved in self-managed teams), coaching support, training and work group relations (Batt, 1999) as well with the extent of deep acting and the display of positive emotions (Totterdell & Holman, 2003). Objective performance measures of call quality and call quantity were recorded by Renn and Fedor (2001), who found that they were positively associated with performance monitoring practices that gave feedback frequently and allowed CSRs to participate in setting their goals. Earley (1988) also confirmed the important role that feedback and goal setting play in improving CSR performance. Sales volume has been linked to team self-regulation, coaching support and level of education (Batt, 1999), while customer satisfaction has been associated with employee behaviours such as empathy, assurance, the authority to deal with requests and, interestingly, the display of negative emotions (Burgers, de Ruyter, Keen & Streukens, 2000; Doucett, 1998).

At the organisational-level, an assumption in the models presented earlier is that optimal performance in mass service and HCS call centres can be achieved through the correct alignment of strategy, customer segment, work organisation and HRM practices. The models assume a contingency theory based argument, i.e. when organisations fit their design to the context they will out perform those that do not. Alternative theories of organisational performance are the universalist perspective, that there is one best way, as well as the resource-based perspective. The resource-based perspective argues that a "best-fit" may not be desirable as it is easily mimicked by other organisations, and that competitive advantage is gained from having unique and hard-to-imitate features (Boxall, 1996).

Batt (2002) adopted a resource-based theory (rather than the contingency theory perspectives implicit in her earlier work) to argue that call centres using high-involvement/ high-commitment practices in mass markets will gain a competitive advantage as such an approach will be rare and "difficult to imitate". In contrast, for call centres serving the large business market, high-involvement practices appear to be the price of entry. Leaving aside the extent to which high-involvement practices are difficult to imitate, the argument implies that high-involvement practices are universally relevant and will provide greater performance benefits in sectors where they remain rare, i.e. mass market segments. This is precisely the opposite hypothesis to that of conventional contingency theory. Batt's empirical tests support this argument as she found that a high involvement index (as described earlier in the section on HRM) was related to sales growth and that the interaction between this and one measure of whether the call centre serves a residential mass market but not another—large business—is highly significant. The interaction between the high-involvement index and a measure of a third sector, small business, is also significant but not as strongly as is the residential. The results demonstrate that, regardless of the type of market, high-involvement practices are associated with higher sales and confer a greater advantage when used in market segments in which they are rare. Batt's results, however, could equally be consistent with an argument that some managers seek to compensate their employees for the routine nature of much of their work by providing them with higher-involvement HRM practices and more empowered jobs than is required according to mass-market operational requirements. In other words, the presence of high-involvement practices may be a result of pragmatic rather than strategic choices.

Batt also found a negative association between the high-involvement index and quit rates. This relationship was unaffected by the customer segment served and thus supported a universalist perspective. In a similar manner, Holman and Wood (2004) found quit rates to be positively associated with low control over work tasks and interaction with customers. They also found that sickness rate and customer satisfaction were both positively associated with performance monitoring, a finding in keeping with the idea expressed earlier that performance monitoring can have positive and negative effects. They did not, however, find that the customer segment moderated these relationships. Other studies of organisational performance have shown that management's ability to reduce waiting times is a key determinant of customer satisfaction (Evenson, Harker & Frei, 1999; Feinberg, Kim, Hokama, de Ruyter & Keen, 2000). Yet, managing call volumes so that resources match demand has proven problematic with current technologies and procedures, particularly when calls are long (Betts et al., 2000). This would indicate that management's ability to control a key determinant of customer satisfaction might be limited.

CONCLUSION

Call centre work is distinctive, as it requires front-line staff to simultaneously:

- Manage customer-interaction on the telephone without reference to the visual cues present in face-to-face interaction.
- Manipulate computer-based packages.
- Rapidly process and retrieve knowledge of products, services and IT systems.
- Monitor and regulate their performance and emotions with regard to multiple criteria.
- Perform repetitive physical movements of the arm, wrist and hand whilst seated.

This combination of activities distinguishes call centre work from other types of office, service and computer-based work, such as shop work or data entry. At the same time, call centre work can be considered in terms of the same job and work characteristics as other forms of work, such as job control, job demand, performance monitoring, social support and HRM practices.

A further feature of call centres is their variety and diversity, and thus it is misguided to view all of them as "electronic sweatshops". One way of approaching this diversity is to understand call centres as possessing characteristics that are representative of two ideal-types—the "mass market" and "high commitment service" call centre; it appears that, in many call centres, the particular alignment of work organisation and HRM practices to customer–employee interaction and customer segment is similar to that posited in the ideal-type mass service and HCS call centres. However, many "anomalies" or non-alignments exist. This may be because the distinction between mass service and HCS call centres is too simplistic, and that a more differentiated taxonomy is needed to capture the diversity of call centre types (see Houlihan (2004) for an alternative taxonomy). There is also a need to understand why alignments and non-alignments occur, in particular the extent to which they are a result of managers' and other stakeholders' strategic decisions and pragmatic responses to conflicting operational demands.

The variety and diversity of call centres should also not mask the fact that, in Europe at least, many call centre jobs are characterised by low levels of job control and variety, relatively high levels of monitoring, and encounter or pseudo-relationship service interactions; this suggests that many call centres may be more akin to mass service call centres. The prevalence of these factors is also likely to explain the general trend of stress being higher in call centre workers. It would seem imperative that further large-scale comparative studies of well-being in call centre workers and other occupations are conducted.

As noted, call centre work has been considered on similar job characteristics to other forms of work, and it is apparent that the underlying causes of stress are similar in both, for example low control, high demand, etc. However, front-line call centre work has a fairly distinctive combination of job characteristics, i.e. cognitive and physical computer-based tasks being conducted simultaneously with telephone-based service interactions. There is a need to examine whether this distinctive combination of factors has a unique effect on employee well-being. Research on well-being in call centres also needs to examine performance monitoring in detail, particularly if there is any trade off between its effect on well-being and performance. In addition, more quasi-experimental redesign studies are needed to compare the performance and well-being effects of different job designs and different performance monitoring systems (Workman & Bommer, 2004). Since call centres are not radically new forms of organisation, job redesign or system redesign methods, including socio-technical methods and the like, that have been successfully used elsewhere, could be applied in a call centre setting (Parker & Wall, 1998).

The choices made about the design of call centre practices are important as they affect employee well-being and performance, and organisational performance. One noticeable aspect of research on the effects of call centre practices is that there is a degree of commonality in the practices that promote employee well-being, employee performance and organisational-level performance. These practices are characteristic of the high-involvement or high-commitment approach and include empowered jobs, high skill levels and skill utilisation, training and development practices, and performance monitoring that is focused on developing employees' skills. One implication is that a high-involvement approach should be universally adopted to increase performance and well-being, and that this may even confer additional competitive advantage to call centres that sell to mass markets (Batt, 2002). But while research on the effects of these practices on employee well-being paints a fairly consistent picture, it is probably too early to draw firm conclusions with regard to their effects on employee performance and organisational performance. At the organisational level in particular, research is needed across a range of sectors, countries and performance indicators. Another important question centres on the cost of high-involvement practices. Although such practices might decrease turnover and increase sales and employee well-being, their overall effect on costs is not known. High-involvement practices typically entail greater investment and if this is seen as especially costly, it might explain their low level of uptake in mass service call centres. If overall costs are cheaper or similar, the presence of cultural factors or managers' "implicit mental models" may explain their prevalence.

In conclusion, this chapter has demonstrated that the design and diversity of call centres emerges from the pragmatic and strategic choices made by various stakeholders, and that the different ways of designing a call centre has profound effects on employee well-being and performance, and organisational performance. This demonstrates that the stakeholders in call centres, and particularly managers, do have a choice in how they run and organise call centres, and that well-being and performance can be designed into call centres.

REFERENCES

ACA Research (2001). *The 2001 Australia and New Zealand call centre industry benchmark study.* Sydney: ACA Research.

Aiello, J. R. & Kolb, K. J. (1995). Electronic performance monitoring and social context: impact on productivity and stress. *Journal of Applied Psychology*, **80**, 339–353.

Aiello, J. R. & Shao, Y. (1993). Electronic performance monitoring and stress: the role of feedback and goal setting. In M. J. Smith & G. Salavendy (Eds), *Human–Computer Interaction: Applications and Case Studies* (pp. 1011–1016). Amsterdam: Elsevier Science.

Alder, G. S. (1998). Ethical issues in electronic performance monitoring: a consideration of deontological and teleological perspectives. *Journal of Business Ethics*, **17**, 729–743.

Bain, P. & Taylor, P. (2000). Entrapped by the "electronic panoptican"? Worker resistance in the call centre. *New Technology, Work and Employment*, **15**, 2–18.

Bain, P., Watson, A., Mulvey, G., Taylor, P. & Gall, G. (2002). Taylorism, targets and quantity–quality dichotomy in call centres. *New Technology, Work and Employment*, **17**, 186–203.

Bakker, A. B., Demerouti, E. & Schaufeli, W. B. (2003). Dual processes at work in a call centre: an application of the job demands–resources model. *European Journal of Work and Organisational Psychology*, **12**, 393–428.

Batt, R. (1999). Work organization, technology and performance in customer service and sales. *Industrial and Labor Relations Review*, **52**, 539–564.

Batt, R. (2000). Strategic segmentation in front line services: matching customers, employees and HRM systems. *International Journal of Human Resource Management*, **11**, 540–561.

Batt, R. (2002). Managing customer services: human resource practices, quit rates and sales growth. *Academy of Management Journal*, **45**, 587–597.

Batt, R. & Appelbaum, E. (1995). Worker participation in diverse settings: does the form affect the outcome, and if so, who benefits? *British Journal of Industrial Relations*, **33**, 353–378.

Batt, R. & Moynihan, L. (2004). The viability of alternative call centre production models. In S. Deery and N. Kinnie (Eds), *Call Centres and HRM Management: A Cross-national Perspective* (pp. 25–53). Basingstoke: Palgrave MacMillan.

Betts, A., Meadows, M. & Walley, P. (2000). Call centre capacity management. *International Journal of Service Industry Management*, **11**, 185–196.

Boddy, D. (2000). Implementing inter-organizational IT systems: lessons from a call centre project. *Journal of Information Technology*, **15**, 29–37.

Bowen, D. E. & Schneider, B. (1988). Services marketing and management: implications for organizational behaviour. In B. M. Staw & L. L. Cummings (Eds), *Research in Organisational Behavior*, Vol. 10 (pp. 43–80). Greenwich: JAI Press.

Boxall, P. (1996). The strategic HRM debate and the resource-based view of the firm. *Human Resource Management Journal*, **6**, 59–75.

Brooke, C. (2002). Information systems at a call centre. *International Journal of Information Management*, **22**, 389–401.

Burgers, A., de Ruyter, K., Keen., C. & Streukens, S. (2000). Customer expectation dimensions of voice to voice service encounters: a scale development study. *International Journal of Service Industry Management*, **11**, 142–161.

Callaghan, G. & Thompson, P. (2001). Edwards revisited: technical control and call centres. *Economic and Industrial Democracy*, **22**, 13–37.

Carayon, P. (1993). Effects of electronic performance monitoring on job design and worker stress: review of the literature and conceptual model. *Human Factors*, **35**, 385–395.

Chalykoff, J. & Kochan, T. (1989). Computer-aided monitoring: its influence on employee job satisfaction and turnover. *Personnel Psychology*, **42**, 807–834.

Chaudhuri, A. & Holbrook, M. B. (2001). The chain effects from brand trust and brand affect to brand performance: the role of brand loyalty. *Journal of Marketing*, **65**, 81–93.

Cherns, A. (1987). Principles of socio-technical design revisited. *Human Relations*, **40**, 153–162.

Clark, J., McLoughlin, I., Rose, H. & King, J. (1998). *The Process of Technological Change: New Technology and Social Change in the Workplace*. Cambridge: Cambridge University Press.

Collin-Jacques, C. (2004). Professionals at work: a study of autonomy and skill utilization in nurse call centres in England and Canada. In S. Deery and N. Kinnie (Eds), *Call Centres and HRM Management: A Cross-national Perspective* (pp. 153–173). Basingstoke: Palgrave MacMillan.

Deery, S. J., Iverson, R. D. & Walsh, J. T. (2002). Work relationships in telephone call centres: understanding emotional exhaustion and employee withdrawal. *Journal of Management Studies*, **39**, 471–496.

Doucett, L. (1998). Responsiveness: emotion and information dynamics in service interactions. Working Paper 98–15, Financial Institutions Center, The Wharton School, University of Pennsylvania.

Earley, P. C. (1988). Computer-generated performance feedback in the magazine subscription industry. *Organizational Behavior and Decision Making Processes*, **41**, 50–64.

Evenson, A., Harker, P. T. & Frei, F. X. (1999). Effective call center management: evidence from financial services. Working Paper 99–110. Financial Institutions Center, The Wharton School, University of Pennsylvania.

Feinberg, R. A., Kim, I-K., Hokama, L., de Ruyter, K. & Keen, C. (2000). Operational determinants of caller satisfaction in the call center. *International Journal of Service Industry Management*, **11**, 131–141.

Ferreira, M. & Saldiva, P. (2002). Computer–telephone interactive tasks: predictors of musculoskeletal disorders according to work analysis and workers' perceptions. *Applied Ergonomics*, **33**, 147–153.

Frenkel, S., Korczynski, M., Shire, K. & Tam, M. (1999). *On the Front-line: Organization of Work in the Information Economy*. Ithaca, NY: Cornell University Press.

Frenkel, S., Tam, M., Korczynski, M. & Shire, K. (1998). Beyond bureaucracy? Work organisation in call centres. *International Journal of Human Resource Management*, **9**, 957–979.

Garson, B. (1988). *The Electronic Sweatshop: How Computers are Transforming the Office of the Future into the Factory of the Past*. New York: Simon & Schuster.

Grandey, A. A. (2000). Emotion regulation in the workplace: a new way to conceptualise emotional labour. *Journal of Occupational Health Psychology*, **5**, 95–110.

Grandey, A. A., Dickter, D. N., & Sin, H-P. (2004). The customer is not always right: customer aggression and emotion regulation of service employees. *Journal of Organizational Behavior*, **25**, 397–418.

Grant, R. A. & Higgins, C. A. (1989). Computerised performance monitors: factors affecting acceptance. *IEEE Transactions on Engineering Management*, **38**, 306–314.

Grebner, S., Semmer, N. K., Faso, L. L., Gut, S., Kalin, W. & Elfering, A. (2003). Working conditions, well-being, and job-related attitudes among call centre agents. *European Journal of Work and Organisational Psychology*, **12**, 341–365.

Grundy, J. (1998). Trust in organizational teams. *Harvard Business Review*, **73**, 40–50.

Gutek, B. (1995). *The Dynamics of Service: Reflections on the Changing Nature of Customer/Provider Interactions*. San Fransisco, CA: Jossey-Bass.

Gutek, B. (1997). Dyadic interactions in organisations. In C. L. Cooper & S. E. Jackson (Eds), *Creating Tomorrow's Organizations Today*. Chichester: Wiley.

Halford, V. & Cohen, H. H. (2003). Technology use and psychosocial factors in the self reporting of musculoskeletal disorder symptoms in call centre workers. *Journal of Safety Research*, **34**, 167–173.

Hochschild, A. (1983). *The Managed Heart: The Commercialization of Human Feeling*. Los Angeles, CA: University of California Press.

Holman, D. (2002). Employee well-being in call centres. *Human Resource Management Journal*, **12**, 35–50.

Holman, D., Chissick, C. & Totterdell, P. (2002). The effects of performance monitoring on emotional labour on well-being in call centres. *Motivation and Emotion*, **26**(1), 57–81.

Holman, D. & Fernie, S. (2000). Employee well-being in call centres. Institute of Work Psychology, Memo No. 260, University of Sheffield.

Holman, D. & Wood, S. (2002). Human resource management in call centres. University of Sheffield, Institute of Work Psychology/Call Centre Association.

Holman, D. & Wood, S. J. (2004). Human resource management and call centre performance in the UK. IWP Memo No. 350, University of Sheffield, Institute of Work Psychology.

Houlihan, M. (2004). Tensions and variations in call centre management. In S. Deery and N. Kinnie (Eds), *Call Centres and HRM Management: A Cross-national Perspective* (pp. 75–102). Basingstoke: Palgrave MacMillan.

Hutchinson, S., Purcell, J. & Kinnie, N. (2000). Evolving high commitment management and the experience of the RAC call centre. *Human Resource Management Journal*, **10**, 63–78.

Ichniowski, C., Kochan, T., Levine, D., Olson, C. & Strauss, G. (1996). What works at work: overview and assessment. *Industrial Relations*, **35**, 299–334.

Incomes Data Services (1997). *Pay and Conditions in Call Centres*. London: Incomes Data Services.

IRS/CCA (Incomes Data Services/Call Centre Association) (2002). Call centres 2002: Reward and work–life strategies. London, Incomes Data Services/Call Centre Association.

Irving, R. H., Higgins, C. A. & Safeyeni, F. R. (1986). Computerised performance monitoring systems: use and abuse. *Communications of the ACM*, August 29, 794–801.

Jensen, C., Finsen, L., Søgaard, K. & Christensen, H. (2002). Musculoskeletal symptoms and duration of computer and mouse use. *International Journal of Industrial Ergonomics*, **30**, 265–275.

Karasek, R. A. & Theorell, T. G. (1990). *Healthy Work: Stress, Productivity and the Reconstruction of Working Life*. New York: Basic Books.

Keefe, J. & Batt, R. (2001). Telecommunications services: union–management relations in an era of industry reconsolidation. In P. Clark, J. Delaney & A. Frost (Eds), *Collective Bargaining: Current Developments and Future Challenges*. IRRA Research Volume. Madison, WI: IRRA.

Kinnie, N. & Parsons, J. (2004). Managing client, employee and customer relations: constrained strategic choice in the management of human resources in a commercial call centre. In S. Deery and N. Kinnie (Eds), *Call Centres and HRM Management: A Cross-national Perspective* (pp. 102–128). Basingstoke: Palgrave MacMillan.

Kinnie, N., Purcell, J. & Hutchinson, S. (2000). Managing the employment relationship in call centres. In K. Purcell (Ed.), *Changing Boundaries in Employment* (pp. 133–159). Bristol: Bristol Academic Press.

Knights, D. & McCabe, D. (1998). What happens when the phone goes wild? Staff, stress and spaces for escape in a BPR telephone banking call regime. *Journal of Management Studies*, **35**, 163–194.

Korczynski, M., Shire, K., Frenkel, S. & Tam, M. (2000). Service work in consumer capitalism: customers, control and contradictions. *Work, Employment and Society*, **14**, 669–687.

Levitt, T. (1972). Production line approach to services. *Harvard Business Review*, **50**, 41–50.

Metcalf, D. & Fernie, S. (1998). (Not) hanging on the telephone: payment systems in the new sweatshops. *Centrepiece*, **3**, 7–11.

Michel, L. P. (2001). Call centres in Germany: employment market and qualification requirements. *Economic and Industrial Democracy*, **22**, 143–247.

Nohria, N. & Eccles, R. G. (Eds) (1992). *Networks and Organizations*. Boston, MA: Harvard Business School Press.

Orlinowski, W. J. (1992). The duality of technology: rethinking the concept of technology in organisations. *Organization Science*, **3**, 398–427.

Parker, S. K. & Wall, T. D. (1998). *Job and Work Design*. London: Sage.

Renn, R. W. & Fedor, D. B. (2001). Development and field test of a feedback seeking, self-efficacy, and goal setting model of work performance. *Journal of Management*, **27**, 563–583.

Rutter, D. R. (1987). *Communicating by Telephone*. Oxford: Pergamon.

Schlesinger, L. & Heskett, J. (1991). Breaking the cycle of failure in services. *Sloan Management Review*, **32**, 17–28.

Schuler, R. S. & Jackson, S. E. (1995). Linking competitive strategies with HRM management strategies. *Academy of Management Executive*, **1**, 207–219.

Shah, V. & Bandi, R. K. (2003). Capability development in knowledge intensive IT enabled services. *European Journal of Work and Organisational Psychology*, **12**, 418–427.

Short, J., Williams, E. & Christie, A. (1976). *The Social Psychology of Telecommunications*. Chichester: Wiley.

Singh, J. & Sirdeshmukh, D. (2000). Agency and trust in consumer satisfaction and loyalty judgements. *Journal of the Academy of Marketing Science*, **28**, 150–167.

Smith, M. J., Carayon, P., Sanders, K. J., Lim, S. Y. & LeGrande, D. (1992). Employee stress and health complaints in jobs with and without monitoring. *Applied Ergonomics*, **23**, 17–27.

Smith, P. R. & Sprigg, C. A. (2001). *Advice Regarding Call Centre Working Practices*. Health and Safety Executive, UK, Local Authority Circular, 94/1 (Rev.).

Sprigg, C. A., Smith, P. R. & Jackson, P. R. (2003). *Psychosocial Risk Factors in Call Centres: An Evaluation of Work Design and Well-being*. HSE Research Report (RR 169). Sudbury, UK: HSE Books.

Stanton, J. M. (2000). Reactions to employee performance monitoring: framework, review and research directions. *Human Performance*, **13**, 85–113.

Sturdy, A. (2000). Training in service—importing and imparting customer service culture as an interactive process. *International Journal of Human Resource Management*, **11**, 1082–1103.

Sturdy, A., Knights, D. & Willmott, H. (Eds) (1992). *Skill and Consent*. London: Routledge.

Taylor, P. & Bain, P. (1999). An assembly line in the head: the call centre labour process. *Industrial Relations Journal*, **30**, 101–117.

Taylor, P. & Bain, P. (2001). Trades unions, workers' rights and the frontier of control in UK call centres. *Economic and Industrial Democracy*, **22**, 39–66.

Taylor, P. & Bain, P. (2003). *Call Centres in Scotland and Outsourced Competition from India*. Scotecon, University of Stirling.

Terry, D. & Jimmieson, N. (1999). Work control and well-being: a decade review. In C. Cooper & I. Robertson (Eds), *International Review of Industrial and Organizational Psychology*, Vol. 14 (pp. 95–148). Chichester: Wiley.

Thompson, P., Callaghan, G. & van den Broek, D. (2004). Keeping up appearances: recruitment, skills and normative control in call centres. In S. Deery and N. Kinnie (Eds), *Call Centres and HRM Management: A Cross-national Perspective* (pp. 129–152). Basingstoke: Palgrave MacMillan.

Tittiranonda, P., Burastero, S. & Rempel, D. (1999). Risk factors for musculoskeletal disorders among computer users. *Occupational Medicine: State of the Art Review*, **14**, 17–38.

Totterdell, P. & Holman, D. (2001). Just trying to keep my customers satisfied: a diary study of emotional dissonance in a call centre. Paper presented at European Congress of Psychology Conference, London, 3 July.

Totterdell, P. & Holman, D. (2003). Emotional regulation in customer service roles: testing a model of emotional labour. *Journal of Occupational Health Psychology*, **8**, 55–73.

TOSCA (Table d'Observation Sociale des Centres D'Appels) (2002). *How Can We Help? Good Practice in Call Centre Employment*. Brussels: European Trade Union Confederation.

Trades Union Congress (2001). *It's Your Call: TUC Call Centre Workers' Campaign*. London: TUC.

van den Broek, D. (2004). Call to arms? Collective and individual responses to call centre labour management. In S. Deery and N. Kinnie (Eds), *Call Centres and HRM Management: A Cross-national Perspective* (pp. 267–284). Basingstoke: Palgrave MacMillan.

Vandevelde, H. (2001). Call centres don't have to be hellish. *Sunday Times*, 25 November, Public Appointments (p. 9).

Waters, R. (1998). *Computer Telephony Integration*. London: Artech House.

Wood, S. (1995). Can we speak of high commitment management on the shop floor? *Journal of Management Studies*, **32**, 215–247.

Workman, M. & Bommer, W. (2004). Redesigning computer call centre work: a longitudinal field experiment. *Journal of Organizational Behavior*, **25**, 317–337.

Wright, P. & McMahon, G. (1992). Theoretical perspectives for strategic HRM management. *Journal of Management*, **18**, 295–320.

Zapf, D., Isic, A., Bechtoldt, M. & Blau, P. (2003). What is typical for call centre jobs? Job characteristics and service interactions in different call centres. *European Journal of Work and Organisational Psychology*, **12**, 311–340.

Zapf, D., Vogt, C., Seifert, C., Mertini, H. & Isic, A. (1999). Emotion work as a source of stress: the concept and development of an instrument. *European Journal of Work and Organisational Psychology*, **8**, 371–400.

CHAPTER 8

Knowledge Management

Harry Scarbrough

Warwick Business School, University of Warwick, Coventry, UK

This chapter considers the impact of knowledge management (KM) on the workplace. This is still a matter of some debate, and the limited evidence currently available makes it difficult to draw any conclusive judgements. Despite this caveat, however, one of the recurring themes of this chapter will be the dramatic contrast between the level of interest and expectation surrounding KM and its concrete achievements at workplace level. The explanations for that contrast are many and various. As we will see, however, they have something to do with the inherent scope of the design of KM systems, but also the limited success of such designs, especially as they relate to the use of IT and the pursuit of management control. While KM's scope clearly extends beyond the conventional aims and criteria of work organization—being largely concerned with relationships and knowledge exchange *between*, rather than *within*, workgroups—the experience of what has been termed "first generation KM" (Blackler, 2000) has often failed to live up to the expectations that this concept has created.

To begin with the scope of KM's aspirations, however, we can observe that while KM notionally has an important impact on employee behaviour, we only have sketchy indications of the evidence for such impact. Much the greater part of the visible impact to date has been on the management community, where KM is associated with important developments in both managerial thinking and practice. In addressing KM's impact, therefore, we need to acknowledge its importance both as a discourse—a way of talking about management—and as a rationale for the use of a diverse array of tools and practices within organizations. Accordingly, this chapter is structured around the following themes: the wider context for KM; the organizational obstacles to KM; KM's impact on management thinking; KM's impact on organizational practice; and finally, KM's implications for HRM.

WIDER CONTEXT FOR KM

Before evaluating its organizational impact, it is important to place KM in a wider context. The emergence of KM can be related to a constellation of changes—some profound, some more cosmetic—in the business environment. These include:

The Essentials *of the New Workplace: A Guide to the Human Impact of Modern Working Practices.*
Edited by David Holman, Toby D. Wall, Chris W. Clegg, Paul Sparrow and Ann Howard. © 2005 John Wiley & Sons, Ltd.

- Long-run shifts in advanced industrial economies, which have led to the increasingly widespread perception of knowledge as an important organizational asset (Castells, 1996).
- The rise of occupations based on the creation and use of knowledge (Reich, 1991), and changes in the management of professional groups within firms (Whittington, 1991; Willcocks, Lacity & Fitzgerald, 1995).
- The convergence of information and communication technologies, and the advent of new tools such as intranets and groupware systems (Alavi & Leidner, 1997).
- Theoretical developments, for example the resource-based view of the firm, which emphasize the importance of unique and inimitable assets, such as tacit knowledge (Grant, 1997).
- New wave approaches to packaging and promoting consultancy services in the wake of business process re-engineering (Willmott, 1995).

Taken together, these developments have prompted a re-thinking of conventional management approaches to knowledge. Since the development of scientific management in the early 1900s, knowledge has generally been viewed by managers not as a resource but as a cost. Indeed, the explicit aim of scientific management was to remove knowledge from the workforce altogether and concentrate it in the heads of managers. Processes of standardization, specialization and de-skilling were the bedrock of the modern organization (Clegg, 1990). Now the development of KM does not seem to signify any lessening of these economic pressures on the creation and exploitation of knowledge. Indeed, the concern to capture knowledge and to make it an organizational resource rather suggests the further intensification of such pressures. Companies seek to recycle knowledge as much as possible, ensuring that local insights and learning are made more widely available throughout the organization. Given these intensifying economic pressures, some commentators have questioned whether KM is fundamentally different to scientific management in its ultimate aims (McKinlay, 2000).

But while KM can certainly be likened to scientific management in its aim of exploiting knowledge for economic ends, it would be wrong to overstate the similarities. Not only is KM a much broader-based movement than that of scientific management, encompassing a wide range of different approaches, its emergence and practice reflect important changes in the business and organizational context, which clearly distinguish it from the narrower efficiency focus of scientific management. Arguably, the key problems that KM attempts to address are those associated with the distribution of knowledge across increasingly fluid social boundaries, for example hierarchical, horizontal, spatial, temporal. Firms introducing KM initiatives seek to improve their exploitation (re-use) and exploration (creation) of knowledge (March, 1991) by providing ways of interconnecting disparate knowledge domains as they restructure (e.g. into flatter, decentralized or networked forms) and reorganize (e.g. around process lines), sometimes on a global scale.

Against this backdrop, KM has become a portmanteau term to designate a number of different strands of managerial activity associated with knowledge. These include, for instance, attempts to value knowledge in financial terms; practices to exploit the intellectual property of the firm; the management of knowledge workers; and the desire to make learning and situated knowledge available throughout the organization. Despite the diversity of settings and practices, however, KM initiatives tend to share a broadly similar prospectus in terms of the utilitarian perspective they bring to the creation and diffusion of knowledge. In simple terms, this prospectus can be defined as the attempt to constitute and exploit knowledge as an organizational resource. This is reflected in many of the definitions of KM which circulate within the literature. For example, KM is variously defined as: "an approach to adding or creating value by more actively leveraging the know-how, experience, and judgement resident within and, in many cases, outside of an organization" (Ruggles, 1998); or "the process of creating, capturing, and using knowledge to enhance organizational performance" (Bassi, 1997); or a "process of continually managing knowledge of all kinds to meet existing and emerging needs, to identify and exploit existing and acquired knowledge assets and to develop new opportunities" (Quintas, Lefrere & Jones, 1997, p. 387). The view of knowledge as an asset, something to be leveraged or captured, is a recurring trope in the literature on KM.

ORGANIZATIONAL OBSTACLES TO KM

Constituting knowledge as a resource has profound implications for management and for organizational practices. These are often neglected in articles dealing with KM which tend to focus on the mechanisms for exploiting knowledge. As many studies have indicated, however, the distributed, tacit and situated character of knowledge makes it difficult to extract and transfer from specific groups and settings (Blackler, 1995; Spender, 1996; Tsoukas, 1996). Moreover, both the creation and the exploitation of knowledge is dependent on the behaviour and work practices of employees, and is thus inextricably linked to the control of labour within the firm.

This intractability and embeddedness of knowledge has long led organizations to seek to economize on its use through specialization and stratification (Grant, 1996). As noted above, the division of labour applied to that end—as reflected in existing hierarchical and functional structures—itself represents a significant obstacle to attempts to constitute knowledge as a resource for the organization as a whole. The exploitation of knowledge as an organizational resource is therefore a complex endeavour which extends across technical, social and economic dimensions, as outlined below:

- In technical terms, KM involves *centralizing* knowledge that is currently scattered across the organization and codifying tacit forms of knowledge. In this more centralized and explicit form, knowledge can be accessed by a variety of groups according to business needs. The development of centralized knowledge databases is one manifestation of this aim.
- In social and political terms, KM involves *collectivizing* knowledge, so that it is no longer the exclusive property of individuals or groups. Knowledge is abstracted from highly situated processes of social learning, such that its use is no longer so closely tied to its creation. This is reflected in the deployment of IT systems, such as intranets and groupware, which seek to enhance knowledge sharing within and between employee groups. It is also manifest in the development of "communities of practice", which seek to improve the sharing of good practice at the occupational level.
- In economic terms, KM is a response to organizations' need to intensify their creation and exploitation of knowledge. This reflects the rising competitive pressures for innovation and the more rapid turnover of new products and services. KM increases the throughput rate for converting knowledge into new products and services.

The tension between these aspirations and existing hierarchical structures and practices for managing labour helps to account for many of the initiatives associated with KM. Thus, to cite one important example, the pressures for more rapid innovation create a need for multi-functional or multi-organizational project teams, spanning organizational boundaries (Clark & Fujimoto, 1989). This in turn leads to demands for more effective ways of sharing knowledge amongst geographically and organizationally dispersed team members and of capturing the knowledge that they have generated. Such demands are aggravated, not resolved, by conventional bureaucratic and hierarchical forms of organization. The latter constrain the lateral flows of knowledge-sharing with vertical authority structures. They have few, if any, mechanisms for capturing or applying knowledge that transcend internal functional divisions.

A variety of KM initiatives, including the development of intranet technology and the cultivation of communities of practice, can be seen as attempts to address this mis-match between the pressures to exploit knowledge more intensively and prevailing hierarchical structures. As these initiatives indicate, constituting knowledge as an organizational resource involves exploiting the ability of new technologies and organizational innovations to transcend social, geographical and organizational boundaries. Their success, however, seems likely to depend not so much on the technologies or innovations *per se* as on the constraining effect of existing structures and practices predicated on the management of labour.

KM'S IMPACT ON MANAGEMENT THINKING

KM has had an important impact on the ongoing debate in the management community about the design of organizations and the use of technology. Indeed, KM has become a fashionable discourse amongst managers, academics and consultants. To present KM as a management fashion is not to understate its importance. Such fashions are, after all, now an established feature of the contemporary scene (Noon, Jenkins & Lucio, 2000). They represent an important vehicle for the diffusion of new ideas and practices amongst managers. As Abrahamson puts it:

> Management fashions are not cosmetic and trivial. Management fashions shape the management techniques that thousands of managers look to in order to cope with extremely important and complex managerial problems and challenges (Abrahamson, 1996, p. 279).

As a management discourse, however, KM is much more loosely defined and ambiguous than other similar concepts, such as TQM and BPR. This reflects the rich array of sources and ideas on which KM has drawn in its emergence as a discourse. The nebulous nature of "knowledge" itself empowers a wide range of approaches and tools. Much debate, for example, centres on the distinction between knowledge, information and data. Here, Earl argues that knowledge is information that is tested and validated. It may or may not be codified, depending on its tacit or explicit nature (Earl, 1996). Others adopt differing views, defining knowledge as, respectively; "a dynamic human process of justifying personal beliefs as part of an aspiration for the truth" (Nonaka, 1994); "information made actionable" (Maglitta, 1995); and "information within people's minds" (Davenport & Marchand, 1999).

KM initiatives within firms are said to focus primarily on relatively broad or intangible objectives, such as the pursuit of competitive advantage, rather than the narrower aims of improving efficiency, quality or productivity. Thus, authors argue that "KM is becoming a

Table 8.1 Perspectives on KM

Cognitive perspective	Community perspective
Knowledge is equated with objectively defined concepts and facts	Knowledge is socially constructed and based on experience
Knowledge can be codified and transferred through text: information systems have a crucial role	Knowledge can be tacit and is transferred through participation in social networks, including occupational groups and teams
Gains from knowledge management include exploitation through the recycling of existing knowledge	Gains from knowledge management include exploration through the sharing and synthesis of knowledge among different social groups and communities
The primary function of knowledge management is to codify and capture knowledge	The primary function of knowledge management is to encourage knowledge-sharing through networking
The critical success factor is technology	The critical success factor is trust and collaboration
The dominant metaphor is the human memory	The dominant metaphor is the human community

core competence that companies must develop to succeed in tomorrow's dynamic global autonomy" (Skyrme & Amidon, 1998). In keeping with this emphasis on relative competitive performance, core KM activities are said to include benchmarking and monitoring knowledge "assets" as well as processes for knowledge capture, creation and distribution (Drew, 1996).

KM's status as a fashionable discourse within the management community makes its impact on management thinking relatively visible. In addressing that impact, however, it is clear that within the diverse array of approaches to KM outlined in the literature, recent years have seen the emergence of two broad perspectives. These perspectives have been given a variety of labels, for example the "engineering" and the "cultivation" approaches (Markus, 2000), but here will be summarily defined as the "cognitive" and the "community" perspectives. Obviously, this distinction between two broad perspectives cannot do justice to the extensive literature relating to KM—particularly, more recent studies on "embodied interaction" (Dourish, 2001) and "embodied mind" (Clark, 1998), which not only challenge the Cartesian mind–body distinction but also help to blur the distinction between "social" and "technical" activities (Scarbrough, 1995). Similarly, studies adopting a "practice-based" view of knowledge are beginning to influence our understanding of the social boundaries to the flow of knowledge (cf. Carlile, 2002). However, this characterization of existing thinking, which is summarized in Table 8.1, is useful in capturing the polarity in the literature between different views of knowledge, i.e. as a cognitive or a community phenomenon.

Cognitive Perspective

This approach to the management of knowledge adopts a cognitive, information-processing view of the firm, where valuable knowledge located inside people's heads or in successful organizational practices is identified, captured and processed, via the use of IT tools, so that it can be applied in new contexts. Tacit knowledge is codified into more explicit forms. The aim, then, is to make the knowledge inside employees' heads or the knowledge embedded in successful routines widely available to the rest of the organization. Indeed the practice of "knowledge management", as seen, is frequently reduced to the implementation of new IT systems for knowledge transfer, for example "the idea behind knowledge management is to stockpile workers' knowledge and make it accessible to others via a searchable application" (Cole-Gomolski, 1997). Knowledge is viewed metaphorically as a physical entity which can be stored, "drilled" and "mined".

Community Perspective

In contrast to the above, organizational theorists have highlighted the need to understand knowledge as also embedded in, and constructed from and through, social relationships and interactions (Blackler, 1995; Nonaka & Takeuchi, 1995). According to this view, knowledge (unlike data) cannot simply be processed; rather, it is continuously recreated and reconstituted through dynamic, interactive and social networking activity. Blackler (1995), for example, draws a categorization of forms of knowledge as: *embedded* in technologies, rules and organizational procedures; *embodied* into the practical activity-based competencies and skills of key members (i.e. practical knowledge or "know-how"); *encultured* as collective understandings, stories, values and beliefs of organizational members; or *embrained* as the conceptual understandings and cognitive skills of key members (i.e. conceptual knowledge or "know-what"). Moreover, where the cognitive perspective emphasizes the codification of knowledge into more explicit forms, here the emphasis is on the communication of knowledge on a basis of shared trust and collaboration.

The community model highlights the importance of relationships, shared understandings and attitudes to knowledge formation and sharing (Kofman & Senge, 1993). It is important to acknowledge these issues, since they help to define the likely success or failure of attempts to implement ICT-based "knowledge management" initiatives. The community model suggests that it is easier to share knowledge between individuals who have the same or similar work practices, because they share a common understanding and belief system.

In the following section, we will review the practical effects of these different approaches to KM, and seek to identify some of the reasons why they often fall short of the expectations they create.

IMPACT OF KM ON ORGANIZATIONAL PRACTICES

There is still little empirical work on the spread and impact of KM at organizational and workplace level. Much of the existing literature operates at a relatively low level of evidence, with more or less uncritical accounts of KM practices in leading firms providing the most substantive empirical material available. Firms such as BP, Skandia, Buckman Labs and Xerox continue to act as role models for the development of KM practices. Where more extensive studies have been undertaken, they have often been carried out by consultancy organizations with a vested interest in promoting KM or particular versions of it. The available evidence is therefore sketchy.

Summarising that evidence, however, leads to the following conclusions:

- KM has had only limited impact at workplace level and in the design of work organization. KM's impact on work organization and on other areas of management seems questionable. Unlike BPR or even total quality management (TQM), KM involves no explicit agenda of radical work redesign. Rather, it is often linked to investments in IT systems, such as intranets or groupware, which are designed to facilitate collaboration around existing forms of work organization. Where other discourses have sought to bring about radical changes in work practice and organizational forms, KM presents a more benign aspect. Its development is often situated *between* work groups and business units, and is frequently aimed at improving their interaction. Thus, many KM initiatives are aimed more globally at transcending existing organizational boundaries—enabling the transfer of best practice across multinational sites, for instance, or promoting knowledge-sharing amongst worldwide "communities of practice". In that sense, therefore, KM is predominantly additive rather than transformative in intent; intensifying but not fundamentally changing the existing work processes within the organization.

- KM's "discursive penetration" (Clark, 2000) into organizations is most advanced in the areas of the design and justification of IT investments. Many KM initiatives have centred on the development of IT systems such as groupware (systems which enable collaborative working between distributed groups and individuals), intranets (internal company communication systems using Internet technologies) and so-called "corporate yellow pages" (used to identify the skills of individual employees). Some evidence for this assessment of KM is provided by existing surveys of KM practice. For example, a KPMG survey in 1998 of 100 leading UK companies of £200 million plus turnover found that 90% had Internet access for employees, two-thirds had developed intranets and document-management systems, 50% had adopted groupware and one third had actually developed data warehousing and decision support systems. Against this evidence on the spread of IT systems related to KM, 43% of the sample claimed to actually have a KM initiative in place. However, only one-quarter of the latter group (i.e. only 10% of the overall sample) were said to be at the implementation stage. Moreover, only one-third of the KM adopters had developed a strategy for KM and/or a budget for KM activities. There is even evidence to suggest that in those areas where KM has penetrated, it has partly involved the relabelling of existing activities. In their study of KM practices in UK R&D functions, for instance, Coombs and Hull (1998) found that KM frequently involved the development or relabelling of existing management practices.
- The scope of KM initiatives is limited to relatively small numbers of employees—not extending beyond knowledge worker groups at the apex of the organization. For example, the CREATE study of 128 firms worldwide in 1999 found that the coverage of KM initiatives varied from 0.5–20% of the workforce.
- At the same time, and reflecting this limited coverage, many management groups are excluded from active involvement in the design of KM initiatives, with top management and Information Systems (IS) management playing the dominant roles. Thus, a survey of European businesses by the Information Systems Research Centre at Cranfield found that KM was seen as having most relevance to the R&D function and least relevance to the HR and finance functions (Cranfield School of Management, 1997). This echoed an earlier survey of 143 organizations worldwide reported in the *International Knowledge Management Newsletter* (November 1997). This found that in most organizations the responsibility for the deployment of KM lay primarily with top management and IS management.

Reflecting the different perspectives noted above, the substantive effects of KM within organizations to date seem to centre on either the IT-based extraction and concentration of knowledge or the development of communities of practice as a social arena for the sharing of knowledge. Some illustrations of these substantive effects are outlined below.

Role of IT Systems in KM

Many of the attempts to relate knowledge to information and data noted above, reflect the literature's predominant concern with the role of IT in KM. The link between IT developments and the discourse of KM is evident in the close coupling of IT and KM, which is a feature of much of the literature (Scarbrough & Swan, 2001; Raub & Ruling, 2001). Yet, despite the stress that many authors place on the use of IT, the evidence for the effective role of IT systems in creating or transferring knowledge is limited. The evidence suggests three major constraints on the use of IT for KM: the embeddedness of knowledge in social networks; the importance of face-to-face interaction for knowledge exchange; and the importance of informal settings for knowledge creation.

On the first point, this is illustrated by studies of the introduction of groupware systems (e.g. Lotus Notes). One such study found that groupware systems tend to reinforce, rather than change, the communication patterns among existing social networks. Thus, the study observed that organization members who communicated regularly and frequently before the introduction of a groupware system continued to do so using the new system. Conversely, the introduction of groupware had no impact on those members who did not communicate with each other before its introduction (Vandenbosch & Ginzberg, 1996). As Nahapiet and Ghoshal (1998) note, "The availability of electronic knowledge exchange does not automatically induce a willingness to share information and build new intellectual capital".

Similar constraints have been observed for other KM technologies. For example, a recent study of a KM initiative found that scientific employees in a pharmaceutical company made little use of a database of "lessons learned" from projects; "this was contrary to sharing tacit knowledge only with one's immediate workgroup and opened up the individual to scrutiny beyond existing structures" (McKinlay, 2000, p. 119). Likewise, a study of corporate intranet development in a global banking organization found that intranets were unsuccessful in persuading employees to share knowledge with those in other divisions (Newell, Scarbrough & Swan, 2001). Rather, a proliferation of intranets across business divisions only reflected and reinforced existing organizational boundaries. Moreover, the most frequent uses cited in this and other cases tend to be the provision of mundane information—inter-site bus timetables or canteen menus—rather than the sharing of knowledge.

Second, the importance of face-to-face contact has been underlined by studies which emphasize the role of trust in the sharing of knowledge (Nahapiet & Ghoshal, 1998).These studies reinforce previous research on management information systems which has highlighted the limitations of IT even for the provision of timely and valued information. One such study suggested that managers acquired two-thirds of their information from face-to-face or phone conversations and the remaining one-third from documents most of which came from outside the organization (Davenport, Jarvenpaa & Beers, 1996).

Third, the limitations of IT in knowledge creation were demonstrated in another study of the application of groupware technology (Ciborra & Patriotti, 1998). This highlighted the distinction between "above-the-line" (i.e. visible to management and colleagues in other units) and "below-the-line" activities (visible only to immediate colleagues). Below-the-line activities are where the most creative aspects of innovation projects take place as new ideas, and insights are tested and refined against the thinking of other trusted colleagues. The study found that the introduction of groupware did not remove this distinction, but rather reinforced it. Tools such as groupware were used primarily for above-the-line uses— communicating results and management reporting. Other communication tools, such as e-mail, phone, paper and fax were seen as more relevant to below-the-line activities.

The implication of these constraints on the use of IT systems in KM is not that IT has no value whatsoever in this context. Rather, a number of authors argue that IT systems need to be viewed as multi-dimensional, enabling technologies, whose use encompasses social and behavioural factors as much as technical ones (Ciborra & Patriotti, 1998). This multi-dimensional view of IT systems has been advanced, for instance, by Bressand and Distler (1995), who identify three layers within such systems: infrastructure, the hardware/software which enables the communication contact between network members; infostructure, the formal rules which govern the exchange between the actors on the network, providing a set of cognitive resources (metaphors, common language) whereby people make sense of events on the network; and infoculture, the stock of background knowledge which actors take for granted and which is embedded in the social relations surrounding work group processes.

Communities of Practice

In the 1990s a number of leading organizations identified the value of "communities of practice" as means of encouraging knowledge sharing across the organization. The origins of this approach can be traced back to studies by Lave and Wenger (1991) and Orr (1990) in the early 1990s. Orr's study of photocopier technicians, for instance, highlighted the importance of story-telling amongst this group as a means of sharing knowledge about repair problems. As Brown and Duguid (2000) put it, "The talk (i.e. amongst Orr's reps) made the work intelligible, and the work made the talk intelligible" (p. 125). "As part of this common work-and-talk, creating, learning, sharing and using knowledge appear almost indivisible" (pp. 125–126). Studies such as these were important in defining the properties of a community of practice. For example, Brown and Duguid (2000, p. 127) define such properties as follows: ". . . in getting the job done, the people involved ignored divisions of rank and role to forge a single group around their shared task, with overlapping knowledge, relatively blurred boundaries, and a common working identity". Unlike other types of so-cial network, communities of practice tend to support the work process directly by allowing individuals to share experience about their work. Such knowledge-sharing is seen as being facilitated by the norms of reciprocity, and levels of trust generated amongst the community.

Although the studies noted above highlight the value of a community approach, it seems to be more difficult for organizations to develop this approach. This may partly be because the cognitive approach tends to fit more neatly with established management practices; the emphasis on individuals and on the use of technology to "capture" knowledge offering a more predictable solution. Conversely, community-based approaches may seem more nebulous to managers. Such groupings do not as a rule appear in organization charts or in the different business processes designed by management (Brown & Duguid, 1998). Whereas project teams, for instance, have leaders, goals, and deliverables, communities of practice are said to be open-ended and free from directive management structures. They are said to be based on a voluntary, collaborative and egalitarian ethos.

The community of practice approach has been widely adopted in a few large organizations—notably in oil companies such as BP and Shell, where it serves to link groups of technicians and engineers who are distributed worldwide. However, the extent of its over-all impact beyond these leading firms is still uncertain, though some evidence exists on the spread of the community discourse amongst managers (Swan, Scarbrough & Robertson, 2001). There are also critical views that highlight the possible exploitative effects of this approach; McKinlay (2000) in the study noted above, analyses communities in terms of "participatory control", i.e. a form of control which requires the active engagement of par-ticipants. In his study of the UK operation of a large pharmaceutical firm, he describes the development of a "lessons learned" database encompassing tips generated by individuals and workgroup briefings at the end of a project. He describes the efforts that managers made "to socialise the digital world and to extend the reach of digital communication into the social world of the workplace" (McKinlay, 2000, p. 117). He views such efforts as an expression of the long-standing managerial desire to access tacit knowledge through the exploitation of communities of practice.

The emergence of communities of practice is seen as linked to a shift in the philosophy of management away from conventional forms of control towards what Wenger (2000) terms "cultivation". These approaches involve opening up social and virtual spaces for knowledge exchange and supporting the dialogic basis of knowledge creation. They might encompass a number of activities, including the following: public events such as knowledge fairs that bring the community together; multiple forms of leadership, including "thought leaders", networkers, and people who document practice; inter-community learning projects; and the creation and dissemination of artefacts such as documents, tools, stories, websites, etc. (Wenger, 2000).

Although they proceed from a very different epistemology to that which usually informs the design of IT systems, communities of practice may still be compatible with the use of such systems. Indeed, many global organizations view them as a means of connecting geographically and culturally disparate communities. In companies such as Buckman Labs and Xerox, IT systems provide a worldwide forum through which employees can share experience and solve problems collectively. In these cases, e-mail systems or intranets allow a conversational exchange of experience about particular problems. Thus, typically, an individual might post a particular problem of practice to a discussion forum. Subsequently, a member of the worldwide community from another continent or country would respond with a suggested solution or tip for dealing with the problem, developing the thread of the exchange. Progressively, others would build on that contribution, refine it and develop it. Brown and Duguid (2000) note that an example of such a system, Xerox's "Eureka" database, currently holds about 30 000 records. They cite what they say is an example of how the database is used. In one case, an engineer in Brazil was about to replace a malfunctioning high-end colour machine at a cost of $40 000. A quick visit to the database, however, produced a tip from a Montreal photocopier representative that led him to replace a 50 cent fuse instead. Xerox were said to have quantified the savings made from this and other uses of the database at around $100 million.

HRM IMPLICATIONS OF KM

Human resource management (HRM) and KM are both broadly defined management dis-courses which encompass a wide variety of different perspectives. On the surface, moreover, they share important similarities in their aim of mobilizing important but sometimes elusive resources for the benefit of the organization's strategic goals. It may seem surprising, then, to note that relatively few articles on KM link it in any meaningful way to the HRM practices of the organization. Beyond a few cursory references to the need for employee commitment or the importance of a "supportive culture", articles on KM make few, if any, links to HRM. Substantive debate on the implications of staple HRM policies to do with recruitment, development and reward is remarkably absent from much of the existing KM literature (Scarbrough & Swan, 2001).

This myopic view certainly reflects the emphasis we find in much KM literature on IT tools and systems. It ignores a considerable body of literature which points to the formative role played by HRM practices in the development of the organization's knowledge base. The scope of this "HRM gap" in the KM debate is signalled by a variety of studies which highlight this important formative role. Under this heading, we might include studies of the impact of career systems on the development of employee knowledge (Lam, 1998), the contribution of training and development to the formation of human capital (Switzer, 1996), and the implications of reward systems for the development of team working and trust relationships within firms.

While such studies are certainly relevant to KM, relatively few studies within the HRM field itself have directly addressed the knowledge dimensions of organizations. This seems to reflect the persistence of the broad conceptual paradigm in which HRM is essentially viewed as the management of labour. This places the emphasis on the motivation and commitment of groups and individuals but neglects the impact of their contribution to the knowledge-base of the organization (Scarbrough, 2003). Of course, employee knowledge is made available through their physical interaction with their work tools and the immediate work environment. However, it is also clear that in many cases it is employees' knowledge, not their physical effort, which is critical to their relationship with the employing firm. Grant, (1991, p. 128) discusses this relationship in terms of a balance of power:

> The degree of control exercised by a firm and the balance of power between the firm and an individual employee depends crucially on the relationship between the individual's skills and organizational routines. The more deeply embedded are organizational routines within groups of individuals and the more are they supported by the contributions of other resources, then the greater is the control that the firm's management can exercise.

Some HRM studies are beginning to explore these knowledge dimensions of the employment relationship. For example, certain studies have addressed the specific problem of HRM practices for knowledge workers (Tampoe, 1993). More generally, other studies have highlighted the role of HRM practices in absorbing and retaining knowledge. The importance of such practices is underscored by the open-ended nature of the employment contract. This not only establishes the potential mobility of human resources, but also a bargaining power that may allow them to appropriate a good deal of the market value that their skills command (Kay, 1993). Existing studies suggest a variety of absorption and learning mechanisms that are available to firms. These include teamwork and firm-specific training (Kamoche & Mueller, 1998). In addition, companies can limit the bargaining power of individuals by preventing any single individual gaining access to the complete corporate stock of knowledge—an approach which is followed, for instance, by Cosworth Engineering in the UK (Kay, 1993).

Appropriating employee knowledge for the organization also involves ensuring that such knowledge is retained by the organization and not lost through turnover or delayering.

HRM practices which may enable such knowledge retention tend to centre on the creation of continuance commitment through employee status, firm-specific training and pensions. The creation of such "human resource barriers" (Capelli & Singh, 1992) may require the development of "backloaded" payment systems rewarding loyalty with seniority and status, promotion systems which lock in high performers, and attractive pension arrangements.

Studies such as these underline the extent to which the processing of knowledge within organizations is intimately linked to the way employees are recruited, developed and rewarded. Setting aside topics which have still to be adequately researched or theorized, it is possible to determine from the existing literature three major areas where KM's links to HRM are beginning to be explored; the links between KM and HRM strategy; the links to commitment and reward; and the links to organization culture.

Links to HRM Strategy

While research on knowledge absorption and retention has highlighted mechanisms and processes through which employee knowledge is appropriated by the organization, relatively few studies have analysed the relationship between such mechanisms and firm-level strategy. One study which attempts to do this, however, is a recent study of consultancy firms in the USA (Hansen, Nohria & Tierney, 1999). Although not specifically concerned with HRM, but with "knowledge management strategy", this study does identify some important relationships between HRM and KM. Hansen *et al.* argue that there are basically two KM strategies: "codification" and "personalization".

- *Codification:* "Knowledge is carefully codified and stored in databases where it can be accessed and used readily by anyone in the company"(p. 107).
- *Personalization:* "Knowledge is closely tied to the person who developed it and is shared mainly through direct person-to-person contacts" (p. 107).

These strategies overlap to some extent with the cognitive and community perspectives outlined earlier. However, the notion of "personalization" places a greater stress on individual rather than community knowledge, reflecting the consultancy context from which these strategies are derived. The different strategies are seen as linked to the HRM and IT management practices of the organization as outlined in Table 8.2.

This analysis does not claim that organizations pursue these strategies exclusively—firms with a codification strategy also engage in personalization to some degree. However, Hansen *et al.* argue that competitive success involves pursuing one strategy predominantly. Success comes from an 80–20 split in strategic emphasis. Failure comes from attempting to "straddle" both strategies equally.

As this study was based on consultancy organizations, its wider generalizability may be limited. The personalization strategy emphasizes the role of individual experts and thus reflects the relatively individualistic nature of consultancy work. However, in other settings groups and communities may play an important role in creating and sharing knowledge. At the same time, the Hansen *et al.* account makes several useful contributions to our understanding of the links between HRM and KM. First, it links both KM and HRM to the competitive strategy of the organization. This is a useful corrective to the many articles which imply that KM can be equated with the development of large IT databases—as if the sheer quantity of "knowledge" communicated and stored was the secret of business

Table 8.2 Knowledge management strategies

	Codification strategy	Personalization strategy
Use of IT	Invest heavily in IT—connect people with re-usable knowledge	Invest moderately in IT—facilitate conversations and exchange of tacit knowledge
Human resources		
Recruitment and selection	Hire new college graduates who are well suited to the re-use of knowledge and the implementation of solutions	Hire MBAs who like problem-solving and can tolerate ambiguity
Training and development	Train people in groups and through computer-based distance learning	Train people through one-to-one mentoring
Reward systems	Reward people for using and contributing to document databases	Reward people for directly sharing knowledge with others

Source: Adapted from Hansen *et al.* (1999).

success. Hansen *et al.* (1999) show that it is not knowledge *per se* but the way it is applied to strategic objectives which is the critical ingredient of competitiveness. Second, this account effectively demonstrates the need to align HRM practices—recruitment, training and reward—to the KM strategy in use. As they note of reward systems, for instance:

> The two knowledge management strategies call for different incentive systems. In the codification model, managers need to develop a system that encourages people to write down what they know and to get those documents into the electronic repository...companies that are following the personalization approach...need to reward people for sharing knowledge directly with other people... (Hansen *et al.*, 1999, p. 113).

The Link to Knowledge-sharing and Rewards

Writers such as Senge (1993), Kofman and Senge (1993) and Nonaka (1991, 1994) all emphasize the importance of commitment to the effective implementation of KM practices. As Nonaka notes:

> in tapping the tacit and often highly subjective insights, intuitions and hunches of individual employees...The key to this process is personal commitment, the employees' sense of identity with the enterprise and its mission (Nonaka, 1991, p. 7).

Moreover, although much of the discussion about KM adopts the perspective of the organization or its senior management, there is ample evidence to suggest that the effectiveness of KM practices ultimately hinges on the response of individual employees. The greater the commitment required of the employee, the greater the need to address the incentives that underpin such commitment. The importance of such incentives was underlined by a KPMG survey of 100 leading UK businesses (KPMG, 1998). This found that 39% of respondents said that their organization did not reward knowledge-sharing, and this was considered one of the most important barriers to storing and sharing knowledge (and, if anything, this figure itself seems something of an underestimate, when we consider the limited evidence of the number of firms who explicitly reward knowledge-sharing).

In addressing reward systems for KM, it is important to note that incentives can take a variety of forms, not all of them necessarily controlled by senior management. If KM systems encourage knowledge sharing between individuals and groups, for example, the rewards for commitment are provided through the *quid pro quo* of the knowledge supplied by work colleagues. There are also intangible rewards in the form of status, reputation and recognition which can be conferred on knowledge leaders in a particular field.

Turning to more tangible incentives, however, the range is equally wide in that knowledge-intensive environments, by their nature, may permit a more innovative approach to rewarding commitment. Instances of innovative rewards being used to foster KM include the example of Hewlett Packard, where free Lotus Notes licenses were distributed to encourage trainers and educators within the organization to submit comments and ideas to knowledge bases. Also, when a new knowledge base was established, 2000 free air miles were offered to the first 50 readers and another 500 miles to anyone who posted a submission. Where knowledge sharing is central to the strategy of an organization, however—as, for example, in many consultancies and R&D organizations—there may be attempts to develop a more formalized approach to incentives. This may be easier to manage where KM is focused on exploiting the expertise of individuals, e.g. long-term achievement within a particular discipline may be rewarded by promoting individuals to senior expert positions within a "dual-career" system. This practice, developed most notably at Fujitsu/ICL, for instance, avoids siphoning off knowledge leaders into mainstream management positions. Rajan, Lank and Chapple (1998) also stress the importance of "soft rewards"; it is "essential that employees can see that sharing means immediate gains, such as less hassle, or easier tasks, reducing working hours or earlier closing" (p. 14). Moreover, in terms of specific links between rewards and knowledge-sharing, they advocate the use of intranet systems, where the number of "hits" per individual employee's website may be used to influence decisions over promotion and reward.

Although a few firms have been won over by the logic of linking rewards to knowledge-sharing, it must be recognized that the vast majority of firms do not attempt to do so. A review of the existing literature, relating not only to KM but also to other management practices, suggests that there remain important constraints on managers' ability to make explicit linkages between knowledge-sharing and reward:

- Knowledge-sharing is difficult to evaluate, since the exchange of knowledge may take place in a variety of ways, many of them tacit, and the nature of what has been exchanged may be difficult to evaluate or quantify *ex ante* (von Hippel, 1990; Williamson, 1986).
- Knowledge is created and shared within communities, and much of the most important knowledge is tacit (Lave & Wenger, 1991; Orr, 1990).
- Any linkage between knowledge-sharing and rewards will encourage employees to be more reflexive and instrumental about their willingness to share knowledge with others. Where the reward system operates in an individualistic way, it may encourage individuals to withhold knowledge from others in their workgroup or community (Robertson & Swan, 1998).
- Linking rewards to knowledge means that the measures of knowledge themselves effectively become a currency. This may lead to a tokenistic emphasis on the measures, rather than the creation or sharing of knowledge *per se* (Rajan *et al.*, 1998).

- To the extent that KM is sensitive to the exchange of knowledge within informal social networks, it may be adversely affected by the introduction of reward systems which impair the operation of such networks (Kohn, 1993).

In short, differential rewards may create dissatisfaction or overly instrumental attitudes, and the reward itself may lead towards an overemphasis on the rewarded behaviour to the detriment of the task at hand. Activities relating to knowledge creation and sharing are seen to depend heavily on the participation and intrinsic motivation of the people involved. Such motivation may actually be undermined by extrinsic rewards (Deci, 1975). Given the limitations on the effectiveness of reward systems in promoting knowledge sharing, a number of authors advocate the importance of aligning the informal norms and values of the organization with the goal of knowledge-sharing. This involves giving greater attention to the role of culture and leadership in influencing behaviour.

The Role of Culture in KM

A number of writers on knowledge-intensive organizations have highlighted the attempts by managers to engineer specific forms of organizational culture; for example, Kunda (1992, p.7) describes the manipulation of culture in one such organization:

> "Culture" is a gloss for an extensive definition of membership role in the corporate community, including rules for thought, behaviour and feeling. For some managers, culture is also the object of their work. There are specified ways of engineering it; making presentations, sending 'messages', running 'bootcamp', writing papers, giving speeches, formulating and publishing the rules....

A number of writers emphasize the role of organizational culture in fostering "normative control" over employee behaviour. This perspective highlights culture as a synthetic instrument of managerial motives, and a subtle means of manipulating meanings and identities. Knowledge-intensive firms are seen as especially prone to this form of cultural control. Although their organic structures actually involve the relaxation of individual commitment to organizational roles, this only ensures a more complete immersion of individual identity in the environing flux of tasks and projects (Alvesson, 1995).

A number of case-studies attest to the importance of culture as both an enabler and inhibitor of KM. One repeated view from the KM literature is to do with the cultural constraints that dog the initial implementation of KM systems. This operates not only in traditional, bureaucratic settings but also in dynamic knowledge-intensive organizations, where a distinct professional sub-culture has emerged. Quinn, Anderson and Finkelstein (1996), in a study of Arthur Andersen, found that major changes in incentives and culture were required to stimulate use of its new electronic network. Similarly, there were even problems in the introduction of KM at Ernst and Young:

> The E&Y consulting culture was traditionally based on pragmatism and experience rather than a conceptual orientation; while the culture was changing there were many consultants who had entered the firm and prospered under the old model and found it difficult to aggressively pursue structured knowledge in systems and documents. (Thomas Davenport website: bus.utexas.edu).

One of the most publicized examples of successful KM also underlines the cultural dimension. The development of KM at Buckman Labs in the USA involved the introduction of a KM system, termed K'Netix, which allowed for the easy transfer of information and learning between the company's many operations worldwide. Although the technology was important, the company's CEO, Bob Buckman, believed that the company's success was "90% cultural change" (Pan & Scarbrough, 1998). To underline the value of knowledge-sharing, Buckman put in place a code of ethics which was issued on a wallet-sized laminated card to every employee. Buckman employees were asked to think about the company as a ship, with the code of ethics as the waterline of the ship.

The cultural change wrought at Buckman Labs rested on more than the issue of laminated cards, however. Leadership, and particularly the symbolic deployment of both rewards and punishments, played a critical role. In particular, Bob Buckman's ability to "manage the managers" and thus enrol them as enthusiastic practitioners of KM was of paramount importance. This helped to overcome resistance to change and dismantle barriers to communication across the organization and between different levels of management.

The role of rewards was significant, but not in an instrumental way. Buckman Labs did not formalize the link between rewards and knowledge-sharing. Incentives were offered on an occasional basis, with the explicit aim of reinforcing desired cultural norms; for example, the group deemed to be the 150 best knowledge sharers were rewarded with a vacation at a fashionable resort. But there was also the hint of sanctions. In the early implementation period of K'Netix, top management wrote to all of those associates who were not willing to participate in the sharing activities.

CONCLUSIONS

This chapter has reviewed the implications of KM on a number of levels. Having situated the discourse within a conducive societal context, it began by acknowledging KM as a currently fashionable discourse in the management community. Setting aside the pejorative implications of management fashion, it is clear that KM has exerted an important impact on management thinking. However, KM has not presented a uniform recipe to managers so much as an array of tools and approaches. As has been noted, such approaches seem polarized between cognitive and community-based perspectives. Each of these approaches has profoundly different consequences for the way KM is practised in organizations; one emphasizing the extraction and concentration of knowledge through technocratic means, and the other stressing the importance of participation and knowledge sharing across communities.

As yet, it is difficult to gauge how far this polarization in the KM literature has affected workplaces. While there are many examples of the application of IT systems for KM, the limited empirical evidence suggests that many of these applications are relatively ineffectual in practice. At the same time, the evidence for the effects of communities of practice is more positive but is limited to a small number of leading firms. Even here, there are suggestions that such communities may be a further development of long-standing managerial interests in exploiting the tacit knowledge of employees (Contu & Willmott, 2000). The evidence on the impact of KM to date, therefore, highlights a number of challenges which still remain to be addressed before any of its variants can begin to satisfy the high expectations that have been created around it. This future agenda for KM is outlined in Table 8.3.

The reasons for the limited impact of KM in practice may be linked to the inherent difficulties confronting any attempt to constitute knowledge as an organizational resource.

Table 8.3 The future agenda for KM

Future challenges	Possible implications for KM
Overcoming the cultural and communication barriers posed by existing division of labour and organization structures	Moving away from a "technocratic" view of knowledge and relating it to the way work and employment is organized
Integrating knowledge from a variety of different contexts within the innovation process	Acknowledging the value of both the cognitive and community perspectives in deepening as well as transferring knowledge
Rewarding the sharing of knowledge as much as the application of effort	Developing KM initiatives within a framework defined by HRM strategies and systems
Linking the development of IT systems to social networks of trust and exchange	Socializing IT systems to encourage dialogue rather than centralization of knowledge
Development of corporate cultures which encourage knowledge-sharing	Linking KM to leadership and programmes of change within organizations
Development of more explicit, holistic and strategic criteria for evaluating the design and success of KM initiatives	Viewing knowledge as a means to an end, not an end in itself. Making KM a general management responsibility with associated metrics

Historically, knowledge within the firm has been fragmented and stratified by the pursuit of efficiency. The process of concentrating and collectivizing knowledge, which is the subtext of many KM initiatives, inevitably clashes with the hierarchical structures, employment practices and subcultures which have evolved within the existing division of labour. This historical legacy of management strategies for economizing on knowledge continues to constrain both the cognitive and community-based approaches to managing knowledge.

Overall, therefore, the available evidence tends to suggest that KM's influence on management thinking has been somewhat greater than its impact on organizational practices. This is partly because the discourse of KM does not empower any specific programme of work redesign. Many KM interventions are situated between work groups or business divisions and are aimed at overcoming the barriers to knowledge sharing posed by existing organizational boundaries. At the same time, KM's potential for change is often channelled through investments in IT systems which are de-coupled from any wider process of organizational change. The limited success of such systems—at least, those that have been the subject of academic research—may reflect not only the limitations of the cognitive perspective on knowledge, but also the absence of wider management involvement in their design and implementation. The relative lack of HRM involvement, in particular, seems likely to inhibit the levels of employee commitment and trust which are critical to the development of knowledge sharing amongst groups and individuals.

In this context, it seems significant that few, if any, examples of successful KM are focused on the use of IT systems. Rather, as the evidence from consultancy organizations and firms such as Buckman Labs seems to underline, successful KM initiatives proceed above all from the determination of business strategy. Whether or not they are labelled "knowledge management", such initiatives are developed at top management level and are linked to a wider programme of organizational change, encompassing HRM policies and cultural change, in which the ruthless exploitation of knowledge is the focal axis of management practice. This holistic approach empowers the kind of innovation that transcends existing internal and external boundaries and enables knowledge to be more fully appropriated as an organizational resource.

REFERENCES

Abrahamson, E. (1996). Management fashion. *Academy of Management Review*, **21**, 254–285.

Alavi, M. & Leidner, D. (1997). *Knowledge Management Systems: Emerging Views and Practices from the Field. INSEAD Working Paper Series*. Paris: INSEAD.

Alvesson, M. (1995). *Management of Knowledge-intensive Companies*. Berlin: Walter de Gruyter.

Bassi, L. J. (1997). Harnessing the power of intellectual capital. *Training and Development*, **51**, 25–30.

Blackler, F. (1995). Knowledge, knowledge work and organizations: an overview and interpretation. *Organization Studies*, **16**, 1021–1046.

Blackler, F. (2000). Knowledge management. *People Management*, **March**, 34–38.

Bressand, A. & Distler, C. (1995). *La Planete Relationelle*. Paris: Flammarion.

Brown, J. S. & Duguid, P. (1998). Organizing knowledge. *California Management Review*, **40**, 90–98.

Brown, J. S. & Duguid, P. (2000). *The Social Life of Information*. Cambridge, MA: Harvard Business School Press.

Capelli, P. & Singh, H. (1992). Integrating strategic human resources and strategic management. In D. Lewis, O. Mitchell & P. Sherer, (Eds), *Research Frontiers in Industrial Relations and Human Resources*, (Chapter 5) Washington, DC: International Industrial Relations Association.

Carlile, P. R. (2002). A pragmatic view of knowledge and boundaries: boundary objects in new product development. *Organization Science*, **13**(4), 442–455.

Castells, M. (1996). *The Rise of the Network Society*. Oxford: Blackwell.

Ciborra, C. & Patriotti, G. (1998). Groupware and teamwork in R&D: limits to learning and innovation. *R&D Management*, **28**, 1–10.

Clark, A. (1998). *Being There*. Cambridge, MA: MIT Press.

Clark, K. B. & Fujimoto, T. (1989). Overlapping problem-solving in product development. In K. Ferdows (Ed.), *Managing International Manufacturing* (pp. 127–152). Amsterdam: North-Holland.

Clark, P. (2000). *Organizations in Action*. London: Routledge.

Clegg, S. (1990). *Modern Organizations*. London: Sage.

Cole-Gomolski, B. (1997). Users loathe to share their Know-how. *Computerworld*, **12**(3), 6–15.

Contu, A. & Willmott, H. (2000). Comment on Wenger and Yanow. Knowing in practice: A delicate flower in the organizational learning field. *Organization*, **7**, 269–276.

Coombs, R. H. & Hull, R. R. (1998). Knowledge management practices and path dependency. *Research Policy*, **27**, 237–253.

Cranfield School of Management (1997). *Cranfield Surveys*. Cranfield: Cranfield School of Management.

Davenport, T. H., Jarvenpaa, S. L. & Beers, M. C. (1996). Improving knowledge work processes. *Sloan Management Review*, 53–65.

Davenport T. H. & Marchand, S. (1999). Is KM just good information management? *Financial Times*, Mastering Information Management, 8 March.

Deci, E. L. (1975). *Intrinsic Motivation*. New York: Plenum.

Dourish, P. (2001). *Where the Action Is*. Cambridge, MA: MIT Press.

Drew, S. (1996). Strategy and intellectual capital. *Manager Update*, **7**, 1–11.

Earl, M. J. (1996). *Information Management: the Organizational Dimension*. Oxford: Oxford University Press.

Grant, R. M. (1991). The resource-based theory of competitive advantage: implications for strategy formulation. *California Management Review*, **34**, 114–135.

Grant, R. M. (1996). Toward a Knowledge-based theory of the firm. *Strategic Management Journal*, **17**, 109–122.

Grant, R. M. (1997). The knowledge-based view of the firm: implications for management practice. *Long Range Planning*, **30**, 450–454.

Hansen, M. T., Nohria, N. & Tierney, T. (1999). What's your strategy for managing knowledge? *Harvard Business Review*, 106–116.

Kamoche, K. & Mueller, F. (1998). Human resource management and the appropriation-learning perspective. *Human Relations*, **51**, 1033–1060.

Kay, J. (1993). *Foundation of Corporate Success: How Business Strategies Add Value*. Oxford: Oxford University Press.

Kofman, F. & Senge, P. (1993). Communities of commitment: the heart of learning organizations. *Organizational Dynamics*, **22**, 5.

Kohn, A. (1993). Why incentive plans cannot work. *Harvard Business Review*, 54–63.

KPMG Consultants (1998). *Survey Report on ICTs and KM*. KPMG web-site: www.kpmg.co.uk

Kunda, G. (1992). *Engineering Culture: Control and Commitment in a High-tech Corporation*. Philadelphia: Temple University Press.

Lam, A. (1998). Tacit knowledge, organisational learning and innovation: a societal perspective. British Academy of Management Conference, Nottingham.

Lave, J. & Wenger, E. (1991). *Situated Learning: Legitimate Peripheral Participation*. Cambridge: Cambridge University Press.

Maglitta, J. (1995). Smarten up. *Computerworld*, 4 June, 84–86.

March, J. G. (1991). Exploration and exploitation in organizational learning. *Organization Science*, **2**, 171–187.

Markus, L. (2000). Knowledge management. Warwick Business School Seminar Series, University of Warwick, August, 2000.

McKinlay, A. (2000). The bearable lightness of control. In C. Prichard, R. Hull, M. Chumner & H. Willmott (Ed.), *Managing Knowledge: Critical Investigations of Work and Learning* (pp. 107–121). Basingstoke: Macmillan.

Nahapiet, J. & Ghoshal, S. (1998). Social capital, intellectual capital and the organizational advantage. *Academy of Management Review*, **23**, 242–266.

Newell, S., Scarbrough, H. & Swan, J. (2001). From global knowledge management to internal electronic fences: contradictory outcomes of intranet development. *British Journal of Management*, **12**, 97–111.

Nonaka, I. (1991). The knowledge-creating company. *Harvard Business Review*, 96–104.

Nonaka, I. (1994). A dynamic theory of organisational knowledge creation. *Organization Science*, **5**(1), 14–37.

Nonaka, I. & Takeuchi, H. (1995). *The Knowledge Creating Company*. New York: Oxford University Press.

Noon, M., Jenkins, S. & Lucio, M. M. (2000). Fads, techniques and control: the competing agendas of TPM and TECEX at the Royal Mail (UK). *Journal of Management Studies*, **37**, 499–520.

Orr, J. (1990). Sharing knowledge, celebrating identity: war stories and community memory in a service culture. In D. Middleton & D. Edwards (Eds), *Collective Remembering: Remembering in a Society*. London: Sage.

Pan, S. L. & Scarbrough, H. (1998). A socio-technical view of knowledge sharing at Buckman Laboratories. *Journal of Knowledge Management*, **2**, 55–66.

Quinn, J. B., Anderson, P. & Finkelstein, S. (1996). Managing professional intellect: making the most of the best. *Harvard Business Review*, **74**, 71–80.

Quintas, P., Lefrere, P. & Jones, G. (1997). Knowledge Management: a strategic agenda. *Long Range Planning*, **30**, 385–391.

Rajan, A., Lank, E. & Chapple, K. (1998). *Good Practices in Knowledge Creation and Exchange*. Tunbridge Wells: Create.

Raub, S. & Ruling, C. C. (2001). The knowledge management tussle—speech communities and rhetorical strategies in the development of knowledge management. *Journal of Information Technology*, **16**, 113–130.

Reich, R. (1991). *The Wealth of Nations: Preparing Ourselves for 21st Century Capitalism*. London: Simon and Schuster.

Robertson, M. & Swan, J. (1998). Modes of organizing in an expert consultancy: a case study of knowledge, power and egos. *Organization*, **5**, 543–564.

Ruggles, R. (1998). The state of the notion: knowledge management in practice. *California Management Review*, **40**, 80–89.

Scarbrough, H. (1995). The social engagement of social science. *Human Relations*, **48**, 1–11.

Scarbrough, H. (2003). Knowledge management, HRM and the innovation process. *International Journal of Manpower*, **24**(5), 501–516.

Scarbrough, H. & Swan, J. (2001). Explaining the diffusion of knowledge management: the role of fashion. *British Journal of Management*, **12**, 3–12.

Senge, P. (1993). *The Fifth Discipline: the Art and Practice of the Learning Organization.* New York: Century Business.

Skyrme, D. J. & Amidon, D. M. (1998). New measures of sucess. *Journal of Business Strategy*, **19**(1), 20–24.

Spender, J. C. (1996). Organizational knowledge, learning and memory: three concepts in search of a theory. *Journal of Organizational Change Management*, **9**, 63–78.

Swan, J., Scarbrough, H. & Robertson, M. (2001). The construction of "communities of practice" in the management of innovation, *Management Learning*, **33**(4), 477–496.

Switzer, J. (1996). Managing human capital. *Banking Strategies*, **72**, 50–51.

Tampoe, M. (1993). Motivating knowledge workers: the challenge for the 1900s. *Long Range Planning*, **26**.

Tsoukas, H. (1996). The firm as a distributed knowledge system: a constructionist approach. *Strategic Management Journal*, **17**, 11–25.

Vandenbosch, B. & Ginzberg (1996). Understanding strategic learning. Academy of Management Meeting, Boston, MA.

von Hippel, E. (1990). The impact of "sticky data" on innovation and problem-solving. Cambridge, MA: Sloan School of Management, MIT.

Wenger, E. (2000). Communities of practice and social learning systems. *Organization*, **7**, 225–246.

Whittington, R. (1991). Changing control strategies in industrial R&D. *R&D Management*, **21**, 43–53.

Willcocks, L., Lacity, M. & Fitzgerald, G. (1995). IT outsourcing in Europe and the USA: assessment issues. Oxford: Oxford Institute of Information Management, Templeton College.

Williamson, O. E. (1986). *Economic Organisation: Firms, Markets and Policy Control.* Brighton: Wheatsheaf.

Willmott, H. (1995). BPR and Human Resource Management. *Personnel Review*, **23**, 34–46.

CHAPTER 9

Employee Involvement: Utilization, Impacts, and Future Prospects

George S. Benson
College of Business Administration, University of Texas at Arlington, Arlington, TX, USA

and

Edward E. Lawler III
Marshall Business School, University of Southern California, Los Angeles, CA, USA

By all accounts there has been a significant increase in the use of employee involvement practices in firms over the last 10–15 years. Practices including self-managed teams, problem-solving groups, gainsharing and cross-training have been written about by the business press and studied extensively by academics. By the mid-1990s several studies suggested some form of formal employee involvement, labeled as "innovative" or "high-performance" practices, had been embraced by a significant number of firms worldwide, including roughly half of all US firms and some two-thirds of the Fortune 1000 (Cooke, 1994; Freeman, Kleiner & Ostroff, 2000; Gittleman, Horrigan & Joyce, 1998; Kling, 1995; Lawler, Mohrman & Ledford, 1998; Locke, Kochan & Piore, 1995; Osterman, 1994). However, there is some recent evidence that the rate of growth in the adoption of employee involvement practices in the Fortune 1000 leveled off in the late 1990s (Lawler, Mohrman & Benson, 2001). This leads to the question of where the utilization of employee involvement practices is headed. Has the diffusion of employee involvement peaked and begun to decline? Have we seen the heyday of employee involvement? It also strongly raises the issue of the long-term effectiveness of employee involvement practices.

ADOPTION OF EMPLOYEE INVOLVEMENT

Employee involvement has generated a great deal of interest from organizational researchers and theorists for decades. Employee involvement has a history going back to the 1950s with some notable early experiments in Europe and the USA. From its beginnings in "industrial

The Essentials *of the New Workplace: A Guide to the Human Impact of Modern Working Practices.*
Edited by David Holman, Toby D. Wall, Chris W. Clegg, Paul Sparrow and Ann Howard. © 2005 John Wiley & Sons, Ltd.

democracy" and "participative management", employee involvement has evolved into an integrated approach to work system design that supports employees having decision-making authority (Argyris, 1957; Likert, 1961; McGregor, 1960). Lawler (1986, 1992, 1996) argues for the design of organizations in which employees are equipped with the skills and resources they need to make informed decisions and implement them effectively. He argues that effective employee involvement requires corporate practices that distribute power and business information, create incentive rewards and provide employees with the skills and knowledge they need in order to make decisions. He further argues that, in order for employees to feel involved, they must feel that they are in control of their work, have accurate feedback concerning their performance and be rewarded for that performance. Employee involvement theorists typically argue that lower level employees should have opportunities to make decisions concerning the conduct of their jobs and to participate in the business as a whole (Cotton, 1993; Lawler, 1992).

Employee involvement was not widely embraced by industry until the 1980s (Blasi & Kruse, 2001; Cappelli & Neumark, 2001; Parks, 1995). At that time, union-management quality of work life programs became popular, as did "greenfield" high-involvement manufacturing plants (Guest & Hoque, 1996; Katz, Kochan & Gobeille, 1983; Katz, Thomas, Kochan & Weber, 1985; Lawler, 1992; Poole, Lansbury & Wailes, 2001). Several large, multi-company studies showed a significant growth in "participative", "flexible", "high-performance" or "high-involvement" work practices in the early 1990s. In 1994, two large national representative sample surveys of establishments (actual work locations as opposed to business units or firms) estimated that work teams were being used in one-third to one-half of all establishments in the USA (Gittleman *et al.*, 1998; Osterman, 1994). In a 1994 study of large companies, the number using self-managed teams was estimated at two-thirds (Lawler *et al.*, 1998). Estimates of the percentage of US firms using job rotation ranged from 24% (Gittleman *et al.*, 1998) to 43% (Osterman, 1994). Representative surveys in Europe and Australia showed similar adoption rates for employee involvement. In 1998, 42% of British establishments reported using quality circles and 65% had some sort of formally designated teams (Cully *et al.*, 1999). An Italian survey during this same period found that 56% of firms reported some type of job rotation (Locke *et al.*, 1995).

Part of the interest in new work systems during the 1980s and early 1990s was the result of a perceived competitiveness gap between US industry and the major Japanese manufacturing firms. A great deal of interest developed in total quality management (TQM) programs, and many companies began making use of quality circles. At the same time that foreign competition and technological changes were placing real competitive pressures on many firms, trends in re-engineering and corporate restructuring led many corporations to reassess the way they organized work (Hammer & Champy, 1988). The result was that many US firms introduced work teams and reduced their management overhead by giving more responsibility to front-line employees. In Europe and Australia the process was driven by both public policy and a transition away from traditional union-dominated industrial relations. Despite differences in national settings, increasing globalization and international competition during this time appears to have driven the adaptation of local employment practices towards employee involvement (Locke *et al.*, 1995).

Reviewing the research on employee involvement is challenging because of the considerable number of practices that have been labeled as "high-involvement" or "high-performance"; for example, Becker and Gerhart (1996) found 27 different variables in a review of only five studies. Among the different theories of employee involvement, however, practices are commonly categorized by those that put the power to make decisions in the hands of employees, provide incentives to take responsibility for their jobs, and provide the skills or information needed to make informed decisions (Cotton, 1993; Lawler, 1986, 1992, 1996). Some also include practices that promote job security (Kochan & Osterman, 1994; Levine & Tyson, 1990). Employee involvement theory suggests that the different types of practices are complementary and need to occur together in order to create an effective work system. Research on employee involvement, therefore, is different from the vast amount of research that has been conducted on the effectiveness of the multitude of individual management practices that are part of the employee involvement approach. For example, so much academic research has examined participative decision-making that it has been the subject of more than a dozen reviews in the past 30 years (Wagner, 1995). The employee involvement research studies reviewed in this chapter involve more than decision-making power. This review focuses on the studies examining some combination of teamwork, training, job design, and contingent rewards.

Research at the work unit level confirms the importance of viewing practices as complementary. Ichniowski, Shaw and Prennushi (1995) examined steel-finishing lines and concluded that systems of practices that included work teams, flexible assignments, training and incentive pay increased productivity over plants with "traditional" control-orientated work systems. Individual practices in isolation showed no effect on productivity. However, the exact combination or "bundles" of practices required in order to create an effective high-involvement approach is uncertain and may be industry-specific (Cappelli & Neumark, 2001; Pils & MacDuffie, 1996). As a result, most of the research conducted on cross-industry data has used scales representing multiple practices, categorized by factor or cluster analysis to cope with the variation of practices used by firms and the specific interaction patterns of practices within firms (Fernie & Metcalf, 1995; Huselid, 1995; Koch & McGrath, 1996; Lawler, Mohrman & Ledford, 1995; Lawler et al., 1998, 2001; Scholarios, Ramsay & Harley, 2000; Wood & de Menezes, 1998). While the specific practices included in these scales varies by study, they all support employee decision-making, incentive rewards, access to information on business performance, and providing workers with appropriate skills.

Table 9.1 shows the characteristics of the major surveys that have been done over the past 20 years to investigate the performance effects of employee involvement practices across a diverse group of firms or establishments in Anglophone countries around the world. In the UK and Australia, worker participation surveys have generally been conducted by government agencies. In the USA, the only government survey was conducted by the Bureau of Labor Statistics (BLS). However, surveys conducted by Columbia University, the Center for Educational Quality of the Workforce (EQW), as well as the first survey conducted by the Center for Effective Organizations (CEO) were done in cooperation with US government agencies. The remainder were conducted privately. It is not a complete list. There are several other studies that have examined adoption of practices as well as outcomes for workers, for example John Goddard conducted a telephone survey of Canadian establishments that examined outcomes for employees of involvement practices. In the USA, both the National Organizations Survey (NOS) conducted in 1991 and the National Longitudinal Survey of Youth (NLSY) 1992 supplement asked questions concerning workplace changes, including adoption of several employee involvement practices (for a complete summary of US studies of the adoption of practices, see Blasi and Kruse, 2001; for a bibliography of studies based on the UK Workplace Employee Relations Survey, see Millward, Woodland, Bryson, Forth and Kirby 1999).

Table 9.1   Surveys used to research EI and organizational performance

Conducted by	Year	Sample	Responses
Columbia University	1984	Public firms	495 (6%)
Michigan Industrial Training Institute	1989	20+ Establishments	2431 (70%)
Mark Huselid	1992	Public firms	968 (28%)
	1994	Public firms	740 (20%)
British Workplace Employee Relations Survey (WERS)	1990	25+ Establishments	2061 (83%)
	1998	10+ Establishments	2191 (80%)
Australian Workplace Industrial Relations Survey (AWIRS)	1995	20+ Establishments	2001 (75%)
Center for the Educational Quality of the Workforce	1994	20+ Establishments	2954 (66%)
	1997	20+ Establishments	4139 (59%)
Cheri Ostroff / SHRM	1993	SHRM members	373 (11%)
Bureau of Labor Statistics (SEPT)	1994	20+ Establishments	7895 (71%)
Center for Effective Organizations	1990	Fortune 1000 firms	313 (32%)
	1993	Fortune 1000 firms	279 (28%)
	1996	Fortune 1000 firms	212 (22%)
	1999	Fortune 1000 firms	143 (15%)

Early Studies

Cappelli and Neumark (2001) note that the first large-scale survey of "transformed" work practices was conducted in 1982 by the New York Stock Exchange. The survey included all public firms with more than 100 employees. The survey had a 26% response rate and asked about 17 categories of practice. In 1986 the US Department of Labor and researchers at Columbia University surveyed 7765 business units with a 6.5% response rate (Ichniowski, 1990). They estimated that 45% of firms had established some form of participation program and that 39% (unionized firms) to 54% (non-union firms) had profit sharing in place. The Michigan Industrial Training Institute (Cooke, 1994) followed this study with a survey of manufacturing firms in Michigan, which investigated teamwork and incentive compensation plans, including gainsharing and profit-sharing. Data on the adoption of practices was similar, in that approximately 45% of firms in Michigan were using teams for some portion of their workers. The proportion of firms that reported using incentive compensation was between 36% (unionized firms) and 52% (non-union firms).

The early studies differed significantly in their survey samples, but the results tended to show that employee involvement practices, including teams and incentive compensations, were in use in one-third to one-half of US firms. However, these studies also suggest that the early adopters of these practices may not have fully embraced employee participation, for example Delaney, Lewin and Ichniowski (1989) found that only 2% of the units surveyed in 1984 had work groups that were allowed to manage themselves.

EQW

In 1992 Paul Osterman at Wharton's Center for the Educational Quality of the Workforce (EQW) conducted a national telephone survey of manufacturing establishments with more than 50 employees that received approximately a 65% response rate. Osterman (1994) reported that one-third of organizations had an active quality program and 26% had job rotation for core employees. Approximately two-thirds of organizations at this time employed some type of contingent pay practices (e.g. gainsharing or skill-based pay). The survey also found that 40% of establishments had self-directed teams, which indicates a greater degree of employee involvement than earlier studies.

In 1994 the EQW teamed with the US Census Bureau on a national representative survey of establishments with more than 20 employees, called the National Establishment Survey (NES). This survey asked about the adoption of practices among all employees, rather than "core" employees, as was done in the original study. A follow-up to the 1994 survey was conducted in 1997. This second administration of the telephone survey was not a panel sample, but nonetheless indicated some significant increases in the adoption of certain practices. Capelli and Neumark (2001) report that a comparison of the 1994 and the 1997 data suggest growth in each of the involvement practices. Blasi and Kruse's (2001) analysis of the two surveys found that the percentage of establishments with self-managed teams had increased modestly from 31.8% to 34%. Adoption rates in the two NES surveys (1997 and 1994) are most likely to be lower than those reported by Osterman in his 1992 survey, because the NES sample includes all establishments with more than 20 employees, as opposed to the organizations with 50 or more employees that were sampled in the earlier survey. Generally, there is a relationship between organizational size and adoption. Taken together these three surveys indicate that employee involvement practices were firmly in place in the early 1990s and continued to grow slowly though the early part of the decade.

WERS and AWIRS

The 1990s also saw major survey efforts undertaken in the UK and Australia which were designed to assess the changes in industrial relations. The Workplace Employee Relations Survey (WERS) series in the UK has addressed several aspects of employee involvement in the two most recent administrations of the survey in 1990 and 1998. Studies conducted before 1990 indicated that no more than 2% of UK establishments used quality circles or problem-solving teams and there was relatively little use of employee involvement overall (Locke et al., 1995). A similar survey in Australia, called the Workplace Industrial Relations Surveys (AWIRS), was conducted in 1990 and 1995. The 1990 surveys in both countries consisted of cross-sectional samples and contained a number questions concerning communication and employee participation, but was dominated by union-representation issues. The 1998 WERS and the 1995 AWIRS present a more detailed picture of the adoption of employee involvement practices. Both of these surveys were extremely comprehensive, as they included all establishments in either the UK or Australia with more than 10 employees and had 75–80% responses. Based on these two surveys, Scholarios et al. (2000) reported that nearly half of workplaces in the UK (41%) and Australia (49%) have some form of contingent pay. Problem-solving teams are in place in 46% of UK establishments and 34% of Australian establishments. The latest UK and Australian establishment surveys are also unique in that they include a complement of employee surveys within a sample of establishments that measure attitudes and reactions to involvement practices.

BLS–SEPT

In 1993 the Bureau of Labor Statistics conducted the Survey of Employer Provided Training (SEPT), a comprehensive study of training practices in US establishments with 50 or more employees (Gittleman *et al.*, 1998). In addition to training data, a number of questions were asked about the establishments' work practices. This survey sample included 7500 establishments and enjoyed a 71% response rate. The survey found that 32% of establishments used team-based work for at least a portion of their employees. TQM programs were in place in 46%, and 16% used quality circles. One-quarter of the establishments had job rotation. These estimates are similar but generally smaller than the findings of the NES survey conducted around the same time.

CEO Fortune 1000 Surveys

A major research program of the Center for Effective Organizations at the University of Southern California has examined the adoption of employee involvement practices in the Fortune 1000 since 1987 with a total of five surveys (Lawler *et al.*, 1995, 1998, 2001). The first survey was conducted in conjunction with the US General Accounting Office (GAO). Mail surveys were sent to the executive office of each company and asked what percentage of employees were covered by a number of practices. These surveys provide a unique look at the adoption of practices over time. Unfortunately, the sample does not provide a true firm-by-firm longitudinal look, due to changes in the composition of the Fortune 1000. Lawler *et al.* (2001) note, however, that when they looked at a constant sample of firms their results were the same.

Findings from this series of surveys show a sharp increase in the use of many employee involvement practices in the early 1990s (Lawler *et al.*, 1998, 2001). For example, the number of companies reporting the use of self-managed teams for at least 20% of employees increased from 8% in 1987 to 32% in 1996. By the same measure, the use of individual incentive pay increased from 38% to 57% of companies (Lawler *et al.*, 1998). The findings from the most recent surveys, however, indicate that in the late 1990s growth in the adoption of employee involvement practices declined and their use may have remained constant since 1996 (Lawler *et al.*, 2001). The use of many practices, including quality circles, gainsharing and profitsharing, and cross-training, has remained relatively stable since the mid-1990s. In the case of TQM, the results indicate a significant decrease in use. In 1993, an average of 50% of employees participated in TQM activities, compared with 32% in 1999 (Lawler *et al.*, 2001).

EMPLOYEE INVOLVEMENT AND ORGANIZATIONAL PERFORMANCE

The adoption of employee involvement practices sparked dozens of research studies on their effectiveness. The relationship between employee involvement practices and firm performance has been addressed from many perspectives, including strategic management (Koch & McGrath, 1996), labor economics (Black & Lynch, 1997; Ichniowski, Kochan, Levine, Olsan & Strauss, 1996), human resources (Huselid, 1995; Huselid & Becker, 1996;

Wright *et al.*, 2001), and industrial/organizational psychology (Vandenberg, Richardson & Eastman, 1999). The level of analysis differs between the studies, since some are based on establishment surveys, while others are firm-level surveys. This raises the question of the appropriate level of analysis for examining the relationship between practice and firm performance. Employee involvement practices, such as self-managing teams and flexible job design, are seldom applied to 100% of employees in an organization. This means that the performance benefits of employee involvement practices are localized and apply to some fraction of the total employees of a firm. Organizational performance, on the other hand, is most often measured at the firm level.

BUSINESS UNIT STUDIES

Although there have been many studies that have examined organizational performance at the business-unit or establishment level, the effort (and firm cooperation) required to collect unit level data means that these studies tend to be case study, single industry, or small sample studies (Adler, Goldoftas & Levine, 1997; Bailey, 1993; Cutcher-Gershenfeld, 1991; Ichniowski *et al.*, 1995; MacDuffie, 1995; Youndt, Snell, Dean & Lepak, 1996). Ichniowski *et al.* (1996), Appelbaum and Batt (1995) and Appelbaum *et al.* (2000) all provide excellent overviews of these studies. Each of these reviews finds that the results of employee involvement are generally positive. Recent studies by Appelbaum, Bailey, Berg and Kallenberg (2000) and Brown and Appleyard (2001) report positive effects for involvement practices through in-depth case studies and surveys in industries as diverse as steel manufacturing, apparel, medical imaging and semiconductor fabrication. Although it is dangerous to generalize from single-firm and industry studies, there have been so many studies in so many different sectors of the economy that it is safe to conclude that the productivity benefits of employee involvement are real and robust, particularly in manufacturing firms.

MULTI-INDUSTRY STUDIES

It is one thing to show that employee involvement affects productivity, it is another to show they contribute to the profitability of firms in different industries. This issue has been addressed by large-scale, multi-industry studies. The decade of the 1990s saw a significant amount of research into the effects of HR systems on firm performance, based on large cross-industry studies.

Ichniowski (1990) examined 176 firms from the Columbia University survey and found that firms that used HR practices, including training and flexible job design, had higher sales per employee and higher firm performance as measured by Tobin's Q. Tobins's Q is the difference between the market value of the firm and its total assets and has been used as a proxy for the value of the firm's intangible assets, such as human capital and managerial effectiveness (Chung & Pruitt, 1994). Ichniowski (1990) suggested that employee involvement practices have the potential to impact business performance in addition to individual productivity, but it required complementary practices being implemented together. Using data from the same survey Koch and McGrath (1996) also found a significant relationship between employee involvement practices and sales per employee. They conclude that labor productivity is positively related to a firm's willingness to invest in innovative human resource management practices.

Cooke (1994) used data on 841 manufacturing firms in Michigan and concluded that group incentives and employee participation programs had a positive effect on value-added per employee. The findings for the various practices were affected by whether or not the firm was unionized. Self-managed teams and quality circles coupled with profit-sharing and gainsharing plans had positive effects on productivity. He found that although these practices tended to increase wages, that increase was less than the value-added. Among non-unionized firms, Cooke (1994) estimated that companies with teams, incentive compensation or both pay roughly 6–7% higher wages that firms without these employee involvement practices. Even with this increase in labor costs, however, he reported that firms with employee involvement practices enjoyed 21% better net performance, as measured by value-added per employee less wage costs.

Huselid (1995) surveyed 3452 public companies and received responses from 968 firms. Based on a factor analysis of responses, he constructed two indices of work practices. The first, which he labeled "skills and work structures", includes items such as individual job design, employee participation programs, and skills training. The second index, labeled "motivation", includes measures of performance appraisals and merit-based rewards programs. Controlling industry, firm size, capital intensity, R&D concentration, sales growth, union presence, and firm-specific risk, Huselid showed significant relationships between his human resource indices, sales per employee, and firm performance, as measured by gross return on assets. He also estimated that a one standard deviation increase in practice adoption was associated with an additional $27 000 additional in sales per employee per year—a 16% increase. The same change in practice adoption was also associated with a $3800 increase in gross return on assets per employee per year. In addition, significant relationships were also found with the stock market valuation of the firm, as measured by Tobin's Q.

Around the same time, Fernie & Metcalf (1995) used data from the 1990 British Workplace Industrial Relations Survey to examine the effects of participation and contingent pay on workplace performance in nearly 1500 establishments. Performance was measured as management perception of the establishment's labor productivity relative to its competitors and perceived changes in productivity over the past 3 years. They categorized workplaces between "employee involvement", "collective bargaining" and "authoritarian", based on the levels of communication, representation and contingent pay. Fernie and Metcalf found that managers in employee involvement workplaces reported the highest productivity levels. In addition, they found that establishments that had undertaken recent efforts to increase employee involvement reported the strongest relationships with the perceptual performance measures. More recent work by Addison and Belfield (2001), however, fails to replicate these results using the 1998 sequel survey and raises questions about this technique for investigating the link between involvement and performance.

For large firms, studies conducted by the Center for Effective Organizations have found consistent relationships between the adoption of employee involvement in the Fortune 1000 and several measures of financial and market performance (Lawler *et al.*, 1995, 1998, 2001). Using data on the adoption of a number of employee involvement practices, four indices were created, representing the distribution of decision-making power, access to information, level of employee training and the existence of contingent rewards. Employee involvement indices explained a small but significant amount of variance in the return on investment, return on assets and sales per employee of Fortune 1000 firms. Organizational performance was predicted in the current and following years in 1993, 1996 and, to a lesser extent, in 1999. In 1996, Fortune 1000 firms with high adoption rates of employee involvement practices (more than one standard deviation higher) had an average return on assets of 12.3%, compared with 9.2% for those firms with low adoption rates (Lawler *et al.*, 1998).

Taken together, the multi-industry studies indicate that employee involvement practices are positively correlated with firm performance, using perceptual measures, and a variety of accounting and market performance measures, including sales per employee, Tobin's Q, market returns and return on assets. However, these studies leave some important questions unanswered. Most importantly the findings from these studies raise the question of causality. Did the practices lead to the superior performance of the firms that adopted them, or did firms with the resources and flexibility provided by superior performance choose to embrace employee involvement practices? This potential problem has been labeled alternatively as a "heterogeneity bias" (Huselid & Becker, 1996) and a "self-selection bias" (Ichniowski *et al.*, 1996). Simply put, are there unmeasured management practices or other firm characteristics (such as higher quality managers and employees) that are positively related to both employee involvement and firm performance? If so, the estimates of the performance effects reviewed above may be overestimating the true impact of the employee involvement practices.

Huselid and Becker (1996) attempted to address this question with a longitudinal analysis using data from a second administration of Huselid's survey to the original sample. They used panel data collected in 1992 and 1994 to control for firm heterogeneity through a fixed effects model. In this case the estimated performance effects were substantially smaller than Huselid's (1995) original cross-sectional estimates and not statistically significant. They argue that these differences are due to measurement error common to all surveys of human resource practices; primarily that the use of a panel sample focuses the analyses on the firms that adopted employee involvement or "high-performance" practices during the study period, which in this case was only 2 years. The variance examined through this type of analysis comes from the firms that reported changes in the rates of adoption of the practices over the two survey administrations. In this case, the number of companies that reported changes was significantly smaller than those that had adopted the practices in the original survey. Although Huselid and Becker use various methods to correct this bias and conclude that the actual effects are similar to their cross-sectional estimates, their findings might also be interpreted as evidence of firm heterogeneity leading to firm performance, rather than employee involvement practices (Cappelli & Neumark, 2001).

Further evidence for the importance of firm heterogeneity in determining the performance effects of employee involvement comes from Black and Lynch (1997), who find that practices by themselves do not contribute to labor productivity, but depend on multiple contextual factors or firm contingencies for success. Using data from the National Employers Survey (NES), Black and Lynch (1997) use repeated observations of the characteristics and performance of the firm over time, rather than repeated measures of work practices. Using data collected in 1992, they assume that the use of the practices within the firms has been stable for the previous 4 years. They construct a "within estimator" using firm size, investment and labor measures for the period 1988–1993. This estimator is the residual of a regression predicting firm performance with as many firm-specific characteristics as possible. This residual is then regressed on work practices and finds that employee involvement practices explain a significant part of the variance in firm performance not explained by the control variables over time. Black and Lynch (1997) conclude that the adoption of practices alone does not contribute to productivity. They argue that the performance effects of employee involvement practices depend significantly on contextual factors, such as the educational level of workers and the use of information technology by non-managerial workers. This suggests that the effects of employee involvement depend on how practices are implemented, which in turn depends on firm characteristics, such as high-quality management and highly skilled workers. In another argument for the importance of firm heterogeneity, Wood and de Menezes (1998), in an analysis of British establishment data, found that the managers perceived the highest levels of performance in firms with either above-average or below-average use of "high-commitment" work practice, and suggest firm strategy as a critical contextual variable that might moderate the impact of these practices on firm performance.

Although the research results regarding the positive relationship between employee involvement and organizational performance have been consistent since 1990, the studies by Huselid and Becker (1996) and Lynch and Black (1998) illustrate that interpretations of these findings are not unanimous. Capelli and Neumark (2001) recently suggested that the evidence does not show conclusively that high-performance work practices contribute to the profitability of companies. They note that although the practices contribute to labor productivity, they also increase the cost of labor and wages. According to them, "The findings are suggestive of important effects but, taken as a group, remain inconclusive" (Cappelli & Neumark, 2001, p. 737). With data from two waves of the NES conducted in 1992 and 1997, they use a longitudinal design and conclude that "high-performance" work practices do not impact on labor productivity as measured by output per dollar spent on labor, and therefore have little potential effect on firm performance. These findings are supported by Freeman and Kleiner (2000), who analyzed data from the 1993 SHRM survey conducted by Ostroff to examine the performance effects of employee involvement (Freeman *et al.*, 2000). They conclude, based on analysis of 273 firms, that employee involvement practices have no significant effects on output per worker. Finally, with regards to perceptual measures of performance, Addison and Belfield (2001) analyzed the 1998 British WERS and were unable find significant effects for employee involvement practices, and call into question the findings of Fernie and Metcalf (1995) and their conclusions based on the 1990 WERS.

The findings from these recent studies raise important questions regarding the true effect of employee involvement on firm performance. The theoretical and methodological problems associated with this line of research have been documented (Ichniowski *et al.*, 1996; Becker & Huselid, 1998) and debated (Gerhart, Wright, McMahan & Snell, 2000; Huselid & Becker, 2000; Gerhart, Wright & McMahan, 2000). Some of these problems are particularly vexing, such as deciding on the most appropriate unit of analysis and the measurement errors associated with assessing the adoption of practices across a large and diversified organization. Data for companies is most often collected from a single respondent. Although this is less of a problem for small companies or establishments, the potential for measurement error is significant in large companies (Wright *et al.*, 2001). The contextual variables examined should be expanded and methods for research in multi-industry studies should be improved in order to address some of the problems with the existing research.

However, the best approach to getting at the real effects of employee involvement may be to make a closer examination of the actual mechanisms through which these practices affect firm performance.

HOW DOES EI TRANSLATE INTO ORGANIZATIONAL PERFORMANCE?

In the organizational behavior literature, employee involvement practices are theorized to act on organizational performance through some combination of creating more efficient work processes and increasing the motivation of workers (Huselid, 1995; Ichniowski *et al.*, 1996; Lawler, 1986). Vandenberg *et al.* (1999) label these two mechanisms "cognitive" and "motivational" models. They argue that the positive effects of employee involvement on organizational performance come from the increased utilization of the knowledge and skills of employees. The increased efficacy of workers then motivates them to give extra effort, resulting in higher productivity coupled with lower absenteeism, grievances and turnover, which ultimately impact the bottom line.

From the economic efficiency perspective, employee involvement increases the value of the firm's stock of human capital that it can apply to manufacturing products or providing services. Viewing the skills and abilities of individual employees in terms of human capital has a long tradition in labor economics (Becker, 1964) and there have been multiple recent research efforts to link investment in human capital with firm performance (Bassi, Lev, Low, McMurrer & Seisfeld, 1999; Blundell, Dearden, Meghir & Sianest, 1999; Bouillan, Doran & Orazem, 2001). The notion that employee involvement creates economic efficiencies in work has dominated research on the performance effects of HR practices until recently. Studies of the performance effects of employee involvement or high-performance practices have most often made arguments that employee involvement practices improve labor productivity by better use of the knowledge and skills of employee through efficient work processes. However, they have tended to look past the effects of involvement practices on employees and have focused on their attention on organizational outcomes, such as sales per employee, return on assets, and market returns. Studies of the effects of employee involvement on firms have generally taken an economic or efficiency perspective and left the individual "intervening" effects unmeasured and assumed (Ichniowski, 1990).

All of the studies reviewed above examine direct relationships between employee in-volvement work practices and organizational outcomes. When outcomes such as turnover (e.g. Huselid, 1995) or labor productivity (e.g. Cooke, 1994) are examined, the motivations of the workers are assumed. When organizational outcomes such as profitability and market returns are studied, the effect of the work practices on employees is left as a "black box" (Gardner, Moynihan, Park & Wright, 2000). For example, training in TQM and statistics is assumed to lead to constant improvement of work processes and teamwork. Communi-cation skills are thought to help identify potential problems, while cross-training and decision-making authority are thought to allow employees to act quickly when a problem does arise. Self-managed teams mean that fewer middle managers are needed to schedule and monitor individual work.

While studies of the performance impact of employee involvement have generally viewed the effects of employee involvement in terms of economic efficiencies and firm strategy, the original impetus for advocating employee involvement was based more on its effect on individual motivation and extra effort. Employee involvement is based on the notion that those closest to the actual work of the company should be responsible for as many aspects of their work as possible, because this will motivate them to perform better. That is, if employees are given challenging work that involves serving customers and contributing to the business, they will be motivated to improve their job performance. Based on a needs-satisfaction or intrinsic motivation view of the workplace, giving people responsibility and allowing them to feel part of a well-performing organization increases performance motivation.

Some of the recent research on employee involvement is moving back towards a motivation model to better explain the effects of employee involvement on firm performance. Specifically, it suggests that the link between practices and organizational performance may depend on a worker's interpretation of the practices (Meyer & Smith, 2000; Kinicki, Carson & Bohlander, 1992; Koys, 1988). Research suggests that involvement practices that promote positive employee attitudes, such as organizational commitment, may, in turn, contribute to extra-effort (Cappelli & Rogovsky, 1998), prosocial behavior (O'Reilly & Chatman, 1986), work performance (Meyer, Paunonen, Gellatly, Goffin & Jackson, 1989), customer satisfaction (Oakland & Oakland, 1998; Bowen & Schneider, 1999), safety (Probst & Brubaker, 2001) and employee retention (Koys, 2001). Examining the effects of employee involvement on employee attitudes and behavior as an intermediate step between the practices and organizational performance gets back to the foundations of employee involvement as a motivational approach.

Other studies have examined different employment relationships and HR "climates" and concluded that particular configurations of HR practices (such as employee involvement systems) are associated with higher commitment and greater discretionary effort on the part of employees (Liao & Chuang, 2004; Rogg, Schmidt, Shull & Schmitt, 2001). Other studies have shown significant relationships between HR strategies such as "high-performance" or "high-commitment" work systems and employee attitudes (Arthur, 1994; Lam & White, 1998; Scholarios, *et al.*, 2000; Tsui, Pearce, Porter & Tripoli, 1997). Employee attitudes are critical in light of other studies that indicate that positive attitudes are associated not only with organizational outcomes, such as absenteeism and turnover, but also with objective measures of performance.

Vandenberg *et al.* (1999) illustrate this new approach towards examining the performance effects of employee involvement. Based on motivation theory, they predict that employee involvement leads to positive employee attitudes, which in turn leads to improved individual and organizational performance. In a study of 3500 insurance company employees in 49 organizations, they found that the level of employee involvement affected the commitment and satisfaction of workers. These attitudes, in turn, were associated with higher levels of customer satisfaction for the units, and higher individual performance rankings for the employees. Similarly, Morrison (1995) and Koys (2001) found that employee attitudes, organizational citizenship behavior and turnover mediate the effects of employee involvement and other HR practices on customer satisfaction and organizational effectiveness. Gelade and Ivery (2003) use a similar approach and conclude that work climate partially mediates the effects of HRM practices on business performance in a chain of retail banks.

Such multi-level studies have been advocated but not widely pursued (Becker & Huselid, 1998, Gardner *et al.*, 2000; Guest, 1997). If this line of research is extended and proves to be explanatory of the relationship between employee involvement and firm performance, the implications for the future adoption and effects of work practices are significant. It means that a causal mechanism between practices and performance is their impact on employees. Recent theoretical work by Bowen and Ostroff (2004) details some of the mechanics through which the 'strength' of a system of practices might explain how individual employee outcomes accumulate to affect organizational effectiveness. It may explain, in part, the differences in the success of practices across similar firms.

IMPACT ON EMPLOYEES

There is evidence that attitudes such as organizational commitment are dependent on how the employee interprets the reasons for practices. Kinicki *et al.* (1992) found that employees only responded to certain HR practices with organizational commitment if they interpreted those practices as indications of the firm's genuine interest in their well-being. Employees who felt that the HR practices were instituted only to protect the company from lawsuits did not report higher levels of organizational commitment. In a similar study, Meyer and Smith (2000) found that the relationship between "employee-friendly" HR practices and organizational commitment was mediated by perceptions of organizational support.

This suggests that workers need to interpret employee involvement as genuine efforts to improve employee well-being in terms of job satisfaction, positive workplace relations and employee benefits, in addition to company performance. This can be particularly challenging if involvement practices are implemented through a large structural reorganization (Morgan & Zeffane, 2003). Preuss and Lautsch (2002), for example, found that a history of downsizing may mute the effectiveness of employee involvement practices unless employees perceive management effort to maintain job security. There is evidence that employees tend to respond positively to increased opportunities to share ideas and contribute on the job. In 1994 the Worker Representation and Participation Survey collected phone surveys from a representative sample of all US private sector employees regarding individual reactions to employee involvement practices. Freeman and Rogers (1999) report that 79% of non-managerial participants in employee involvement programs report having "personally benefited from [their] involvement in the program by getting more influence on how [their] job is done". Based on this survey, Freeman *et al.* (2000) conclude that employee involvement practices are associated with increased job satisfaction and greater trust in management. Guest reports similar findings from two studies of a 1996 survey of 1000 British employees collected by the Institute of Personnel and Development (Guest; 1999; Guest & Conway, 1999). Goddard (2001) finds that involvement has positive relationships with satisfaction, commitment and belongingness among Canadian employees. There is also evidence that high-involvement workplaces tend to provide additional training to employees (Leigh & Gifford, 1999). Finally, Chadwick and Fister (2001) suggest that at least some employee involvement practices (including self-managed teams and job rotation) are correlated with greater fringe benefits for employees.

But are work life improvements, fringe benefits and access to training enough to sustain employee involvement practices? Models of employee involvement have generally assumed that employees are not willing to put forth the increased effort and suggestions for improvement required to make the system work if they do not feel that they are justly rewarded (Lawler, 1986) and that the firm is not committed to them over the long term (Kochan & Osterman, 1994; Levine & Tyson, 1990; Osterman, 2000). Osterman (2000) suggests that a real examination of employee welfare needs to include the effects of employee involvement on employee wages. If employees are asked to be more responsible for the performance of the firm, are they compensated for their increased involvement? However, whether or not employee involvement practices increase wages is an open question. There is some evidence that it does. Freeman and Lazear (1994) examined participative decision-making through works councils and found that it not only increased the total rent produced by the firm, but also had a positive effect on the wages of employees. Cooke (1994) also found higher wages in companies with teams and incentive pay. Chadwick and Fister (2001) found that wages were positively related to the use of self-managed teams. Helper, Levine and Bendoly (2002) found employee involvement practices in US and Canadian auto suppliers had raised wages by 3–5% during the 1990s.

Osterman (2000), on the other hand, argues that while the use of employee involvement practices dramatically increased in the 1990s, "aggregate measures of employee welfare do not show commensurate gains" (Osterman, 2000, p. 180). Osterman (2000) notes that the rise of "high-performance" practices during the 1980s and 1990s was heralded as a trend towards the "mutual-gains" enterprise, in which both companies and workers would share the benefits. However, in contrast to the findings of Freeman and Lazear (1994) and Cooke (1994), Osterman (2000) finds that there was no corresponding increase in workers' wages to reflect these gains and increased responsibilities. In addition, those companies with employee involvement practices in place were more likely to experience lay-offs in the years following. This finding suggests that employees may resist employee involvement in the future because they do not see it having a positive impact on wages or job security.

EMPLOYEE INVOLVEMENT: FUTURE PROSPECTS

What is the future of employee involvement? Employee involvement is not right for every firm, and it is becoming clearer where it fits and where it does not. It may well be that the slow-down in the adoption of employee involvement practices in the late 1990s is a very rational reaction to the popular rush towards the practices in the earlier part of the decade. In the future we are more likely to see employee involvement practices adopted by firms with employees and work processes that are suited to involvement. There will be fewer firms who adopt involvement practices because everyone is doing it, or because of pressure from investors. Because of the wealth of research and experience that exists concerning employee involvement, it is also unlikely that there will be as many naïve adopters in the future. It is now clear that what once looked like an easy route to improvement is a complex change that requires more commitment and investment than some firms are willing to make. This suggests that adoption may be less frequent but more successful in the future.

Just as relatively little is known about why employee involvement programs impact on firm performance, very little is known about why firms adopt employee involvement. There is some evidence emerging that it is more likely to be adopted by large firms and that it is particularly likely to be adopted in industries that require skilled human capital. A developed view of who adopts employee involvement and why is needed. Further understanding of adoption behavior is important because it is a precursor to organizations making intelligent adoption decisions and, ultimately, to effective implementation of employee involvement.

The future adoption of employee involvement may also be limited if it is not clear that employees gain from the practices. It is increasingly apparent that involvement practices are only successful under circumstances where employees embrace the practice and respond with increased motivation and commitment to the organization. For employees to embrace involvement practices, they need to see the benefits and react positively in terms of job satisfaction, commitment and organizational citizenship.

A clear threat to the future of employee involvement is the possibility that firms will use it in an exploitative way, i.e. they will install some of the practices, but manage them and the organization in a way that leads to gains being accrued by the organization but not by the employees. The more often this happens, the less likely it is that employees will accept involvement practices. This can be particularly problematic in unionized workplaces with a history of labor/management antagonism.

Because it is increasingly apparent that the success of employee involvement practices depends on how the practices are interpreted by employees, future research should also address the role of employee involvement in the overall employment relationship. A particularly interesting issue here concerns the importance of job security. It is not clear that employees need to have job security in order to respond favorably to involvement efforts, but some writers have suggested that it is. If it is necessary, given the turbulent economic times, this may prove to be a major limitation on the successful adoption of employee involvement programs and their survival over the long-term.

Finally, despite the large number of studies that have examined the performance effects of employee involvement, there is clearly a need for further research. A number of directions appear to be worth exploring. First and foremost, studies are needed that look at why a connection exists between the adoption of employee involvement practices and the performance of firms. More probing needs to take place to define the mechanisms at work in the "black box" between involvement and organizational performance. This probing should include a focus on how the adoption of different patterns of involvement practice affect individual attitudes and performance. Equally, we need to know how changes in individual performance changes affect organizational performance. A better understanding of the connection between practices and organizational performance should lead to a clearer understanding of how employee involvement systems should be designed and implemented, as well as where and when they are likely to be effective. It is not enough to know that involvement practices generally work; more knowledge needs to be developed concerning when, where and how they work.

Findings from several national cross-industry studies show the economic benefits of employee involvement practices, notwithstanding the well-documented limitations. However, viewing the effects of employee involvement practices from a purely economic perspective simplifies the analysis of the effects by putting the practices into a cost vs. benefits equation in terms of labor productivity and labor expense. The problem is that it may be hard to quantify the true benefits to an organization of having a highly involved workforce. Even if the costs and benefits of implementing employee involvement practices appear to cancel each other on the balance sheet, there are additional benefits in terms of positioning the firm strategically and competitively. For example, firms that use employee involvement practices may be more "agile" or "ambidextrous" (Gibson & Birkinshaw, 2001; Shafer, Dyer, Kilty, Amos & Ericksen, 2001). In highly competitive industries, where long-term performance is determined by the ability to adapt to rapidly changing market conditions and product quality, employee involvement may prove to be an important asset that, over the long-term, is difficult to quantify. Future research should address these additional potential benefits of employee involvement.

Many questions remain concerning the future of employee involvement practices. These work practices have received a very considerable amount of attention over the past 20 years, with many large-scale studies to assess their adoption and effectiveness in industry. The bottom line, however, is that employee involvement has only been strongly embraced by a minority of firms. Given that successful work practices that yield a consistent competitive advantage are likely to be imitated by other firms, there is good reason to believe that employee involvement practices will continue to be utilized. What may change is whether they are adopted as part of a specific program. It may well be that, rather than being part of a major employee involvement change effort, practices that are associated with employee involvement may simply become standard operating procedures in companies. Ultimately, rather than being seen as part of a new approach to management, they will be seen as the right way to manage an effective organization.

REFERENCES

Adler, P., Goldoftas, B. & Levine, D. (1997). Ergonomics, employee involvement, and the Toyota production system: a case study of NUMMI's 1993 model introduction. *Industrial and Labor Relations Review*, **50**(3), 416–438.

Addison, J. & Belfield, C. (2001). Updating the determinants of firm performance: estimation using the 1998 UK Workplace Employees Relations Survey. *British Journal of Industrial Relations*, **39**(3), 341–366.

Appelbaum, E. & Batt, R. (1995). *The New American Workplace: Transforming Work Systems in the United States*. Ithaca, NY: ILR Press.

Appelbaum, E., Bailey, T., Berg, P. & Kallenberg, A. (2000). *Manufacturing Advantage: Why High-performance Work Systems Pay Off*. Ithaca, NY: ILR Press.

Argyris, C. (1957). *Personality and Organizations*. New York: Harper & Row.

Arthur, J. (1994). Effects of human resource systems on manufacturing performance and turnover. *Academy of Management Journal*, **37**(3), 670–687.

Bassi, L., Lev B., Low, J., McMurrer, D. & Seisfeld, T. (1999). Corporate investments in human capital. In M. Blair & T. Kochan (Eds), *The New Relationship: Human Capital in the American Corporation*. Washington DC: Brookings Institution Press.

Bailey, T. (1993). Organizational innovation in the apparel industry. *Industrial Relations*, **32**, 30–48.

Becker, B. & Gerhart, B., (1996). The impact of human resource management on organizational performance: progress and prospects. *Academy of Management Journal*, **39**(4), 779–801.

Becker, B. & Huselid, M. (1998). High performance work systems and firm performance: A synthesis of research and managerial implications. *Research in Personnel and Human Resources*, **16**, 53–101.

Becker, G. S. (1964). *Human Capital*. New York: National Bureau of Economic Research.

Black, S. & Lynch, L. (1997). *How to Compete: the Impact of Workplace Practices and Information Technology on Productivity*. Working Paper No. 6120. Cambridge: National Bureau of Economic Research.

Blasi, J. & Kruse, D. (2001). High performance work practices at century's end: incidence, diffusion, industry group differences and the economic environment. Unpublished manuscript, Rutgers University.

Blundell, R., Dearden, L., Meghir, C. & Sianest, B. (1999). Human capital investment: the returns from education and training to the individual, the firm, and the economy. *Fiscal Studies*, **20**(1), 1–23.

Bouillon, M., Doran, M. & Orazem, P. (2001). Human capital investment effects on firm returns. *Journal of Applied Business Research*, **12**(1), 30–41.

Bowen, B. & Schneider, D. (1999). Understanding customer delight and outrage. *Sloan Management Review*, **41**(1), 35–45.

Bowen, D. & Ostroff, C. (2004). Understanding the HRM–firm performance linkages: the role of "strength" of the HRM system. *Academy of Management Journal*, **29**(2), 203–221.

Brown, C. & Appleyard, M. (2001). Employment practices and semiconductor manufacturing performance. *Industrial Relations*, **46**(3), 436–471.

Cappelli P. & Neumark, D. (2001). Do "high-performance" work practices improve establishment-level outcomes? *Industrial and Labor Relations Review*, **54**(4), 737–775.

Cappelli, P. & Rogovsky, N. (1998). Employee involvement and organizational citizenship: implications for labor law reform and "Lean production". *Industrial and Labor Relations Review*, **51**(4), 633–653.

Chadwick, C. & Fister, T. (2001). Innovative human resource practices and outcomes for workers. Unpublished manuscript, University of Illinois at Urbana-Champaign.

Chung, K. & Pruit, S. (1994). A simple approximation of Tobin's Q. *Financial Management*, **23**(3), 70–74.

Cooke, W. (1994). Employee participation programs, group-based incentives, and company performance: a union-nonunion perspective. *Industrial and Labor Relations Review*, **47**(4), 594–609.

Cotton, J. (1993). *Employee Involvement*. Newbury Park, CA: Sage.

Cutcher-Gershenfeld, J. (1991). The impact on economic performance of a transformation in workplace relations. *Industrial and Labor Relations Review*, **44**(January), 241–260.

Cully, M., O'Reilly, A., Millward, N., Forth, J., Woodland, S., Dix, G. & Bryson, A. (1999). *The 1998 Workplace Employee Relations Survey: First Findings*. London: Department of Trade and Industry.

Delaney, J., Lewin, D. & Ichniowski, C. (1989). *Human Resource Policies and Practices in American Firms*. Bureau of Labor–Management Relations and Cooperative Programs, US Department of Labor, BLMR 137. Washington, DC: US Government Printing Office.

Fernie, S. & Metcalf, D. (1995). Participation, contingent pay, representation and workplace performance: evidence from Great Britain. *British Journal of Industrial Relations*, **33**(3), 380–415.

Freeman, R., Kleiner, M. & Ostroff, C. (2000). *The Anatomy of Employee Involvement and Its Effects on Firms and Workers*. Working Paper No. 8050. Cambridge: National Bureau of Economic Research.

Freeman, R. & Lazear, E. (1994). *An Economic Effects of Works Councils*. Working Paper No. 4918. Cambridge: National Bureau of Economic Research.

Freeman, R. & Rogers, J. (1999). *What Workers Want*. Ithaca, NY: Cornell University Press.

Gardner, T., Moynihan, L., Park, H. & Wright, P. (2000). Unlocking the black box: examining the processes through which human resource practices impact business performance. Unpublished manuscript, Cornell University.

Gelade, G. & Ivery, M. (2003). The impact of human resource management and work climate on organizational performance. *Personnel Pschology*, **56**, 383–404.

Gerhart, B., Wright, P., McMahan, G. & Snell, S. (2000). Measurement error in research on human resources and firm performance: how much error is there and does it influence effect size estimates? *Personnel Psychology*, **53**, 803–834.

Gerhart, B., Wright, P. & McMahan, G. (2000). Measurement error in research on the human resources and firm performance relationship: further evidence and analysis. *Personnel Psychology*, **53**, 855–872.

Gibson, C. & Birkinshaw, J. (2001). Contextual determinants of organizational ambidexterity. Unpublished manuscript, University of Southern California.

Gittleman, M., Horrigan, M. & Joyce, M. (1998). "Flexible" workplace practices: evidence from a nationally representative survey. *Industrial and Labor Relations Review*, **52**(1), 99–115.

Goddard, J. (2001). High performance and the transformation of work? The implications of alternative work practices for the experience of outcomes at work. *Industrial and Labor Relations Review*, **54**(4), 776–805.

Guest, D. (1997). Human resource management and performance: a review and research agenda. *International Journal of Human Resource Management*, **8**(3), 263–276.

Guest, D. (1999). Human resource management—the worker's verdict. *Human Resource Management Journal*, **9**(3), 5–25.

Guest, D. & Conway, N. (1999). Peering into the black hole: The downside of new employment relations in the UK. *British Journal of Industrial Relations*, **37**(3), 367–389.

Guest, D. & Hoque, K. (1996). National ownership and HR practices in UK Greenfield sites. *Human Resource Management Journal*, **6**(4), 50–74.

Hammer, M. & Champy, J. (1988). *Reengineering the Corporation*. New York: Harper Business.

Helper, S., Levine, D. & Bendoly, E. (2003). Employee involvement and pay at US and Canadian auto suppliers, *Journal of Economics and Management Strategy*, **11**(2), 329–377.

Huselid, M. (1995). The impact of human resource management practices on turnover, productivity, and corporate performance. *Academy of Management Journal*, **38**(3), 635–672.

Huselid, M. & Becker, B. (1996). Methodological issues in cross-sectional and panel estimates of the human resource-firm performance link. *Industrial Relations*, **35**(3), 400–422.

Huselid, M. & Becker, B. (2000). Comment on "Measurement error in research on human resources and firm performance: how much error is there and does it influence effect size estimates?" by Gerhart, Wright, McMahan, and Snell. *Personnel Psychology*, **53**, 835–854.

Ichniowski, C. (1990). *Human Resource Management Systems and the Performance of US Manufacturing Businesses*. Working Paper No. 3449. Cambridge: National Bureau of Economic Research.

Ichniowski, C., Shaw, K. & Prennushi, G. (1995). *The Impact of Human Resource Practices on Productivity*. Working Paper No. 5333. Cambridge: National Bureau of Economic Research.

Ichniowski, C., Kochan, T., Levine, D., Olson, C. & Strauss, G. (1996). What works at work: overview and Assessment. *Industrial Relations*, **35**(3), 299–333.

Katz, H., Kochan, T. & Gobeille, K. (1983). Industrial relations performance, economic performance, and QWL programs: an inter-plant analysis. *Industrial and Labor Relations Review*, **37**, 3–17.

Katz, H., Thomas, P. Kochan, T. & Weber, M. (1985). Assessing the effects of industrial relations systems and efforts to improve quality of working like on organizational effectiveness. *Academy of Management Journal*, **28**(3), 509–526.

Kinicki, A., Carson, K. & Bohlander, G. (1992). Relationship between an organization's actual human resource efforts and employee attitudes. *Group & Organization Management*, **17**(2), 135–152.

Kling. J. (1995). High performance work systems and firm performance. *Monthly Labor Review, May*, 29–36.

Koch, M. & McGrath, R. (1996). Improving labor productivity: human resource management policies do matter. *Strategic Management Journal*, **17**, 335–354.

Kochan, T. & Osterman, P. (1994). *The Mutual Gains Enterprise*. Boston: Harvard Business School Press.

Koys, D. (1988). Human resource management and a culture of respect: effects on employees' organizational commitment. *Employee Rights and Responsibilities Journal*, **1**, 57–67.

Koys, D. (2001). The effects of employee satisfaction, organizational citizenship behavior, and turnover on organizational effectiveness: a unit-level longitudinal study. *Personnel Psychology*, **54**, 101–114.

Lam, L. & White, L. (1998). Human resource orientation and corporate performance. *Human Resource Development Quarterly*, **9**(4), 351–364.

Lawler, E. (1986). *High-involvement Management: Participative Strategies for Improving Organizational Performance*. San Francisco, CA: Jossey-Bass.

Lawler, E. (1992). *The Ultimate Advantage: Creating the High Involvement Organization*. San Francisco, CA: Jossey-Bass.

Lawler, E. (1996). *From the Ground Up: Six Principles for Creating the New Logic Organization*. San Francisco, CA: Jossey-Bass.

Lawler, E., Mohrman, S. & Benson, G. (2001). *Organizing for High Performance: the CEO Report on Employee Involvement, TQM, Re-engineering, and Knowledge Management in Fortune 1000 Companies*. San Francisco, CA: Jossey-Bass.

Lawler, E. Mohrman, S. & Ledford, G. (1995). *Creating High Performance Organizations: Practice and Results of Employee Involvement and Quality Management in Fortune 1000 Companies*. San Francisco, CA: Jossey-Bass.

Lawler, E., Mohrman, S. & Ledford, G. (1998). *Strategies for High Performance Organizations: Employee Involvement, TQM, and Re-engineering Programs in Fortune 1000 corporations.* San Francisco, CA: Jossey-Bass.

Leigh, D. & Gifford, K. (1999). Workplace transformation and worker upskilling: the perspective of individual workers. *Industrial Relations*, **38**(2), 174–191.

Levine, D. & Tyson, L. (1990). Participation, productivity, and the firm's environment. In A. Blinder (Ed.), *Paying for Performance: a Review of the Evidence* (pp. 183–243). Washington, DC: Brookings Institution.

Liao, H. & Chuang, A. (2004). A multilevel investigation of the factors influencing customer service performance and customer outcomes. *Academy of Management Journal*, **47**(1), 41–58.

Likert, R. (1961). *New Patterns of Management.* New York: McGraw-Hill.

Locke, R., Kochan, T. & Piore, M. (1995). Reconceptualizing comparative industrial relations: Lessons from international research. *International Labour Review*, **134**(2), 139–162.

Lynch, L. & Black, S. (1998). Beyond the incidence of employer-provided training. *Industrial and Laser Relations Review*, **52**(1), 64-81.

MacDuffie, J. (1995). Human resource bundles and manufacturing performance: organizational logic and flexible production systems in the world auto industry. *Industrial and Labor Relations Review*, **48**(2), 197–222.

McGregor, D. (1960). *The Human Side of the Enterprise.* New York: McGraw-Hill.

Meyer, J., Paunonen, S., Gellatly, I., Goffin, R. & Jackson, D. (1989). Organizational commitment and job performance: it's the nature of the commitment that counts. *Journal of Applied Psychology*, **74**, 152–156.

Meyer, J. & Smith, C. (2000). HRM Practices and organizational commitment: test of a mediation model. *Canadian Journal of Administrative Sciences*, **17**(4), 319–331.

Millward, N., Woodland, S., Bryson, A., Forth, J. & Kirby, S. (1999). *A Bibliography of Research Based on the British Workplace Industrial Relations.* Survey Series. London: Department of Trade and Industry (available at http://www.dti.gov.uk/er/emar/1998wers.htm).

Morgan, D. & Zeffane, R. (2003). Employee involvement, organizational change and trust in management. *International Journal of Human Resource Management*, **41**(1), 55–75.

Morrison, E. (1995). Organizational citizenship behavior as a criticl link between HRM and service quality. *Human Resource Management*, **35**, 493–512.

Oakland, J. & Oakland, S. (1998). The links between people management, customer satisfaction and business results. *Total Quality Management*, **9**(4, 5), 185–190.

O'Reilly, C. & Chatman, J. (1986). Organizational commitment and psychological attachment: the effects of compliance, identification, and internalization on prosocial behavior. *Journal of Applied Psychology*, **71**, 492–499.

Osterman, P. (1994). How common is workplace transformation and who adopts it? *Industrial and Labor Relations Review*, **47**(2), 173–189.

Osterman, P. (2000). Work restructuring in an era of restructuring: trends in diffusion and effect on employee welfare. *Industrial and Labor Relations Review*, **53**(2), 179–196.

Parks, S. (1995). Improving workplace performance: historical and theoretical contexts. *Monthly Labor Review*, **May**, 18–28.

Pils. F. & MacDuffie, J. (1996). The adoption of high involvement work practices. *Industrial Relations*, **35**(3), 423–455.

Poole, M., Lansbury, R. & Wailes, N. (2001). A comparative analysis of developments in industrial democracy. *Industrial Relations*, **40**(3), 490–525.

Preuss, G. & Lautsch, B. (2002). The effect of formal versus informal job security on employee involvement programs. *Canadian Industrial Relations*, **57**(3), 517–539.

Probst, T. & Brubaker, T. (2001). The effects of job insecurity on employee safety outcomes: cross-sectional and longitudinal explorations. *Journal of Occupational Health Psychology*, **6**(2), 139–159.

Rogg, K., Schmidt, D., Shull, C. & Schmitt, N. (2001). Human resource practices, organizational climate, and customer satisfaction. *Journal of Management*, **27**, 431–449.

Scholarios, D., Ramsay, D. & Harley, B. (2000). "High-commitment" management practices and employee outcomes: evidence from Britain and Australia. Working Paper in Human Resource Management, ER, and OS, Number 9. University of Melbourne.

Shafer, R., Dyer, L., Kilty, J., Amos, J. & Ericksen, J. (2001). Crafting a human resource strategy to foster organizational agility: a case study. *Human Resource Management*, **40**(3), 197–211.

Tsui, A., Pearce, J., Porter, L. & Tripoli, A. (1997). Alternative approaches to the employee-organization relationship: does investment in employees pay off? *Academy of Management Journal*, **40**(5), 1089–1121.

Vandenberg, R., Richardson, H. & Eastman, L. (1999). The impact of high involvement work practices on organizational effectiveness: a second-order latent variable approach. *Group & Organization Management*, **24**(3), 300–339.

Wagner, J. (1995). Participation's effects on performance and satisfaction: a reconsideration of the research evidence. Academy of Management Review, **19**, 312–330.

Wood, S. & de Menezes, L. (1998). High commitment management in the UK: evidence from the Workplace Industrial Relations Survey, and Employers' Manpower and Skills Practices Survey. *Human Relations*, **51**(4), 485–515.

Wright, P., Gardner, T. M., Moynihan, L., Park, H., Gerhart, B. & Delery, J. (2001). Measurement error in research on human resources and firm performance: additional data and suggestions for future research. *Personnel Psychology*, **54**, 875–901.

Youndt, M., Snell, S., Dean J. & Lepak, D. (1996). Human resource management, manufacturing strategy, and firm performance. *Academy of Management Journal*, **39**, 836–866.

CHAPTER 10

Managing Virtual Workers and Virtual Organisations

David Lamond

Sydney Graduate School of Management, University of Western Sydney, NSW, Australia

Kevin Daniels

Loughborough University Business School, UK

and

Peter Standen

Department of Management, Edith Cowan University, Western Australia

Telework[1] is a growing work practice whereby employees work at a site(s) remote from their office(s) for at least part of the week. Common arrangements include work done at home or in the field, by teleworkers in a range of sales and service occupations. As such, telework is one of the most radical departures from standard working conditions in the suite of flexible work practices now gaining widespread acceptance, and presents unique challenges to both managers and employees.

Recent figures indicate between and eight and nine million teleworkers in the USA (Glosserman, 1996; Rourke, 1996). Huws, Jagger and O'Regan (1999) conclude that 5% of the UK workforce can be classified as teleworkers. Meanwhile, Australian Bureau of Statistics (2001) figures indicate that, as of June 2000, 3% of employees mainly worked at home, with two-thirds (64%) using information technology in the job. The European Commission (1998) estimates that the number of teleworkers rose from 0.8% to 3.1% of the workforce between 1997 and 1998. The increased interest in teleworking among managers and employees is also reflected in the literature on the subject, with more than 1000 articles being published in the period 1999–2001 (Proquest, 2001). It is worthy of note that, again from examination of the database (Proquest, 2001), the term "telecommuting" appears to be almost exclusive to the articles published in the North American media, while "teleworking" appears to be the preferred term in European publications.

There are many reasons to expect organisations and their employees to experiment with this type of work organisation, particularly given the rapid growth of affordable

---

[1] Telework or teleworking is also referred to as "telecommuting" and "homeworking". The specific choice of the term "teleworking" is explained in the chapter. To avoid confusion, all references are to teleworking, even where other authors use different terms.

The Essentials *of the New Workplace: A Guide to the Human Impact of Modern Working Practices.*
Edited by David Holman, Toby D. Wall, Chris W. Clegg, Paul Sparrow and Ann Howard. © 2005 John Wiley & Sons, Ltd.

telecommunications technology. For organisations, the benefits are seen in terms of the positive impact on what are often their two largest overheads—their work force and accommodation costs: and so teleworking has been linked to improved productivity, improved employee retention, greater staffing flexibility and more efficient use of office space (e.g. Cascio, 2000). Specific individual benefits are thought to include: more flexible working hours; more time for home and family; reduced commuting; greater job autonomy; less disturbance whilst working; and the chance to remain in work despite moving home, becoming ill or taking on family care roles (IRS, 1996). Many of these direct benefits would have indirect consequences for job and life satisfaction and possibly physical health. The list of perceived societal benefits includes increased community stability; increased entrepreneurial activity; less pollution; and more efficient use of energy resources (Cascio, 2000).

While this list of perceived benefits is impressive, the potential negative consequences of teleworking, including fewer chances for development or promotion, increased conflict between work and home and social isolation have also been acknowledged (e.g. Gainey, Kelley & Hill, 1999; Gillespie, Richardson & Cornford, 1995; Hamblin, 1995). Then there are the negative organisational consequences, which may include increased selection, training and support costs, along with health and safety consequences (cf. Cascio, 2000).

The future of teleworking depends on whether employers provide the opportunity to telework and whether workers take advantage of this opportunity. As Cascio (2000) points out, for example, not all employees are suited to spend their scheduled work hours away from their primary business locations, while not all managers are suited to manage employees with telework arrangements. However, most of the literature on telework to date has involved prescriptions based heavily on the experience of individuals and does not use existing theory or recent research.

To address this issue, this chapter presents a comprehensive framework for understanding the psychology of teleworkers and telework management, based on both organisational behaviour theory and recent empirical evidence. Embedded in this framework is an examination of the relationship between organisation structure and teleworking, in order to identify the organisational structures that are most likely to support teleworking. We begin by considering teleworking in general, with a brief examination of the various uses of the term "teleworking", and present a definition and a framework that take account of its multidimensional nature. We then explore the organisational and individual factors that impinge on the telework process. Theoretical and empirical considerations from the literature are used to develop predictions about how these factors impact on the various forms of telework. These predictions set an agenda for future research aimed at building a body of empirical knowledge that ultimately researchers and practitioners alike can use to make informed decisions about telework and teleworking.

TELEWORKING AND TELEWORKERS: DEFINITIONS AND TYPOLOGY

Teleworking

Despite its growing popularity, there is still no "official" definition of teleworking (Baruch, 2001). As a result, discussions on the issue of teleworking tend to cover a variety of different working practices and to overlap into related areas such as homeworking, including where the term is used to refer to unskilled workers receiving piece rates for manual tasks (cf. Felstead & Jewson, 2000). Based on an extensive review of the literature, we characterise teleworking not just as a structure or function defined primarily in terms of where work is done or what equipment is used, but as a process that involves several variables (see also Daniels, Lamond & Standen, 2000, 2001; Lamond, Daniels & Standen, 1997a, 1997b):

- *Location*—the amount of time spent in the different locations: traditional office, home, remote office/telecottage, nomadic.
- *ICT usage*—extent of use of telecommunications/ICT links—home/mobile computer, fax, modem, phone, mobile phone, use of WWW sites.
- *Knowledge intensity*—extent of knowledge required, ease of output measures and autonomy of work.
- *Intra-organisational contact*—extent (range and intensity) of intra-organisational contact.
- *Extra-organisational contact*—extent (range and intensity) of extra-organisational contact.

This set of variables, summarised in Table 10.1 together with exemplar jobs, allows us to say that:

- Teleworking is best viewed as a process which involves a bundle of practices.
- There is no *one* form of teleworking and, as a corollary, there is no *one best way* of teleworking.
- Teleworking is best thought of as a multidimensional phenomenon, its character varying across five major variables: ICT usage; knowledge intensity; intra-organisational contact; extra-organisational contact; and location.

These five variables can be used as the basis of describing and making predictions about teleworking in different organisational contexts.

Much of the literature in this area focuses on "teleworkers" rather than the process of teleworking. Following Daniels *et al.* (2001), we consider a teleworker to be someone:

1. Who spends a fraction of working time, no matter how small, within a defined period at home, at a remote office or engaged in nomadic working.
2. For whom a fraction of work tasks, no matter how small, necessitate the use of ICTs, even if this is simply a telephone.

This provides a minimum threshold for teleworking, and is less restrictive than attempts to define teleworkers by an arbitrary threshold of time spent in given locations (cf. Qvortrup, 1998). Nevertheless, the exact form of telework should be described according to levels on all five variables.

A FRAMEWORK FOR THE STUDY OF TELEWORKING

Teleworking is a set of work practices that exists at the juncture of a wide variety of organisational, social, individual and historical forces (Daniels *et al.*, 2001). In this and the following sections we present a comprehensive framework for the study of teleworking, beginning with the macro-level context set by national variations in legislation,

Table 10.1 Types of telework and sample jobs

Location	ICT usage	High knowledge intensity				Low knowledge intensity			
		Intra-organisational contact				Intra-organisational contact			
		High		Low		High		Low	
		Extra-organisational contact		Extra-organisational contact		Extra-organisational contact		Extra-organisational contact	
		High	Low	High	Low	High	Low	High	Low
Home-based	Low ICT usage	Sales managers	Management accountant	Lawyer	Translator	Phone operator	Bookkeeper	Phone sales	Proof-reader
	High ICT usage	Public relations	Programmer	Financial analyst	IS developer	Customer enquiries	Secretarial/clerical	Market research	Data processing
Remote office	Low ICT usage	Sales managers	Management accountant	Lawyer	Translator	Phone operator	Bookkeeper	Phone sales	Proof-reader
	High ICT usage	Public relations	Programmer	Financial analyst	IS developer	Customer enquiries	Secretarial/clerical	Market research	Data processing
Nomadic	Low ICT usage	Sales managers	Internal management consultant	Community nurse	Architect	Service persons	Bookkeeper	Sales representative	Proof-reader
	High ICT usage	Engineer	Internal IT consultant	Auditor	IS developer	Service persons	Secretarial/clerical	Delivery staff	Data processing

Source: Reproduced by permission from Daniels et al., 2001. © 2001 Blackwell Publishers.

geography, culture and industrial relations. We then move to the organisational-level factors of culture and structure, and looking within organisations to social and group factors such as socialisation and communication. Next, we consider individual factors, such as personality, the psychological character of work including the nature of the psychological contract and motivation, job characteristics and well-being, and the home/work interface. Finally, we consider the impact of human resource management practices on the social, group and individual variables, and the outcomes of teleworking programs.

Figure 10.1 captures schematically what we consider to be the major factors which impact on, and are in turn impacted by, teleworking—national characteristics, the context of organisational structure and culture, human resource management practices, group factors within organisations, and individual factors. In subsequent sections, we speculate on some of the relationships between these influences. In some cases, the factors we discuss can be seen to moderate the impact of telework on outcomes, while in others the impact of telework on outcomes is mediated through the impact on, for example, job characteristics. Although we would expect to see mediating effects more frequently, this does not preclude the possibility of moderating effects in more specific models of telework and behaviour.

National Context

It is clear that some countries are making more use of telework than others, and differential growth rates exist (Tregaskis, 2000). For example, in Europe the Scandinavian countries and the UK appear to have greater uptake than the central and southern countries (Tregaskis, 2000). There are many factors that contribute to these differences (Tregaskis, 2000), which we consider linked to four major categories of variables: legislative factors; culture and attitudes; industrial factors; and geography. The exact form of teleworking adopted by organisations will partly depend on the conflation of such national factors, with different forms of teleworking encouraged by different combinations of national context factors, operating directly on the form of teleworking adopted or in conjunction with other contextual factors linked to organisational structures and cultures (see Daniels *et al.*, 2000, 2001, for a fuller discussion).

Organisational Context—Structure and Culture

Organisational structures and cultures are likely to influence the kinds of teleworking practices adopted by organisations. However, there are two factors specific to organisations that are necessary but not sufficient conditions for the adoption of teleworking practices. The first of these, obviously, is the suitability of work tasks for teleworking. Jobs that are suitable for teleworking are those that require the interpretation, communication and manipulation of information. The number of such jobs in an organisation places an upper limit of the number of people that can engage in teleworking practices. Second, relevant decision-makers within an organisation must realise the benefits of teleworking relative to the costs, and have sufficient power over other stakeholders to allow teleworking practices (Daniels *et al.*, 2001). Teleworking is also more likely to be implemented alongside other changes, such as relocation, since implementation of teleworking is likely to be less costly where there are changes to other fixed costs (van Ommeren, 1998).

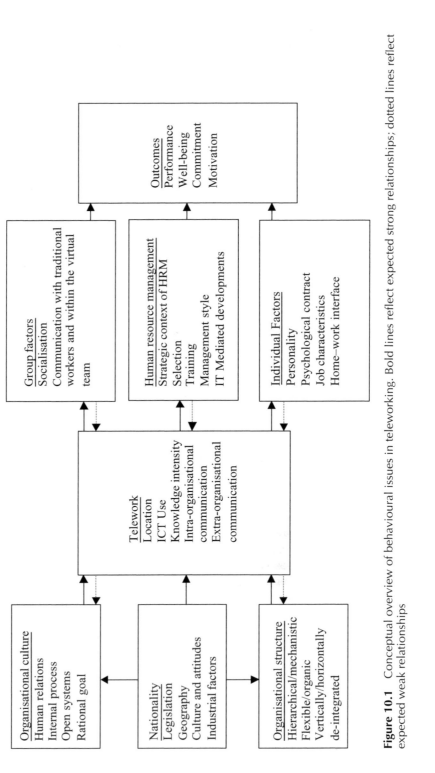

Figure 10.1 Conceptual overview of behavioural issues in teleworking. Bold lines reflect expected strong relationships; dotted lines reflect expected weak relationships

Structure

Over the last decade, we have been witnesses to a number of trends that have affected organisational structure: downsizing; delayering; process re-engineering; replacement of traditional functional departments with team-based or project-based structures; the shift to a core/periphery model with a greater role for contingent workers; growth in inter-organisational networks; and boundaryless designs (Ashkenas, Ulrich, Jick & Kerr, 1995). These recent changes in organisational structure may encourage the adoption of teleworking practices (Daniels *et al.*, 2001). The reasons appear to be twofold.

First, the rise in knowledge work and the increased sophistication of information technology make it easier for organisations to develop structures that transcend traditional space and time limits (Reich, 1992). These structures can often be characterised as loose federations of groups and individuals. Building on the contingency approach to organisational structure (e.g. Lawrence & Lorsch, 1967), it could be expected that such flexible, "organic" organisations are more likely to move towards teleworking and are more likely to have effective teleworkers. A reciprocal relationship may exist here too, as growth in teleworking encourages wider experimentation with flexible structures. For example, Travic (1998) found a positive relationship between the amount of ICT usage and the existence of non-traditional organisational structures, and invoked the notion of an "organic, informated organisation" (cf. Figure 10.1 "organic/flexible").

Second, teleworking might be introduced by organisations where the primary attraction is the promised cost reductions through downsizing and delayering the organisation, and geographical relocation of the remaining employees and functions (cf. Figure 10.1 "hierarchical/mechanistic"). In this context, the impact on teleworking could be quite different to that of the organic orientation. For instance, there may be a distinct lack of interest in flexibility issues and notions of "re-engineering" may be code for cost-cutting, and teleworking introduced with stringent electronic controls and greater use of contingent workers (Daniels *et al.*, 2001).

Culture

A number of predictions follow from the view that teleworking forms are related to organisational cultures. We have utilised Quinn's (1988) competing values framework as a basis for classifying cultures. Quinn's (1988) framework identifies organisations on two dimensions—flexibility vs. control and internal vs. external focus—creating four potential organisational archetypes. An adapted version of Quinn's (1988) framework is presented in Table 10.2, which also includes some of the predicted impacts on forms of teleworking.

HRM authorities emphasise the importance of supportive organisational cultures for flexible working practices (e.g. Guest, 1990). Accordingly, organisations whose internal processes are characterised by flexibility, trust and openness (see the Human Relations model in Table 10.2) would be expected to move towards home-based or remote office teleworking practices for all types of workers (Standen, 1997). Organisations whose cultures have an external focus (open systems) are similarly more likely to support telework when the cultures are also more flexible. These organisations are focused on expansion

Table 10.2 Predicting forms of telework from Quinn's (1988) competing values framework

	Internal focus	External focus
	Human relations model	Open systems model
Flexibility	*Goal*: human commitment *Values*: human resources, training, cohesion, morale *Telework*: Types A and B; all types of intra- and extra-organisational contact; all locations	*Goal*: expansion and adaptation *Values*: adaptability, readiness, growth, resource acquisition, external support *Telework*: Knowledge intensive; all types of intra- and extra-organisational contact; bias towards nomadic
	Internal process model	Rational goal model
Control	*Goal*: consolidation and continuity *Values*: information management, communication, stability, control *Telework*: Limited low knowledge intensity; home, remote office, telecottage	*Goal*: maximization of output *Values*: productivity, efficiency, planning, goal setting *Telework*: Limited knowledge intensive; extra-organisational contact; mainly nomadic

and adaptation and may see telework as a competitive business tool to increase flexibility and communication, and so may be biased toward forms of teleworking that emphasise flexible task completion most, for example high-knowledge-intensity, mobile teleworking, especially with high extra-organisational contact.

Conversely, cultures focused on flexible external goals but which have a bureaucratic control-based internal focus (rational goal), are likely to support only knowledge-intensive telework. Clerical and other non-professionals may not be considered to be trustworthy off-site, thus reducing possibilities for teleworking. Finally, organisations lacking flexibility in both internal and external perspectives (internal process) are focused on stability and would be considered least likely to experiment with radical practices like telework. With both types of control-orientated cultures, low-knowledge-intensity teleworkers may be very rare. Where such teleworkers are employed, it is likely to be only in home-based or remote office contexts, where outputs from workers can be easily monitored. For all types of workers, control-orientated organisations may only employ teleworkers where other factors (such as structure) support such practices.

As in the case of organisational structure, there are reciprocal relationships between teleworking and culture—moving towards teleworking practices necessitates changes in people's attitudes, and therefore can affect culture. It is likely, however, that most telework programs are currently small scale and that "feedback" effects will be found more in the future. At the same time, there will be limits on the influence of organisational cultures; for example, nomadic workers (sales staff and consultants) get to work off-site more from practical necessity, which may override cultural factors (Standen, 2000). Indeed, these groups were allowed to roam off-site long before telework was considered as an organising strategy.

GROUP PROCESSES, THE INDIVIDUAL, HRM PRACTICES AND TELEWORK

According to the preceding analysis, the initiation and development of a teleworking project is related, at least in part, to national contexts and the cultures and structural dynamics of the organisations in which they are initiated. The expected outcomes of these teleworking processes, summarised in Figure 10.1, are improvements in variables such as employee performance, commitment, motivation and well-being. However, as also shown in Figure 10.1, the impact of teleworking on these outcome variables will be moderated by three critical areas of organisational behaviour: (a) group and social processes that include teleworkers; (b) characteristics of individual teleworkers; and (c) human resource management practices.[2] We now examine these three areas.

Social and Group Processes

Socialising Teleworkers

In examining strategies for creating and maintaining a committed workforce, Aryee (1991) points to the importance of linking socialisation practices to business strategy. He also discusses the different types of employees and organisational roles that need to be taken into account in determining the most appropriate approach. The extent to which teleworkers participate in social networks is strongly affected by the extent of time spent off-site, but for the purposes of analysis we will consider arrangements with a high degree of off-site work (e.g. three or more days per week). Such teleworkers do not have the same opportunities for social contact as traditional workers and are not as immersed in the organisational culture. However, there are probably differences between workers engaged in different types of telework. For instance, teleworkers with high intra-organisational contact, or who regularly use real-time telecommunication media (e.g. telephones), are more likely to be socialised through natural processes. In contrast, teleworkers with low intra-organisational contact and that use non-real-time telecommunications (e.g. e-mail), are less likely to be socialised through natural means. Therefore, this group of workers is more likely to need socialisation interventions, yet many of the usual socialisation factors are not relevant.

With at least some groups of teleworkers, then, this poses an interesting problem as managers seek to use socialisation into organisational cultures as an important tool for management control of teleworkers in place of more traditional but impractical direct supervision. There are potential solutions to this problem. First, managers can begin by selecting teleworkers whose values are already close to those of the organisational culture (Billsberry, 2000). Second, it is also possible that teleworkers need less socialisation initially than a typical worker to be functional off-site. Some evidence (Omari & Standen, 1996) suggests that many teleworkers value autonomy more than other workers and resist socialisation, except where it coincides with personal values related to work achievement.

---

[2] It is recognised that, as with other organisational level variables, there is potential for feedback effects whereby there might be reciprocal relationships between teleworking and changes in social processes, some individual factors and human resource management practices more broadly in the organisation beyond the direct impact of the telework program.

Beyond initial socialisation, maintaining social networks is crucial to the success of teleworking programs. Organisations need to consider options such as regular meetings, minimum requirements for office attendance, including teleworkers in social programs, and developing off-site social events. It will be important to include teleworkers' co-workers in such events, so that contact is maintained across the team to which the teleworker belongs.

Communication between Teleworkers and Traditional Office Workers

A related issue to socialisation is the types of communication between traditional office workers and teleworkers, and the possible evolution of separate subcultures. Face-to-face communication is likely to be highest between managers and traditional workers, and lowest between managers and teleworkers. At the same time, in-group communication is likely to be highest amongst traditional workers and amongst remote office-based workers, leading to the possibility of separate and conflicting cultures emerging. Full use of information technology should overcome some barriers, supplemented by regular socialisation events that involve all workers.

Whilst teleworkers with lower intra-organisational communication requirements to perform their work tasks may experience fewer problems with task-related communication, as intimated in the previous section, communication can have an important function beyond direct facilitation of work. Therefore, it is important to be sure that managers and co-workers are happy with low levels of contact and that team cohesion is not lost. In some cases where there is otherwise little intra-organisational communication, a separate "cyberspace" sub-culture based on mutual support and information sharing may be beneficial to teleworkers. The next section elaborates on the issues of communication *within* the virtual team.

Communication for Decision Making within the Virtual Team

Another related but distinct problem (especially for knowledge-intensive teleworking) is the use of electronically mediated communication to make decisions. There is evidence (Hiemstra, 1982) that people prefer face-to-face communication that enables use of subtle facial and body signals in the visual channel, and the para-linguistic signals conveyed by intonation, voice, pitch, pause and pace of speech, all of which are lost in text-based media. This does not exclude the possibility that, over a period of time, teams linked by electronic media can communicate effectively (cf. Harper, 2000; Walther, 1995). Indeed, Duxbury and Nuefeld's (1999) analysis of data from two Canadian federal government departments suggests that part-time telework arrangements need not substantially change the way in which teleworkers communicate with managers, subordinates, colleagues and clients. The explosive growth of "cyberspace" as a (mostly) non-work communication medium suggests that many people will readily trade the limitations of new media for its benefits, and will find new ways to encode non-textual signals in text, for example the use of signs such as ":-)" (smiley face) and ";-)" (wink), or simple graphics (cf. Lea & Spears, 1992).

The optimal communication networks and the optimal media (e-mail, telephone, etc.) for effective decision making need to be explored further. However, it is clear that the effectiveness of each network and medium depends on the nature of the work that is being performed and the characteristics of the organisation and the team (Harper, 2000). For example, for knowledge-work characterised by a high need for intra-organisational communication to coordinate tasks across a work team, all-channel networks and frequent and informal real-time contact (e.g. by telephone) may be more suitable for home-based or remote office teleworkers. In contrast, nomadic teleworkers who spend time working face-to-face with clients may prefer multi-channel, asynchronous (i.e. non-real time) communication via voice mail or e-mail from colleagues, so as not to disturb time spent with clients.

Individual Factors

As well as group factors, a number of individual factors will also affect the performance and satisfaction of teleworkers. These are personality, motivation and the psychological contract, job characteristics and their impact on psychological and physical health, and the home/work interface.

Personality, Competencies and Telework

Telework will not suit all workers equally. One way in which to examine the degree of fit between teleworking practices and personal characteristics is to explore personality in the context of teleworking. One popular approach to personality indicates that personalities can be summarized or classified in terms of five basic dimensions (the "Big Five")— extraversion, emotional stability, agreeableness, conscientiousness, and openness to experience (Barrick & Mount, 1991). This model, amongst others, might be suitable for making predictions about which types of people adapt better to teleworking (Lamond, 2000a).

   In the teleworking context, the importance of personality may be intensified, given that the feedback and correction processes afforded by direct supervision are often not present or present to only a minimal degree. We may then expect research that indicates aspects of personality that predict good performance in non-teleworking contexts not only to generalise to teleworking contexts, but the extent of predictive relationships to be strengthened. For example, the characteristics associated with conscientiousness, such as persistence, care, capacity for hard work and being responsible, have been shown to influence the accomplishment of work tasks. We would also expect that people who work in jobs with high levels of intra- and/or extra-organisational communication are likely to be more successful if they are higher on extraversion, agreeableness and openness to experience. Personality can also be important with regard to how knowledge about aspects of teleworking is gained, since distance learning, again with minimum supervision, is an attractive training option for teleworkers for a variety of reasons (Salmon, Allen & Giles, 2000; see below). In this respect, extraversion, openness to experience and conscientiousness are important, since these dimensions are related to performance on training programs (Barrick & Mount, 1991; Behling, 1998). Behling's (1998) concurrent conclusion, that intelligence is positively related to work performance, while unsurprising, reminds us that intelligence is likely also to be a predictor in regard to teleworker training outcomes in regard to success, perhaps especially for high-knowledge-intensity, high-ICT-usage jobs.

   Townsend, DeMarie and Hendrickson (1998) describe the shift to "virtual interaction"— e-mail and document sharing replaces face-to-face meetings and geographic proximity—as new ways of communicating and interacting that enable teleworking and coordination of teleworkers. They point out that virtual team members still need traditional teamwork skills—effective communication skills, goal clarity and performance orientation—but they need to learn new ways to express themselves and understand others in an environment with a "diminished sense of presence". In this sense, personality factors associated with membership of successful teams might be especially important in the context of "virtual teams", where correcting social factors might be less evident. Such personality factors include higher levels of extraversion, agreeableness, emotional stability and conscientiousness (Lamond, 2000a). Further, given the fluidity of membership of virtual teams and that they more easily transcend functional, organisational and national boundaries (Townsend *et al.*, 1998), there is a greater need to adapt quickly to novel situations, and so the personality dimension of openness to experience may be associated with better adaptation to virtual teamworking.

As well as personality, competencies may be influential in adaptation to teleworking. Several authors have established lists of teleworking competencies (e.g. Omari & Standen, 2000; Sparrow & Daniels, 1999). These lists include competencies that can be grouped into four major clusters:

1. *Personal competencies*, such as self-discipline, self-direction, self-motivation, capacity for self-assessment, tough-mindedness, tenacity, personal integrity and self-confidence.
2. *Inter-personal competencies*, such as strong verbal and written communication skills, negotiation skills, trusting others and assertiveness.
3. *Generic task competencies*, such as organisation skills, practical orientation, basing decisions on facts, flexibility, ability to take independent decisions, time management skills, and possessing consistent, productive and organised work habits.
4. *Technical competencies*, such as information and communications technology literacy and good subject-matter knowledge.

Several recent studies have considered the interaction of some of these competencies with attitudes towards teleworking (Raghuram, Wiesenfeld & Garud, 2003; Workman, Kahnweiler & Bommer, 2003). Raghuram *et al.* (2003) report on a cross-sectional survey of 723 employees who worked from home at least half a day per week (home-based teleworkers by our definition). They considered the impact of perceived teleworking self-efficacy and extent of home-based teleworking (in terms of days per week at home) on self-reported structuring behaviour (extent of planning their own work at home) and self-reported adjustment to teleworking (teleworking satisfaction). They found that women, employees who undertake more home-based telework and those with greater perceived self-efficacy, plan their own work at home to a greater extent. They also found that adjustment to teleworking is better for women, for those with more teleworking experience, for those who undertook a greater extent of teleworking and those with higher perceived teleworking self-efficacy. Perceived teleworking self-efficacy is moderated by the extent of teleworking, such that more time spent teleworking is associated with greater perceived self-efficacy.

Workman *et al.* (2003) have examined the effects of cognitive style and media richness (frequency and elaborateness of ICT use, including real-time and face-to-face communications through videoconferencing) on commitment to home-based telework and virtual teams. They carried out their investigation by way of a cross-sectional self-report survey of 261 teleworkers in 21 virtual software development teams undertaking high knowledge intensity work with high (team-based) intra-organisational communication. Workman *et al.* (2003) found that cognitive style moderated the relationships between ICT media richness and commitment to telework and to virtual teams. In conditions of richer ICT media, there is more commitment to telework for people who prefer to solve problems by themselves, while those who like to solve problems through group interactions were more committed to the team. At the same time, for those who prefer order, structure and compliance with existing rules, there is more commitment to telework and to the virtual team in conditions of richer ICT media, while people who prefer novelty and innovation don't seem to be affected by ICT media richness. Meanwhile, for people who prefer concrete detail and less abstract thinking, there is more commitment to telework in conditions of richer ICT media. These results are, on the one hand, consistent with our views concerning ICT usage; richer ICT media appear to benefit some people without harming others, as least in terms of commitment to virtual working. At the same time, they point to the view that it is reasonable to expect individual differences in adaptation to teleworking, and such individual differences have clear implications for selecting teleworkers (see below). Apart from the work of Raghuram *et al.* (2003) and Workman *et al.* (2003) there has been very little systematic research examining the conjoint impact of different teleworking practices and personality dimensions or competencies on the performance of teleworkers or other indicators of successful adaptation. Such research is needed before any practical benefits can be truly realised.

Motivation and the Psychological Contract

Along with the broad trend towards greater flexibility in HRM, there has been a movement away from the traditional psychological contract where employers have offered career and employment stability (e.g. Sparrow & Cooper, 1998). Instead, the emerging psychological contract emphasises flexibility and mobility, where employees should expect to be flexible in their work practices, be prepared to take responsibility for their own training and career development, and be prepared to move jobs regularly. This new psychological contract brings potential problems of motivation and commitment (Sparrow & Cooper, 1998) and these could be exacerbated amongst teleworkers, who might experience hitherto unknown forms of contract violation (Sparrow, 2000) and who lack the support of office networks, unions and counselling services, along with the visibility that being in the office brings. Whilst effective socialisation may overcome some of these problems, moves towards providing clearer career paths and training opportunities may encourage employee retention and motivation without necessarily affecting the establishment of a mutually beneficial, flexible psychological contract.

Three qualifications to this picture are noted. First, although there is no clear information on the extent to which teleworking promotes non-traditional contracts, some Australian data (McClennan, 1996) does show that most home-based workers to date are in service areas where traditional employment contracts never existed, and they are on casual conditions. It is not possible to determine how many of these are engaged in telework, but one might ask whether teleworking will create a net drop in the number of traditional psychological contracts focused on career and employment stability.

The second qualification is that teleworkers may not always show the problems of their in-office counterparts with respect to psychological contracts—and telework might offer other benefits to compensate for reductions in employment and career stability. In one study (Omari & Standen, 1996), teleworkers were more likely to report feeling highly valued by the organisation and to appreciate receiving a benefit not widely available. In another study,

Igbaria and Guimares (1999) found that teleworkers had lower satisfaction with promotion opportunities (and their peers), yet reported less role conflict and role ambiguity and tended to be happier with their supervisors and more committed to their organisation.

Third, and more generally, there may be differences in the experience of those engaged in knowledge-intensive and low-knowledge-intensity telework. For example, it is noted that professionals tend to show more commitment to their profession than to their employers (cf. Mintzberg, 1979) and so they may have different reactions to those with different labour market power and career involvement.

Employee Well-being and the Impact of Job Characteristics

Based on a review of current empirical knowledge in this area, Daniels (2000) has identified how different forms of teleworking might influence the development of psychologically healthy or harmful job conditions. Daniels' review was based on Warr's (1987) Vitamin Model, in which psychologically healthy jobs are characterised generally by: greater opportunities for control, through task discretion or participation in decisions; greater skill use; greater variety in work; balanced demands from work; high clarity concerning tasks, performance feedback and job security; higher wages; better physical working conditions; more support and contact with others; and greater social value accorded to the nature of the work.

Daniels considers that task discretion, skill use and variety are more likely to be reduced in telework with low knowledge intensity, possibly due to increased opportunities for electronic monitoring of outputs if such work is routinised. Lack of variety is likely to be exacerbated for home-based and satellite office teleworkers. In contrast, nomadic teleworkers at least have the opportunity to move to different locations. Daniels has suggested autonomy over scheduling of work tasks and task rotation as means of redesigning teleworking jobs to prevent these problems.

Due to remote working, opportunities for participating in decision making might be reduced in most teleworking jobs, except for jobs in which there is high extra-organisational contact and high knowledge intensity. In this latter case, contact with customers or suppliers gives access to information that other organisational members—including managers—do not have. To use this information, organisations may then require such teleworkers to participate in decisions (Daniels, 1999). Notwithstanding, frequent visits to the main organisational location to attend meetings might be one way of increasing participation, as might use of electronic means of communication between team members.

Increased demands have been reported in home-based and nomadic teleworking. In both cases, increased opportunities for workers to enact demands might lead to escalation if other contributory factors are in place. For example, any increase in demands might be accentuated for workers with high degrees of intra- and extra-organisational contact and who use several electronic media that allow many channels for information to be exchanged. Technical problems with equipment can add further to problems. One suggestion to combat these problems is for teleworkers and their line managers to establish a diary of realistic routines and tasks (Ingham, 1995). Daniels (2000) has also suggested time management and prioritisation skills training in conjunction with improvements in technology to prioritise messages.

Teleworkers often report a reduction in the quality of information they receive, especially that related to performance feedback, organisational politics and organisational strategy

(Crossan & Burton, 1993), although such problems may not be as great in a satellite office with a significant number of people from the same organisation. We have discussed some ways of enhancing communication earlier in this chapter. With respect to enhancing well-being in particular, various authors have made a number of suggestions. Cox, Griffiths and Barker (1996) point to the establishment of clear goals and objectives and implementation of reporting systems as a way to prevent problems of reduced clarity for teleworkers. Daniels (2000) suggests that, provided they do not lead to information overload, establishing communication channels amongst co-workers can also provide information networks, although regular office visits provide perhaps the best access to informal networks (cf. Daniels, 1999).

Some of the strategies for improving information clarity may also help to reduce the social isolation reported by many teleworkers, especially home-based teleworkers and those with little intra- and extra-organisational contact (Daniels, 2000). Other strategies that can help reduce social isolation include social activities other than regular visits to the main office, and well-designed systems for providing managerial and technical support.

Poor physical working conditions are a problem for all teleworkers, especially low-knowledge-intensity teleworkers, who are more likely to engage in repetitive display screen work (Cox, Griffiths & Barker, 1996). Moreover, those low-knowledge-intensity teleworkers based at home are less likely to live in accommodation where a designated work-space can be easily established. Clearly, such working conditions can influence physical as well as psychological health (Huws, 1994). Gray, Hodson and Gordon (1993) suggest a number of strategies for dealing with these problems, including providing allowances for teleworkers to buy suitable equipment or adapt premises; establishing a designated space for work; inspection of premises for health and safety purposes; and health and safety training.

Daniels (2000) considers low-knowledge-intensity workers to be at risk from poor well-being caused by lower wages and lower social value attached to their work, especially as such work is more likely to be of a contingent nature (see earlier). Ensuring teleworkers' pay is comparable to traditional workers in similar jobs and establishing support networks might help prevent problems of poor well-being for low-knowledge-intensity teleworkers. Daniels also considers that most knowledge-intensive teleworking can also suffer from lower social value because of a lack of visibility that limits the opportunities for promotion often valued by knowledge-intensive workers. Again, establishing support networks might enhance visibility, as would regular visits to the main office. Regular information exchanges through remote media can also help establish greater visibility.

Home/Work Interface

Teleworkers working from home face a range of issues not met by in-office or other off-site workers. These issues derive from the ability of the worker to create physical and social conditions in the home that adequately support work. For homeworkers without family, the issues are chiefly to do with creating an appropriate physical space and restricting the impact of the wider community through regulating contacts from neighbours, friends, businesses, salespeople and so on.

Those with family or other co-residents face additional problems (Standen, Daniels & Lamond, 1999). The boundary between work and family spheres is highly permeable in the home (Ahrentzen, 1990). Consequently, "segmentation" theories of work/family relationships, which assume no interaction, are particularly inappropriate in the case of teleworkers.

Lambert (1990) has proposed, in the traditional (office) work context, that spillover from each sphere impacts on the other, in terms of both the objective and subjective conditions of work. In the case of telework, the objective impact might be where the physical conditions of work (e.g. working hours) impact on family life, either positively or negatively, or where the physical conditions of family life (e.g. need to transport children to school) impact on work performance. Subjective (psychological) effects can also be identified, such as changes in well-being and changes in the levels of work–family conflict (Standen *et al.*, 1999). Lambert (1990) contends that these impacts can cause workers to reduce their involvement in either sphere, either by compensation (e.g. where a man with a dissatisfying job becomes more orientated to the family), or accommodation (e.g. where a woman may limit her involvement in work to accommodate family; Lambert, 1990).

Although research on *nomadic teleworkers* is in its infancy, one study reports more work vs. non-work conflict (Daniels, 1999). This might be reduced by interventions that allow mobile workers to filter information more effectively—so that remote contact can be established with home and managers trained to be sensitive to the demands placed on nomadic workers. In asking and answering the question "Does it matter where you work?", a more recent study by Hill, Ferris and Martinson (2003) carried out a comparison of how three work venues (traditional office, virtual office, and home office) influence aspects of work and personal/family life through a self-report cross-sectional survey of 4315 traditional workers, 767 mobile workers, and 441 home workers (n = 6133). In general, their results show that home-based teleworkers report better work–life balance than mobile and office workers, while mobile workers report more motivation but less work–life balance than office workers.

Human Resource Management

One set of management practices explicitly aimed at managing the dynamics of groups and individuals in order to achieve the organisation's goals are those subsumed under the heading of human resource management (cf. Lamond 1995, 1996). Here, we cover some of the ways in which human resource management strategies can impact on the outcomes of teleworking.

Selecting Teleworkers

Earlier observations on socialisation, personality, competencies, job features and the home–work interface suggest that teleworker selection should be a systemic process involving more than just matching personal characteristics to those of the job (Omari & Standen, 2000). From our discussion so far in this chapter, we can suggest at least three strategies for selecting teleworkers: (a) assess the congruence of personal values with organisational culture; (b) assess the likely impact of teleworking practices on the home/work interface, job characteristics and the psychological side of work (and home where relevant); (c) match personality and competencies to the requirements of the job and form of teleworking. This would entail far wider assessment of organisational, task, personal and teleworking factors than is usual for selection into more traditional forms of work.

Management Style and Management Control

There is increasing recognition of the need for managers to develop new and different skills to manage effectively into this new millennium (cf. Lamond, 1996). Management of teleworkers is no exception to this general rule. However, it is unlikely that there will emerge a uniformly effective way of managing teleworkers (Lamond, 2000b). Consequently, the usual adage of managing teleworkers by outputs—in of and by itself—may prove inappropriate for teleworkers, possibly leading to problems such as reduced well-being, reduced trust and low-quality work (Sparrow, 2000; van Ommeren, 2000). We do, however, consider it important that managers pay close attention to the social context of teleworking (Daniels *et al.*, 2000), because this is important for establishing support networks, ensuring opportunities for communication and establishing the trust necessary for organisational learning to occur (Tregaskis & Daniels, 2000).

Likewise, telework practitioners (Gray *et al.*, 1993) recommend that managers should endeavour to provide supportive teleworking environments. Earlier, we noted the importance of congruence between organisational cultures and telework practices—human resource managers should be aware of the cultures and contexts in each area of their organisation and should endeavour to ensure that telework schemes, workers and managers suit those cultures and contexts (since changing the cultures and contexts to suit teleworking is a longer-term strategy). This necessitates selection and training of managers of teleworkers. In many ways, perhaps the best people to manage teleworkers are other teleworkers, since they are already familiar with the special circumstances of teleworking and the skills and supports needed for successful teleworking (Hilthrop, 2000).

Training and Telework

Training and development are just as important or more important for telework than more traditional forms of work (Salmon *et al.*, 2000). Indeed, there are many areas in which training may benefit teleworkers, for example corporate values, communication, self-management and time management, health and safety requirements off-site, company security policy, legal, tax and insurance requirements of homework, computer operation and maintenance, as well as any job-specific needs, such as the use of communications software. Counsellors, career advisers, managers and on-line support services may also help address problems that are often classified as training issues. It is likely that some of this training will itself be available off-site, particularly through CD-ROM, the Internet or traditional open learning media. Indeed, training for on-line workers might be best achieved on-line through a variety of media, as this will provide experience with the context of telework and the media that will be used eventually for work (Salmon *et al.*, 2000).

Training managers should also consider targeting telework managers or supervisors, and the colleagues of teleworkers, all of whom may need to understand office policy and the practicalities of telework, and to be aware of the need to manage by results and to maintain support, communication and socialisation. Indeed, establishing the importance of training and development may help to institutionalise greater organisational learning in itself, and make managers more aware of the need to develop the skills and working relationships necessary for organisational learning (see Tregaskis & Daniels, 2000).

Electronically-Mediated Interventions

New developments which may assist teleworkers include face-to-face (video) communication technology, on-line data bases, www sites, virtual reality, and new software capabilities found in groupware, decision-support systems, executive support systems, on-line tutors and so on. These may improve communications amongst teleworkers, assist support from other teleworkers, help the management control of telework, and deliver flexible training packages. Improving telecommunications will also make it easier to coordinate virtual teams across current boundaries set by distance and time. Improvements in ICTs may also enable greater opportunities for organisational learning, e.g. through access to electronic archives and bulletin boards (Townsend *et al.*, 1998). In a recent study, Venkatesh and Johnson (2002) have examined the impact of different teleworking ICT systems on the experienced social richness of the media, telepresence (the sense that one is psychologically present with others during virtual communication), and attitudes to the technology. New teleworking ICT systems, utilizing varying combinations of video conferencing and virtual reality technologies (to enhance social richness), were installed at three sites, with each site having a different combination of systems. A total of 527 employees were involved across the three sites. Experienced social richness of the media, telepresence and attitudes to the technology were measured three months after the new systems were introduced, while systems use (measured through a "time logged on" system) was assessed on several occasions for up to one year after training with the new systems. Their findings support the view that virtual reality technologies increase social richness and telepresence, which, in turn, increases positive attitudes to the system and, in turn, increases use of the system.

CONCLUSION: THE CHALLENGE OF MANAGING TELEWORKERS

In this chapter we have examined telework as a contemporary working practice and the impact it has had on how people work and their experience of work, together with the human resource management implications of telework. How telework will evolve in the future is the subject of great speculation in the media and the academic press. However, as industries become more knowledge-intensive and telework becomes more central to business processes, there are ways to prevent the worst that the future might have to offer, or at least to buffer organisations and teleworkers against it (Daniels *et al.*, 2000).

Effective management does not mean a narrow focus on productivity. As we have noted earlier and elsewhere (Daniels *et al.*, 2000), managing teleworkers by outputs is often not a sensible option while relying purely on developments in technology to improve productivity and coordination. Indeed, the technological methods that allow managers to monitor the actions of teleworkers as closely as they could monitor on-site workers have been associated with low employee morale (Fairweather, 1999). At the same time, there is a need for an ethical approach to managing teleworkers (Fairweather, 1999; Moon & Stanworth, 1997), so that telework is *not* used to worsen employees' terms and conditions. It is clear that, instead of simply managing the outputs of teleworkers or the teleworking process, the most appropriate approach is to manage the outputs, the process and the context of teleworking.

Placing greater emphasis on the management of teleworkers can have benefits for both organisations and teleworkers, while paying attention to context and processes can help technologically-driven innovations enhance communication and organisational learning capability, through proper use of technology and creation of the right social environment. At the same time, managers must make an effort to build the supportive environments, organisational cultures and the trust needed to ensure the best results from teleworking. Managers need to confront and overcome not only the problem of trying to use organisational culture as an important tool for management control, but also the other inherent problems of alternative work arrangements—an increase in structure and flexibility, a focus on both individuals and teamwork, and an increase and decrease in control (Pearlson & Saunders, 2001).

We have touched briefly on the issue, but further consideration of communication for decision making for virtual teams presents some very interesting possibilities in regard to the different roles of text, voice, paper (fax, mail, courier) and video media, interactivity, manipulability (e.g. ability to enter digital communications in a database, groupware features as in Lotus Notes) and synchronicity of media (cf. Venkatesh & Johnson, 2002). One might also ask whether new models of decision-making are emerging: do these new technologies promote more or less democratic modes, e.g. by minimising status-conferring signals of dress, voice and physical size? Do they change the type of communication and social skills needed to be a good team member?

Teleworking is most likely to be successful where teleworking forms part of a coherent and integrated human resource management system that supports organisational strategy (Daniels et al., 2000). This means ensuring that telework programmes are compatible with organisational strategies, structures and cultures, and which are suited to prevailing economic and social contexts. Analysis of the organisation and its environment is important for deciding whether teleworking is appropriate for current conditions, or whether organisational structures, cultures and processes need to be changed to suit teleworking practices. Various strategies can help achieve a match between teleworking practices and the macro-economic, organisational, social and psychological environments, including those related to technology management, socialisation processes, job design, psychological contracting and career management, selection systems, training and development practices and performance management. As noted by Hamel and Prahalad (1993), effective organisational performance comes not just from fitting the environment, but also by developing and using organisational resources in new and more effective ways. For these reasons, human resource management has a wider responsibility than ensuring that teleworking fits its place in the organisation; it should also ensure that the possibilities of teleworking are explored to develop what is possible with teleworking.

This chapter has presented a framework for advancing understanding of telework, using organisational behaviour theory to fill the gaps in empirical knowledge. However, theory alone is not enough—prescriptions of "best practice" based on limited empirical knowledge and theory developed in other areas of organisational psychology must be applied in an informed, context-sensitive manner. There are, therefore, two challenges to be met in ensuring the effective management of teleworkers.

The first challenge is to practitioners. They need to reflect on the insights and prescriptions offered here and elsewhere and apply them in ways that are sensitive to their own organisational contexts. They then need to assess the impact of these prescriptions carefully and adapt them as necessary in the light of their findings. A key part of this process is to establish ongoing two-way lines of communication (in all its myriad forms) with those involved in telework, including those involved with research on this new and radical form of work.

The second challenge, then, is to researchers, to continue to develop theoretical and empirical knowledge of teleworking as a basis for reflective practice. Most of this research is in its initial phases and has, to date, been limited by what we now know to be a narrow and partial view of telework and teleworking. The presentation here of our dimensional model of telework and the overview of the attendant issues has moved us closer to a state of conceptual clarity, and so provides clear pointers for future research in all areas that we have covered in this chapter. Our framework perhaps raises as many questions as it answers, but, to the extent that it sharpens the focus of those questions, it provides a basis for developing specific theoretical models of the major issues involved in teleworking (e.g. Standen *et al.*, 1999; Daniels *et al.*, 2001). Without such detailed theoretical knowledge, research in this area will not be able to build in a cumulative fashion and empirical work will continue to be dominated by case studies and surveys that have no particular focus, other than to compare teleworkers with "traditional" workers. Consequently, the research community will not be able to inform practitioners, in any useful and generalisable way, of the circumstances in which different forms of teleworking are likely to be adopted by organisations, and the circumstances in which different forms of teleworking have specific causal effects on organisations, workers and their families.

The initial qualitative and survey research has been valuable in helping to inform the field but the emphasis should now shift from the small scale exploratory work that still dominates the area, to larger-scale confirmatory work. Whilst the qualitative methods are useful, in so far that they sharpen theoretical development and add new perspectives, many recently published reports appear to repeat familiar themes. Further, the small number of larger-scale quantitative studies that are appearing seem to rely on cross-sectional self-report methods that are complicated by other design problems (use of single-item scales, omission of important features of teleworking, inappropriate data analysis). At the same time, there appears to be some tightening up of which kinds of teleworking are being researched: authors seem to be getting better at differentiating, for example, home-based teleworking from nomadic teleworking, and being clear that the amount of teleworking in a given domain can vary—rather than talking about teleworking as a general, undifferentiated concept. However, in general, studies need to be much tighter in specifying the characteristics of their samples in respect to the kinds of facets of teleworking we have indentified. Surveys should incorporate longitudinal elements and test specific causal hypotheses, whilst qualitative work should be used in a reflexive way to critique and sharpen theoretical perspectives. Researchers also need to consider quasi-experimental evaluation of intelligently designed telework interventions. Given the rapid change in technology and the expected changes in work practices, new research approaches may be required and these will need to be sensitive to the multiple forms of teleworking and realities those forms encompass.

As we noted in our introduction, the future of teleworking depends on whether employers provide the opportunity to telework and whether workers take advantage of this opportunity. To realise the full benefits of telework, there must be a dialogue between teleworkers, those that manage teleworkers and researchers. The new communications media that support telework also allow researchers to interact with management and teleworker communities in new ways, bringing exciting possibilities for the research community to assist in the evolution of this new work practice.[3]

---

[3] An interesting aside for the reader is that all the collaboration on this chapter between the authors has been "virtual"—it has been carried out via extensive e-mail contact. Indeed, although the team now has a considerable publication record together, two of the authors have never met face to face.

REFERENCES

Ahrentzen, S. B. (1990). Managing conflict by managing boundaries: how professional home workers cope with multiple roles at home. *Environment and Behavior*, **22**, 723–752.

Aryee, S. (1991). Creating a committed workforce: linking socialisation practices to business strategy. *Asia Pacific Human Resource Management*, **29**, 102–112.

Ashkenas, R., Ulrich, D., Jick, T. & Kerr, S. (1995). *The Boundaryless Organization: Breaking the Chains of Organizational Structure*. San Francisco, CA: Jossey-Bass.

Australian Bureau of Statistics (2001). *Locations of Work, Australia*. Cat. No. 6275.0. Canberra: Australian Government Publishing Service.

Barrick, M. R. & Mount, M. K. (1991). The big five personality dimensions and job performance. *Personnel Psychology*, **44**, 1–26.

Baruch, Y. (2001). The status of research on teleworking and an agenda for future research. *International Journal of Management Reviews*, **3**, 113–129.

Behling, O. (1998). Employee selection: will intelligence and conscientiousness do the job? *Academy of Management Executive*, **12**, 77–86.

Billsberry, J. (2000). Socialiszing teleworkers into the organization. In K. Daniels, D. Lamond & P. Standen (Eds), *Managing Telework: Perspectives from Human Resource Management and Work Psychology*. London: Thomson Learning.

Cascio, W. F. (2000). Managing a virtual workplace. *Academy of Management Executive*, **14**, 81–90.

Cox, T., Griffiths, A. & Barker, M. J. (1996). *Teleworking: Health and Safety Issues in the Member States of the European Union*. Dublin: European Foundation for the Improvement of Living and Working Conditions.

Crossan, G. & Burton, P. F. (1993). Teleworking stereotypes: a case study. *Journal of Information Science Principles & Practice*, **19**, 349–362.

Daniels, K. (1999). Home based teleworking and mobile teleworking: a study of job characteristics, well-being and negative carry-over. Work Science Report Series, *13/14* (pp. 1535–1536). Tokyo: Institute of Science of Labour.

Daniels, K. (2000). Job features and well-being. In K. Daniels, D. Lamond, & P. Standen (Eds), *Managing Telework: Perspectives from Human Resource Management and Work Psychology*. London: Thomson Learning.

Daniels, K., Lamond, D. A. & Standen, P. (Eds) (2000). *Managing Telework: Perspectives from Human Resource Management and Work Psychology*. London: Thompson Learning.

Daniels, K., Lamond, D. & Standen, P. (2001). Teleworking: frameworks for organizational research. *Journal of Management Studies*, **38**, 1151–1186.

Duxbury, L. & Nuefeld, D. (1999). An empirical evaluation of the impacts of telecommuting on intra-organizational communication. *Journal of Engineering and Technology Management*, **16**, 1–28.

European Commission (1998). *Status Report on European Telework*. Luxembourg: Office for Official Publications of the European Communities.

Fairweather, N. B. (1999). Surveillance in employment: the case of teleworking. *Journal of Business Ethics*, **22**, 39–49.

Felstead, A. & Jewson, N. (2000). *In Work, at Home*. London: Routledge.

Gainey, T. W., Kelley, D. K. & Hill, J. A. (1999). Telecommuting's impact on corporate culture and individual workers: examining the effect of employee isolation. *S.A.M. Advanced Management Journal*, **64**, 4–10.

Gillespie, A. E., Richardson, R. & Cornford, J. (1995). *Review of Teleworking in Britain: Implications for Public Policy*. London: Parliamentary Office of Science and Technology.

Glosserman, B. (1996). How green is my cyberspace? *Japan Times Weekly International Edition*, **36**(44), 15.

Gray, M., Hodson, N. & Gordon, G. (1993). *Teleworking Explained*. Chichester: Wiley.

Guest, D. (1990). Human resource management and the American dream. *Journal of Management Studies*, **27**, 377–397.

Hamblin, H. (1995). Employees' perspectives on one dimension of labour flexibility: working at a distance. *Work, Employment and Society*, **9**, 473–498.

Hamel, G. & Prahalad, C. K. (1993). Strategy as stretch and leverage. *Harvard Business Review*, **March–April**, 75–84.

Harper, R. (2000). Communication and collaboration at a distance. In K. Daniels, D. Lamond and P. Standen (Eds), *Managing Telework: Perspectives from Human Resource Management and Work Psychology*. London: Thomson Learning.

Hiemstra, G. (1982). Teleconferencing, concern for face, and organizational culture. In M. Burggon (Ed.), *Communication Yearbook 6*. Beverly Hills, CA: Sage.

Hill, E. J., Ferris, M. & Martinson, V. (2003). Does it matter where you work? A comparison of how three work venues (traditional office, virtual office, and home office) influence aspects of work and personal/family life. *Journal of Vocational Behaviour*, **63**, 220–241.

Hilthrop, J. M. (2000). Preparing people and organizations for teleworking. In K. Daniels, D. Lamond, & P. Standen (Eds), *Managing Telework: Perspectives from Human Resource Management and Work Psychology*. London: Thomson Learning.

Huws, U. (1994). *Teleworking*. Brussels: European Commission's Employment Task Force (Directorate General V).

Huws, U., Jagger, N. & O'Regan, S. (1999). *Teleworking and Globalisation*. Report No. 358. Brighton: Institute for Employment Studies.

Igbaria, M. & Guimares, T. (1999). Exploring differences in employee turnover intentions and its determinants among telecommuters and non-telecommuters. *Journal of Management Information Systems*, **16**, 147–164.

Ingham, C. (1995). *Working Well at Home*. London: Thorsons.

IRS (1996). Teleworking in Europe: part three. *European Industrial Relations Review*, **271**, 18–23.

Lambert, S. J. (1990). Processes linking work and family: a critical review and research agenda. *Human Relations*, **43**, 239–257.

Lamond, D. A. (1995). The art of HRM: human relationship management. Presented at the Australian and New Zealand Academy of Management Conference, Townsville, Queensland, 3–6 December.

Lamond, D. A. (1996). Karpin on management: is that all managers should be doing? Journal of the Australian and New Zealand Academy of Management, **2**(1), 21–35.

Lamond, D. (2000a). Personality and telework. In K. Daniels, D. Lamond & P. Standen (Eds), *Managing Telework: Perspectives from Human Resource Management and Work Psychology*. London: Thomson Learning.

Lamond, D. (2000b). Managerial style and telework. In K. Daniels, D. Lamond & P. Standen (Eds), *Managing Telework: Perspectives from Human Resource Management and Work Psychology*. London: Thomson Learning.

Lamond, D. A., Daniels, K. & Standen, P. (1997a). Virtual working or working virtually? an overview of contextual and behavioural issues in teleworking. *Proceedings of the Fourth International Meeting of the Decision Sciences Institute*, Part II, 477–481.

Lamond, D. A., Daniels, K. & Standen, P. (1997b). Defining telework: what is it exactly? *Proceedings of the Second International Workshop on Telework*, Amsterdam, The Netherlands.

Lawrence, P. R. & Lorsch, J. W. (1967). *Organization and Environment: Managing Differentiation and Integration*. Boston, MA: Graduate School of Business, Harvard University.

Lea, M. T. & Spears, R. (1992). Paralanguage and social perception in computer-mediated communication. *Journal of Organizational Computing*, **2**, 321–341.

McClennan, W. (1996). *Persons Employed at Home, Australia*. Australian Bureau of Statistics, Catalogue No. 6275.0. Canberra: AGPS.

Mintzberg, H. (1979). *The Structuring of Organizations*. Englewood Cliffs, NJ: Prentice Hall.

Moon, C. & Stanworth, C. (1997). Ethical issues in teleworking. *Business Ethics: A European Review*, **6**, 35–45.

Omari, M. & Standen, P. (1996). The impact of home-based work on organisational outcomes. Paper presented at the Australian and New Zealand Academy of Management Conference, Wollongong, NSW, 4–7 December.

Omari, M. & Standen, P. (2000). Selection for telework. In K. Daniels, D. Lamond, & P. Standen (Eds), *Managing Telework: Perspectives from Human Resource Management and Work Psychology*. London: Thomson Learning.

Pearlson, K. E. & Saunders, C. S. (2001). There's no place like home: managing telecommuting paradoxes. *Academy of Management Executive*, **15**(2), 117–128.
Proquest Information and Learning Company (formerly UMI Company) (2001). *ABI/Inform Global Edition, January 1999–August 2001*. Ann Arbor, MI: Proquest.
Quinn, R. (1988). *Beyond Rational Management: Mastering the Paradoxes and Competing Demands of High Performance*. San Francisco, CA: Jossey-Bass.
Qvortrup, L. (1998). From teleworking to networking: definitions and trends. In P. J. Jackson & J. M. Van der Wielen (Eds), *Teleworking: International Perspectives, from Telecommuting to the Virtual Organization*. London: Routledge.
Raghuram, S., Wiesenfeld, B. & Garud, R. (2003). Technology enabled work: the role of self-efficacy in determining telecommuter adjustment and structuring behaviour. *Journal of Vocational Behaviour*, **63**, 180–198.
Reich, R. (1992). *The Work of Nations*. New York: Vintage.
Rourke, J. (1996). A few good tips for telecommuters and their employers. *Rural Telecommunications*, **15**(5), 8.
Salmon, G., Allen, J. & Giles, K. (2000). Training and development for on-line working. In K. Daniels, D. Lamond & P. Standen (Eds), *Managing Telework: Perspectives from Human Resource Management and Work Psychology*. London: Thomson Learning.
Sparrow, P. (2000). Teleworking and the psychological contract: a new division of labour. In K. Daniels, D. Lamond & P. Standen (Eds), *Managing Telework: Perspectives from Human Resource Management and Work Psychology*. London: Thomson Learning.
Sparrow, P. R. & Cooper, C. L. (1998). New organizational forms: the strategic relevance of future psychological contract scenarios. *Canadian Journal of Administrative Sciences*, **15**, 356–371.
Sparrow, P. R. & Daniels, K. (1999). Human resource management and the virtual organization: mapping the future research issues. In C. L. Cooper & S. E. Jackson (Eds), *Trends in Organizational Behavior*, Vol. **6**. Chichester: Wiley.
Standen, P. (1997). Home, work and management in the information age. *Journal of the Australian and New Zealand Academy of Management*, **3**, 1–14.
Standen, P. (2000). Organizational culture and telework. In K. Daniels, D. Lamond & P. Standen (Eds), *Managing Telework: Perspectives from Human Resource Management and Work Psychology*. London: Thomson Learning.
Standen, P., Daniels, K. & Lamond, D. (1999). The home as a workplace: Work–family interaction and psychological well-being in telework. *Journal of Occupational Health Psychology*, **4**, 368–381.
Townsend, A. M., DeMarie, S. & Hendrickson, A. R. (1998). Virtual teams: technology and the workplace of the future. *Academy of Management Executive*, **12** (August), 17–29.
Travic, B. (1998). Information aspects of new organizational designs: exploring the non-traditional organization. *Journal of the American Society for Information Science*, **49**, 1224–1244.
Tregaskis, O. (2000). Telework in its national context. In K. Daniels, D. Lamond & P. Standen (Eds), *Managing Telework: Perspectives from Human Resource Management and Work Psychology*. London: Thomson Learning.
Tregaskis, O. & Daniels K. (2000). Organizational learning. In K. Daniels, D. Lamond & P. Standen (Eds), *Managing Telework: Perspectives from Human Resource Management and Work Psychology*. London: Thomson Learning.
van Ommeren, J. N. (1998). Telework in Europe. In *Teleworking Environments: Proceedings of the Third International Workshop on Telework*. Turku, Finland.
van Ommeren, J. (2000). Performance management and compensation. In K. Daniels, D. Lamond & P. Standen (Eds), *Managing Telework: Perspectives from Human Resource Management and Work Psychology*. London: Thomson Learning.
Venkatesh, V. & Johnson, P. (2002). Telecommuting technology implementations: a within- and between-subjects longitudal field study. *Personnel Psychology*, **55**, 661–687.
Walther, J. B. (1995). Relational aspects of computer-mediated communication: experimental observations over time. *Organization Science*, **6**, 186–202.
Warr, P. B. (1987). *Work, Unemployment and Mental Health*. Oxford: Oxford University Press.
Workman, M., Kahnweiler, W. & Bommer, W. (2003). The effects of cognitive style and media richness on commitment to telework and vitural teams. *Journal of Vocational Behaviour*, **63**, 199–219.

CHAPTER 11

Organisational Performance and Manufacturing Practices

Stephen Wood

Institute of Work Psychology, University of Sheffield, UK

Total quality management, just-in-time, total preventive management and supply-chain partnership are all seen as modern manufacturing practices. They are often subsumed under umbrella concepts, such as Womack, Jones and Roos's (1990) lean production, Dean and Snell's (1991) integrated manufacturing, and Schonberger's (1986) world class manufacturing. Total quality management (TQM) may itself be one such umbrella concept (Cooney & Sohal, this book). Within social theory they have been viewed as a vital part of the post-Fordist model, "Toyotaism" in some people's terms (Wood, 1989). The contrast is often drawn between this new approach to management and the excessively rigid Fordist system, which was based on Taylorist principles of job design, with a narrow division of labour, highly functional management and low role demands for the mass of workers. Womack *et al.* (1990) encouraged the differentiation of lean production from mass production, while TQM has been portrayed by some as a major cultural force—an enterprise lifestyle (McCloskey & Collett, 1993)—which represents a radical change in the way organisations operate.

Portrayed in such terms, lean production and TQM became in the late 1980s panaceas for management and the ills of Western economies: the low productivity, poor quality and industrial conflict. Their extension to all fields of industry and commerce was urged. Womack *et al.* (1990, p. 277), indeed, proclaimed that lean production would become "the standard global production system of the twenty-first century", seemingly taking it for granted that their exhortations would be heeded. Having conceived the management methods of lean production literally as a machine, they effectively turned it into a juggernaut that would eliminate in one fell swoop many, if not all, of the production, organisational and personnel problems associated with post-war Western economies.

Prescriptive packages of practices tend to be all-embracing concepts that offer a fresh way of thinking, as well as urgently needed practices. In the case of lean production, the emphasis is on viewing the organisation in the context of its suppliers and customers and in terms of a flow of activities pulled by the customer. The aim is to eliminate all elements of this system that add no value to the customer. Lean production and other such approaches were part of a movement to elevate operational management within the overall concerns of management (Abernathy, Clark & Kantrow, 1984). Prior to this, the over-riding emphasis of

The Essentials *of the New Workplace: A Guide to the Human Impact of Modern Working Practices.*
Edited by David Holman, Toby D. Wall, Chris W. Clegg, Paul Sparrow and Ann Howard. © 2005 John Wiley & Sons, Ltd.

corporate strategy, in theory and practice, was on the development of products and markets, with some consideration given to technology. As an antidote to this, lean production and TQM have often been presented as if they could (and should) become the business strategy of the organisation.

Nonetheless, they are perhaps more limited than their architects imply. First, within them certain practices are given prominence, for example just-in-time (JIT) in lean production, decentralisation of quality control in TQM. Second, the practices themselves are likely to be orientated towards specific objectives, for example JIT to cost reduction and customer responsiveness. Third, they have evolved as reactions to past omissions in operational management theory and the problems that arose in its application. Problems of inventory management and integration were ill-considered within the Fordist and Taylorist theories of mass production. In practice, Fordist mass production was plagued by certain nagging and recurring problems: poor quality, bottlenecks, rigidities, difficulties of balancing the work of operators, and the unreliability of suppliers. Lean production was a novel way of addressing the loose ends of Fordism in theory (Walker, 1989, p. 65) and in practice (Wood, 1993). Similarly, TQM emerged to overcome the quality problems that the functional approach to quality control had either created or failed to address.

Finally, there is a tendency for the proponents of the packaged programmes of manufacturing practices to concentrate on the technology to the neglect of human and social issues. This means they under-consider two things: (a) the vital role of employee involvement in their programmes, and (b) the problems of implementation. What are sometimes called the "soft" or "people-orientated" practices, such as teamworking or continuous improvement methods, are integral to the programmes but often presented in a sanitised way, on a par with a measurement instrument, when in fact they are the conduits through which the techniques are applied. Moreover, the problems of implementation run deeper than getting people to administer the techniques competently. They involve overcoming the existing forms of commitment, control and conflict that past systems of management, and particularly their functional roots, have created. In the quest to present manufacturing practices as the means of achieving leanness, total quality or world class status, authors skate over whether they can fully resolve the tensions within organisations, between groups, and between job demands and employee satisfaction (see Delbridge, Chapter 2, this volume).

The fundamental question then raised by the portrayal of manufacturing practices as the saviour of Western economies is: how are they faring? This involves at least three issues: (a) to what extent are they diffusing?; (b) to what extent do the practices associated with lean production, TQM and high involvement coexist, or is there a mirroring of the theorists' over-emphasis on techniques of operational management to the neglect of the organisational and personnel practices?; (c) is their use leading to the superior performance prophesied? No one study has thus far addressed all these questions together. Indeed, the number of studies that includes operational and human resource practices is very small. My purpose in this chapter is to overview these studies in order to take stock of what we have by way of answers to the three questions.

The literature discussed is from two areas: production management and human resource management. In the former, primacy is given to the operational practices, JIT and TQM, and the human and organisational elements are conceived as infrastructrual supports for the successful adoption of these, while in the latter, the emphasis is placed on employee involvement and then the issues are: (a) the extent to which the operational management models have spurred and shaped its development; and (b) whether "employee involvement without TQM practices is less likely to affect performance positively and vice versa" (Lawler, Mohrman & Ledford, 1995, p. 144). If successful, the combined use of modern manufacturing and involvement methods should result in employees being flexible, expansive in their perceptions and willing to contribute proactively to innovation. Their main effect on performance is thus through work restructuring, innovation and learning, not through employee commitment.

THE DIFFUSION OF MANUFACTURING PRACTICES

Bolden, Waterson, Warr, Clegg and Wall (1997, p. 1114), at the Institute of Work Psychology (IWP), Sheffield, developed a list of 70 modern manufacturing practices based on the literature and experts' views. They range from the very specific (e.g. computer-aided design) to the abstract (e.g. company vision and organisational culture). The studies thus far have, though, concentrated on those most connected with lean production, integrated manufacturing and TQM, such as JIT, decentralised quality control and computer-integrated manufacturing.

Following directly from Bolden *et al.*'s (1997) conceptual work, the IWP team (Waterson *et al.*, 1999) investigated the use of some of the key practices that they identified in this. The survey, conducted in 1996, was based on a sample of 564 UK manufacturing companies with more than 150 employees. It confirmed that most of the practices were "new", as most had been introduced recently. In over 75% of the companies that used business process re-engineering, TQM, team-based working, empowerment and a learning culture, the practice had been introduced in the 1990s, While in the case of all other practices—JIT production, integrated computer-based technology, supply-chain partnering, total productive maintenance, concurrent engineering, manufacturing cells—the figure was over 60%, with one exception, outsourcing, where only 39% of the users had introduced it in the 1990s.

In 2000, the IWP team (Wood, Stride, Wall & Clegg, 2004) conducted a follow-up study of 126 of the companies in the 1996 study. They focused on the seven most prevalent practices in 1996, namely: total quality management, just-in-time production, integrated computer-based technology, supply-chain partnering and team-based working, empowerment and learning culture. The results, based on use scores in a five-point scale running from "not at all" to "entirely", showed that the average use of all seven practices had increased significantly but that the rank-ordering had remained almost unchanged. Learning culture and empowerment remained the least used. The most significant increases were in the use of integrated computer manufacturing and supply-chain partnerships. However, it was evident that the increase was disproportionately accounted for by greater use by those firms that already used the practice in 1996, rather than new users. Indeed, the proportion of companies reporting not using a practice at all, which ranged from 12.0% for total quality management to 30% for empowerment, had not changed significantly between 1996 and 2000. The small number of new users observed was as likely to have moved straight to high use as to have started their use gradually. There is thus evidence of polarization in the use of modern manufacturing practices, and little to suggest that the use of practices is ephemeral or inevitably wanes over time.

An earlier more limited study by Wood and Albanese (1995, p. 234) showed an increasing use of practices between 1986 and 1990 in a sample of 135 manufacturing plants in the UK. The percentage of plants where operators were responsible for their quality and inspection, a key TQM practice, had increased from 51% to 76% in that period, while those having flexible job descriptions had increased from 38% to 69%, with teamworking from 41% to 62%, and with quality circles from 8% to 16%.

For the USA we also have similar evidence. In Osterman's (1994) data set of 871 establishments with 50 or more employees in both manufacturing and services, there was information on the date of introduction for four key practices—teams, job rotation, cross-training and statistical process control. Analysis showed that their usage for the core occupational grouping in workplaces had increased considerably in the 10 years prior to the survey, which was conducted in 1992.[1] Osterman (2000) resurveyed 457 of the original establishments in 1997. The trend of increased usage continued for job rotation but not for teams. He did not, however, report the usage for cross-training and statistical process control; but he did show that the use of quality circles and TQM increased considerably between 1993 and 1997. The proportion in the sample using quality circles, job rotation and TQM had more than doubled by 1997, to 59%, 47% and 51% respectively. The use of teams had increased one percentage point from its figure of 40% in 1993.

Lawler, Mohrman and Ledford (1998, p. 60), using samples ranging from 32% to 22% of the Fortune 1000 largest manufacturing and service companies, also reported a similar trend. The use of key modern manufacturing practices—self-inspection, statistical process control for front-line employees, JIT deliveries, cell-production, employee participation groups—increased both across the economy and within these firms in the 1990s. Quality circles, however, decreased slightly in this period.

THE COMBINED USAGE OF MANUFACTURING PRACTICES

If the operational and human resource practices form a system we would expect them to coexist and, perhaps more importantly, for this coexistence to reflect an underlying managerial orientation toward integrated manufacturing. Studies addressing this question are limited in number and scope, as they concentrate simply on the association between the usage of practices. Wood (1999) and his colleagues (de Menezes, Wood & Lasaosa, 2002) have, however, made the examination of whether any association between them reflects an underlying integrated approach to management a core concern. The research thus far has mainly concentrated on TQM, JIT and high-commitment practices, with some attention being given to computer-based manufacturing.

Osterman

Osterman (1994) attempted to gain a picture of the combined use of TQM and human resource (HR) practices by aggregating their usage. Four practices were measured: TQM, quality circles, teams and job rotation. Osterman examined all possible combinations of the four practices constituting his measure and found that 36% of the workplaces used none of these, while 14% used only teams and 7% used only job rotation. All the other subsets, including the use of all four practices, were each to be found in less than 5% of the establishments. From this, Osterman concluded that no single major dominant cluster of practices

---

[1] This is based on the author's own analysis of Osterman's data.

emerged from the data and, by implication, that HR and TQM practices do not necessarily go together.

Lawler, Mohrman and Leford

Lawler *et al*. (1995) acquired information on both TQM and employee involvement practices in their 1993 company-level survey. TQM practices were grouped into two main categories: core- and production-oriented. Core practices included quality improvement teams, cross-functional planning and customer satisfaction monitoring; while production-orientated practices consisted of self-inspection, JIT deliveries and work or manufacturing cells. Information was collected for four types of employee involvement practices, grouped under the following headings: information-sharing, training and skills, reward systems, and power-sharing.

Lawler *et al*. used simple pair-wise correlations to examine the relationship between the individual TQM measures and the four indices of employee involvement, as well as an overall index based on the average scores across the indices. The correlations on a high proportion of all pairs involving the information-sharing, skills, and power-sharing indices were all significantly above zero, but the rewards index was only (weakly) related to one of the TQM practices, self-inspection. The correlations on the three other indices ranged from 0.47 to 0.08. Lawler *et al*. (1995, p. 58), somewhat over-zealously, concluded that "most companies have both employee involvement and TQM initiatives" and that they "are most frequently coordinated or managed as one integrated program". The size of the correlations between the use of particular TQM practices and the employee involvement indices was not consistently high enough to suggest that the dominant pattern is a fully integrated TQM and employee involvement. Neither was the frequency of use of many of them: while most firms used at least some of the practices, the typical firm used most of the practices with only 1–20% of its employees. In the absence of further analysis, it is not in fact possible to conclude that TQM and employee involvement practices tend to coexist or form a unified package. In a second survey in 1996, the correlations were again varied and not especially high (Lawler *et al*., 1998, p. 68).

Wood, Stride, Wall and Clegg

Wood *et al*. (2004) also examined the association between practices in the two IWP surveys of 1996 and 2000 and whether this had changed between the two time points. As their measure of the extent of use was on an ordinal scale and the data was not normally distributed, they could not employ factor analysis to assess whether correlations among practices reflected a unified use. As an alternative, they tested the hypothesis of a segmented use of practices, and more specifically that operational and human resource practices are distinct groups, by examining if the rank correlations amongst each pair of practices in the operational group were significantly different from the human resource group. There was no evident grouping for either 1996 or 2000, and there was no tendency for operational practices to be used in isolation of human resource practices, and vice versa. However, the correlations amongst the practices increased significantly between 1996 and 2000, the average being 0.32 in 2000, compared with 0.18 in 1996. This, along with the general increase in practice use that Wood *et al*. observed, demonstrates that the joint use of practices has increased over the last decade.

Patterson, West and Wall

For the UK, Patterson *et al.* (2002), in another study at the Institute of Work Psychology, went beyond the focus on TQM or JIT by including computer-based manufacturing—a form of advanced manufacturing technology (AMT)—in their study. Following Dean and Snell (1991), they took these to be the core of integrated manufacturing. They investigated these three practices in relation to two dimensions of empowerment, job enrichment and skill enhancement.

Patterson *et al.* collected their data in a sample of 80 manufacturing firms in the UK, drawn mainly from metal goods, mechanical engineering and the plastics and rubber sectors. They were all single-site companies selected on this basis in order to get performance data from publicly available accounts that would tally with the best level for collecting data on practices, namely the workplace. Patterson *et al.* did not simply rely on the responses to structured questions of the managers or employees in the firms. They first collected data from interviews conducted on site that typically involved the chief executive, the production director, the finance director and the personnel director. Different respondents were used for different practices. Patterson and his colleagues then supplemented this with information from relevant company documents and their own observations of work practices. Given this "wide array of information" (Patterson *et al.*, 2002, p. 14), the researchers scored the practices on the basis of their own ratings, using the information from all three sources.

None of the five measures—AMT, JIT, TQM, job enrichment and skill enhancement— were heavily correlated. Patterson *et al.* (2002, p. 20) concluded that this does not justify treating any of them as "composite constructs" i.e. as part and parcel of the same phenomenon. Nonetheless, subsequent multiple regression analysis of the association between the three manufacturing techniques and the two human resource practices revealed that TQM and JIT were significantly related to both job enrichment and skill enhancement, while AMT was related to skill enhancement but not enrichment. This adds support, within the limits of cross-sectional data, for the idea that production concepts drive the human resource practices, as well as that they enhance jobs, rather than de-skill them.

Sakakibara, Flynn, Schroeder and Morris

From the production management literature, Sakakibara *et al.* (1997) investigated in the USA a set of practices that they viewed as either constituting JIT manufacturing or its infrastructure. For JIT, six practices were identified: set-up time reduction, scheduling flexibility, maintenance, equipment layout, *kanban*, and JIT supplier relationships; while five types of infrastructure practices were identified: product design for manufacturability, workforce practices geared towards flexibility, organisation characteristics relating to the reallocation of decision rights, quality management and manufacturing strategy.

Forty-one plants were sampled (representing a 60% response rate) and within each of them 21 questionnaires were completed by a variety of managers and workers in three industries (transport components, electronics and machinery). The average of the scores for each sub-practice was taken as the plant usage of the practice. To create the overall superscales, the average score over the sub-practices for each type of practice was calculated. So the JIT score was based on the above six practices. The reliability of each scale was over the conventional 0.60 level, which suggests that the various practices tend to coexist. In investigating their coexistence, Sakakibara *et al.* (1997) adopted a correlational analysis similar to that of

Lawler *et al.* (1995). The JIT scale was significantly correlated with the infrastructure scales—product design, workforce management, organisational characteristics, quality management and manufacturing strategy. The correlations were all at the 0.45–0.51 level, with the exception of workforce management, which was 0.61. The weakest correlations involved product design and quality management. The correlations between the infrastructure scales were, however, generally higher, these ranging from 0.52 (product design and workforce management) to 0.85 (product design and manufacturing strategy). Sakakibara *et al.* (1997) concluded that this "implies that a plant that shows strengths in quality management and manufacturing strategy is very likely to have good practices in other areas".

Wood

In making the examination of the relationship between practices a core concern, Wood went beyond correlational analysis since, for him, this alone is not the defining criterion of a system. Rather, coexistence implies a need to investigate further and assess the nature of any underlying orientation that explains the associations between the practices. Addressing this amounts to an investigation of whether umbrella concepts like lean production and integrated manufacturing represent identifiable phenomenon. *In the absence of confirmation of this, they remain simply part of the discourse of management thought, or practices may simply be being used in an ad hoc way.* The central research question Wood addresses is, then, whether the relations amongst a set of operational and human resource practices reflect one of three possibilities:

1. Differing degrees of usage of an integrated management system combining both types of practices.
2. The operational and human resource dimensions are separate and thus, for example, TQM or JIT and high-involvement management are pursued as distinct approaches.
3. Practices are adopted in an *ad hoc* way rather than as part of a systematic approach.

Having earlier concentrated on human resource practices (Wood & Albanese, 1995; Wood, 1996; Wood & de Menezes, 1998), Wood (1999) examined the link between these and manufacturing practices using Osterman's data. It appeared to Wood that Osterman's conclusion that there was no dominant system, on the basis that there was a wide diversity of combinations of practices in use in his sample of firms, was too hasty. This diversity does not necessarily mean that there was no underlying pattern to the data.

Wood examined the pattern of association that existed between the set of total quality and human resource practices in Osterman's data set to see if it reflected an integrated quality and human resource approach, using latent variable modelling, as developed by Bartholomew (1987) and others. This assesses whether any association between items (i.e. the use of practices in a workplace) can be explained by a common factor or factors. Factor analysis is the most well-known latent variable model, but in this case the practices were binary and thus Wood attempted to fit latent trait models, in which the latent variable is, as in factor analysis, continuous, but the manifest variables are binary or categorical. Wood used more than the four practices that Osterman used as, in addition to quality circles, teamworking and job rotation, there was data on cross-training, human relations skills as a selection criterion, internal recruitment, employment security policy and statistical process control. He also excluded TQM, as the question treated it as a generic concept, not a practice.

Initially, a two-factor model fitted the data best. One factor loaded on quality circles, statistical process control and teamworking, all practices associated with TQM, and the other loaded on the two practices associated with labour flexibility, job rotation and cross-training, and to a lesser extent teamworking. This suggested that the first measure was a quality dimension and the second a human resource one, and that the use of quality and human resource practices reflected distinct approaches. This was supported by the fact that the first was correlated with the reported use of TQM but the second was not.

An examination of the distribution of the workplaces in the sample on the two scales revealed, however, that the workplaces divided into clearly recognisable groupings, and that the two groups were separated by whether or not they had quality circles. Given that quality circles were an important source of differentiation between establishments, a further latent trait analysis was conducted without this item being included. This time a one-factor model fitted the data well and the average score on this one-factor latent scale was significantly higher for those establishments claiming to use TQM than it was for those not pursuing it. The results of this second stage of analysis suggested that the two-factor model in the first stage was a false resolution and was misleading. Wood thus concluded that the latent variable is measuring an integrated high-involvement quality management.

Wood's re-analysis of Osterman's data revealed a picture that is more complicated than the three possibilities that he conceived at the outset. There was no fragmentation between quality and human resource practices. But quality circles have been shown to be distinct from the other practices, which Wood suggested is likely to be a reflection of the ambiguity towards them within management circles. Overall, the results suggest that something akin to an integrated total quality high involvement is an identifiable phenomenon.

De Menezes, Wood and Lasaosa

Wood's work has been extended, with his colleagues de Menezes and Lasaosa (de Menezes *et al.*, 2002), through an analysis of the UK Workplace Employee Relations Survey of 1998 (WERS98). The focus was on high-involvement management in the context of TQM. First, their definition of high involvement as a task-centred approach to participation reflected the lean production/TQM model. It involved:

1. The combined use of managerial practices for working flexibly and producing innovation.
2. An orientation on the part of employers to develop and harness the human capital of the organisation.

At its core were task-level practices, such as quality circles, job flexibility and team working. But it involved two types of support practices:

1. Individual supports, through which individuals are given training and information to engage successfully in such practices.
2. Organisational-level supports—practices such as minimal status differences and job se-curity, which are directed at the recruitment and retention of people who are able to work in a high-involvement manner.

Second, there should be a relationship between high-involvement management (HIM) and modern operational management methods, and particularly TQM. Consequently, de Menezes *et al.* (2002) examined the pattern of relationships amongst core HIM practices, the two types of supports and TQM techniques.

The WERS98, which they used, consists of a sample of 2191 workplaces with 10 or more employees across the whole economy, representing a response rate of 80% of the targeted sample. From WERS98 de Menezes *et al.* developed four measures of the task HIM practices—team working, functional flexibility, quality circles and suggestion schemes; five individual supports—induction procedures, team briefing, information disclosure, appraisal, and training in human relations; and six organisational supports—survey feedback method, commitment as a major selection criterion, internal recruitment, single status between managers and non-managers, job security guarantees, and variable pay. They measured TQM by seven practices: self-inspection; quality monitored by records of faults and complaints; quality monitored through customer surveys; records on quality of product or service that are not confidential to management; quality targets set; training on quality control; and training in problem solving. In addition, they used a measure of the use of JIT procedures.

A number of the variables were dichotomous by nature (e.g. single status) or recorded as binary in WERS98 data. The others were based on questions that asked for the percentage of employees covered by the practice, and de Menezes *et al.* (2002) found that the distributions of these practices were either multi-modal or skewed, so the variables were redefined as binary. Again adopting latent variable modelling, de Menezes *et al.* fitted latent trait and latent class models to the data. Motivation as a selection criterion and JIT were not related to any great extent to the other practices and were excluded from their main analysis. Initial stages of a step-wise procedure produced models that did not fit well and the source of the problems was diagnosed to be all the organisational supports. These practices were consequently not crucial for an integrated high-involvement quality system that is grounded in an underlying managerial orientation, and therefore were excluded from the final analysis. Latent class models, which included different combinations of both high-involvement and total quality practices, fitted the data better than any latent trait model. This means that the orientation underlying their use was best measured in terms of three grades, i.e. on a discontinuous, not continuous, scale. The population was divided into three homogeneous groups, which were identified as low, medium and high, i.e. on a discontinuous, not continuous, scale.

However, four latent class models were identified that were equally valid statistically. One model simply contained all the high-involvement practices. The three others incorporated elements of TQM and thus supported a broader and integrated concept of high-involvement management. These varied in emphasis; one was very biased towards TQM, another gave more weight to information dissemination, and the third favoured a more integrated (involvement–quality) approach. Within these models, the common core practices were self-inspection and customer surveys, and their likelihood of usage clearly increased proportionately from the low through the medium to the high class. All four classifications correlated with a measure of the degree to which employee involvement was embedded in an organisation that was based on the manager's self-report.

What underlies the finding of four observationally-equivalent models is uncertain. On the one hand, the diversity may be indicative of different managerial orientations, i.e. just as in academia, there may be no consistent perspective on the high involvement–TQM link, there are differences between managements across the economy. Some managements may see them as distinct, while those that see a connection may view this link in different ways. On the other hand, the diversity of models may simply reflect the sparseness of the data, for even with seemingly a large data set like WERS98 there was a large number of patterns of responses that were observed only once. While de Menezes *et al.* (2002) could not say which of the two possibilities explained the variety of models, they did suggest that there were signs that, with a larger data set, the integrated high-involvement–quality management

(HIQM) model might very well outperform others. Their study certainly implies that high involvement management (HIM) and TQM are overlapping concepts. So, despite the indeterminacy in the results, this study points to the value of the TQM–HIM model and suggests that:

1. The task practices are being used in conjunction with quality practices and may well be part of TQM.
2. The core of high involvement in the UK are the task practices associated with TQM carrying with it the implication of an underlying management orientation centred on continuous improvement.

Overall, the evidence from the studies reviewed on the nature of the relationships amongst modern manufacturing practices is limited. Correlations alone may be misleading. However, there is sufficient in the results, particularly in the results of the latent variable studies, to suggest that the usage of practices is not *ad hoc*. The extent to which they are combined under one truly integrating concept is unclear, but it would appear that if any one such concept underlies management's use of these practices, it extends across the operational and human resource boundaries.

MANUFACTURING PRACTICES AND PERFORMANCE

Most of the research linking manufacturing practices to performance has concentrated on assessing which, if any, of TQM, JIT, HIM or other human resource practices have the most effect. Each of these has typically been measured by a number of sub-practices. Researchers have also attempted to see whether any performance effects depend on other practices being used, or at least are enhanced when they are present, i.e. to test for any synergistic relations amongst practices. If this is the case, it is the interaction effect between practices, and not the practices themselves, that should explain most of the variation in performance. In this way, a system could be identified as the set of practices that has strong performance effects. Since any reactive effect between the practices will occur regardless of whether they tend in general to coexist, it is an alternative concept to that underlying the latent variable analysis of Wood and his colleagues. Their notion, that integrated management is ultimately an underlying orientation, implies that the practices form a coherent system that reflects management's use of them as a package, albeit to varying degrees, and does not imply synergistic effects between practices but rather, as we have seen, that this coexistence will be explained by a common factor. Moreover, it may well be that although the practices form an integrated set, their collective use may not result in superior performance to other packages that reflect other integrated approaches. It is thus necessary to differentiate between synergistic and orientation-type arguments. We shall review the literature, first presenting the research which has attempted to examine synergy, ordering this according to the extent to which it has found any, before concluding with the one study based on orientations.

Patterson, West and Wall

Patterson *et al.* (2002), uniquely, used official accounting data to measure performance. Two indices were used, labour productivity and profit. Labour productivity was measured as the logarithm of the financial value of net sales per employee, divided by labour productivity for the sector, to make it relative to the sector. Profit (before tax) was measured as the financial value of sales less costs per employee. Both productivity and profit were measured for a period of three financial years prior to the collection of the data on practices and for the financial year in the year following this. Patterson *et al.* (2002) were able to assess the association between five practices—TQM, JIT, AMT, job enrichment and skill enhancement—and the level and rate of change of both productivity and profits.

Using multiple regression analysis, the study showed that of the three operational practices, only AMT was significantly related to productivity. It was not, however, related to profits, the implication being that the effect of AMT on productivity is countered by investment costs. But both job enrichment and skill enhancement were related to both. Close examination of this revealed that the effect on profits of these two human resource practices was accounted for by its effects on productivity. Similar results were found when the change in productivity and profit was considered. Analysis of the interaction between the practices revealed no significant or meaningful results. There was thus no evidence of any synergistic relationship between integrated manufacturing and empowerment practices.

Lawler, Mohrman and Ledford

Lawler *et al.* (1995, pp. 87–92) examined the issue of synergy at the company level, using their data from the Fortune 1000 largest manufacturing and service companies. They analysed the effects of employee involvement (EI) and TQM on measures of economic and financial performance. The measures were total productivity, sales per employee, return on sales, return on assets, return on investment, and total return to investors. They conducted multiple regression analysis of the effects of EI and TQM, controlling for industrial sector and capital. EI and TQM variables were most strongly related to return of equity and return on assets, while all of the other outcome measures were significantly, but weakly, related to their usage, with the exception of the total return on investment. The percentage of corporate performance variance that was accounted for by EI and TQM practices was, however, relatively small; nonetheless, because of the wide range of performance, small movements in these practices could have translated into a relatively large effect on performance. A one standard deviation increase in EI and TQM practices would, Lawler *et al.* (1995) estimated, mean an additional 30% of employees within a company being covered by them, and this would have had quite big effects on five of the six performance indicators.

For the 1996 data, Lawler *et al.* (1998, pp. 142–153) did not report the results of a regression analysis on the effects of the combined use of EI and TQM on financial performance, as they did in 1993. It was, however, shown to be the case that the high users of both EI and TQM did in fact perform better on return on sales, return on assets, return on investment, and return on equity. A regression analysis of EI usage on its own showed that it was related to sales per employee and return on assets, as it was in 1993. Additionally, it was related to return on investment. However, it was not, as was the case in 1993, related to return on sales and return on equity. TQM usage, when assesssed in isolation of EI, was related to return on sales, return on assets and return on equity, which was not the case for 1993. The strength of the overall conclusion of the studies, that financial performance was affected by the use of EI and TQM, was enhanced by time-lagged analysis which showed that the use of practices in 1993 was related to financial performance in 1996, although no information was given to show that financial performance in 1993 was unrelated to the use of practices in 1996. So overall, Lawler's research, within the limits of its methodology, offers some support for the argument that HIM and TQM both constitute what Lawler *et al.* want to see as the high-performance system.

MacDuffie

MacDuffie (1995) conducted a single-industry study based on the 62 final assembly plants in the major car-producing countries, using data from the MIT Future of the Auto Industry project, the birthplace of the lean production concept. His work was a major attempt within the programme to investigate the human resource or high-involvement (Pil & MacDuffie, 1996) side of lean production. He measured the extent to which the production regime was lean, or bufferless, by the percentage of total assembly area space dedicated to final assembly repair, the average number of vehicles in the work-in-process buffer between the paint and assembly areas (as a percentage of one shift's production), and the average level of inventory stocks for a sample of eight key parts (weighted by the cost of each part). MacDuffie differentiated two types of HR practices, which he labelled "innovative work system practices" and "innovative HRM practices/policies". He measured the former by practices that are often associated with TQM: the existence of work teams, problem-solving groups, job rotation, decentralisation of quality-related tasks, and an effective system for employee suggestions. The HRM policies included such high-involvement practices as selection criteria geared towards openness to learning, interpersonal and teamworking skills, a contingent pay system, and minimum status differentials.

Through cluster analysis, MacDuffie identified three discrete types of plants. At the extremes were lean plants or flexible production systems with few buffers and the characteristics of both innovative work systems and human resource systems, and traditional buffered plants, which made little use of innovative work or high-involvement practices, hired on the basis of a simple match to the job requirements and trained very little. Between these was an intermediate group, which used buffers and innovative human resource practices to an extent that was half-way between the two other systems, but its usage of innovative work systems was at a similar low level to the traditional "mass" plant.

MacDuffie assessed the relative performance of plants within the three clusters on two dimensions: productivity, measured by the number of hours taken to build a vehicle (adjusted to allow for factors such as size of vehicle, number of welds and absenteeism) and quality, measured by consumer reports of defects per vehicles, as collected by a market-research company. Lean production plants were superior on both performance criteria, while the intermediate plants also performed better than the traditional ones on both these measures, although their quality levels were far closer to the traditional than they were to the lean plants. All the three elements of the lean production system, the non-use of buffers, the work system and human resource management, were related to productivity, and moreover, there was a strong interactive effect between them. The results for quality were less strong. For while work system and human resource practices were related to quality, the low use of buffers was not, neither was there an interaction effect between work system and human resource practices. Nevertheless, there was an interaction effect between having low buffers and the work system practices, suggesting that JIT was only working when work organisation was based on TQM principles. The interaction between buffers and human resource practices was significant but negative, and thus not as expected, the implication being that lean production was working best when not allied with high-involvement practices.

Taking the work system practices as indicative of TQM, the evidence on both performance criteria could be taken as support for the argument that there is a synergistic relationship between TQM and JIT. The added effect of human resource practices on productivity may add credence to MacDuffie's claim that the three practices should be treated as part of the same phenomenon. The evidence of the effects on quality, however, was not so clear-cut as it implies that human resource practices have the opposite effect to those expected or even intended by those introducing them. The factor analysis of the practices that MacDuffie reported also implies these can not be seen as an integrated set of practices on the basis of their joint usage. The limited number of plants with the bufferless system and high-commitment practices in the sample may have affected the results.

Flynn, Sakakibara and Schroder

Flynn *et al.* (1995) evaluated the effects of JIT and TQM on what they called JIT performance and TQM performance. In their study, JIT practices were of four types: *kanban*; lot size reduction practices; JIT scheduling; and set-up time reduction practices. TQM practices were classified into three types: statistical process control (SPC); product design for quality; and customer focus practices. Infrastructure practices were practices that have typically been seen as "supporting both JIT and TQM" (Flynn *et al.*, 1995, p. 328). They pertained to five domains of manufacturing: information feedback, plant maintenance, management support, supplier relationships, and workforce management.

Flynn *et al.* (1995) started from the premise that TQM practices should be the prime determinant of TQM performance and JIT of JIT performance, but they also argued that TQM will affect JIT performance and JIT, TQM performance. For example, TQM can reduce manufacturing process variance, which will reduce the need for inventory and shorten cycle times, and these are the key measures of JIT performance. Similarly, JIT practices may be used to reduce lot sizes and this may impact on quality performance, since the potential rework and scrap resulting from process failure will affect batches of smaller sizes.

Flynn *et al.* (1995) tested two sets of related hypotheses, one for JIT performance and one for TQM performance. They ordered the sets hierarchically. Since, in Flynn *et al.*'s terms, common infrastructure practices lay the foundation for the use of the unique practices, these formed the first tier of both hierarchies: common infrastructure practices are positively related to TQM or JIT performance. The second rung was the practice that corresponds to the performance outcome, thus TQM for the TQM performance equation and JIT for the JIT performance one. Finally, the last step was the inclusion of the less proximal practice: JIT positively affects TQM performance and TQM is positively related to JIT performance.

Flynn *et al.* (1995) tested these hypotheses using data from a stratified sample of 75 manufacturing plants in the US electronics, transportation components and machinery industries. They acquired information on the practices from a range of selected informers in the plants—operatives and managers—using questionnaires. Information was acquired on a number of practices falling under the 12 dimensions that Flynn *et al.* (1995) identified, for example three in the case of customer focus, statistical process control and most JIT methods, and nine for workforce management. They omitted two infrastructure sets of practices (information feedback and work management) and one JIT practice (set-up time reduction practices) on the grounds that they were relatively highly correlated with other independent variables, which might not have been necessary on statistical grounds as the correlations were not above 0.60.

Reflecting the way that they had organised the hypotheses, Flynn *et al.* (1995) conducted hierarchical regression analysis on the data. The first stage of the analysis of JIT performance revealed that a significant part of the variance could be explained by the infrastructure practices, the second stage that JIT practices added significantly to this, but the third stage revealed that the TQM measures had no significant effect. The final equation showed that management support had by far the greatest effect, while lot size was weakly related. A third factor, supportive plant environment, was also significantly related to JIT performance but the relationship was negative, not positive as expected.

Tests for interaction effects between practices suggested that having a supportive plant environment did, however, enhance the effects of (a) statistical process control, (b) JIT scheduling, and (c) lot size reduction practices. In addition, having supportive management and a customer focus both also strengthened the effect of JIT scheduling. The interaction between supportive management and *kanban* was negative, which Flynn *et al.* suggest may mean that they were operating as substitutes.

The analysis of TQM performance revealed even stronger effects from infrastructure practices ($R^2 = 0.51$ for stage one). The additional R^2 for the next two stages was not, however, significant. In the final model only the infrastructure practices were significant, management support and supplier relationship both were more strongly related to TQM performance than the third practice, plant environment, which was positively, albeit weakly, related to it. The sign of JIT scheduling was in fact negatively related to quality. Interaction analysis revealed that supportive management enhanced the effect of JIT scheduling and that supplier relations, likewise, intensified the effect of product design and JIT scheduling.

The few significant interaction effects between the supports and TQM (and JIT) practices did not suggest that they have joint effects. The research in fact showed that infrastructural supports have important effects on performance in their own right. Managerial support was especially significant. JIT scheduling was especially important for both JIT and TQM performance but its effects were not realisable without the infrastructural supports. Overall, TQM practices appear to have little effect on the basis of this study. But statistical process control will, in the context of a supportive plant environment, affect JIT performance, while product design, when coupled with supplier relations, has an effect on TQM.

Nonetheless, the conclusion that Flynn *et al.* (1995, p. 1354) draw from their study is "that there is a relationship between TQM and JIT practices and performance" and "that although TQM and JIT function effectively in isolation, their combination yields synergies that lead to further improvements". Given that no unconditional effects of either JIT or TQM were found, nor were any significant synergies between any two types of JIT or TQM practices, this is clearly wrong. Moreover, it appears that the infrastructural practices had an independent effect in isolation of the existence of JIT or TQM practices.[2] Since the

---

[2] Flynn *et al.* (1995, p. 1351) appear to have concluded that there is an effect of TQM on the grounds that the results reflect the ordering that the variables were inserted in the hierarchical regression analysis. So, while the inclusion of TQM practices in the TQM performance equation, for example, added little to the starting model that just included infrastructure supports, had these formed the first stage they may well have been significant. But this is insufficient to justify a TQM effect. While the R^2 associated with TQM practices may be greater if they were included first, any significant regression coefficients for TQM at this stage would not survive the inclusion of the other variables. Flynn *et al.* (1995, p. 1350) also argued that the low addition to the R^2 following the inclusion of the TQM set may have reflected the fact that there is an overlap between the unique TQM variables and the common infrastructure. The precise meaning of this in substantive terms was, however, unclear, especially as it was being gauged from an analysis of the practices' effects.

managerial support measures were biased towards quality rather than JIT, it would appear from this study that it is having a philosophy geared to quality and not the practices *per se* that is crucial for quality and JIT.

Cua, McKone and Schroeder

Cua *et al.* (2001) investigated the effects of three operational practices, TQM, JIT and total productive maintenance (TPM). In a similar vein to Flynn *et al.* (1995), they distinguished the key practices that are uniquely associated with each of these from those that are common to them, and which in their terms are "supporting" mechanisms (Cua *et al.*, 2001, p. 680) that strengthen the impact of operational practices on performance.

In their study, unique TQM practices were cross-functional product design, process management, supplier quality management, and customer involvement; unique JIT practices were set-up time reduction, pull system production, JIT delivery by suppliers, equipment layout, and daily schedule adherence; and TPM practices were autonomous and planned maintenance, technology emphasis and proprietary equipment development. The common practices were, in Cua *et al.*'s (2001, p. 679) terms, human- and strategic-orientated practices, and were committed leadership, strategic planning, cross-functional training, employee involvement, and information and feedback. Data was gathered from a survey of 163 manufacturing plants in five countries (USA, Japan, Italy, Germany and the UK), which were randomly selected in each country from three industries, electronic, machinery and transportation parts suppliers. In each plant, 26 respondents completed a questionnaire (12 were direct labourers and 14 were managers) and multiple observations of a practice were averaged to form a score for each practice. The data on performance was collected from one source, the plant manager. He/she was asked to rate the plant's performance relative to its competitors on four dimensions: cost efficiency, quality of product conformance, on-time delivery, and volume flexibility. In addition, a composite performance measure based on a weighted sum of the four performance measures was developed, where the weights reflect the strategic importance that the plant places on the performance dimension.

Cua *et al.* (2001) first divided the plants into high and low performance and then conducted discriminant analysis to assess which practices discriminated between the two groups. First, they created four composite measures of all the four types of practices, TQM, JIT, TPM and common or support practices, and then investigated their relative importance in discriminating between the high and low performers. The discriminant loadings for all four composite measures were all high, 0.53–0.85, over all five performance indicators, and the overall model fit was good for all equations. JIT was most significant for cost efficiency, and TQM was more important for quality and volume flexibility and even for on-time delivery. TPM was the least significant for all measures, except for the weighted measure, where JIT was slightly less significant than it, the implication being that cost efficiency was weighted highly in the measure. The discriminant loadings for the common practices were either the top or very close to the top-rated practices for all the performance measures.

Second, the authors conducted a similar analysis using the individual practices that made up the TQM, JIT, TPM and support practices. The results confirmed that at least one practice from each of these "sets" had an impact on all the performance measures. For TQM, all four were important for on-time delivery, all but customer involvement were important for quality and the overall performance measure, customer involvement was the only practice significant for volume flexibility, while it and supplier management were important for cost efficiency. For JIT practices, JIT delivery from suppliers was the only important item for all the performance measures, but set-up time reduction and pull production were also significant in the case of cost efficiency. Technology emphasis was the only TPM practice that was important for all performance measures, while planned maintenance was significant for cost efficiency and on-time delivery. In the case of the supports, committed leadership was a highly significant practice in all performance models. In the case of volume flexibility, it was the only such practice of any significance. For on-time delivery all the other supports were significant; for cost efficiency all but strategic planning were; for quality, only strategic planning and employer involvement were significant common practices. Finally, for weighted performance, only strategic planning was significant.

Overall the study suggests that high performance is dependent on the use of practices across the range of JIT, TQM and TPM, as well as social and strategic mechanisms. The authors concluded that these practices are mutually supporting. But this is straying too far from their analysis, since their methodology did not allow them to test for interaction effects between the common practices and hence to see whether the common practices were complementing the operational practices. In fact, the common practices appear to be playing a main role. Moreover, their second analysis implied that the main effects on performance were from the use of specific practices within each program, not all elements.

Shah and Ward

Shah and Ward (2003) examined the three elements of lean production that Cua *et al.* (2001) investigated (JIT, TPM, TQM) but explicitly treated HRM as a fourth dimension. They treat each dimension as a "bundle" of complementary and interrelated set of practices, simultaneous implementation of which has synergistic effects on organisational performance, particularly on operational measures such as quality and waste reduction.

Shah and Ward's analysis is based on data from an annual survey of manufacturing managers conducted by Penton Media Inc., the publishers of *IndustryWeek*, and PricewaterhouseCoopers, the accountancy and consultancy firm. This data set comprises answers from 1757 respondents to a mail questionnaire sent to approximately 28,000 subscribers of *IndustryWeek* and other manufacturing-related publications, representing a response rate of 6.7%. The unit of analysis is the manufacturing plant and the sample covers the full range of industries but is somewhat biased in favour of paper, chemicals, primary metal, electrical and electronic equipment, and transportation equipment.

Twenty-two practices were included in the study. Those representing JIT were lot size reduction, JIT/continuous flow production, pull system, cellular manufacturing, cycle time reductions, focused factory production systems, agile manufacturing strategies, quick changeover techniques, bottleneck/constraint removal, reengineered production processes; the TPM bundle included predictive or preventive maintenance, maintenance optimization, safety improvement programs, planning and scheduling strategies, and new process equipment or technologies; TQM consisted of competitive benchmarking, quality management programs, total quality management, process capability measurements, and formal continuous improvement; finally, HRM was captured by self-directed work teams and a flexible, cross-functional workforce. Practice use was measured on a three-point scale ranging from "no implementation" to "extensive implementation" with "some implementation" representing the mid-point. Shah and Ward used principal component analysis to empirically validate the bundles, that is to see if the correlations between the use of practices reflect an underlying grouping of practices that corresponds to their initial four-fold classification of the practices. Four principal components were identified and they reflected the four assumed bundles perfectly, with one exception: competitive benchmarking loaded almost equally on TPM and TQM. Shah and Ward decided to locate it in the TQM bundle and develop measures of JIT, TPM, TQM and HRM based on the use of the practices included in each bundle. Operational performance was measured as a five-year change in six items: manufacturing cycle time, scrap and rework costs, labour productivity, unit manufacturing costs, first pass yield, and customer lead time. In a principal component analysis the six items loaded on one factor, and thus the authors constructed a uni-dimensional measure of performance based on the factor scores (Shah & Ward, 2003, p. 138).

Using hierarchical regression analysis, Shah and Ward showed that the inclusion of the four lean bundles resulted in a statistically significant incremental change of 0.231 in the R^2 in the prediction of performance from a model that included only controls for industry, union presence, and size and age of plant. Each bundle contributed to the effect, with JIT and TPM having a slightly more significant effect than TQM and HRM. There was no support for the hypothesis that these effects were contingent on the four contextual variables measured in the study (industry, unionisation, plant size and plant age) as none of the interactions between these variables and the bundles were significant.

Shah and Ward (2003, p. 145) conclude rightly that "a separate and identifiable incremental effect can be attributed to the four major lean practices areas". The all-embracing nature of their results does differentiate their study from the others reported here. They go on to claim that the "findings provide unambiguous evidence of synergistic effects on performance amongst the four lean bundles". Like Cua et al. (2001), this is, though, going a step beyond their analysis because they did not test for interaction effects between either the practice bundles or individual practices within bundles.

Wood, de Menezes and Lasaosa

Wood and his colleagues (de Menezes et al., 2002) investigated whether the three different classes identified in their latent class model using WERS98 data were associated with different levels of performance. They considered three performance indicators: financial performance, labour productivity, and change in labour productivity. De Menezes et al. (2002) ran regression models in which there were two dummy variables indicating membership of particular latent classes, the minimal and partial high-involvement quality management, or high-involvement management (depending on the model). In each regression model de Menezes et al. (2002) controlled for all other types of practice that were not included in the specific latent class model being tested; for example, in the model based on high-involvement practices only, all the organisational supports and a measure of total quality management were included. Other control variables such as the size of the establishment were also included.

Membership of the high (third) class resulted in a significant increase in the change in labour productivity in the case of all four models. There were no significant effects on labour productivity. The results are consistent with the TQM/lean production theory, since it is centred on the importance of continuous improvement and thus the performance variable that is most significant to it is the rate of productivity change. This is itself not strongly linked to the other outcomes.

Finally, de Menezes *et al.* (2002) tested a key element of the theory of lean production, namely that it will reverse the tendency for there to be a trade-off between productivity and quality, that chasing high quality will result in low productivity (see Womack *et al.*, 1990). Analysis of whether high-involvement–quality management produced this virtuous combination of high productivity and quality revealed that it did, as it had the greatest effect on the relationship between the level of both. The effect was more pronounced for the integrated model than for high involvement management alone (the model that excluded quality practices).

DISCUSSION AND CONCLUSIONS

There is little doubt that the studies reviewed here are addressing important issues for our understanding of the new workplace. But when taken together, they do not offer any conclusive evidence on the diffusion, nature and effects of modern manufacturing practices. The limited studies of the changing use present a consistent picture of increased use over the past decade, and they suggest that this is not largely, if at all, reflecting faddism. Whether it is sufficient to represent the institutionalisation of lean production, TQM and high-involvement management implied by Womack *et al.*'s (1990) forecast is impossible to tell on the basis of the studies to date.

The evidence on the integrated use of the practices that we have reviewed is uneven. It is first uneven in quality, reflecting different methods of analysis; and second, in results, as some of the correlational analysis points to a limited coexistence between practices, while some of it implies a stronger collective use. The most systematic studies of the inter-relationship between practices by Wood and his colleagues have yielded promising results. In the case of the US (Osterman) data, Wood's analysis suggests that TQM (albeit with a limited number of measures) and HR practices may reflect some underlying integrated orientation on the part of management. In the UK (WERS98) case, the results are less clear-cut but certainly suggest that TQM and HIM are not unrelated phenomena and may well be (or even more than likely are) inseparable. This study suggests though that JIT may not be so integrated across the whole economy or even within manufacturing.

The findings on the performance effects are even more mixed. First, we have the Patterson *et al.* (2002) study, showing that it is the high-involvement (empowerment) elements of integrated manufacturing that are affecting labour productivity. Second, the evidence of the Lawler *et al.* (1995, 1998) and MacDuffie (1995) studies imply—more strongly in the case of the latter—that the various types of practices have positive synergistic effects on performance. Third, we have the three studies by Cua *et al.* (2001), Flynn *et al.* (1995) and Shah and Ward (2003), which conclude that similar synergistic effects have been found, when in fact either their statistical model does not test for this or the results do not support this conclusion. At best, Cua *et al.* show that that all three of TQM, JIT and TPM practices have effects, while Shah and Ward confirm this but also show that TPM may have significant effects. In the case of Flynn *et al.* (1995), consistent with Patterson *et al.*, it is the human resource elements that are important, and seemingly the managerial philosophy, not the use of specific practices, that has the most effect. Finally, de Menezes *et al.* (2002), in suggesting that the combined use of TQM and HIM may well reflect an underlying "holistic" orientation on the part of management, also put emphasis on management's approach rather than the practices *per se*, these being reflections of this.

Aside from the different results, the studies vary on a range of dimensions. First, they differ according to which practices they included. Second, they differ in the way that the practices were measured, some being measured continuously, others dichotomously. Third, some have relied on a single respondent for the measures of practices, others have used multiple respondents. Fourth, studies differ according to whether or not they attempted to assess the relationship between the practices before they measured their performance effects. Fifth, the unit of analysis differs between studies, and in particular whether they were conducted at the company or workplace/establishment level. Finally, the type of performance measures used in the studies varies, with some concentrating on manufacturing measures, others productivity or financial performance data. There is also a difference between the types of measurement of these indices, as most studies relied on the assessment of relative performance by a representative of the organisation, while only Patterson *et al.* (2002) used published company data.

Since the studies vary so markedly between each other, it is not possible to do any systematic comparison of them. Nonetheless, it is clear, even without this, that the marked differences between the results of the studies does not reflect in any systematic way the underlying concepts or designs of the studies.

A number of lessons can be drawn from this review. First, the minimum that we can take from it is that the study of operational and human resource practices are best not separated. Second, if we are to progress this area of study, it seems that we need a greater consistency of concepts and research design. At the same time we need to design studies that allow us to test between alternative possible ways in which the practices may be used and having an effect. The two-stage strategy followed in some studies, and most strongly by de Menezes *et al.* (2002), seems vital. We need: (a) to investigate the association between practices to assess whether they are in fact used in concert and whether their use is indicative of an underlying management orientation, and if so the nature of this; and, if their use is found to be systematic then (b) to measure whether the underlying orientation(s) is correlated with performance. Testing for synergy between practices is a separate activity. It clearly makes less sense if the practices form part of the same phenomenon.

Third, there are a number of limitations in all the studies, which will need to be addressed as research progresses. In many ways these mirror the limitations of the HRM–performance studies that Wood and Wall (2002, pp. 263–270) highlight. The main methodological one is that they are cross-sectional, although in the case of Patterson *et al.* (2002) they do link practices to future performance. All but Patterson *et al.* (2002) are based on performance data that relied on the judgements of managers, and in some cases of a single manager, and the samples have been small and in many cases not representative. Only the WERS98 study used weights to correct any bias. Yet, the uncertainty in the results of the WERS98 study provide a salutary lesson in relying on small samples. Even with what would seemingly appear to be a large sample, we are not able to decide conclusively in favour of the integrated high-involvement quality model.

Conceptual limitations in the studies include a lack of attention to: (a) the mechanisms that link the practices to performance; (b) the effectiveness or depth of the use of the practices; and (c) the contingent nature of the effects of use on performance. Attending to these issues will inevitably take us to the nuances underlying the theoretical discussions surrounding manufacturing methods. Four seem especially important.

First is the possible existence of different managerial perspectives on the relationship between the various types of practices. Even if it is subsequently discovered that, for the UK, the integrated high-involvement–quality model does reflect the UK situation best, this still leaves open two possibilities: (a) that managers differ in their view of its links to JIT and other practices not included in the study, and (b) there are different perspectives between countries. Second, there is the possibility of different types of lean production, TQM or high-involvement systems, in theory and practice; for example Sitken, Sutcliffe and Schroeder (1994) distinguish between TQM systems that are focused on controlling processes and add little involvement and those orientated towards organisational learning. Or there is the distinction between team-based systems that rely on heavy supervision and those based on self-managed teams (Appelbaum & Batt, 1994; Wood, 1990, p. 181). Third, there is also the question of the link between manufacturing practices and job enrichment, so central to this book. The research (Dean & Snell, 1991; Wood, 1993) specifically on this supports an additional conclusion of de Menezes *et al.*'s (2002) study, that core high involvement practices are being used alongside non-enriched jobs and that re-design of the basic tasks of a job does not seem to be central to integrated manufacturing. De Menezes *et al.* also found that there were no extra performance gains from enriching the jobs when using high-involvement quality management. This analysis is tentative and needs much more research and conceptual thought. Finally, while incorporating the high-involvement practices in the analysis of operational techniques goes some way to addressing the human resource issues associated with their implementation, the focus and the methodology adopted in the studies may need to be extended if all the issues of conflict within organisations are to be addressed.

The burden of this review is that the limitations of the studies reviewed reflect, as much as anything, the fact that the debate is still in its infancy. So, while the methodological problems point to the need for a "big science" model for future research in this area, the conceptual limitations imply "little science" will also play a decisive role.

Acknowledgements

I would like to thank David Holman and Malcolm Patterson for their comments on an earlier draft of this chapter; Lilian de Menezes and Ana Lasaosa for their contribution to my ideas and the joint work I have reported above; and the Economic and Social Research Council of the UK's support for that work (Grant No. R000238112). I would also like to thank Paul Osterman for making his data available to me.

REFERENCES

Abernathy, W. J., Clark. K. B. & Kantrow, A. H. (1984). *Industrial Renaissance: Producing a Competitive Future for America*. New York: Basic Books.

Appelbaum, E. & Batt, R. (1994). *The New American Workplace: Transforming Work Systems in the United States*. Ithaca, NY: Cornell IR Press.

Bartholomew, D. (1987). *Latent Variable Models and Factor Analysis*. London: Charles Griffin.

Bolden, R., Waterson, P. E., Warr, P. B., Clegg, C. W. & Wall, T. D. (1997). A new taxonomy of modern manufacturing practices. *International Journal of Operations and Production Management*, **17**(11), 1112–1130.

Cua, K. O., McKone, K. E. & Schroeder, R. (2001). Relationships between implementation of TQM, JIT, and TPM and manufacturing performance. *Journal of Operations Management*, **19**(6), 675–694.

Dean, J. W. & Snell, S. A. (1991). Integrated manufacturing and job design: moderating effects of organizational inertia. *Academy of Management Journal*, **34**(4), 774–804.

Flynn, B., Sakakibara, S. & Schroeder, R. (1995). Relationship between JIT and TQM: practices and performances. *Academy of Management Journal*, **38**(5), 1325–1360.

Lawler, E. E., Mohrman S. A. & Ledford, G. E. Jr (1995). *Creating High Performance Organizations*. San Francisco, CA: Jossey-Bass.

Lawler, E. E., Mohrman, S. A. and Ledford, G. E. Jr (1998). *Strategies for High Performance Organizations*. San Francisco, CA: Jossey-Bass.

McCloskey, L. A. & Collett, D. N. (1993). *TQM*. Methuen, MS: Coal/OPC.

MacDuffie, J. P. (1995). Human resource bundles and manufacturing performance: organizational logic and flexible production systems in the world auto industry. *Industrial and Labor Relations Review*, **48**(2), 197–221.

de Menezes, L., Wood, S. & Lasaosa, A. (2002). The Foundations of Human Resource Management in the UK. Mimeo, Institute of Work Psychology, University of Sheffield.

Osterman, P. (1994). How common is workplace transformation and who adopts it? *Industrial Relations and Labour Relations Review*, **47**(2), 173–188.

Osterman, P. (2000). Work reorganization in an era of restructuring: trends in diffusion and effects on employee welfare. *Industrial Relations and Labor Relations Review*, **53**(2), 179–196.

Patterson, M., West, M. A. & Wall, T. D. (2002). Integrating manufacturing, empowerment and company performance. *Journal of Organizational Behavior*, **25**(5), 641–665.

Pil, F. K. & MacDuffie, J. P. (1996). The adoption of high-involvement work practices. *Industrial Relations*, **35**(3), 423–455.

Sakakibara, S., Flynn, B. B., Schroeder, R. G. & Morris, W. T. (1997). The impact of just-in-time manufacturing and its infrastructure on manufacturing performance. *Management Science*, **43**(9), 1246–1257.

Schonberger, R. J. (1986). *World Class Manufacturing: the Lessons of Simplicity Applied*. New York: Free Press.

Shah, R. & Ward, P. T. (2003). Lean manufacturing: context, practice bundles, and performance. *Journal of Operations Management*, **21**(1), 129–149.

Sitken, S. B., Sutcliffe, K. M. & Schroeder, R. G. (1994). Distinguishing control from learning in total quality management: a contingency perspective. *Academy of Management Journal*, **19**(3), 537–564.

Walker, R. (1989) Machinery, labour and location. In S. Wood (Ed.), *The Transformation of Work* (pp. 1–43). London: Unwin Hyman.

Waterson, P. E., Clegg, C. W., Bolden, R., Pepper, K., Warr, P. B. & Wall, T. D. (1999). The use and effectiveness of modern manufacturing practices: a survey of UK industry. *International Journal of Production Research*, **37**(10), 2271–2292.

Womack, J., Jones, D. & Roos, D. (1990). *The Machine that Changed the World*. New York: Rawson.

Wood, S. (1989). The transformation of work. In S. Wood (Ed.), *The Transformation of Work*, (pp. 1–43). London: Unwin Hyman.

Wood, S. (1990). Tacit skills: the Japanese management model and new technology. *Applied Psychology*, **39**(20), 169–190.

Wood, S. (1993). The Japanization of Fordism. *Economic and Industrial Democracy*, **14**(4), 535–555.

Wood, S. (1996). High commitment management and payment systems. *Journal of Management Studies*, **32**(11), 83–77.

Wood, S. (1999). Getting the measure of the transformed high-performance organization. *British Journal of Industrial Relations*, **37**(2), 391–417.

Wood, S. & Albanese, M. (1995). Can you speak of a high commitment management on the shop floor? *Journal of Management Studies*, **32**(2), 215–247.

Wood, S. & De Menezes, L. (1998). High commitment management in the UK: evidence from the Workplace Industrial Relations Survey, and Employers' Manpower and Skills Practices Survey. *Human Relations*, **51**(4), 485–515.

Wood, S. J., Stride, C. B., Wall, T. D. & Clegg, C. W. (2004). Revisiting the use and effectiveness of modern management practices. *Human Factors and Ergonomics in Manufacturing*, **14**(4), 415–432.

Wood, S. & Wall, T. D. (2002). Human Resource Management and Business Performance. In P. Warr (Ed.), *The Psychology of Work* (pp. 351–374). Harmondsworth: Penguin.

CHAPTER 12

Organizational Performance in Services

Rosemary Batt and Virginia Doellgast

School of Industrial and Labour Relations, Cornell University, NY, USA

Competition in service activities has intensified over the last two decades and corporations have responded by making radical changes in their strategies and organizational structures. On the demand side, national product market deregulation has encouraged price competition and facilitated the internationalization of service activities. On the supply side, advances in information technologies have expanded remote service options and automated processes, while heightened international immigration has increased the availability of labor for traditionally low-wage, as well as high-wage, service jobs.

In this context, the quest for more efficient and effective service delivery systems has become a central topic among academics and industry practitioners. While leading management theorists in the 1970s advocated competing on price by applying industrial models of production to services (Levitt, 1972), quality service and customer relationship management have emerged as dominant themes since the mid-1980s (Heskett, Sasser & Schlesinger, 1997).

The question of performance in service activities and occupations is important for several reasons. First, over two-thirds of employment in advanced economies is in services. Second, productivity growth in most service industries is historically low, lagging far behind manufacturing and limiting the potential for wage growth in production-level service jobs. In addition, labor costs in service activities are often over 50% of total costs, whereas in manufacturing they have fallen to less than 25% of costs. This raises the question of whether management practices that have improved performance in manufacturing, such as investment in the skills and training of the workforce, may be more difficult or costly to apply to service activities. Yet these practices, referred to as "high-involvement" or "high-commitment" practices, may be even more important for performance in services because employees often interact directly with customers and shape their buying behavior. Third, the role of the customer in production makes the process of service delivery fundamentally different from that found in goods production. Thus, it is useful to focus on the factors affecting performance in services, the topic of this chapter.

To discuss competition and performance in services, we first briefly review the nature and extent of change in market institutions, technologies and business strategies. We

The Essentials *of the New Workplace: A Guide to the Human Impact of Modern Working Practices.*
Edited by David Holman, Toby D. Wall, Chris W. Clegg, Paul Sparrow and Ann Howard. © 2005 John Wiley & Sons, Ltd.

conclude that while there is variation within and across service industries and across countries, most firms have responded to intensified price competition with cost reduction rather than quality-enhancing strategies. Where quality and relationship management strategies are adopted, they are typically reserved for business or high-valued added customers. To examine the predictors of performance, we turn to empirical studies within organizations regarding the link between management practices and performance outcomes, and then to empirical studies of causal mechanisms. Our literature review covered quantitative studies from 22 journals between 1995 and 2001. Conclusions follow.

CHANGING MARKETS, TECHNOLOGIES AND BUSINESS STRATEGIES

Competition in services has intensified as markets that were once local and regional have become national and international in scope. This expansion has been facilitated by a growing demand for services as inputs into global manufacturing, advances in information technology that have increased the speed and volume of electronic transactions, and political movements to deregulate and privatize service industries. We reviewed changes in markets, technologies and business strategies in five industries—airlines, financial services, telecommunications, hotels and health care. In each case, heightened price competition, increased scope of the market, and increased concentration in ownership structures have contributed to a focus on cost cutting and the use of customer segmentation strategies.

Price competition has accelerated in airlines, financial services and telecommunications, primarily due to deregulation and privatization of national product markets. In airlines, deregulation began in the USA in 1978 and spread quickly to the UK, New Zealand, Chile, Canada and Australia (Oum & Yu, 1998). Most European nations began a more gradual process of deregulation in the mid-1980s (Doganis, 2000). In financial services, deregulation and privatization began in most OECD countries in the 1970s and early 1980s in response to high inflation, the internationalization of banking and the abandonment of fixed foreign exchange rates. It continued in the 1980s due to international debt crises and the entrance of new financial actors such as mutual funds and credit card companies. In telecommunications, the UK and US undertook deregulation and privatization in the early 1980s, and within a decade almost all other countries around the globe were doing the same (Katz, 1997).

The hotel industry, by contrast, experienced economic difficulties due to overbuilding of capacity in the late 1980s and early 1990s. In the USA, in particular, thousands of hotels were foreclosed and several major chains filed for bankruptcy. Competition has intensified as national and global chains have gobbled up more traditional, independently owned and operated hotels (Lattin, 1998, pp. 96–98).

In health care, rising costs have threatened funding systems in most countries, although there is great variation due to the variety of national systems of funding and the high level of government involvement in health care. The USA faces the greatest crisis, with health care costs rising at two or three times the rate of inflation in recent years, due to factors such as new technology, an aging population, the rise of medical malpractice suits, overspecialization, and the cost of poor quality (Gaucher & Coffey, 1993).

Regardless of the source of pressure, organizations in these industries have responded by focusing heavily on cost-cutting strategies. In industries undergoing deregulation, new entrants to the market typically have lower cost structures than established companies due to fewer sunk costs in obsolete technologies and a lower-wage, non-union workforce. The established firms have responded to new entrants by investing in new technology and by cutting labor costs. In airlines, for example, US companies: downsized; established two-tier wage structures; demanded concessions in work rules; established low-cost subsidiaries with lower wage scales and more flexible terms; and outsourced activities such as aircraft cleaning and maintenance, passenger handling, in-flight catering and accounting. European airlines followed suit by the late 1980s and early 1990s (Doganis, 2000, pp. 112–119).

In banking, companies began offering a range of new products, such as insurance, credit cards, cash management, and pension and mutual funds. US banks led the way in shifting the business focus from service to sales maximization and reducing labor costs through labor-saving technologies, such as automatic teller machines, new back-office data-processing technologies, and telephone and Internet banking. Banks in other OECD countries have followed many of these practices. There is some evidence that these changes have had a negative impact on customer satisfaction, as in a Norwegian study that found that cost-cutting and restructuring led to significant declines in service quality and to customer defection (Lewis & Gabrielson, 1998).

In telecommunications, the old monopolies responded by investing heavily in digital technologies and slashing labor costs through downsizing. Following deregulation, sales maximization replaced the historic goal of providing a universal service to the public. These patterns varied by country, with more market-driven strategies in the USA, UK, and Australia and more union-mediated strategies in the European countries and Japan (Katz, 1997).

In the hotel industry, globalization has allowed firms to maintain low labor costs through the utilization of large numbers of low-wage immigrant workers. Hotels have also adopted labor-saving technologies such as property management systems, Internet booking, and automated check-in and check-out. In health care, organizations have attempted to constrain spending and seek more efficient organizational and funding strategies (Howard & MacFarlan, 1994). The USA has shifted from "patient-driven" to "payer-driven" competition, which has led to a decline in the influence of the medical profession over health care management and the rise of control by for-profit financial interests (Dranove & White, 1999). This market-orientated strategy distinguishes the USA from other industrialized nations, which responded to increases in health care costs by adopting more centralized, budget-driven approaches (Dranove & White, 1999, p. 34). While the USA appears to be experiencing the greatest crisis in health care, restructuring to reduce costs is occurring in most countries (Sochalski, Aiken & Fagin, 1997).

Some studies show that cost cutting has had negative results in health care. For example, a study of re-engineering at a large US hospital found that it had extremely negative results for employees and patients. Using three waves of employee surveys, researchers found significant increases in depression, anxiety, emotional exhaustion, job insecurity, workloads and team work. Workers also reported significant declines in the overall quality of care they gave (Woodward et al., 1999). A survey of nurses from over 700 hospitals in the USA, Canada, England, Scotland and Germany in 1998–1999 found a high rate of dissatisfaction and experiences of job-related strain in all countries except Germany (Aiken, Sean, Clarke, Sloane & Sochalski, 2001). They found a high level of discontent associated with negative perceptions of staffing adequacy and workforce management policies.

In addition to cutting labor costs and investing in labor-saving technologies, service companies have responded to heightened competition by consolidating organizations and ownership structures. While deregulation is designed to increase the number of industry players, it has led to rising concentration of ownership across OECD countries in airlines (Oum & Yu, 1998), banking (Hunter, 1999) and telecommunications (Katz, 1997). In the hotel industry, concentration has also increased, with the USA leading the way with new forms of chains, franchising, hotel development and management. Hotels in other countries are replicating US practices such as international franchising and alliances (Lattin, 1998, pp. 54–56). The USA also has led the world in the consolidation of health care facilities, as managed care organizations assume a growing role and independent hospitals are incorporated into for-profit chains (Dranove & White, 1999).

Another popular service management strategy is customer segmentation, in which companies stratify customers by their ability to pay. Segmentation allows companies to compete on quality and relationship management for high value-added customers, such as business clients, but to adopt a cost-minimizing or industrial model of service provision in the mass market. In airlines, for example, business customers pay a premium for quality service, while the bulk of consumers complain about cramped seating arrangements, poor baggage handling and automated reservation systems. Segmentation strategies are more problematic in banking because of the difficulty of identifying the future value of customers. Nonetheless banks distinguish between high net worth and mass-market sectors in personal banking; and large, medium and small sectors in business banking (Hunter, 1999). In telecommunications, segmentation strategies have become widespread, with different levels of customer service and human resource strategies for workers serving various tiers of business customers and the mass market (Batt, 2000). Similarly, hotels are typically classified into three basic strata: upscale, mid-scale, and budget/economy. Management practices and labor strategies differ across the strata, with some attention to recruitment, training and compensation at upscale hotels, but little or none in mid-scale or economy hotels. The "mass market" approach in the lower tier of the market emphasizes rationalization and intensification of work for the bulk of low-wage workers. Nonetheless, even at the high end, labor investment strategies tend to focus on front office employees and managers, not the three-quarters of hotel workers who occupy "low-level" service occupations, such as maid, janitor, food server or hotel clerk (Bernhardt, Dresser & Hatton, 2003; Cobble & Merrill, 1994, pp. 455–457).

The use of workplace innovations or human resource strategies that invest in the workforce are relatively undeveloped in service organizations. National surveys show that service industries have lagged behind manufacturing in the use of high-commitment work practices, at least in the USA. For example, a 1993 national survey of establishments by the US Bureau of Labor Statistics found that 56% of manufacturing plants used at least one innovative practice (use of teams, TQM, job rotation or quality circles), but only 36% of retail firms and 41% of all service firms did (Gittleman, Horrigan & Joyce, 1998). Hunter's (2000) analysis of a US national establishment survey found that service establishments were roughly half as likely as manufacturing establishments to use TQM and self-managed teams. Exceptions, such as Southwest Airlines, are notable.

More generally, where companies have experimented, it is with a particular type of innovation. In airlines, for example, employee stock ownership plans (ESOPs) have become popular since their introduction by United Airlines. They are designed to motivate workers to have a stake in the company by offering equity in exchange for pay and work rule concessions. All major US airlines now have ESOPs and employee representation on their boards (Doganis, 2000, pp. 121–122). In banking, studies have found examples of work reorganization that provide workers with a broader set of skills for service and cross-selling of a variety of products (Baethge, Kitay & Regalia, 1999, pp. 7–14). In telecommunications, a handful of US companies experimented with TQM and self-directed teams in the 1980s, but soon after abandoned them (Katz, 1997). And in health care, there is widespread interest in the application of TQM principles to hospitals, a trend that began in the USA in the 1980s but which is spreading throughout OECD countries. However, Ennis and Harrington (2001) found that only 25% of the hospitals they surveyed had formal TQM programs, and half of those had started in the year prior to the survey.

Our brief review of several major service industries suggests that firms have responded to intensified competition primarily by cutting costs and using new technologies to compete on product and process innovation. They have made relatively little use of innovative human resource practices, and where they have, these are in workplaces serving business or high-value-added customers. The question, then, is how and why quality service strategies and high-commitment practices can lead to better performance in a broader array of service activities, particularly in the mass market.

MANAGEMENT PRACTICES AND PERFORMANCE OUTCOMES

We identified a range of models for service management that vary on a continuum from those designed exclusively to reduce labor costs to those focused on quality professional service. Industrial models of service production are designed to maximize volume and minimize cost by emphasizing mechanization, individually designed jobs with low skills and discretion, and intense monitoring and rule enforcement (Levitt, 1972). At the other end of the spectrum are relationship management strategies modeled after professional service (Gutek, 1995; Heskett *et al.*, 1997). They are characterized by high levels of specialization and education, independent judgment, long-term personal relationships between providers and consumers, and intense focus on quality, loyalty and customization. Between these two extremes is a range of strategies characterized by some mix of attention to cost and quality—what some have termed "mass customization" (Pine, 1993; Frenkel, Korczynski, Shire & Tam, 1999). They involve some level of automation and process re-engineering found in industrial models, coupled with some level of attention to service quality and customer loyalty found in the professional model.

Implicit in these models is the assumption that there is an inverse relationship between cost and quality. By contrast, TQM theory assumes that costs and quality may be jointly maximized by involving workers in problem-solving to lower defect rates. However, the investments in training and high relative pay for skilled workers under TQM, lean production, or other high-commitment production models, means that labor costs are higher in these systems (Cappelli & Neumark, 2001). Thus, whether there is a net performance gain from high-commitment systems is an empirical question that is likely to vary with the relative labor intensity of an activity. The labor-intensive nature of services coupled with tight profit margins may limit the utility of high-commitment practices in mass markets.

Evidence that the effectiveness of high-commitment practices is contingent on a quality or up-market strategy is inconclusive. On the one hand, a study of 209 hotels in the UK showed that investment in HRM was ineffective where cost control was the business strategy, but effective for hotels pursuing a quality strategy (Hoque, 1999). On the other hand, Delery and Doty (1996) studied banks in the USA and found that while some high-commitment HR practices had contingent effects on performance, universal effects were stronger. Batt's

(2002) research on call centres found that an index of high-commitment practices had significant positive effects overall, but that the effects were *more* powerful in the mass market, where price competition dominates. Finally, using archival data from 525 US nursing homes, Mukamel and Spector (2000) found that the relationship between cost and quality was not linear. Rather, they found an inverted U relationship between quality and costs, suggesting that there are quality regimens in which higher quality is associated with lower costs. This evidence from a highly labor-intensive and cost-constrained industry supports the idea that cost and quality can be jointly maximized in mass market service activities, as TQM theory predicts.

In the remainder of this section, we review the evidence on management practices and performance in three areas: the use of technology and skills, the organization of work, and HR incentive and control systems. We then turn to studies that integrate these dimensions and examine the processes linking management practices to organizational performance. Most of the studies included use objective measures of operational outcomes, such as productivity and quality, defined in contextually-specific ways or measured by managers or customer reports. We also included several studies of employee attitudes and behaviors that shed light on explanatory mechanisms as well as the limits of current research.

Information Technology and Skills

In the 1980s, service firms began investing heavily in information technology to improve historically low productivity levels. However, in the USA where technology investments in service industries outpaced those in other countries, aggregate data revealed no productivity gains in the 1980s and early 1990s (compared to manufacturing, where technology-related productivity grew significantly). Researchers referred to this phenomenon as the productivity paradox (National Research Council, 1994). By the mid-1990s, however, evidence began to shift. In a major review of the literature, Brynjolfsson and Yang (1996) concluded that the main benefits from using computers were improved quality, variety, timeliness and customization—none of which are well measured in official productivity statistics. These findings held across manufacturing and service industries. In recent research, Brynjolfsson and colleagues surveyed over 400 large firms and found that greater levels of IT are significantly associated with higher skill levels, investments in training and the reorganization of work to emphasize decentralization and the use of teams. These factors, both independently and interacting with each other, lead to higher productivity. These findings, however, were not disaggregated by sector (Bresnahan, Brynjolfsson & Hitt, 2002).

Other studies specific to service industries reach similar conclusions. Pennings (1995), for example, examined 10 years of data from 107 banks on product and process innovations (ATMs, computers). He found that both had a significant positive effect on efficiency and effectiveness indicators, with computer innovations having a stronger effect on internal measures of performance and ATMs on external measures. He also found that mimetic or late adopters of IT enjoyed fewer performance advantages than their innovating competitors who "left the pack early". Reardon, Hasty and Coe (1996) found that IT contributes as much on the margin towards the creation of output as spending on additional selling space in retail establishments. They concluded that retailers are underutilizing IT. Quinn (1996) reviewed government and service industry data and identified alternative benefits from investments in IT that do not show up in "productivity" data: maintaining market share, avoiding catastrophic losses, creating greater flexibility and adaptability, handling complexity, improving service quality, creating an attractive work environment, and increasing responsiveness and predictability of operations.

These studies suggest a variety of potential benefits of IT adoption, but fail to test interactions with other elements of work design—a strength of the work by Brynjolfsson cited above. Moreover, the *relative* contribution of new technology and work organization strategies is not well understood. In a study of Danish banks and local government offices, for example, Nielsen and Host (2000) found that the most significant predictor of service quality was a job design variable including skill variety, task identity, task significance, autonomy, and feedback; internal marketing initiatives and IT support did not play a major role.

The Organization of Work

Choices regarding technology may influence, but not entirely predict, the organization of work. Managers can design individual jobs to enhance or to limit employees' use of skills through greater decision-making discretion or breadth and variety of tasks. Managers most also decide whether to organize work as an individual or interdependent function. While most manufacturing technologies imply task interdependence, the extent of technically-required interdependence is more varied and less obvious in service settings where "products" are more intangible. Managers, therefore, have considerable choice in the extent to which they emphasize work as an individual or collaborative process in such areas as customer service, banking, retail sales, airline reservations and service, hotels and health care.

Discretion, Participation and TQM

Prior reviews of the literature on job design have shown that individual employee autonomy, "empowerment", or participation in off-line teams are generally associated with better employee attitudes, such as satisfaction, but either modest positive or no objective performance outcomes (Cotton, 1993). Findings from our review of articles since 1995 are consistent with this evidence. On the one hand, Harel and Tzafir (1999) found a positive correlation between participation and manager-reported performance in a study of service organizations in Israel. Similarly, Hunter and Hitt (2001) found that higher levels of worker discretion in retail banks were associated with significantly higher objective productivity and sales. On the other hand, King and Garey (1997) reported that empowerment had no significant correlation with guest satisfaction ratings in hotels. Rodwell, Kienzle and Shadur (1998) found no evidence that employee participation in decision-making predicts self-rated performance in a study of an Australian IT company. Other research showed that participation in off-line quality teams had no relationship to subjective and objective performance criteria for field technicians (Batt, 2001) or call center workers (Batt, 1999). In fact, in the latter case, greater autonomy was significantly negatively associated with self-reported quality. Preuss (1997, 2003) studied similar issues in hospitals, and found that greater discretion for nursing assistants led to higher rates of patient errors, while greater discretion for nurses led to lower rates. Employee involvement in personnel decisions such as scheduling, training and assignments had no effect on patient error rates.

Several studies of Total Quality Management have also shown mixed results. TQM generally includes two dimensions of job redesign. One is delegation of decision-making discretion to lower organizational levels, so that employees with tacit knowledge closest to the "the point of production" can make operational decisions. The second is the use of off-line quality improvement groups (quality circles and the like) to solve problems. Douglas and Judge (2001) found a significant positive relationship between financial performance and the degree of implementation of TQM in a study of 193 hospitals. Hospitals that implemented a comprehensive array of TQM practices outperformed those that had less well-developed programs. Lammers, Cretin, Gilman and Calingo (1996) found that commitment to TQM philosophy and the number of active teams explained 41% of the variance in perceived quality improvement in 36 medical centers. However, in another study of TQM involving 3000 patients in 16 hospitals, Shortell and colleagues (2000) observed that while there were two- to four-fold differences in all major clinical outcomes, little of the variation was explained by TQM. Patients in hospitals scoring high on TQM were more satisfied but also more likely to have hospital stays greater than 10 days. And in a study of TQM in 61 hotels in the UK, Harrington and Akehurst (1996) found that only 22% of those that had a formal quality policy reported return on capital rates of more than 10% in a 3 year period (1989–1992). There was no evidence of a statistically significant relationship between company adoption of a quality orientation and their rates of return on net assets. These inconsistent results suggest that the value of individual worker discretion, participation or TQM varies across workplace and industry settings and thus must be examined in contextually specific ways.

Teams and Group Collaboration

In contrast to the ambiguous findings for TQM, researchers have found fairly consistent positive associations between the use of groups or collaborative forms of work organization and performance (Cohen and Bailey, 1997). Cohen and Bailey's review, however, contained only a handful of studies of work teams in services, and these showed inconsistent results. Since that review, new studies of semi-autonomous teams in frontline services have found more positive performance results. In a study of knowledge workers in financial services, Campion, Papper and Medsker (1996) found that Hackman and Oldham's (1980) model of job characteristics, measured at the work group level, significantly predicted better self-reported and managerial ratings, and archival data on performance. Similarly, Batt (1999) found that self-directed teams of customer service representatives had 9.2% higher monthly sales and higher self-reported quality than traditionally supervised groups. Langfred (2000) studied 1000 workers at two service workplaces: a social service agency and the Denmark military. He found that both group and individual autonomy predicted the quality and accuracy of group outcomes as reported by managers. Uhl-Bien and Graen (1998) studied 400 public sector workers and found that individual self-management showed a strong, positive relationship with team effectiveness (as reported by managers) in functional work units, but a weak, negative relationship with effectiveness in cross-functional teams.

Other research has examined the importance of inter-group relations in services, particularly among project and product development teams, where much of the original research on this topic emerged (Cohen & Bailey, 1997). More recent studies, however, have shown the importance of inter-group coordination among frontline service workers, for example Gittell, found that cross-functional coordination was a significant predictor of objective performance measures in airline (Gittell, 2001) and health care settings (Gittell *et al.*, 2000). In sum, there is growing evidence that opportunities for group work and collaboration are associated with better performance in frontline service work.

Similar to the literature on technology, researchers increasingly recognize that group effectiveness depends not only on the design of groups, but on a series of supportive management practices that create a coherent set of directions and incentives. Arguably, these management practices are more important in service workplaces, because the justification for group-based work rests less on interdependent task characteristics and more on intangible aspects, like information sharing and learning. Most of the studies of service teams, discussed above, found that group effectiveness was enhanced by supportive management practices, such as training, supervisory support, rewards and work group relations.

In one influential study, for example, Cohen, Ledford and Spreitzer (1996) tested a structural equation model of performance as predicted by four dimensions of the work environment: group work design; encouraging supervisor behavior; group characteristics, such as coordination and expertise; and "employee involvement" context (information, feedback, training, resources and recognition). They found significant relationships between all four dimensions and four outcome variables: satisfaction, self-rated and manager ratings of performance, and absenteeism. One of their strongest findings was that the context variables significantly predicted employee satisfaction and manager ratings of performance, but encouraging supervisor behavior was significantly negatively related to manager ratings. They attribute the latter finding to the possibility that supervisors interfere more often in worse-performing teams or that supervisors who intervene in teams may actually undermine performance because workers are better situated to know what to do.

HR Incentive and Control Systems

Incentive and control systems may be usefully classified as either behavior-based or outcome-based (Eisenhardt, 1985). Behavior-based systems rely on supervisory monitoring and enforcement of rules and are typically utilized for jobs that are defined as low-skilled or routine and relatively easy to monitor. Outcome-based systems rely more on performance-based pay and are typically utilized for jobs that do not have easily programmable tasks and are difficult to monitor.

Classic mass production control systems are usually behavior-based, and thus rely heavily on monitoring and rules. High-commitment systems, in which jobs are defined as more complex and less programmed, typically rely on outcome-based incentives, such as performance-based pay. If work systems require group work, then group-based pay is the logical concomitant. If firms adopt outcome-based systems, then, in theory, supervisory responsibilities should change, from disciplining employees and enforcing rules to facilitating support, resources, employee development and coordination across work groups.

Service jobs that involve customer interaction—the bulk of employment in services—should in theory have outcome-based control systems because the customer introduces uncertainty and variability into the production process, and thus tasks are not easily programmed. Sales jobs, for example, have historically relied heavily on commission pay. In reality, however, many firms have adapted mass production models to services, from call centers to fast food. In these settings, behavior-based controls are viewed as even more important than in manufacturing, because current technology limits the extent to which standardization can be accomplished through machine-pacing. Thus, service managers also must set standardized routines for interacting with customers, coupled with supervisory monitoring. In recent years, technological advances have allowed electronic monitoring systems to be used in a much broader array of service jobs, reducing the number of supervisors while maintaining high levels of surveillance.

Empirical research on the performance effects of alternative incentive systems is quite undeveloped. For example, there is limited research on the relationship between electronic monitoring, supervisory monitoring, and performance. On the one hand, electronic monitoring may replace supervisors, thereby reducing indirect labor costs and improving organizational efficiency. On the other hand, intense electronic monitoring has been found to cause emotional exhaustion and burnout (Carayon, 1993; Holman, Chissick & Totterdell, 2002), which may negatively affect productivity. In addition, supervisory monitoring may be a complement to electronic monitoring, as in research by Holman *et al.* (2002), who found that supervisor support moderated the negative effects on workers of electronic monitoring.

Similarly, research on supervisors is theoretically and empirically undeveloped. Often researchers include a measure of supervisor support (positive feedback, fair treatment of workers) when they study management practices, but fail to examine what supervisors actually do. These studies typically show that supervisors influence employee attitudes but not necessarily performance; for example, Cunningham and MacGregor (2000) found that supervisor support was a significant predictor of employee satisfaction, intention to quit, and absenteeism in a study of 750 Canadian telephone and service station workers. However, in an international survey of 400 call center workers, supervisor support and team member support had a significant relationship with job satisfaction but not employees' commitment or reported capacity to satisfy customers (Sergeant & Frenkel, 2000). Singh (2000) found that task control was more important than supervisor support as a resource for call center workers in financial services, and King and Garey (1997) found that positive supervision and leadership in hotels had little correlation to guest ratings of responsiveness and slight negative correlations to welcoming and helpfulness.

A second set of issues concerns the ratio of supervisors to workers: are new forms of work organization a complement to or substitute for supervision? One group of studies has shown that self-managed teams are an effective substitute for supervisors. A meta-analysis of research on self-managed teams, for example, found that teams without supervisors performed better than those with supervisors (Beekun, 1989). In a recent study of call center workers, Fernie and Metcalf (1999) found that team-based pay systems and low supervisor–worker ratios were associated with higher self-reported productivity and financial performance. Batt (2001) found that field technicians in self-managed teams absorbed the monitoring and coordination tasks of supervisors in one-third of the time required by supervisors, thereby reducing indirect labor costs without adversely affecting objective quality and productivity. In theory, teams that develop the capacity to be self-regulating and do without supervisors will perform better. Cohen, Cheng and Ledford (1997) tested this idea using data from 900 employees in self-managed and traditionally supervised work groups in a telecommunications firm. They found that self-managed teams scored higher on leadership dimensions and that these dimensions predicted employee satisfaction and self-rated effectiveness. They also found that these leadership behaviors were applicable to traditionally supervised groups.

Other researchers argue that supervisors are a complement to new forms of work organization. In a study of an airline company, for example, Gittell (2002) found that higher supervisor:worker ratios predicted better performance, and that the supervisory effect acted through its positive impact on workers' cross-functional communication. She attributes this effect to the fact that small spans of control allow supervisors to provide intensive coaching.

Thus again, the relationship between supervision and teamwork appears to be quite context specific, varying based on the nature of group tasks and the need for coordination across groups. The empirical research on alternative pay systems also provides relatively little clarity about what predicts better outcomes, in part because of the many different types of plans and the fact that outcomes are contingent on the specifics of the plan (the fairness of the formula for payouts, the tightness of the link to performance, the type of behavior rewarded, and the combination of individual and group-level criteria, etc.). Outcomes also vary according to the relationship between the pay system and other factors (such as the design of work and performance management). Recent comprehensive reviews of the compensation literature provide some evidence that linking pay to performance leads to better individual and organizational performance (Milkovich & Newman, 2002; Gerhart & Rynes, 2000). The strength and persuasiveness of the empirical evidence, however, varies considerably by the type of compensation plan. A few reliable studies show that gainsharing or work group-based plans produce higher performance, but the findings depend on the formula for payouts. The few studies of skill-based pay plans suggest that they encourage more learning, which in turn positively affects quality. A handful of reliable studies on merit pay provide some evidence that it leads to better performance (Milkovich & Newman, 2002). Some research also shows that firms have better financial performance when they link pay to operational or financial goals (Gerhart & Rynes, 2000). However, a meta-analysis of research on financial incentives conduded that they were unrelated to performance quality, but significantly related to performance quantity (Jenkins, Mitra, Gupta & Shaw, 1998).

A particularly relevant study for service and sales workplaces is a 6 year study of performance-based pay at 34 outlets of a large retail organization in the USA. The researchers tracked an experiment in which roughly half of the retail stores switched to an incentive plan that rewarded workers with individual bonuses for sales over a given target. Notably, it also threatened termination if they failed to meet the target for two successive quarters. Supervisory monitoring declined in the experimental stores; and sales, customer service and profits grew significantly. This provides some support for the idea that behavior-based and outcome-based systems are inversely related. Performance outcomes also were higher in stores serving higher-valued customer markets, consistent with the idea that outcome-based systems are more appropriate for more unprogrammed service interactions (Banker, Lee, Potter & Srinivasan, 1996). However, it is unclear whether the improved performance in this case was due to the pay plan or the threat of termination.

In sum, there is evidence that investments in information technology, coupled with high relative skills and collaborative work design, can yield better performance in frontline services. There is also evidence that some types of performance-based pay are associated with better performance. The evidence is not overwhelming, however, and appears to be quite contingent on the nature of the industry, task, occupation and organizational context.

SYSTEMS AND MECHANISMS LINKING MANAGEMENT PRACTICES AND OUTCOMES

Explanations regarding how and why management practices lead to better performance may be classified as primarily psychological, on the one hand, or economic and sociological on the other. While studies in organizational behavior historically focused on worker satisfaction and commitment, more recent research considers a broader array of emotional and affective outcomes, including positive responses, such as pro-social or citizenship behaviors, and trust; and negative responses, such as emotional exhaustion, stress, withdrawal (quits, absences) and other forms of resistance. Research based in economic and sociological explanations has focused on the importance of human capital, social capital and knowledge-sharing and learning on the job.

Psychological Explanations

Affective models build on the large psychological literature on work design, which has demonstrated systematic relationships between enhanced job characteristics (e.g. autonomy, variety, ability to complete a whole task; Hackman and Oldham, 1980) and worker satisfaction, as have the studies of autonomous teams (Cohen & Bailey, 1997). However, these studies have failed to find that happier workers are more productive. More recently, a study of over 500 Canadian workers found that the use of high-commitment practices had contradictory effects on workers, bringing greater intrinsic rewards, such as satisfaction and commitment, but also greater reported stress (Godard, 2001). An analysis of the 1998 UK Workplace Employee Relations Survey by Ramsay, Scholarios and Harley (2000) also casts doubt on the idea that the HR–performance link is mediated through workers' emotional and affective reactions. They found significant positive relationships between a comprehensive measure of high-performance work practices and several performance outcomes as reported by managers, including labor productivity, quality, financial performance, absenteeism and turnover. They then tested whether worker perceptions of discretion, management relations, pay satisfaction, commitment, security and job strain mediated the relationship between management practices and performance. They report mixed and modest mediating effects, and conclude that there is no strong evidence that performance outcomes flow via workers' attitudinal outcomes. Neither of these studies differentiated between manufacturing and service organizations, however.

Several management theorists, nonetheless, have pursued this line of research on the hunch that worker attitudes are more important in customer-contact jobs because they can more readily spill over into customer interactions—positively or negatively. The most elaborate theory (the service profit chain) links human resource practices to employee satisfaction and loyalty, which in turn inspires customer satisfaction and loyalty, ultimately resulting in higher profits (Heskett *et al.*, 1997). Loveman (1998) was the first to empirically demonstrate correlations along several links in this chain (HR practices; employee satisfaction and loyalty; and customer satisfaction, loyalty and profits), based on employee and customer data from 479 branches of a multi-site regional bank.

Schneider and his colleagues have taken a similar approach by measuring workers' reports of management practices and the extent to which they support a positive "service climate" (Schneider, Parkington & Buxton, 1980). The measures in Schneider's service climate survey have parallels with those used in the high-commitment literature. Recent studies provide evidence that a significant positive relationship exists between worker perceptions of service climate, worker attitudes, and customer reports of service quality (Schmit & Allscheid, 1995; Johnson, 1996; Peccei & Rosenthal, 2000; Borucki & Burke, 1999) and financial performance (Borucki & Burke, 1999). In a longitudinal study of 134 bank branches, Schneider, White and Paul (1998) found that their measure of service climate was significantly associated with higher customer reports of service quality. Moreover, in cross-lagged analyses of data over three years, they found a reciprocal effect for service climate and customer perceptions of quality. However, the causal relationships are not entirely clear in this line of research, as some studies have found that customer satisfaction leads to worker satisfaction (Ryan, Schmit & Johnson, 1996). Other research suggest that these relationships may be context specific, such as a study by Somers and Birnbaum (1998) that found no relationship between commitment and objective measures of performance among hospital employees.

A growing area of research concerns the boundary-spanning role of service workers as they are positioned between management and the customers. One study of a Canadian bank, for example, found that the employee–customer interface was the most important predictor of a worker's prosocial behavior (Chebat & Kollias, 2000). This boundary-spanning position, however, is vulnerable to role ambiguity and conflict because management and customers may place contradictory demands on workers. A good example is in call centers, where management may seek to limit call-handling time, while customers demand more time. Similarly, "service workers" increasingly play a dual role of service and selling—roles that require opposite skill sets and approaches to customers and thus can create additional stress for employees. In a study of restaurant workers, Babin and Boles (1998) found that role stress negatively affected customer–server interactions and increased workers' intentions to quit. Hartline and Ferrell (1996) surveyed several hundred managers, workers and customers at 279 hotels and found that role conflict contributed significantly to employees' frustration in their attempt to fulfill their jobs. In a major meta-analysis of research on role ambiguity and role conflict, Tubre and Collins (2000) found a significant negative relationship between role ambiguity and performance, but a negligible relationship between role conflict and performance.

Another emerging line of research seeks to understand the relationship between management practices, worker well-being and performance. Several studies of call center workers have found that routinized work design and high levels of electronic monitoring lead to stress, anxiety, depression, emotional exhaustion and burnout (Carayon, 1993; Holman, 2001; Holman et al., 2002; Deery, Iverson & Walsh, 2002; Singh, 2000). Deery et al. (1999) found that customer interactions, scripts, routinization, workloads and managerial emphasis on quantity predicted emotional exhaustion, which in turn predicted absenteeism. Singh (2000) found that worker burnout with customers is associated with lower self-reported service quality. With increasing levels of burnout, call center workers were able to maintain their productivity levels, but their self-reported quality was lower. Other organization-level studies also show that electronic monitoring predicts higher quit rates (Shaw, Delery, Jenkins & Gupta, 1998; Batt, Colvin & Keefe, 2002).

Economic and Sociological Explanations

A second set of explanations focuses on how management practices influence the use of human capital and knowledge at work. Implicit or explicit in these approaches is Gary Becker's work on human capital (1964) and the idea that productivity hinges on the effective use of the skills and abilities of workers. Human capital theory predicts that high-commitment or high-performance systems should produce better organizational performance and wages because they provide opportunities and incentives for employees to use their skills more effectively. More recently, resource- and knowledge-based views of the firm have gained popularity as theoretical models that focus on employee skills and knowledge as the basis for sustained competitive advantage (Barney, 1991; Grant, 1996).

In customer contact settings, firm-specific human capital is particularly important, because employees manage the boundary between the firm and the customer and their behavior shapes customers' buying behavior. Employees need to manage firm-specific information and knowledge in at least three domains: products, customers and processing protocols. Product knowledge covers specific features, service agreements, pricing, packaging and legal regulations. Customer-specific knowledge includes an understanding of demand characteristics of particular individuals or segments and the ability to use that knowledge to customize service or sales. Workflow and processing protocols require specific knowledge of information processing systems and capabilities and how these affect each customer and product offering.

Research supports the idea that firm-specific human capital positively affects service performance. In a study of a department store chain, for example, Sharma, Levy and Kumar (2000) found a significant positive relationship between sales experience and performance, which they attributed to the knowledge structures of workers with greater expertise. In a meta-analysis of 22 studies of job experience, Quinones, Ford & Teachout (1995) found a 0.27 correlation between experience and performance.

One study of high-commitment practices in service and sales centers found that they influenced organizational performance in two ways: directly, via the effect on employee performance, and indirectly, via employee attachment to the firm (Batt, 2002). High quit rates not only increased the costs of recruitment and selection but also negatively affected performance, because new employees face a learning curve. Long-term employees have the tacit firm-specific skills and knowledge—and often personal relationships with customers—to be more effective. In a micro-level follow-up study, Moynihan and Batt (2001) found that the design of group-based work, recognition and rewards led to greater knowledge sharing among workers, which in turn was correlated with objective service quality in call centers.

Another study in this vein focused on the importance of the quality of information in health care settings, where uncertainty is high and the quality of information is extremely important (Preuss, 1997, 2003). Preuss found that information quality is critical in this setting because patients' health status changes constantly and thus must be updated regularly. Based on a sample of 1100 nursing employees on 50 acute care hospital units, Preuss found that units with lower medical errors were those that relied on nurses with higher levels of formal education, higher levels of experience and broader task responsibilities. Units that gave more responsibilities to lower-skilled employees had significantly higher medical errors. The quality of information mediated the relationship between work design and staffing decisions and medical errors.

A similar approach Gittell (2000) focuses on the importance of communication and relationships among employees in service workplaces, particularly in settings characterized by high levels of uncertainty and time constraints. Based on her fieldwork in airlines and health care, Gittell developed a measure of "relational coordination"—the extent to which employees communicate and have positive relationships with one another within and across departments. She found that several management practices, including selection, cross-functional and flexible work design and supervisor support, shape the extent of coordination among workers. In a study of orthopedic hospital units, the extent of relational coordination predicted significantly lower post-operative pain, shorter lengths of stay and better patient-reported care (Gittell *et al.*, 2000). In airlines, relational coordination led to lower gate time, staff time, customer complaints, lost bags and late arrivals (Gittell, 2001). Another recent study has focused on the knowledge-creation capability of the firm. Drawing on a sample of managers and employees from 136 high-technology firms, Collins and Smith (2004) found that a set of high performance work practices significantly improved sales growth and stock performance by creating a social environment that facilitates knowledge sharing. Specifically, they found that the management practices were significantly related to both the social networks between core employees (tie strength and number of friendship contacts) and the social climate of the organization (trust, cooperation, shared codes and language), and these social factors worked to positively affect firm performance by increasing core employees motivation to share knowledge with one another. Collins and Clark (2003) also studied the internal and external network of top management teams in 73 high-technology companies and found that a set of network-building HR practices was significantly related to the sales growth and stock performance through their effect on the range and tie strength of external networks and range and size of internal networks.

Together, these studies point to the importance not only of individual human capital, but also of networks of human capital, or organizational social capital (Leana & Van Buren, 1999). Organizational social capital may be thought of as an asset embedded in the relationships among employees. While these ideas are at initial stages of conceptual and methodological development, recent research points to the importance of communication networks and relationships of trust among employees as important sources of organizational performance.

DISCUSSION AND CONCLUSIONS

In this chapter, we have reviewed the literature on the restructuring of service industries and concluded that organizations have focused much more attention on cost-cutting strategies and investments in technology than on work redesign or human resource strategies. We then examined quantitative studies of the predictors of performance in services. This research has been conducted in a wide range of contexts and levels of analysis—across industries, firms, establishments and work groups.

At the most general level, researchers across many disciplines—from economics to psychology to sociology—have concluded that various dimensions of management practices must be understood in relation to one another, or as systems. Students of IT, for example, have demonstrated that investments in IT, when coupled with complementary high-commitment practices, are associated with higher productivity, innovation, customization and quality in services. Researchers in organizational behavior have similarly determined that group effectiveness is contingent on the presence of complementary management practices. However, despite this recognition, most studies do a poor job of understanding relationships among management practices. For example, with a few exceptions, students of organization studies and human resources have not integrated an understanding of IT into their work. As a result, at the level of work groups and organizations, we know relatively little about how the differentiated uses of IT (such as electronic monitoring or the availability of software programs and databases) interact with the organization of work and human resource management practices to produce different results. Similarly, our understanding of the relationship between alternative forms of work organization and incentive systems is undeveloped.

Our review of research on work organization found growing evidence that collaborative forms of work organization predict better performance in service contexts. Service organizations that create opportunities and incentives for collaboration within and across groups appear to perform better than those that do not. This finding is important, because in many service settings the relationship between employees and customers appears to be more salient than the relationship among employees. Sales work, for example, has typically been defined as individual. Field technicians usually work alone. However, the service process frequently depends on coordination among workers who are located in different job classifications, work groups, locations or functional departments, as in airlines, hotels or telecommunications. It also depends on collaboration across hierarchically-defined occupational groups, as in health care. In these settings, where interdependence is important but not self-evident or necessarily in the self-interest of employees, managers must create mechanisms and incentives for employees to collaborate and cooperate. However, the effectiveness of specific types of coordinating mechanisms—whether more or less autonomous work groups, cross-functional groups, or virtual teams—is likely to depend on the nature of work, technology, and industry setting.

The search for general findings with respect to the performance effects of incentive and control systems is more elusive. There are two quite different theories about whether supervisors are substitutes or complements to new forms of work organization. While some research suggests that electronic monitoring and team-based systems are substitutes for supervision, other studies suggest that they are complements. It could be that both alternatives produce equally good outcomes or contingency perspectives may instead prevail. Supervision in the form of coaching and support may be particularly important in service settings because of high levels of uncertainty and emotional labor in customer–provider relations. Further research is needed to untangle the answers to these questions.

Empirical research on pay systems is also undeveloped. While some form of performance-based pay appears to be associated with better organizational performance, the devil is in the details. We know relatively little about the differentiated effects of incentive vs. at-risk pay, about systems that combine different types of incentives or about how these systems affect employees at different income levels.

Finally, research on causal mechanisms linking management practices to outcomes is still quite undeveloped. Scholars in organizational behavior have shifted their focus from satisfaction and commitment to a wider array of worker attitudes and emotional outcomes. This work needs to move to the next step of linking worker outcomes to objective performance. The research on human capital, knowledge sharing and social capital is particularly promising, but needs to be developed theoretically and expanded empirically to cover a wider array of occupations and work settings.

In sum, while researchers have begun to identify the ways in which work organization and human resource practices influence service performance, our theoretical models are undeveloped and our empirical evidence is piecemeal. Without clear evidence to the contrary, managers have little reason to shift from tried and true strategies of competing on cost. Interdisciplinary research projects over the next decade must do a much better job of explicating the relationship between management practices and service performance in more systematic and contextually-specific studies of industries and occupations.

REFERENCES

Aiken, L. H., Sean P. Clarke, S. P., Sloane, D. M. & Sochalski, J. A. (2001). Nurses' reports on hospital care in five countries. *Health Affairs*, **20**(3), 43–53.

Babin, B. J. & Boles, J. S. (1998). Employee behavior in a service environment: a model and test of potential differences between men and women. *Journal of Marketing*, **62**, 77–91.

Baethge, M., Kitay J. & Regalia, I. (1999). Managerial strategies, human resources practices, and labor relations in banks: a comparative view. In M. Regini, J. Kitay & M. Baethge (Eds), *From Tellers to Sellers: Changing Employment Relations in Banks* (pp. 3–30). Cambridge, MA: MIT Press.

Banker, R. D., Lee, S. Y., Potter, G. & Srinivasan, D. (1996). Contextual analysis of performance impacts of outcome-based incentive compensation. *Academy of Management Journal*, **39**(4), 920–949.

Barney, J. (1991). Firm resources and sustained competitive advantage. *Journal of Management*, **17**, 99–120.

Batt, R. (2000). Strategic segmentation in front-line services: matching customers, employees and human resource systems. *International Journal of Human Resource Management*, **11**(3), 540–561.

Batt, R. (1999). Work organization, technology, and performance in customer service and sales. *Industrial and Labor Relations Review*, **52**(4), 539–564.

Batt, R. (2001). The economics of teams among technicians. *British Journal of Industrial Relations*, **39**(1), 1–24.

Batt, R. (2002). Managing customer services: human resource practices, turnover, and sales growth. *Academy of Management Journal*, **45**(3): 587–59.

Batt, R., Colvin, A. & Keefe, J. (2002). Employee voice, human resource practices, and quit rates: evidence from the telecommunications industry. *Industrial and Labor Relations Review*, **55**(4): 573–591.

Becker, G. (1964). *Human Capital*. New York: Columbia University Press.

Beekun, R. I. (1989). Assessing the effectiveness of sociotechnical interventions: antidote or fad? *Human Relations*, **42**(10), 877–898.

Bernhardt, A., Dresser, L. & Hatton, E. (2003). The coffee pot wars: unions and firm restructuring in the hotel industry. In E. Appelbaum, A. Bernhardt & R. Murnane (Eds), *Low Wage America: How Employers are Reshaping Opportunity in the Workplace*. New York: Russell Sage.

Borucki, C. C. & Burke, M. J. (1999). An examination of service-related antecedents to retail store performance. *Journal of Organizational Behavior*, **20**, 943–962.

Bresnahan, T. F., Brynjolfsson, E. & Hitt, L. M. (2002). Information technology, workplace organization, and the demand for skilled labor: firm-level evidence. *Quarterly Journal of Economics*, **117**(1), 339–376.

Brynjolfsson, E. & Yang, S. (1996). Information technology and productivity: a review of the literature. *Advances in Computers*, **43**, 179–214.

Campion, M. A., Papper, E. M. & Medsker, G. J. (1996). Relations between work team characteristics and effectiveness: a replication and extension. *Personnel Psychology*, **49**(2), 429–459.

Cappelli, P. & Neumark, D. (2001). Do "high-performance" work practices improve establishment-level outcomes? *Industrial and Labor Relations Review*, **54**(4), 737–772.

Carayon, P. (1993). Effect of electronic performance monitoring on job design and worker stress: review of the literature and conceptual model. *Human Factors*, **35**, 385–395.

Chebat, J. & Kollias, P. (2000). The impact of empowerment on customer contact employees' role in service organizations. *Journal of Service Research*, **3**(1), 66–81.

Cobble, D. S. & Merrill, M. (1994). Collective bargaining in the hospitality industry in the 1980s. In Voos, P. B. (Ed.), *Contemporary Collective Bargaining in the Private Sector*. Industrial Relations Research Association Series, Madison, Wisconsin.

Cohen, S. G., Cheng, L. & Ledford, G. E. (1997). A hierarchical construct of self-management leadership and its relationship to quality of work life and perceived work group effectiveness. *Personnel Psychology*, **50**(2), 275–308.

Cohen, S. G. & Bailey, D. E. (1997). What makes teams work: group effectiveness research from the shop floor to the executive suite. *Journal of Management*, **23**(3), 239–290.

Cohen, S. G., Ledford, G. E Jr. & Spreitzer, G. M. (1996). A predictive model of self-managing work team effectiveness. *Human Relations*, **49**(5), 643–676.

Collins, C. J. & Clark, K. D. (2003). Strategic human resource practices, top management team social networks, and firm performance. *Academy of Management Journal*, **46**(6), 740–751.

Collins, C. J. & Smith, K. G. (2004). Constructing a social environment for knowledge sharing: the role of human resource management practices creating competitive advantage in high technology firms. Unpublished draft.

Cotton, J. L. (1993). *Employee Involvement: Methods for Improving Performance and Work Attitudes*. Newbury Park, CA: Sage.

Cunningham, J. B. & MacGregor, J. (2000). Trust and the design of work: complementary constructs in satisfaction and performance. *Human Relations*, **53**(12), 1575–1591.

Deery, S., Iverson, R. & Walsh, J. (2002). Work relationships in telephone call centers: understanding emotional exhaustion and employee withdrawal. *Journal of Management Studies*, **39**(4), 471–497.

Delery, J. E. & Doty, D. H. (1996). Modes of theorizing in strategic human resource management: tests of universalistic, contingency and configurational performance predictions. *Academy of Management Journal*, **39**, 802–835.

Doganis, R. (2000). *The Airline Business in the Twenty-first Century*. London: Routledge.

Douglas, T. J. & Judge, W. Q. Jr (2001). TQM implementation and competitive advantage: the role of structural control and exploration. *Academy of Management Journal*, **44**(1), 158–169.

Dranove, D. & White, W. D. (1999). *How Hospitals Survived: Competition and the American Hospital*. Washington, DC: AEI Press.

Eisenhardt, K. (1985). Control: organizational and Economic Approaches. *Management Science*, **31**, 134–149.

Ennis, K. & Harrington, D. (2001). Quality management in Irish healthcare. *Service Industries Journal*, **21**(1), 149–168.

Fernie, S. & Metcalf, D. (1999). *Agent Don't Lose that Number . . . Payment Systems, Monitoring, and Performance in Call Centers*. London: Centre for Economic Performance, London School of Economics.

Frenkel, S., Korczynski, M., Shire, K. & Tam, M. (1999). *On the Front Line: Organization of Work in the Information Economy*. Ithaca, NY: Cornell University Press.

Gaucher, E. J. & Coffey, R. J. (1993). *Total Quality in Healthcare: From Theory to Practice*. San Francisco, CA: Jossey-Bass.

Gerhart, B. & Rynes, S. (eds) (2000). *Compensation in Organizations: Progress and Prospects*. San Francisco, CA: New Lexington Press.

Gittell, J. H. (2000). Organizing work to support relational coordination, *International Journal of Human Resource Management*, **11**(3), 517–534.

Gittell, J. H. (2001). Relational coordination: communicating and relating for the purpose of task integration (Unpublished draft).

Gittell, J. H. (2002). Supervisory span, relational coordination and flight departure performance: a reassessment of post-bureaucracy theory. *Organization Science*, **12**(4), 367–82.

Gittell, J. H., Fairfield, K. M., Bierbaum, B., Head, W., Jackson, R., Kelly, M., Laskin, R., Lipson, S., Siliski, J., Thornhills, T. & Zuckerman, J. (2000). Impact of relational coordination on quality of care, postoperative pain and functioning, and length of stay. *Medical Care*, **38**(8), 807–819.

Gittleman, M., Horrigan, M. & Joyce, M. (1998). "Flexible" workplace practices: evidence from a nationally representative survey. *Industrial and Labor Relations Review*, **52**(1), 99–114.

Godard, J. (2001). High performance and the transformation of work? The implications of alternative work practices for the experience and outcomes of work. *Industrial and Labor Relations Review*, **54**(4), 776–805.

Grant, R. M. (1996). Prospering in dynamically-competitive environments: organizational capability as knowledge integration. *Organization Science*, **7**, 375–387.

Gutek, B. (1995). *The Dynamics of Service: Reflections on the Changing Nature of Customer/Provider Interactions*. San Francisco, CA: Jossey-Bass.

Hackman, J. R. & Oldham, G. (1980). *Work Redesign*. Boston, MA: Addison-Wesley.

Harel, G. & Tzafir, S. (1999). The effect of human resource management practices on the perceptions of organizational and market performance of the firm. *Human Resource Management*, **38**(3), 185–200.

Harrington, D. & Akehurst, G. (1996). Service quality and business performance in the UK hotel industry. *International Journal of Hospitality Management*, **15**(3), 283–298.

Hartline, M. D. & Ferrell, O. C. (1996). The management of customer-contact service employees: an empirical investigation. *Journal of Marketing*, **60**(4), 52–70.

Heskett, J. L., Sasser, E. W. & Schlesinger, L. A. (1997). *The Service Profit Chain*. New York: Free Press.

Holman, D., Chissick, C. & Totterdell, P. (2002). The effects of performance monitoring on emotional labour and well-being in call centres. *Motivation and Emotion*, **26**(1): 57–81.

Holman, D. (2001). Employee stress in call centres. Conference on Call Centres and Beyond: the Human Resource Management Implications, Kings College, London, 6 November.

Hoque, K. (1999). Human resource management and performance in the UK hotel industry. *British Journal of Industrial Relations*, **37**(3), 419–443.

Howard, O. & MacFarlan, M. (1994). Health care reform: controlling spending and increasing efficiency. Economics Department Working Paper No. 149. Paris: OECD.

Hunter, L. W. (1999). Transforming retail banking. In Peter Cappelli (Ed.), *Employment Practices and Business Strategy* (pp. 53–192). New York: Oxford University Press.

Hunter, L. W. (2000). The adoption of innovative work practices in service establishments. *International Journal of Human Resource Management*, **11**(3), 477–496.

Hunter, L. W. & Hitt, L. (2001). What makes a high-performance service workplace? Evidence from retail bank branches (Unpublished draft).

Jenkins, G. D. Jr, Mitra, A., Gupta, N. Shaw, J. D. (1998). Are financial incentives related to performance? A meta-analytic review of empirical research. *Journal of Applied Psychology*, **83**(5), 777–787.

Johnson, J. W. (1996). Linking employee perceptions of service climate to customer satisfaction. *Personnel Psychology*, **49**(4), 831–851.

Katz, H. C. (1997). Introduction and comparative overview. In Harry Katz (Ed.), *Telecommunications: Restructuring Work and Employment Relations Worldwide* (pp. 1–30). Ithaca, NY: ILR Press.

King, C. A. & Garey, J. G. (1997). Relational quality in service encounters. *International Journal of Hospitality Mangement*, **16**(1), 39–63.

Lammers, J. C., Cretin, S., Gilman, S. & Calingo, E. (1996). Total quality management in hospitals: the contributions of commitment, quality councils, teams, budgets, and training to perceived improvement at veterans health administration hospitals. *Medical Care*, **34**(5), 463–478.

Langfred, C. W. (2000). The paradox of self-management: individual and group autonomy in work groups. *Journal of Organizational Behavior*, **21**, 563–585.

Lattin, G. W. (1998). *The Lodging and Food Service Industry*, 4th Edn. Lansing: Educational Institute of the American Hotel and Motel Association.

Leana, C. R. & Van Buren III, H. J. (1999). Organizational social capital and employment practices. *Academy of Management Review*, **24**, 538–555.

Levitt, T. (1972). Production-line approach to service. *Harvard Business Review*, **September–October**, 41–52.

Lewis, B. R. & Gabrielsen G. O. S. (1998). Intra-organization aspects of service quality management: the employees' perspective. *Service Industries Journal*, **18**(2), 64–89.

Loveman, G. W. (1998). Employee satisfaction, customer loyalty, and financial performance: an empirical examination of the service profit chain in retail banking. *Journal of Service Research,* **1**(1), 18–31.

Milkovich, G. & Newman, J. (2002). *Compensation,* 7th Edn (pp. 279–304). Boston, MA: McGraw Hill.

Moynihan, L. & Batt, R. (2001). Knowledge sharing and performance of teams in call centers. Paper presented at the 2000 Academy of Management meetings, Toronto, Ontario, August 6–9.

Mukamel, D. & Spector, W. D. (2000). Nursing home costs and risk-adjusted outcome measures of quality. *Medical Care,* **38**(1), 78–89.

National Research Council (1994). *Information Technology in the Service Sector: a 21st Century Lever.* Washington, DC: National Academy Press.

Nielsen, J. F. & Host, V. (2000). The path to service encounter performance in public and private 'bureaucracies'. *Service Industries Journal,* **20**(1), 40–60.

Oum, T. H. & Yu, C. (1998). *Winning Airlines: Productivity and Cost Competitiveness of the World's Major Airlines.* Boston: Kluwer Academic.

Peccei, R. & Rosenthal, P. (2000). Front-line responses to customer orientation programs: a theoretical and empirical analysis. *International Journal of Human Resource Management,* **11**(3), 562–590.

Pennings, J. M. (1995). Information technology and organizational effectiveness. In Harker P. T. (Ed.), *The Service Productivity and Quality Challenge.* Boston, MA: Kluwer Academic.

Pine, B. (1993). *Mass Customization.* Cambridge, MA: Harvard Business School Press.

Preuss, G. (1997). Labor, skills, and information in service delivery: an examination of hospital care. *Proceedings of the 57th Annual Meeting of the Academy of Management* (pp. 282–286). Boston, MA: Academy of Management.

Preuss, G. A. (2003). High performance work systems and organizational outcomes: the mediating role of information quality. *Industrial and Labor Relations Review,* **56**(4), 590–605.

Quinn, J. B. (1996). The productivity paradox is false: Information technology improves services performance. In T. A. Swartz, D. E. Bowen & S. W. Brown (Eds), *Advances in Services Marketing and Management,* Vol. 5 (pp. 71–84). Greenwich, CT: JAI Press.

Quinones, M. A., Ford, K. J. & Teachout, M. S. (1995). The relationship between work experience and job performance: a conceptual and meta-analytic review. *Personnel Psychology,* **48**(4), 887–911.

Ramsay, H., Scholarios, D. & Harley, B. (2000). Employees and high-performance work systems: testing inside the black box. *British Journal of Industrial Relations,* **38**(4) 501–531.

Reardon, J., Hasty, R. & Coe, B. (1996). The effect of information technology on productivity in retailing. *Journal of Retailing,* **72**(4), 445–461.

Rodwell, J. J., Kienzle, R. & Shadur, M. A. (1998). The relationships among work-related perceptions, employee attitudes, and employee performance: the integral role of communication. *Human Resource Management,* **37**(3 and 4), 277–293.

Ryan, A. M., Schmit, M. J. & Johnson, R. (1996). Attitudes and effectiveness: examining relations at an organizational level. *Personnel Psychology,* **49**(4), 853–882.

Schmit, M. J. & Allscheid, S. P. (1995). Employee attitudes and customer satisfaction: making theoretical and empirical connections. *Personnel Psychology,* **48**(3), 521–537.

Schneider, B., Parkington, J. & Buxton, V. (1980). Employee and customer perceptions of service in banks. *Administrative Science Quarterly,* **25**, 252–267.

Schneider, B., White, S. S. & Paul, M. C. (1998). Linking service climate and customer perceptions of service quality: test of a causal model. *Journal of Applied Psychology,* **83**(2), 150–163.

Sergeant, A. & Frenkel, S. (2000). When do customer contact employees satisfy customers? *Journal of Service Research,* **3**(1), 18–34.

Sharma, A., Levy, M. & Kumar, A. (2000). Knowledge structures and retail sales performance: An empirical examination. *Journal of Retailing,* **76**(1), 53–69.

Shaw, J. D., Delery, J. E., Jenkins, G. D. Jr & Gupta, N. (1998). An organization-level analysis of voluntary and involuntary turnover. *Academy of Management Journal,* **39**(5), 1–15.

Shortell, S., Jones, R. H., Rademaker, A. W., Gillies, R. R., Dranove, D. S., Hughes, E. F. X., Budetti, P. P., Reynolds, K. S. E. & Huang, C. (2000). Assessing the impact of total quality management and organizational culture on multiple outcomes of care for coronary artery bypass graft surgery patients. *Medical Care,* **38**(2), 207–217.

Singh, J. (2000). Performance productivity and quality of frontline employees in service organizations. *Journal of Marketing*, **64**(2), 15–34.

Sochalski, J., Aiken, L. H. & Fagin, C. M. (1997). Hospital restructuring in the United States, Canada, and Western Europe: an outcomes research agenda. *Medical Care*, **35**(10, Suppl.), OS13–OS25.

Somers, M. J. & Birnbaum, D. (1998). Work-related commitment and job performance: it's also the nature of the performance that counts. *Journal of Organizational Behavior*, **19**, 621–634.

Tubre, T. C. & Collins, J. M. (2000). Jackson and Schuler (1985) revisited: a meta-analysis of the relationships between role ambiguity, role conflict, and job performance. *Journal of Management*, **26**(1), 155–169.

Uhl-Bien, M. & Graen, G. B. (1998). Individual self-management: analysis of professionals' self-managing activities in functional and cross-functional work teams. *Academy of Management Journal*, **41**(3), 340–350.

Woodward, C. A., Shannon, H. S., Cunningham, C., McIntosh, J., Lendrum, B., Rosenbloom, D. & Brown, J. (1999). The impact of re-engineering and other cost reduction strategies on the staff of a large teaching hospital. *Medical Care*, **37**(6), 556–569.

Author Index

Subject Index